Unicorns from Emerging Economies

In business terms, a 'unicorn' is a privately owned start-up company valued at over $1 billion. While unicorns have predominantly been a feature of well-developed economies, such as the United States and Europe, recent years have seen their increase in emerging economies – to the extent that these markets now host one-third of the world's unicorns. The emergence of unicorns from the Global South represents a transformative shift in the global business and innovation landscape. Despite limited systematic knowledge on this novel phenomenon, high-growth, innovation-driven companies from emerging economies are rapidly positioning themselves at the forefront of technology and business model innovation. These firms challenge the traditional dominance of established markets, asserting their influence on a global scale. This book offers an in-depth analysis of this fast-evolving process, covering a wide geographical range of unicorns. These dynamic new players have the impact and potential to reshape the future of business worldwide.

VENETA ANDONOVA is a professor and the former dean of the Universidad de los Andes School of Management, Colombia. She serves on UN PRME and GBSN International Advisory Boards. Professor Andonova's research on the topic of multilatinas and the Latin American business environment is collated in the edited volume *Multilatinas: Strategies for Internationalisation* (Cambridge University Press, 2017).

DIEGO FINCHELSTEIN is an associate professor at the Universidad de San Andrés and a researcher at Argentina's National Research Agency (CONICET). His research focuses on institutions, internationalisation and innovation from emerging markets. He was the executive director of the Emerging Multinationals Research Network (EMRN) and is a member of the executive board at the Latin American and Caribbean Chapter of the Academy of International Business (AIB-LAC). He has also performed consultancy work for multilateral agencies.

JUANA GARCÍA DUQUE is a professor at the Universidad de los Andes School of Management, Colombia. She was a visiting scholar from 2019 to 2020 at the David Rockefeller Center for Latin American Studies (DRCLAS). Her research activity in international development includes the role of international cooperation and the private sector in peace building and the study of internationalisation and emerging economies. She was the executive director of the Emerging Multinationals Research Network (EMRN) and is a member of the academic board at the EMI Emerging Markets Institute Cornell S. C. Johnson College of Business, Cornell University.

Unicorns from Emerging Economies

Creating Value through Technology and Innovation

Edited by

VENETA ANDONOVA
Universidad de los Andes, Colombia

DIEGO FINCHELSTEIN
Universidad de San Andrés, Argentina

JUANA GARCÍA DUQUE
Universidad de los Andes, Colombia

CAMBRIDGE
UNIVERSITY PRESS

CAMBRIDGE
UNIVERSITY PRESS

Shaftesbury Road, Cambridge CB2 8EA, United Kingdom

One Liberty Plaza, 20th Floor, New York, NY 10006, USA

477 Williamstown Road, Port Melbourne, VIC 3207, Australia

314–321, 3rd Floor, Plot 3, Splendor Forum, Jasola District Centre, New Delhi – 110025, India

103 Penang Road, #05-06/07, Visioncrest Commercial, Singapore 238467

Cambridge University Press is part of Cambridge University Press & Assessment, a department of the University of Cambridge.

We share the University's mission to contribute to society through the pursuit of education, learning and research at the highest international levels of excellence.

www.cambridge.org
Information on this title: www.cambridge.org/9781009469258

DOI: 10.1017/9781009469210

When citing this work, please include a reference to the DOI 10.1017/9781009469210

First published 2026

Cover image: Brochure template layout, cover design, business annual report, flyer, magazine – stock illustration / bgblue / Getty Images

A catalogue record for this publication is available from the British Library

Library of Congress Cataloging-in-Publication Data
Names: Andonova, Veneta editor | Finchelstein, Diego editor | García Duque, Juana editor
Title: Unicorns from emerging economies : creating value through technology and innovation / edited by Veneta Andonova, Universidad de los Andes, Colombia, Diego Finchelstein, Universidad de San Andrés (Argentina), Juana García Duque, Universidad de los Andes, Colombia.
Description: Cambridge, United Kingdom ; New York, NY, USA : Cambridge University Press, 2025. | Includes bibliographical references and index.
Identifiers: LCCN 2025025317 (print) | LCCN 2025025318 (ebook) | ISBN 9781009469258 hardback | ISBN 9781009469234 paperback | ISBN 9781009469210 epub
Subjects: LCSH: Business enterprises–Developing countries | Entrepreneurship–Developing countries
Classification: LCC HD2932 .U53 2025 (print) | LCC HD2932 (ebook)
LC record available at https://lccn.loc.gov/2025025317
LC ebook record available at https://lccn.loc.gov/2025025318

ISBN 978-1-009-46925-8 Hardback

Contents

Figures

Tables

Vignettes

Contributors

JOSÉ ERNESTO AMORÓS
Tecnológico de Monterrey, EGADE Business School, Mexico City, Mexico & Universidad del Desarrollo, School of Business and Economics, Santiago, Chile
Dr Amorós is a professor and associate dean of faculty and research at the EGADE Business School, Tecnológico de Monterrey, Mexico. Until December 2015, he was the executive director of the Entrepreneurship Institute at the Universidad del Desarrollo, Chile. He is a member of the Global Entrepreneurship Monitor, Mexico. He holds a PhD in management sciences from the ESADE Business School, Spain. He has a bachelor's degree in business administration and MSc in marketing from Tecnológico de Monterrey, Mexico.
He is a member of several academic organisations and the vice president of the Iberoamerican Academy of Management. His research interests are entrepreneurship and competitiveness, high growth new business, entrepreneurship and regional development and corporate entrepreneurship.

VENETA ANDONOVA
Universidad de los Andes School of Management, Bogotá, Colombia
Dr Andonova is an associate professor of strategy and entrepreneurship and former dean of Universidad de los Andes School of Management in Colombia. She obtained her doctoral degree in management from the Universitat Pompeu Fabra, Spain and has taught for some of the top business schools in Latin America. She is an accomplished educator, entrepreneurial mentor and researcher. Her scientific contributions have been published in highly ranked international journals in economics and management, and she is a co-author and co-editor of three successful books: *Multilatinas: Strategies for Internationalization* (2017), *Entrepreneurial Ecosystems in Unexpected Places* (2019) and *Cases on Entrepreneurship and Innovation* (2024).

ARMANDO BORDA

ESAN University Graduate School of Business, Lima, Peru

Dr Borda (PhD, Florida International University) is an assistant professor at the Graduate School of Business of ESAN University in Peru. His area of interest focuses on the internationalisation of Latin American firms and on exploring how the rôle of reputation, business group affiliation and institutional context affects the process itself and selected outcomes such as survival, reputation and performance. His work has been published in the *Journal of International Business Studies, Journal of World Business, Journal of Business Research* and in *Multinational Business Review.*

RICARDO BUITRAGO

EGADE Business School, Tecnológico de Monterrey, Monterrey, Mexico

Dr Buitrago (PhD,Università degli Studi di Palermo) currently serves as an associate research professor in strategy and international management at the EGADE Business School, Tecnológico de Monterrey. Before joining EGADE, he held various leadership roles as the program head and dean at several Colombian universities and has been a visiting professor at multiple institutions across Latin America. With research interests at the intersection of international political economy, institutions, strategy and international business, he has been an editor and reviewer for various top-tier journals, including the *Journal of Business Research, International Business Review* and *European Management Journal*, among others. He serves as an academic advisor for Cornell's Emerging Markets Institute and currently is the president of the Business Association for Latin American Studies.

FERNANDA CAHEN

Escola Superior de Propaganda e Marketing, São Paulo, Brazil

Fernanda Cahen (PhD, Universidade de São Paulo) is a professor of international business and innovation and the head of entrepreneurship and innovation for all academic programs at *Escola Superior de Propaganda e Marketing*, Brazil. She was a visiting researcher at USC Marshall, Lloyd Greif Center for Entrepreneurial Studies and a post-doctoral fellow at the Kelley School of Business, Indiana University. Dr Cahen has a PhD degree from the Universidade de São Paulo in business administration, and she specialises in international entrepreneurship with focus on strategy and innovation of high-tech ventures and digital companies. Her latest publications include articles in the *Journal of International Management, R&D Management* and *Journal of Business Research*, among others. She is a member of the Emerging Multinationals Research Network at the Emerging Market Institute at Cornell University.

LOURDES CASANOVA
Emerging Markets Institute, Cornell S.C. Johnson College of Business, Cornell University, Ithaca, USA
Lourdes Casanova is the Gail and Rob Cañizares Director of the Emerging Markets Institute and a senior lecturer at Cornell S.C. Johnson College of Business, Cornell University. Formerly at INSEAD, in 2024 she was awarded the Euroknowledge Global Thought Leader by the Foreign Investment Network. Dr Casanova was named one of the top 50 most influential Iberoamerican intellectuals and one of the top 30 most influential Iberoamerican women intellectuals by Esglobal. A Fulbright scholar, Dr Casanova has a master'sdegree from the University of Southern California and a PhD from the University of Barcelona. Her research focuses on the inter nationalisation of emerging market multinationals. She is a co-editor with F. Cahen and A. Miroux of the book *From Copycats to Leaders: Innovation from Emerging Markets* (2021) and with A. Miroux of *The Era of Chinese Multinationals* (2019). She is the author of the *Emerging Market Multinationals Report* (2016 to 2024); co-author with P. Corneliusand S. Dutta of *Entrepreneurship and the Finance of Innovation in Emerging Markets* (2018); co-author with J. Kassum of *The Political Economy of an Emerging Global Power: In search of the Brazilian Dream* (2014) and author of *Global Latinas: Latin America's Emerging Multinationals* (2009). Dr Casanova is a former member of the Global Agenda Council; Competitiveness in Latin America World Economic Forum; B20 Task Force in G20 summit, Los Cabos (2012) and a board member of the Boyce Tompson Institute. She is a co-founder of Ithaca Hub of Global Shapers; an op-ed writer for *Latin Trade*; Agenda Publica contributor to *CNN en E spañol, El País* and *The Economist*; and Latin America Advisor of The Dialogue and Voice of America.

EDUARDO AVANCCI DIONISIO
Universidade Estadual de Campinas, Limeira, Brazil
Dr Eduardo Avancci Dionisio is a postdoctoral researcher in administration at the Universidade Estadual de Campinas (UNICAMP) (2024). He has a PhD in science and technology policy from UNICAMP (2023). He has a master's degree in production and manufacturing engineering from UNICAMP (2017), a bachelor's degree in economics from the Universidade Cruzeiro do Sul (2023) and a degree in technology in business management from the Faculty of Technology of the State of São Paulo (FATEC) (2012). He has been a professor in business and civil engineering courses at the Federal Institute of Education, Science and Technology of São Paulo and a professor in the human resources management course at FATEC.

JUANA GARCÍA DUQUE
Universidad de los Andes, School of Management, Bogotá, Colombia
Dr García Duque is an associate professor at the School of Management at the Universidad de los Andes, and she is the director of the Strategy and Entrepreneurship area. She is a member of the Academic Committee of the Master's in Peacebuilding and the Master's in Regeneration and Sustainable Development. She was a visiting scholar at the David Rockefeller Center for Latin American Studies at Harvard University (2019–2020). Her research and teaching have focused on international development, with a focus on two aspects: the development and internationalisation of emerging economies and the role of other actors such as businesses and international cooperation entities in peacebuilding. She leads two of the university's research groups: Emerging Competitiveness and Organisations & Peacebuilding. She is a member of international networks, such as the Emerging Markets Research Network and the Microeconomics of Competitiveness at Harvard Business School. She is a member of the International Board of the Emerging Markets Institute at Cornell University. She served as a coordinator of the Emerging Multinationals Research Network. She has published in *Business Horizons, Third World Quarterly, Transnational Corporations Review* and the *Canadian Journal of Development*, among others, and book publications and book chapters in academic publishers such as Cambridge University Press, Palgrave and Uniandes, among others.

DIEGO FINCHELSTEIN
Universidad de San Andrés, Victoria, Argentina
Dr Finchelstein is an associate professor at the Universidad de San Andrés in Argentina and a researcher at Argentina's National Research Agency. He holds a PhD from Northwestern University. His main areas of expertise are in the relation between institutional environments, state action and internationalisation, as well as innovation from emerging markets. His research has been published in prestigious international journals. Dr Finchelstein has accepted invitations to teach in different universities from Latin America, Europe and the United States. He served as an executive director of the Emerging Multinationals Research Network, and he is currently a member of the executive board at the Latin American and Caribbean Chapter of the Academy of International Business. He has served as a consultant for the Argentine Secretariat of Energy and the Inter American Development Bank.

LILIANE OLIVEIRA GUIMARÃES
Pontifícia Universidade Católica de Minas Gerais (PUC MINAS), Belo Horizonte, Brazil
Dr Liliane de Oliveira Guimarães is a professor of the Postgraduate Program in Administration at PUC MINAS and coordinator of the Research Center for Entrepreneurship, Innovation and Territorial Development. She holds a PhD in management sciences from the Getúlio Vargas Foundation of São Paulo and was a visiting scholar at Indiana University, Bloomington campus. She has a bachelor's degree in business administration and MSc in business from the Gerais Centro de Pós-graduação e Pesquisas em Administração, Universidade Federal de Minas Gerais (CEPEAD-UFMG), Brazil. She is a founding member of the National Association for Studies in Entrepreneurship and Small Business Management. Her research interests include entrepreneurship, technology-based entrepreneurship, entrepreneurship and immigration, innovation, networks and clusters, governance of mining regions and regional development.

MICHEL HERMANS
IAE Business School, Universidad Austral, Pilar, Argentina
Michel Hermans (PhD, Cornell University) is a professor of organisational behaviour at the IAE Business School, Universidad Austral in

Argentina and a visiting professor at the EGADE Business School, Tecnológico de Monterrey in Mexico. His research interests lie at the intersection of the strategic management of people and international business. Specifically, he focuses on connections between organisational strategies, human resources management practices, capabilities development and performance outcomes. His research has been published in outlets such as the *Journal of International Business Studies, Long Range Planning, Human Resource Management Journal, Journal of Business Research* and the *European Business Review.*

JAMES HOADLEY
Center for International Business Education and Research (CIBER), Scheller College of Business, Georgia Tech, Atlanta, USA
James Hoadley, Associate Director of CIBER at Georgia Tech, has extensive experience in international business and education. He created the International Practicum course in 2005 while an MBA student and president of the MBA International Business Club. With eight years of experience in Japan working with Seiko EPSON Corporation and time at a Japanese auto parts supplier in South Carolina, Mr. Hoadley brings deep expertise in Japanese business. He co-chairs the Programs Committee of the Japan America Society of Georgia, has served on the board of JapanFest and is active in global trade initiatives through the Metro Atlanta Chamber of Commerce and ORBATL. A published researcher and international presenter, his work focuses on Japanese foreign direct investment, innovation in education, study abroad programs and the role of language and culture in business education.

EDMUNDO INÁCIO JÚNIOR
Universidade Estadual de Campinas (UNICAMP), Limeira, Brazil
Dr Edmundo Inácio Júniorholds a bachelor's degree in business administration from the State University of Maringá (1996), a master's degree in business administration (Uem/Uel) from the Universidade Estadual de Maringá (2002), a master's degree in computer science from the Federal University of Paraná (2003) and a doctorate in science and technology policy from the Universidade Estadual de Campinas (UNICAMP) (2008). He taught management studies at the Air Force Academy (2005–2012) in Pirassununga for seven years and is currently a professor at the School of Applied Sciences at

UNICAMP. He is an associate professor at the Postgraduate Program in Administration and the Postgraduate Program in Science and Technology Policy. He has experience in management, with an emphasis on technological innovation and focus on entrepreneurship, entrepreneurial behaviour, development of science and technology and innovation indicators and their applications.

AYMAN ISMAIL
Onsi Sawiris School of Business, T he American University in Cairo, Cairo, Egypt
Dr Ismail is an international expert in entrepreneurship and economic development. He is the Abdul Latif Jameel Endowed Chair of Entrepreneurship at The American University in Cairo (AUC) Onsi Sawiris School of Business and the founding director of the AUC Venture Lab, the top start-up accelerator in the Middle East and Africa. He is also the founder of AUC Innovation Hub, a platform to connect industry and academia around innovation and R&D. He is the chairman of the Board of Egypt Ventures (VC) and PayMob (digital payments) and a co-founder, angel investor and board member in fast-growing tech start-ups and financial institutions. Previously, he was a research fellow at the Harvard Kennedy School, a consultant at McKinsey & Company's New York office and the World Bank, a co-founder and managing partner at Enovio Consulting and a Young Global Leader at the World Economic Forum. He received his PhD in international economic development from the Massachusetts Institute of Technology (MIT). He has degrees in engineering, business, city planning and information technology from AUC and MIT.

KALMAN KALOTAY
ELTE CERS Institute of World Economics, Budapest, Hungary
Dr Kalotay is a part-time external research fellow of the ELTE CERS Institute of World Economics, Budapest, Hungary, as well as Honorary Professor of the Corvinus University in Budapest. From 1990 until his retirement in 2021, he worked for the United Nations Conference on Trade and Development (UNCTAD), Geneva, Switzerland. From 1996 to 2010 and again from 2016 to 2021, he worked for the World Investment Report group and for the editorial team of the *Transnational Corporations* journal. Between 2010 and 2016, he was in UNCTAD's Investment Policy Review group,

providing advice to national policy makers. From 2001 to 2019, he also taught investment strategies for UNCTAD's policy programs. From 1990 to 1996, he was a policy analyst of economic cooperation among developing countries at the UNCTAD secretariat. Prior to joining UNCTAD, he had taught international economics at the Corvinus University (1983–1990). He holds a PhD from the same university. Dr Kalotay's research was supported by the National Research, Development and Innovation Office of Hungary, under Grant No. FK-146590.

SHERIF KAMEL
Onsi Sawiris School of Business, The American University in Cairo, Cairo, Egypt
Dr Kamel is a professor of management at the Heikal Department of Management and the dean of the Onsi Sawiris School of Business at The American University in Cairo. Previously, he served as the university vice president for information management. Before joining the university, he was the director of the Regional Information Technology Institute and managed the training department of the Cabinet of Egypt Information and Decision Support Center. He serves as the chair of the board of directors of the Association to Advance Collegiate Schools of Business (AACSB) and vice chair of the Global Alliance in Management Education (CEMS). He serves on the board of directors of the Central Bank of Egypt, the Global Business Schools Network and Education for Employment Egypt. He is a member of the Egypt-US Business Council and the Egyptian Center for Economic Studies. He is a founding member of the Internet Society of Egypt. He served as the president of the board of governors of the American Chamber of Commerce in Egypt. He co-chaired the board of stewards of the African Women Entrepreneurship Cooperative. He served on the international board of the Association of MBAs and the Business Graduate Association. His teaching and research interests include digital transformation, information technology transfer to emerging economies, decision support systems and entrepreneurship. He has authored many academic and business articles and book chapters and three edited books. He authored the book *Leading Change in Challenging Times: Lessons of Disruption and Innovation from Egypt – Thoughts, Observations, and Reflections* and the *NileView* article series.

Dr Kamel is an Eisenhower Fellow. He holds a PhD in information systems from the London School of Economics, an MBA, an MA in Islamic Art and Architecture and a BA in business administration from The American University in Cairo.

JOHN R. MCINTYRE

Center for International Business Education and Research (CIBER), Scheller College of Business, Georgia Tech, Atlanta, USA

John R. McIntyre is the founding director of the Georgia Tech CIBER, a national center of excellence and a professor of management (strategy and innovation) in the Scheller College of Business with a courtesy appointment in international relations in Georgia Tech's Sam Nunn School of International Affairs. He received his graduate education at Northeastern University, Strasbourg University and McGill University, completing his PhD at the University of Georgia. Prior to joining Georgia Tech, he was a research associate and fellow at the Dean Rusk Center of the University of Georgia Law School. Author or co-author of sixteen books, he is the recipient of the State of Georgia Governor's International Award in international business education in 2009; the French National Order of Merit (Knight) awarded by the President of France, 2009; and the Georgia Tech-wide Steven Denning Faculty Award for Global Engagement, 2015. He was made Honorary Professor at ICN Graduate School of Business, University of Lorraine, France, 2017.

ANNE MIROUX

Cornell S. C. Johnson College of Business, at Cornell University, Ithaca, USA

Anne Miroux is a faculty fellow at the Emerging Market Institute, Cornell S. C. Johnson College of Business at Cornell University, a former Director of the Division on Technology and Logistics in the United Nations Conference on Trade and Development (UNCTAD) and Head of the Secretariat of the UN Commission on Science and Technology for Development (CSTD). With over thirty years of experience in international trade and finance and STI policies, she began her career in New York in the United Nations Centre on Transnational Corporations where she was involved in the negotiations on the UN Code of Conduct on Transnational Corporations. In UNCTAD, she directed for several years the World Investment Reports (WIR), the UN flagship report on foreign direct investment (FDI) and transnational corporations and served as the editor of the UN Transnational Corporations Journal. She has authored many publications on debt, FDI, technology and innovation and emerging economies, including with Lourdes Casanova on the Emerging Market Multinationals Reports (2016 to 2024) and *The Era of Chinese Multinationals* and as a co-editor with Fernand Cahen and Lourdes Casanova on *From Copycats to Leaders: Innovation from Emerging Markets.* Anne Miroux graduated from HEC, Ecole des Hautes Etudes Commerciales and from IEP (Institut d'Etudes Politiques, Paris). She holds a PhD in Economics from Paris I-Sorbonne.

CRISTIANO MORINI
Universidade Estadual de Campinas (UNICAMP), Limeira, Brazil
Since 2012, Dr Morini has been a full-time professor at the Universidade Estadual de Campinas (UNICAMP), Brazil, where he became a Distinguished Teaching Professor in 2023. Dr Morini has actively contributed to applied research on topics such as trade facilitation, customs administration and digital entrepreneurship. He has contributed to implementing the Brazilian Single Window as a consultant for the Inter American Development Bank (IADB). He has participated in multiple professional and academic associations with frontline experts over the last twenty-seven years. Currently, he is leading a four-year research project funded by the São Paulo Research Foundation.

FRED OLAYELE
Crandall University, Department of Graduate Studies, Moncton, Canada
Dr Fred Olayele is an associate professor of management at the Department of Graduate Studies, Crandall University and a senior fellow at the Norman Paterson School of International Affairs, Carleton University. A seasoned economist, development finance executive and innovation strategy leader with a diverse career focused on global business, finance, public policy, development and academia, his expertise covers trade policy, innovation strategy, foreign direct investment, urban policy, political economy and inclusive development. He has taught courses in four Canadian universities and served as a visiting professor and guest speaker across universities and academic institutions abroad. He previously served as chief economist and

senior vice president at the New York City Economic Development Corporation, where he oversaw a wide range of economic policy initiatives to help position New York as a global model for inclusive growth and innovation. Prior to that, he advised the Canadian provincial governments of British Columbia and Saskatchewan on economic development and energy policy. Earlier in his career before joining academia, he was a global trade finance specialist with Citigroup. He sits on the academic advisory board of the Emerging Markets Institute at Cornell University. He is a member of the international advisory board of the International Economic Development Council in Washington, DC. He chairs the board of directors of the Economic Club of Africa Network and the governing board of Blue Global Canada Institute. Dr. Olayele hosts the Global Recast podcast, a series of curated conversations with global leaders on grit, courage, and economic optimism in a fractured world. He holds a PhD in economics from Lancaster University, United Kingdom, and an MA in economics from the University of Victoria in British Columbia, Canada.

MOACIR DE MIRANDA OLIVEIRA JR
Universidade de São Paulo, Department of Business Administration, São Paulo, Brazil
Moacir de Miranda Oliveira Jr is a full professor in the Department of Business Administration at the Universidade de São Paulo (USP) and Otto Mønsted Visiting Professor at the Copenhagen Business School (2023–2025). Dr Oliveira is currently the president of the Triple Helix Association (from 2024), the president of the Endowment Fund of USP (from 2024) and the head of the USP Partnerships Office (from 2022). He is also Scientific Coordinator of the Innovation and Technology Management Program at USP (PGT-USP) (from 2022) and Innovation Director of the ARIES Center for Research, Innovation and Dissemination in Antimicrobial Research (from 2023). He is currently a member of the Steering Committee of the Center for Artificial Intelligence of IBM + USP (from 2020); Academic Network Partner of the Global Innovation Index (from 2020); member of the Global Steering Committee of the Emerging Markets Institute, Cornell University (from 2016); Director for Latin America at the Center for Global R&D and Innovation (GLORAD) (from 2016) and a founding member of Emerging Multinationals Research Network (from 2015). Dr Oliveira has published 6 books and over 100 papers in academic journals. His most recent book is *Startups and Innovation Ecosystems*

in Emerging Markets (2019). As a consultant in the field of strategy, innovation and international business, he has worked for some of the largest corporations and several governments for over thirty years.

ANDREI PANIBRATOV
EMLV Business School, Léonard de Vinci Pôle Universitaire, Paris, France
Dr Andrei Panibratov is a professor at the EMLV Business School, *Léonard de Vinci Pôle Universitaire* in Paris. His research focuses on the internationalisation and political activity of emerging market firms and on emerging market multinational enterprises' challenges including green transformation, migration and diasporas, populism and economic sanctions. He has published in the *British Journal of Management, International Business Review, Journal of International Business Policy, Journal of World Business, Management and Organization Review* and *Multinational Business Review*, among others. He has authored *Russian Multinationals* (2012) and *International Strategy of Emerging Market Firms* (2017). Dr Panibratov was elected as the first National Representative of Russia and as a board member of the European International Business Academy. He is the recipient of grants funded by the government and corporations. He serves on the editorial and review boards of several top international journals.

MZUKISI QOBO
Wits School of Governance, University of the Witwatersrand, Johannesburg, South Africa
Dr Qobo is South Africa's Ambassador to the World Trade Organisation and a visiting professor at the Wits School of Governance, University of the Witwatersrand. He previously served as the head of the Wits School of Governance and as a member of President Cyril Ramaphosa's Economic Advisory Council from 2019 to 2024. Dr Qobo's work spans international relations, geopolitics, and the political economy of green and digital transitions. He holds a PhD from the University of Warwick (UK), an MA from Stellenbosch University, and a BA from the University of Cape Town.

RAVI RAMAMURTI
Northeastern University, Boston, USA
Dr Ramamurti is a university distinguished professor of international business and strategy and founding director of the Center for Emerging

Markets at Northeastern University. He got his MBA from IIM-Ahmedabad (gold medalist) and his DBA from Harvard University. He studies strategy and innovation in emerging markets. Dr Ramamurti has been a visiting professor at Harvard Business School, the Wharton School, the MIT-Sloan School, the Fletcher School, CEIBS-Shanghai and IMD-Switzerland. He was elected a Fellow of the Academy of International Business in 2008 and has served as Deputy Dean of the AIB Fellows (2020–2023). His nine books include three published by Cambridge University Press on the internationalisation of emerging-market firms and one published by HBR Press on reverse innovation in healthcare. A Stanford study includes Dr Ramamurti among the top 2 per cent of all scientists in the world based on citations, and he is among the top 5 most cited scholars working on emerging markets. He has studied or consulted with dozens of public and private firms in twenty emerging economies and was chief consultant to the World Bank's board on its privatisation strategy in developing countries.

LEANDRO LIMA DOS SANTOS
Universidade de São Paulo, São Paulo, Brazil
Leandro Lima dos Santos holds a PhD in management (2023) and a master's degree in management (2018), both from the Universidade de São Paulo (USP). Dr Santos holds a bachelor's degree in business administration from the Universidade Federal do Pará (2016) and another in computer science from the Centro Universitário do Estado do Pará (2009). During his PhD studies he was a visiting scholar at the Copenhagen Business School, Denmark. He has expertise in innovation management, international business and strategy in multinational subsidiaries in emerging markets. He served as an editorial assistant for *Innovation & Management Review* and has been a member of the Centre for Global R&D and Innovation research network. Currently he is a postdoc researcher and focuses on innovation and entrepreneurship for healthcare.

ERIK STAM
Utrecht University School of Economics, Utrecht, the Netherlands
Dr Stam is a professor of strategy, organisation and entrepreneurship; board member of Strategic Research Theme Institutions for Open Societies; academic director of the Center for Entrepreneurship at Utrecht University and Extraordinary Professor at Stellenbosch

University (South Africa). He was the dean of the Utrecht University School of Economics and held positions at Erasmus University Rotterdam, the University of Cambridge, the University of Oxford, the Max Planck Institute of Economics (Jena, Germany), the IMT School for Advanced Studies (Lucca, Italy) and the Netherlands Scientific Council for Government Policy. He is the editor of the journals *Entrepreneurship Theory and Practice, Small Business Economics* and *Foundations and Trends in Entrepreneurship*. He is a leading scholar of entrepreneurial ecosystems, engaged in the science and practice of entrepreneurship-led development, both locally and globally. Next to his scientific work he is often consulted by governments, at the local, regional, national and international level (European Commission, OECD, G20, African Union, World Bank) and by start-ups, investors and corporates on innovation and entrepreneurship.

JAN JACOB VOGELAAR
Utrecht University School of Economics, Utrecht, the Netherlands
Jan Jacob Vogelaar is a PhD candidate at the Utrecht University School of Economics. He holds an MSc in economic geography from Utrecht University and an MA in public policy from Central European University. His research focuses on innovative entrepreneurship, with a particular interest in the role of governments in fostering it. Alongside his academic work, Mr Vogelaar serves as an economic policy maker in the Netherlands.

XINGQI YE
University of California, Berkeley, USA
Xingqi Ye is a PhD student at the University of California in Berkeley, with a master's degree from Cornell University, studying healthcare management. She holds a Bachelor of Science degree from Imperial College London. Her research interests include digital transformation, the evolution of innovation ecosystems and creative entrepreneurs in emerging markets.

1 Entrepreneurial Ecosystems from Emerging Markets and Their Unicorns: An Overview

JUANA GARCÍA DUQUE, VENETA ANDONOVA AND DIEGO FINCHELSTEIN

1.1 Unicorns, Their Origin and Impact on Emerging Economies

Until a few years ago the term 'unicorn' held no meaning for those participating in entrepreneurial ecosystems around the world. A unicorn was just a mythical creature with a horn on its head, found in legends and children's books. Today, however, it refers to a status most start-ups aspire to achieve. In the context of technology-driven companies, the term 'unicorn' refers to privately held start-ups that have reached a valuation of US$1 billion or more.

The concept of a unicorn company emerged in the early 2010s, and the phenomenon has since become a prominent part of the tech and venture capital landscape and culture. Technically, the term 'unicorn' was first coined by the venture capitalist Aileen Lee in a 2013 TechCrunch article (Lee, 2013). Lee used the term to describe the exceptional occurrence of start-ups that achieved valuations of US$1 billion or above, denoting them as creatures as unusual as the mythical unicorns. Lee has received very little credit for her linguistic discovery since then, despite how the term 'unicorn' has become an essential part of the start-up lexicon, symbolising the potential for exponential growth and success in the digital age.

The phenomenon gained attention as more and more tech-based and digital start-ups achieved billion-dollar valuations. The availability of venture capital (VC) and the disruptive potential of digital technologies in various industries were the main drivers of unicorn proliferation. With the number of unicorns increasing at a fast pace, questions about their business models, profitability and sustainability continue to abound. Many of these companies have suffered from growing pains during their transition from a rapid growth to profitability focus, while national and city governments around the world have greeted them with optimism, some even scrambling to lure them in. Unicorns hold the promise of attracting talent, boosting investment and raising the prestige of the cities where they are headquartered. However, when it comes to public policy, measures far beyond tax breaks have proved necessary for successfully pursuing unicorns (BBC Future, 2023). Unicorns also became part of the pulse of global powers over data access, analytics and control over storytelling, dominant narratives and artificial intelligence (AI). Unicorns have turned themselves into a symbol of innovation and disruption in the tech industry and beyond. They continue to attract significant attention from investors as well as the media, political forces and the general public, becoming symbols of economic power, national pride, political and social influence, technological dominance and even fear.

Over time, the definition of a unicorn has evolved to include promising high-growth companies with valuations approaching (but still below) US$1 billion, called 'soonicorns' (see Chapter 9); unicorns with valuations exceeding US$10 billion, known as 'decacorns'; and even higher categories, such as 'hectocorns' for those valued over US$100 billion. There were fifty-three reported unicorns with a valuation of over US$10 billion in the world in 2025 (CB Insights, 2025). The value of unicorns is generally based on how investors and venture capitalists expect them to grow and consolidate industries, so their value comes down to longer-term forecasting and expectations. Unicorns' valuations have little to do with how they perform financially in the short-term, and many of these companies rarely generate any profits during their first few years of existence. The number of unicorns has risen and the number of unicorn companies around the world in 2022 hit the one thousand mark (see Figure 1.1).

Unicorns often embody experimentation and novel practices in business operations as they introduce unique technology-enabled business models and fast-paced growth and scale up. Attaining unicorn status epitomises a pinnacle of distinction, acknowledging the prowess of start-ups in pioneering technologies, devising viable strategies to captivate venture capital and other resources and a capacity to scale up. The international reach of unicorns underscores the globalisation of technology and entrepreneurship, capitalises on the dynamic tech landscape and connectivity and brings their societal and cultural implications across local contexts both in the Global North and South to the

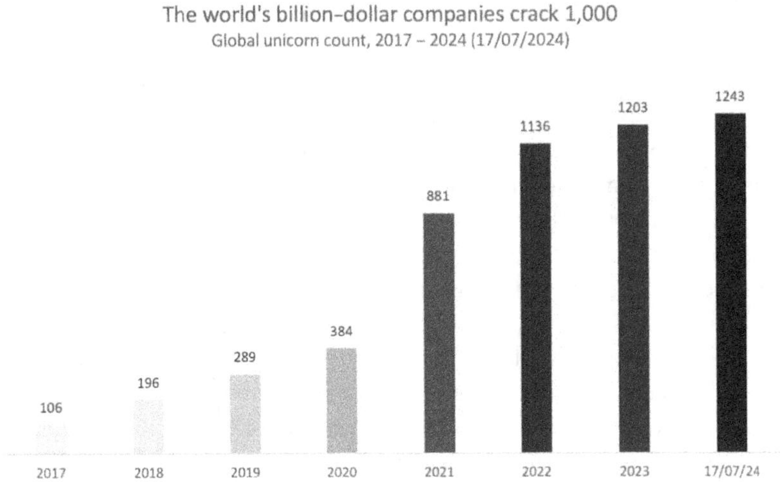

Figure 1.1 Global unicorn count 2017–2024.
Source: Author generated based on CB Insights Research (2024).

fore. Unicorns' successes and failures also hold important lessons for a wide range of stakeholders in the business, entrepreneurship and technology sectors, as well as in the public sphere. They have become particularly important for CEOs of large corporations looking to defend their turf and/or build new revenue streams, bolster resilience and court venture capital resources (Berger de León et al., 2022). They are equally important to policymakers, who strive to understand and direct the economic and social change triggered by the phenomenon of digitalisation and technological transformation that unicorns accelerate (Si et al., 2023).

Unicorns are special because of their potential to disrupt traditional business models by relying on one or more enablers of exponential growth. These can include proprietary innovation, first-mover advantage, digital technology scalability, user-centric processes, network effects, access to capital, global reach, agility, strong branding and entrepreneurial drive, among others. For the Global South's emerging economies, unicorns are also a driver of hope and optimism. They hold the promise of leapfrogging over the educational, infrastructure, institutional and other shortcomings of their local contexts via innovative digital and technology solutions. As of 2023, emerging economies were responsible for more than 50 per cent of the world's economic growth

(CFI Team, 2023). The increasing number of unicorns from the Global South presage a scenario of increased influence and prosperity of emerging economies even though many unknowns still remain before such a prospect can become a reality.

Entrepreneurial ecosystems from the Global South differ in their capacity to enable local innovation-driven start-ups to reach unicorn status and harness their transformational potential. The most prominent entrepreneurial ecosystems as of 2023 included China, India, Southeast Asia, Eastern Europe and Russia, Latin America, the Middle East and Africa. The remainder of this chapter offers a succinct overview of the birthplaces of unicorns from emerging markets and sets the scene for the in-depth analysis offered in the subsequent chapters, which highlight the defining features of specific entrepreneurial ecosystems and signature unicorns.

1.2 The Birthplaces of Unicorns and Soonicorns from the Global South

1.2.1 China

China has shifted economically, politically and culturally since the late twentieth century. After Deng Xiaoping's reforms, the Asian country transitioned towards a more open market economy and prioritised its exporting competitiveness. State institutions promoted the sophistication of the economy and the creation of strong innovation capacity, giving rise to technology-driven innovative ventures. Thus, the technological progress of the twenty-first century and the Chinese government's efforts to promote the transition to a knowledge-based economy boosted the creation, funding and growth of innovative start-ups, many of which attained unicorn status (see Chapter 11).

The Chinese entrepreneurial ecosystem has become the second most relevant in the world in terms of the number of unicorns, behind only the United States (see Chapter 5). There were 162 Chinese unicorns in May 2023, mostly headquartered in big industrial hubs such as Beijing and Shanghai and pertaining to the following industries: healthtech (10 per cent), AI (10 per cent), e-commerce (9 per cent), semiconductors (9 per cent), software-as-a-service (SaaS) (6 per cent) and enterprise services (6 per cent) (Slotta, 2023). Among the most prominent Chinese unicorns were ByteDance (Beijing, 2012; media and entertainment), SHEIN (Shenzhen, 2008; consumer and retail) and Xiaohongshu

ByteDance	SpaceX	OpenAI	SHEIN	Stripe	Databricks	Canva	Revolut	Epic Games	Fanatics	Chime	xAI
USD 225 billion	USD 150 billion	USD 80 billion	USD 66 billion	USD 70 billion	USD 43 billion	USD 25.4 billion	USD 33 billion	USD 22.5 billion	USD 31 billion	USD 25 billion	USD 24 billion

Source: Authors' own elaboration, based on CB Insight 2024.

Figure 1.2 Top twelve most valuable global unicorns.
Source: Author generated from CB Insights (2024).

(Shanghai, 2013; media and entertainment). According to CB Insights (2024), ByteDance and SHEIN were the first and the third highest valued unicorns in the world in 2023. ByteDance had an impressive valuation of US$225 billion, US$75 billion more than the second most valued global unicorn, SpaceX (USA). SHEIN had a valuation of US$66 billion, while Xiaohongshu was the 12th most-valued global unicorn with a US$20 billion valuation (CB Insights, 2024) (see Figure 1.2).

The success of the Chinese entrepreneurial ecosystem in promoting start-up growth and unicorn creation has been attributed to strong government relationships, strategic alliances and founders with unique backgrounds and capabilities (Jinzhi & Carrick, 2019). Notably, the Chinese government has been a fundamental ally, consistently channelling substantial investments into start-up ventures through a myriad of federal, provincial and local investment initiatives. Spanning dozens of direct and indirect programmes, these initiatives furnished nascent companies with crucial resources. Such support mechanisms have been instrumental in catalysing the emergence of thousands of high-growth start-ups (He et al., 2019).

Besides direct funding, the government has used regulation and policy elements to promote investments. The active involvement of the Chinese government profoundly shaped the evolution of the Chinese venture capital community. This influence was exerted through regulatory frameworks that govern the operations of VC entities, as well as through direct interventions such as the establishment of government guidance funds that compete alongside traditional VCs. Additionally, the government participates in VC funds as limited partners, injecting capital into the ecosystem, further influencing its trajectory and sheltering it against geopolitical risks (Chen et al., 2024). Tax deduction has also been an influential regulatory element. The Chinese government implemented significant alterations to tax policies in 2017 and 2018, facilitating a deduction of 70 per cent of the invested capital from taxable income for VC investors (Ho & Lu,

2019). In addition to financial support, human and social capital are two of the most important building blocks for new technology-based companies as they are at the core of competitive advantage; thus, science and education were identified as fundamental drivers of entrepreneurial ecosystem growth (Jinzhi & Carrick, 2019). China's results in this domain have been remarkable as it overtook the United States in terms of the total number of science publications, according to data from the US National Science Foundation (Tollefson, 2018).

Amid geopolitical tensions between the United States and China, China managed to add fifty-six new unicorns in 2023, while the US added seventy (Global Unicorn Index, 2024). Globally, the decline of initial public offerings (IPOs) drives some of this growth, as ventures await the best moment to go public. Most of the Chinese ventures focus on AI, semiconductors and new energy, which attracted VC attention despite a negative trend in global VC investments and the increasing geopolitical uncertainty since 2022. This is especially relevant for such technologies which are sensitive to considerations of state interest.

1.2.2 India

India has also emerged as a prominent leader in the Global South start-up space, currently ranking as the country with the third largest number of start-ups, second only to the United States and China. Yet, a smaller number of Indian start-up ventures have attained unicorn status; the total number of Indian unicorns in 2023 was reported at eighty-three, one less than in 2022 (*The Economic Times*, 2023a). Since 2017, the number of government recognised start-ups in India has experienced rapid growth, climbing from 6,000 to over 113,000 by 2023 (DPIIT, 2024). In addition, the number of unicorns, which was one in 2010, reached 111 in 2023, with a total market valuation exceeding US$345 billion (Jain, 2024). Almost all Indian unicorns are digital businesses as only a few non-digital Indian start-ups have managed to attain unicorn status (Forbes India, 2024).

Start-up activity is primarily concentrated in India's major entrepreneurial hubs, which become homes for the Indian unicorns; Bengaluru, New Delhi and Mumbai accounted for 85 per cent of the country's start-ups in 2022. These ecosystems, populated with dynamic information technology and business process outsourcing companies, also capture 85 per cent of all start-up investment in the country.

Several driving factors have been key to India's prominent place in the global unicorn landscape. The vast and expanding Indian domestic market has been critical to the demand for the products and services offered by Indian unicorns. With 834.29 million people with internet access and 600 million smartphone users, India offers a significant digital market, especially in sectors such as e-commerce, fintech and consumer services. Secondly, India stands out as one of the countries with the largest number of STEM (science, technology, engineering and mathematics) graduates globally, with 34 per cent of students opting for careers in these fields according to data from UNESCO (United Nations Educational, Scientific and Cultural Organization) (Leap, 2024). The abundance of cost-competitive technical talent has been a crucial asset to the local entrepreneurial ecosystem, with elite educational institutions such as the Indian Institute of Technology playing a significant role. With over 27,000 active start-ups in the tech space, abundant and competent technical talent has been a driver for growth and innovation (*The Economic Times*, 2023b). A steady flow of venture capital also played a positive role; until 2022 cumulative investment in tech start-ups in India had reached US$446 billion (Investment in India, 2024). The government has provided targeted support through programmes such as Startup India and Digital India. Initiatives such as Aadhar and the Jan Dhan-Aadhar-Mobile (JAM) banking system have democratised access to financial services and stimulated demand. Recently, geopolitical tensions and trade disputes between China and the USA have created additional opportunities for Indian technology companies. There has been a surge in foreign investments in the Indian entrepreneurial ecosystem which international VCs perceived as less risky than the Chinese equivalent. From a geopolitical perspective, it appears that strengthening US–India technology relations could continue driving foreign investment in Indian research and development (R&D) capabilities.

However, India faces important challenges regarding the exponential growth prospects of its technology-driven ventures. The valuations of companies that went public in 2021 fell by more than 50 per cent in 2022 and smaller IPOs, in the US$300 million range, were anticipated to become more common than multibillion-dollar IPOs. This hinted towards a possible wave of premature IPOs that could be potentially destructive for ventures and the entrepreneurial ecosystem in general. A quick and sizable rebound of 72 per cent was reported in IPO activity in 2023 (Chadha, 2024). At the same time, as many as fifty-five (74 per cent) out of the seventy-four unicorns, analysed by Inc42, incurred a cumulative operating loss of US$5.9 billion in 2022 (Agarwal, 2023). Nevertheless, the Indian entrepreneurial ecosystem has been moving to a more mature stage, with companies focusing on profitability and value creation within specific niches. Despite these challenges, the fundamental factors behind the growth of the start-up ecosystem in India remain robust. The digital revolution in India is in its early stages, with great potential for growth in internet, smartphones, e-commerce and financial services (see Chapter 6).

India came third in the list of countries with the highest number of new unicorns in 2024 (Global Unicorn Index, 2024). The emergence of new unicorns in India appears to be more sensitive to the declining trend in global venture investments than in China. The hopes for the transformational impact of Indian unicorn ventures are strongly linked to the overall growth of the Indian economy.

1.2.3 Southeast Asia

The countries from Southeast Asia, albeit smaller than China and India, have shown remarkable potential for scaling up their technology-driven ventures into unicorns (see Chapter 7). A convergence of factors have propelled the valuation of unicorns including the widespread adoption of smartphones, the rapid digitalisation catalysed by the COVID-19 pandemic, a burgeoning middle class and intensified initiatives by regional governments for fostering digital economies (Yean, 2023). Private equity played a key role as the market allegedly reached a high of US$25 billion in 2021 (Yean, 2023). The Asian Development Bank (ADB) has also supported the region's entrepreneurial ecosystems. For example, in 2022 a project in Indonesia partially funded by the ADB focused on building technology parks to promote research and innovation (ADB, 2022). This project made funding available for technological solutions that could complement the development of scalable start-ups. Still, the region's entrepreneurial ecosystems manifested their vulnerability as the US$25 billion invested in high-growth ventures in 2021 decreased to US$13 million the following year, a decline attributed to global uncertainties, rising interest rates and less attractive exit conditions (Yean, 2023).

The Startup Genome 2023 global start-up ecosystem ranking accounts for a number of parameters including the number of exits, the value of the ecosystem and the success of start-ups. The ranking testified to the capacity of Southeast Asia for supporting its ventures in attaining unicorn status, a capacity that is far from equal among countries. Globally, Singapore came in eighth place, while Indonesia ranked 41st, Malaysia 43rd, Thailand 52nd, Vietnam 58th and the Philippines 59th. The Tech Collective counted forty-two newly minted unicorns in 2022: twenty-five unicorns in Singapore, sixteen in Indonesia, four in Vietnam, three in Thailand and two in Malaysia and the Philippines (Tech Collective, 2023). As of 2023 the region's most prominent unicorns included J&T Express (Indonesia, 2015; Industrials), HyalRoute (Singapore, 2015; Industrials) and Traveloka (Indonesia, 2012; Consumer & Retail). J&T Express was the region's highest-valued unicorn at US$20 billion (CB Insights, 2024) and it was the 13th highest-valued unicorn in the world. HyalRoute has a valuation of US$3.5 billion and Traveloka – US$3 billion (CB Insights, 2024).

Fintech was the industry with the highest numbers of unicorns from the region, mostly influenced by the relatively disproportionate impact of Singapore among the ASEAN (Association of Southeast Asian Nations) countries and its traditionally strong financial industry. More than 40 per cent of Singapore's unicorns were in finance-related sectors (including insurance) and e-commerce. The latter accounted for the largest share of unicorns in Indonesia (Yean, 2023). Growing smartphone usage, young demographics, increased private equity funding and a growing middle class have all enhanced the prominence of fintech unicorns (Tech Collective, 2023). In Indonesia, 51 per cent of citizens had no access to banking or financial services in 2023, while the underbanked, defined as people with access but who choose to use alternative financial services, accounted for 26 per cent of a population of 275 million people (Yean, 2023).

The success of Singapore, the birthplace of the majority Southeast Asian unicorns, would have been impossible without long-standing government support. One example of strategic government intervention was developed in 2017 when the Singaporean government started to develop in-house technical solutions and purchase services from technology start-ups through its Smart Nation Initiative, rather than offering grants to support them (Dekker & Okano-Heijmans, 2020: 20). With this and many other programmes and initiatives, the government of Singapore has promoted innovation and digitalisation and helped Singapore obtain a first-mover advantage in the region as a unicorn powerhouse.

1.2.4 Eastern Europe and Russia

Eastern Europe's former socialist bloc countries, along with Russia, had exhibited an impressive performance regarding unicorn and new venture creation before 2022. According to Crunchbase (CB Insights, 2024), the region directly or indirectly generated a record number of unicorns and even decacorns in 2021 and kept appealing to tech investors. For example, Miro secured a US$400 million investment from leading US investors, boosting its valuation to US$17.5 billion. Originally founded in Perm, Russia in 2011, the visual collaboration company relocated to California. That year, Grammarly, born in Kiev in 2009, reached a valuation of US$13 billion. TradingView, a social network and charting platform for financial markets from Russia, hit a US$3 billion valuation. InDriver, a ride-hailing app founded in Russia in 2012, announced its US$1.23 billion valuation. In addition, PandaDoc from Belarus became a unicorn, closing a large series C round (an advanced stage of capital raising); Russian-founded global graphene nanotube leader OCSiAl reached a US$2 billion valuation; Nexters, a Russian-founded game development company, went public on the Nasdaq through a special purpose acquisition company (SPAC) merger valued at US$1.9 billion; and People.ai, of Ukrainian origin, reached a valuation of US$1.1 billion.

Further west, a similarly prolific period of unicorn creation also took place. The years 2021 and 2022 were particularly robust for billion-dollar companies in Central and Eastern Europe (CEE), with over half of them emerging during this period. As the ecosystem evolved, it garnered increased attention from international investors, fostering more cross-border collaborations between regional venture capital firms (Groszkowska, 2023). Consequently, both the amount and proportion of funding directed towards late-stage start-ups grew significantly. This surge in mega-rounds fuelled the rise of local unicorns. In 2021 alone, fifteen new unicorns were born, followed by eight more in 2022. By the end of the third quarter in 2022, the region had produced a total of forty-four unicorns (Groszkowska, 2023), including Rimac Automobili (Croatia), Nord Security (Lithuania), Glia (Estonia), Payhawk (Bulgaria), Productboard (Czechia), and Veriff

(Estonia). A point worth highlighting is that the scaling process of these unicorns included relocation outside their country of origin, while their back-office operations remained closely linked to the country/region of origin. Many promising start-ups and entrepreneurs have relocated internationally, posing a brain drain in the region.

Many of these unicorns concentrate on digital technologies that need relatively limited capital investment. Consequently, they typically secure smaller amounts of funding and at a later stage compared to their Western counterparts, frequently reaching profitability faster than unicorns from other regions. Naturally, investment companies specialising in high-tech ventures from this part of the world emerged. Examples include the United Venture Company and NRG Ventures.

Somewhat unexpectedly, according to the Startup Ecosystem Index by StartupBlink (2024), Moscow ranked first in Eastern Europe and 32nd globally in 2024, despite the ongoing armed conflict. As of 2022, Russia's population stood at around 143.44 million people, with Moscow being the largest metropolis, boasting 12.5 million inhabitants (Statista, 2023). Specifically, Russia's unicorn companies have enjoyed a burgeoning presence in high-tech industries, encompassing aerospace, nuclear technology, information technology and biotechnology. To bolster innovation and entrepreneurship, the government established the Skolkovo Foundation in 2010, focusing on supporting the development and commercialisation of advanced technologies both within Russia and beyond (WIPO, 2020). The Foundation aspired to be a leading innovation hub specialising in biomedicine, energy, nuclear technologies and space technologies. Additionally, the TechnoSpark deeptech start-up studio in New Moscow was built to foster innovation in areas like robotics and renewable energy. Some Russian universities played an important role in integrating entrepreneurial education into academia, providing expert support and business training to aspiring entrepreneurs.

The armed conflict between Russia and Ukraine started in March 2022 and this profoundly changed the region's entrepreneurial and economic prospects. The case of Yandex (see Chapter 13) exemplifies how geopolitical factors such as sanctions and politics become determinant for the evolution of a unicorn. This case highlights the power of digital technology over the modern-day global power balance. Global geopolitical tensions mould the business environment and strategies of technology companies in a dramatic and immediate way.

This underscores the significance of resilience and adaptability for unicorns navigating challenging geopolitical landscapes.

Moreover, geopolitical tensions exert a substantial impact on talent retention and brain drain within the start-ups and unicorns, and such risks must be carefully assessed in a world in flux.

1.2.5 Middle East and North Africa (MENA)

The Middle East and North Africa region has witnessed a surge of technology-driven entrepreneurship, especially in industries such as e-commerce, transportation, logistics and fintech. From 2023 it featured about 100 Israeli-founded (but not necessarily headquartered in Israel) unicorns and ten unicorns across the other countries in the region: four in the UAE, three in Egypt and three in the Kingdom of Saudi Arabia (see Chapter 9).

Although family-owned small and medium businesses that coexist with multinational corporations have traditionally dominated the regional economies, the region has been taking steps to build vibrant entrepreneurial ecosystems, attracting entrepreneurs and investors from around the globe. With a young and tech-savvy population, supportive government policies and a growing venture capital community, the Middle East and North Africa (MENA) region offers opportunities for technology innovation and ambitious business scaling. According to the Global Start-up Ecosystem Report 2024, Israel is the biggest regional player because Tel Aviv is a consolidated hub for technological innovation. The city globally ranks in fourth place for the performance of its entrepreneurial ecosystem. In 2023, eighty-eight Israeli unicorns were headquartered in the USA, which put Israel into a class of its own, given the very high degree of integration between its entrepreneurial ecosystem and that of the US, which is the most advanced (Si et al., 2023). Unlike those of any other country from the MENA region, Israeli unicorns develop deeptech solutions in AI, big data, analytics, cybersecurity and life sciences.

The MENA region is one of the most diverse in terms of the stage of development and maturity of the countries' entrepreneurial ecosystems, their priorities and ambitions. For example, Dubai hosts a large and diverse expat community boasting a high concentration of technological innovators and entrepreneurs. Egypt has benefited from venture capital funding, government policies geared towards technology-based start-up creation and a growing network of technology incubators and global accelerators that have started to show positive effects. In the Kingdom of Saudi Arabia, the Ministry of Communications and Information Technology, Mohammed bin Salman Foundation 'Misk' and the National Information Technology Development Programme launched a joint national programme (Saudi Unicorns) to empower and support high-growth technology start-ups. These different national efforts are meant to support the attainment of unicorn status for an increasing number of high-growth ventures. Here are some examples:

Swvl is a transportation unicorn created in Egypt in 2018 and later headquartered in Dubai. It focuses on tech-enabled mass transit solutions, particularly bus trips (Rasmal, 2022). Kitopi was created in Dubai and has a presence in sixteen countries with over 6,700 employees (Forbes, 2022). This unicorn raised US$450 million in a Series C round and offers 'ghost kitchen' services, using digital technology to transform supply chains, logistics and delivery for some 100 restaurant brands across the Middle East (Rasmal, 2022). Created in Egypt, Fawry is a fintech company that surpassed the US$2 billion valuation mark in under two years. As an e-payment company, it allows payments of bills for obligations and external services such as traffic fines and water bills. Lastly, Careem was a Dubai-based ride-hailing service with presence in more than fourteen countries. It was acquired by Uber in 2020 for US$3.1 billion, which marked the biggest tech deal in the Middle East as of 2023 (Forbes, 2022).

The rise in MENA unicorn cases has been driven by one main structural strength: more than 55 per cent of the region's population is under the age of thirty and very active in the digital domain. The finance, logistics and real estate sectors are expected to be particularly well suited for a technological disruption and surge in the number of unicorns (Wamda, 2022).

1.2.6 Latin America and the Caribbean

Latin America and the Caribbean have a very strong entrepreneurial tradition compared to other regions, although their firms are small and less likely to grow or innovate (Lederman et al., 2014). In the age of digital transformation, unicorns are expected to change this, despite a few structural limitations that have persisted and weakened the regional entrepreneurial ecosystems. For example, access to digital infrastructure is limited across this vast and rugged region. More than 60 per cent of the population of Latin America and the Caribbean lack access to quality digital infrastructure (Martínez et al., 2020). Education quality and human development in general have made some advancements. Against this backdrop, venture capital was at US$3.9 billion in 2023, down from an all-time-high of US$20.1 billion in 2021 (dealroom.com, 2024).

It is important to stress the role that Latin American governments have played in promoting the growth of technology-driven start-ups by stimulating innovation, entrepreneurship and ultimately the attainment of their unicorn status. Governments have long been interested in fostering innovation. However, arguably, some long-standing policies such as tax subsidies have not had enough bite (Gonzáles & Hernandez, 2021). Tax subsidies for research and development, for example, are hardly relevant as most innovative technology-driven start-ups do not generate profits until years after their innovations occur. Although there have been some efforts to promote time-enduring policies that benefit entrepreneurial activity, there is still a long road ahead.

In a search for alternatives to support the development of start-ups, venture accelerators have been created to boost the number and potential of early stage start-ups (Herman Rodríguez, 2015). Some of the ventures that benefited from these instruments managed to attain unicorn status, and by 2023 the region had potentiated the growth of forty-nine unicorns: twenty-five from Brazil, ten from Argentina, two from Chile, two from Colombia and one from Uruguay (see Chapter 8).

Three of the most impactful unicorns from Latin America in 2023 were Nubank (Brazil, 2013; fintech), Rappi (Colombia, 2015; super app) and Mercado Libre (Argentina, 1999; marketplace). The region suffered an extreme drop in venture capital availability in 2020 triggered by the COVID-19 pandemic. In spite of this, it managed to reach record levels in 2021, indicative of high variability and dependence on foreign VC.

Brazil stands as a compelling example of a thriving start-up ecosystem (see Chapter 12). It is one of the Latin American countries with the highest rate of entrepreneurial creation (Statista, 2023). São Paulo, a major global tech start-up hub and Brazil's largest city, found itself at number twenty-six in the global ranking in 2024, earning the distinction of being the top-ranked ecosystem from Latin America and the only one featured among the global top 30 (Global Startup Ecosystem Report, 2023). Other Brazilian cities such as Rio de Janeiro and Florianópolis have also been rapidly developing their own tech start-up communities, benefiting from the government's legal framework for start-ups.

São Paulo's start-up ecosystem is much more developed than that of most Latin American cities and has positioned itself as an innovative leader in the region. Factors that have enabled this include its status as the largest economy in Latin America, which allows it to have a large local digital market, and the possibility of benefiting from strengthened accelerators and incubators. For example, the accelerator 'Latitud', a platform that supports early-stage founders with training through a selective scholarship programme, offers tailored resources for local start-ups like Latitud Go. It has already invested in more than ninety companies in the region (BBVA, 2022). As a result, the city is home to twelve of the country's seventeen unicorns. It is also remarkable that the combination of public and private support networks, entrepreneurship hubs and talent without borders has given rise to the solid start-up ecosystem of São Paulo, mature enough to withstand future challenges.

Latin American countries have experienced rapid growth in terms of internet access and enjoy high concentrations of internet users and daily digital content use, with an average of 9.3 hours per day (Atlantico, 2023). The region has all the necessary potential to facilitate exponential growth for digital and technology-driven ventures, and it is home to 650 million people. Therefore, efforts must continue in order to move forward to a more robust digital ecosystem while reducing the country's extreme socioeconomic inequality.

1.2.7 Africa

Africa's innovation, technology, entrepreneurship and start-up landscape has experienced a remarkable transformation thanks to digital connectivity and young demographics prone to experimentation and innovation. Observers have noted that entrepreneurship in Africa has experienced an exponential upsurge (Helaly, 2023). The World Economic Forum (WEF) named seven African tech start-ups among the 100 most promising technology pioneers of 2022 (Disrupt Africa, 2023). Among these were Alerzo (Nigeria, 2020; on-demand inventory distribution and financial services), Dove Air (South Africa; urban air mobility technology, 2020) and Vendease (Nigeria; marketplace, 2020).

Africa's technological infrastructure has been undergoing a transformation as governments are taking proactive steps to support business efforts related to innovation and the knowledge economy, benefiting from the digitalisation trend (see Chapter 10). The COVID-19 pandemic sharply accelerated African digital innovation, and demand for more and better digital infrastructure increased across the continent. Industry-related regulatory policy changes made in countries of sub-Saharan Africa during the pandemic emphasised digital accessibility (Feydeau et al., 2022). The result was a rise in the consumption of online services, increased connectivity and the proposal of new, more ambitious approaches to public policies, in the hope that new technologies could provide a leapfrogging opportunity for Africa. African governments are taking proactive steps to support entrepreneurial endeavours, and they have a growing interest in leveraging the region's economic growth with the opportunities offered by technology to boost new business (Business Insider Africa, 2023). Infrastructure development, policy reforms and initiatives to promote digital literacy contribute to the enabling environment for start-ups to flourish. International organisations and private investors also recognise the potential of African businesses and provide support through funding and mentorship programmes.

West Africa attracted the largest proportion of venture capital deal volume in Africa in 2022: 30 per cent. Nigeria was the most active country by volume at 22 per cent and drove up this overall proportion. The most attractive sectors included fintech, health tech, agritech. Most investors in Africa were international, with African investors representing just 23 per cent (Venture Capital in Africa Report, 2022). Of all VC deals in 2022, 78 per cent were in technology-enabled companies operating across a variety of sectors plus fintechs. These absorbed 31 per cent of the deal volume and 42 per cent of the deal value. Besides Nigeria, where Lagos is the African leader in entrepreneurial ecosystems value and early-stage financing, South Africa, Mauritius and Kenya are emerging as promising entrepreneurial hubs.

Nigeria emerges as a reference point for start-up development due to a combination of factors that have boosted its entrepreneurial ecosystem. The country has experienced a surge in investment both from local and international sources, reflecting the growing confidence in its start-up ecosystem. The presence of dynamic tech hubs and incubators, such as Lagos' YabaCon Valley, provides essential support, mentorship and resources for budding entrepreneurs (Hayden, 2022).

Africa reportedly had seven unicorns in 2024: the Nigerian Interswitch, a digital payment and commerce solution and the oldest African unicorn; Flutterwave, a Nigerian application programming interface (API)-driven platform, aggregating payment gateways across Africa; Opay, a mobile payments platform; Wave, a full-stack digital mobile money wallet initially focused on Francophone Africa; Andela, a talent marketplace; Chipper Cash, a cross-border, peer-to-peer money transfer platform; and MNT-Halan, a money lending fintech (Today Africa, 2024).

The world increasingly looks towards innovation and start-ups as drivers of economic growth and transformation. As this happens, Africa hopes to seize the opportunity to not only bridge the digital divide but also become a remarkable success story due to its tech and start-up ecosystems.

1.3 The Importance of Unicorns from Emerging Economies

Emerging economies are characterised by low to middle income per capita and not fully consolidated and competitive industrial sectors. In terms of investment opportunities, emerging markets distinguish themselves by their high returns and low covariance with global market factors, among other things (Goetzmann & Jorion, 1999). Emerging economies were responsible for more than 50 per cent of the world's economic growth in 2023 (CFI Team, 2023). This strong growth translates into huge potential for business opportunities, including unicorns and technology-driven start-ups with exponential transformational impact.

The interconnectedness experienced in the 2000s is partly responsible for this growth and, thus, the emergence of start-ups and unicorns in the Global South. The world experienced a peak in globalisation between 2007 and 2011 in terms of trade and foreign investment. Two of the main factors that drove this increasing interdependence among nations were technology developments and the reduction of communication and transportation costs (Witt, 2019). The increase in trade, foreign investment and communications created opportunities for many emerging economies. In the specific case of unicorns, these companies were created under one of two logics. The first meant taking things that work somewhere and adapting them to work under the unique conditions of the Global South. The second involved building new and better ways of doing things to solve local, regional and global problems. The high degree of interconnectedness, enhanced access to capital and expansion of the technological frontier all contributed to the emergence and increase in the number of unicorns from the Global South.

This chapter has presented a brief overview of the concept of unicorns and explained what makes them unique. On one hand, they are relevant because new technologies and lower costs have allowed scalable and competitive technology-based services to solve specific problems that are intrinsic to the locations in which they are created. These types of new companies offer improved, more attractive solutions or inclusive solutions for traditionally underserved segments. On the other hand, unicorns in emerging markets are different from other companies because, due to the unique conditions of the Global South under which they are created, the need to add value has brought about innovations that lead to disruption in various sectors. Chapter 2 further enriches and expands on these ideas presenting a theoretical framework. Chapter 3 and Chapter 4 focus on understanding the geography and main features of unicorns at a global level. Furthermore, from Chapter 5 to Chapter 13 we zoom into the key determinants of entrepreneurial ecosystems and their unicorns across the emerging economies of the Global South: Latin America, MENA, Eastern Europe and Russia, Africa, India, China, and Southeast Asia. Chapter 14 concludes by systematising the key insights, posing new research questions and outlining a future research agenda.

COVID-19 played a key role in accelerating technological developments in many of these regions. Specific locations stand as central nodal elements in the process of unicorn creation in the Global South among which São Paulo (Brazil), Lagos (Nigeria), Beijing (China) and Singapore (Southeast Asia) stand out. In such places, governments play a key role in enhancing the conditions for start-up creation and unicorn scale up through targeted policies, tax regulation or direct financing to compensate for some of the disadvantages and complement some of the natural advantages of the emerging economies. These advantages can include sizable markets, entrepreneurial spirit, VC capital availability, human talent and training, and a community of determined entrepreneurs. Unicorns from emerging economies have a transformational role in the public and private discourse on human progress and prosperity. The growing number of start-ups founded and located in emerging markets represents a change in how these economies add value. They change the focus from commodity extraction to technology-based services, igniting economic growth, business opportunities, job creation, services exports and other ways of connecting the entrepreneurial ecosystems of the Global South to the global knowledge-based economy. Such a perspective brings hope and new-found confidence to millions of young and creative minds around the world. There is nothing more transformational and important to study and understand than the human spirit that brings change to the world on the wings of a unicorn.

References

Agarwal, M. (2023). *Is profitability a distant dream? 55 of India's most-valued startups remain loss-making in FY22*. Inc42. tinyurl.com/5n6fr68n

Asian Development Bank. (2022). *Projects & tenders*. www.adb.org/projects?terms=Startup

Atlantico. (2023). *Latin America digital transformation report 2023*.

BBC Future. (2023). *Towards industry 4.0: The magic of tech unicorns*. www.bbc.com/storyworks/future/towards-industry-40/tech-unicorns

BBVA Spark. (2022). *Tierra de unicornios e imperio 'fintech': Así es São Paulo, el mayor ecosistema de innovación de Latinoamérica*. tinyurl.com/mcryzb7p

Berger de León, M., Königsfeld, J., Leypoldt, L., and Vollhardt, K. (2022). *How to build a unicorn: Lessons from venture capitalists and start-ups*. McKinsey Digital. tinyurl.com/5hxuuere

Business Insider Africa. (2023). Homepage. africa.businessinsider.com/

Cahen, F., Casanova, L., and Miroux, A. (2021). *Innovation from Emerging Markets*. Cambridge University Press.

CB Insights. (2024). *CB Insights Crunchbase 2024*. www.cbins1ights.com/research-unicorn-companies

(2025). *CB Insights Crunchbase 2025*. www.cbinsights.com/research-unicorn-companies

CFI Team. (2023, 16 May). *Emerging market economy*. Corporate Finance Institute. corporatefinanceinstitute.com/resources/economics/emerging-market-economy

Chadha, S. (2024). *India ranks first in the world in terms of the number of IPOs in 2023*. Business Standard. tinyurl.com/d56hafvw

Chen, J., Gong, K., and Li, J. (2024, 7 May). *Industrial policy in a new era: Government venture capital in the U.S.-China trade war*. SSRN. ssrn .com/abstract=4218297

Dealroom.com. (2024). *Latin America*. dealroom.co/guides/latin-america

Dekker, B., and Okano-Heijmans, M. (2020). *Europe's Digital Decade? Navigating the Global Battle for Digital Supremacy*. Clingendael Institute. www.jstor.org/stable/resrep26543.6

Disrupt Africa. (2023). Homepage. disruptafrica.com/tag/world-economic-forum/

DPIIT. (2024). *Number of government recognized startups from 2016 to 2024*. Statista.

The Economic Times. (2023a). *Slowdown visible in India's startup story as only three unicorns added in 2023: Report*. tinyurl.com/yckh6hm4

(2023b). *India now has nearly 27,000 active tech startups, adds 1,300 last year*. tinyurl.com/wb7hybkewww.statista.com/statistics/1155602/india-start-up-recognized-businesses/

Feydeau, A., Menski, M., and Perry, S. (2022). *Africa's digital infrastructure transformation*. White & Case. tinyurl.com/5e329zu5

Forbes. (2022). *Meet the Middle East's 5 unicorns*. www.forbesmiddleeast .com/innovation/startups/the-middle-easts-5-unicorns

Forbes India. (2024, 20 May). *Unicorns in India: List of startup companies with unicorn status in 2024*. www.forbesindia.com/article/explainers/unicorns-india-list/85309/1

The Global Startup Ecosystem Report. (2023). *Insights, rankings & ecosystem pages*. Startup Genome. startupgenome.com/article/latin-america-insights-rankings-and

Global Unicorn Index. (2024). *Hurun Research Institute*. www.hurun.net/en-US/Info/Detail?num=9K1G2SK5X7CX

Goetzmann, W. N., and Jorion, P. (1999). Re-emerging markets. *The Journal of Financial and Quantitative Analysis 34*(1), 1–32. doi.org/10.2307/2676244

Gonzales, M., and Hernández, M. (2021). *Fostering innovation and entrepreneurship in Latin America and the Caribbean*. IDB. tinyurl.com/3ve6jxwb

Groszkowska, K. (2023). *CEE unicorns: The rise of startup ecosystem in Central & Eastern Europe*. Vestbee. tinyurl.com/48992hn4

Hayden, S. (2022). *Forging Nigeria's future: The young entrepreneurs of 'Yabacon Valley'*. The Irish Times. tinyurl.com/3awt32fx

He, C., Lu, J., and Qian, H. (2019). Entrepreneurship in China. *Small Business Economics 52*, 563–572.

Helaly, H. (2023). *Why Africa is becoming the next serious player in entrepreneurship*. Entrepreneur. www.entrepreneur.com/leadership/why-entrepreneurship-in-africa-is-surging/454910

Herman Rodríguez, J. A. (2015). *Start-up development in Latin America: The role of venture accelerators*. PhD thesis, MIT. dspace.mit.edu/handle/1721.1/99034

Ho, K., and Lu, L. (2019). *New venture tax capital rules and support for inbound investment in China*. International Tax Review. tinyurl.com/2s3n8sc3

Investment in India. (2024). *Indian Brand Equity Foundation*. www.ibef.org/economy/investments

Jain, A. (2024). *From 2014 to 2023: How the startup ecosystem is thriving in India despite all odds? Explained*. Mint. tinyurl.com/b4yyvadf

Jinzhi, Z., and Carrick, J. (2019). The rise of the Chinese unicorn: An exploratory study of unicorn companies in China. *Emerging Markets Finance and Trade 55*(15), 3371–3385. doi.org/10.1080/1540496X.2019.1610877

Leap. (2024). *Where are STEM graduates coming from?* www.insights.onegiantleap.com/blogs/where-are-stem-graduates-coming-from

Lee, A. (2013). *Welcome to the unicorn club: Learning from billion-dollar startups*. TechCrunch+. techcrunch.com/2013/11/02/welcome-to-the-unicorn-club/

Lederman, D., Messina, J., Pianknagura, S., and Rigolini, J. (2014). *El Emprendimiento en América Latina: Muchas Empresas y Poca Innovación*. Banco Mundial. tinyurl.com/3dh542se

Martínez, R., Iglesias, E., and García, A. (2020). *Digital transformation: Infrastructure sharing in Latin America and the Caribbean*. Inter American Development Bank. tinyurl.com/mryacyt5

Rasmal. (2022). *Unicorn startups in the MENA region*. www.rasmal.com/unicorn-startups-in-the-mena-region/

Si, S., Hall, J., and Klein Leichman, A. (2023). *88 Israeli-founded unicorns now have US headquarters*. www.israel21c.org/88-israeli-founded-unicorns-now-have-us-headquarters/

Slotta, D. (2023, 10 January). *China: Industry breakdown of unicorns 2022*. Statista. www.statista.com/statistics/1334654/china-industry-breakdown-of-unicorns/

Statista. (2023). *Startups in Latin America – Statistics & facts*. www.statista.com/topics/4786/startups-in-latin-america/#topicOverview

StartupBlink. (2024). *Startup ecosystem ranking Moscow*. www.startupblink.com/startup-ecosystem/moscow-ru

Tech Collective. (2023, 20 March). *The 8 unicorns of Southeast Asia minted last year*. techcollectivesea.com/2023/03/27/unicorns-southeast-asia-2022/

Today Africa. (2024). *African unicorn: How many in Africa today?* todayafrica.co/african-unicorn/

Tollefson, J. (2018). *China declared world's largest producer of scientific articles*. Nature. www.nature.com/articles/d41586-018-00927-4

Venture Capital in Africa Report. (2022). AVCA. www.avca.africa/media/m3db4yt0/02175-avca-vc-report-2023_4-final-1.pdf

Wamda. (2022). *Mena to witness more than 45 unicorns by 2030*. STV report. tinyurl.com/yyxzhbht

Witt, M. A. (2019). De-globalization: Theories, predictions, and opportunities for international business research. *Journal of International Business Studies 50*, 1053–1077.

WIPO. (2020). *Global innovation index 2020*. www.wipo.int/en/web/global-innovation-index/2020/index

Yean, T. (2023, 12 October). *Rise of unicorns in Southeast Asia*. FULCRUM. fulcrum.sg/aseanfocus/rise-of-unicorns-in-southeast-asia/

2 Unicorns from Emerging Economies: A Framework for Analysing Their Genesis and Nature

VENETA ANDONOVA, JUANA GARCÍA DUQUE AND DIEGO FINCHELSTEIN

2.1 Introduction

Unicorns, only a decade-old phenomenon, are a challenge for researchers. Most attempts to understand their rise, role and impact, including the present one, are preliminary and incomplete. Yet, a number of reasons have provoked interest in these privately held companies, primarily financed by venture capital (VC) and with valuations of at least US$1 billion.

Firstly, on the financial side, the valuations of most unicorns are explained more by market share and strong growth rates than profit margins and high-valued assets. In any case, the median total capital unicorn firms raise through private financing rounds surpasses the median of technology-based initial public offerings (IPOs) (Brown & Wiles, 2015; Bock & Hackober, 2020). Moreover, larger firms that have attained unicorn status typically enjoy easier access to both capital and labour, making them less susceptible to external shocks. This resilience is often reflected in a valuation premium, which investors highly favour (Hammer et al., 2016).

Secondly, such companies have the potential to produce a profound shake up of the industry structure (Divan, 2016) and occasionally act as drivers of deep social changes that redefine societal winners and losers. Meanwhile, public policies intended to balance such developments tend to appear very slowly and often ineffectively. Such risks are especially acute in countries with less robust institutional infrastructure such as in many emerging and developing economies from the Global South (Casanova & Miroux, 2023). Episodes illustrating the disruptive nature of unicorns are numerous, ranging from the working conditions of Rappi (Latin America) and Glovo (Europe, Asia and Africa) collaborators to the lobbying efforts of incumbent taxi companies to block the transportation services offered over platforms such as Uber.

Thirdly, reliable and comparable information regarding unicorns is scarce. Some observers argue that this is a key advantage of maintaining sensitive financial and operational data private for an extended duration under private ownership. This is opposed to IPOs and their associated disclosure procedures (Fenwick & Vermeulen, 2015). For this reason, it is very hard to find a comprehensive and precise list of unicorns for any moment in time; therefore, the lists and rankings offered in Chapter 1 are meant as a proxy rather than precise statistics. In fact, in many fragile institutional settings, companies try to disguise their information or keep it secret. This can come out of fear of extortion, an attempt to maximise benefits in the face of ineffective regulations or a mistrust of the institutions or entities that could opportunistically expropriate or facilitate the expropriation of targeted business ventures. The rise of unicorns coincides with the rise of digitisation, digital platforms and artificial intelligence (AI) technology integrated into business models. Such models enjoy an enormous market but also social and political leverage. As a result, unicorns are very sensitive to social and political dynamics and vulnerable to state action, as they may occasionally be seen to put fundamental interests, geopolitical advantages and civil rights and liberties at risk, as in the case of social media platforms (see Chapter 13).

It seems that some unicorns are key players in a high stake, winner-takes-it-all game of geopolitical influence and technological and economic dominance. The case of accusations that Chinese TikTok was a national security risk causing the app to be banned in the United States mirrored the ban on Google in mainland China; both TikTok and Google used to be unicorns. Many look hopefully to unicorns from emerging economies in anticipation of a similarly strong impact on other countries' development paths. For example, mobile payments were widely adopted in China in 2021, with over 904 million people (roughly 64 per cent of the population) using them. Digital wallets facilitated about 54 per cent of all e-commerce transactions, far surpassing cash payments, which accounted for only 10 per cent. By the close of 2022, digital payments in China totalled approximately US$3.5 trillion, almost double the amount in the United States. China stood out as a global leader in embracing a mobile-first economy, showcasing the rapid advancement and widespread acceptance of mobile payment technology. The exponential growth of unicorns in fintech and other digital domains, as well as their relationship to higher value activities, supports the conjecture that emerging economies can accelerate the catch-up to developed economies' processes and move their economic and social progress forward. By the same token, spill-over effects are expected from unicorns; they create new, better paying jobs and greater research and development (R&D) investments and outcomes. Yet, it has not been easy to separate correlation and causation in building a solid base for such arguments.

Finally, the unique conditions that are common to emerging economies reinforce the need to study this specific class of high-growth venture. Limited access to capital and technology, weaker institutional support and precarious infrastructure are all factors that could act as important barriers to attaining unicorn status but are commonly shared by the emerging economies of the Global South. Start-ups from emerging economies have not only successfully addressed such challenges but also neutralised and used them in their favour by innovating and offering unique business models (Casanova et al., 2021).

In such a context, emerging economies such as China, India and others (see Chapter 1) have managed to facilitate the birth of a growing number of unicorns, some of which have become leaders in their respective industries. In essence, countries from the Global South are leveraging their local specificities to build bubbling entrepreneurial ecosystems (EE) in the hope of producing unicorn ventures. All these reasons lead to a burning need for policymakers to understand unicorns, specifically those from the emerging and growing economies of the Global South. This is equally important for investors, managers of incumbent companies, entrepreneurs and citizens because unicorns have the potential to profoundly shake up everyone's way of life. Notably, citizens living in countries with less robust institutional effectiveness must become acutely aware of the risks and opportunities the unicorn phenomenon offers; such contexts are more permissive regarding infringement on civil rights and privacy.

In line with previous research, we assert that the valuation and success factors for the emergence of unicorns diverge from those influencing typical ventures. This distinctiveness makes unicorns a specialised phenomenon, prompting the need for specialised research to uncover the factors that drive the likelihood of attaining unicorn status (Bock & Hackober, 2020). There are a broad range of factors that play a role in attaining unicorn status. Namely, the realities of global geopolitical and power balances, which interact with the global race for technological developments such as AI. In addition, the structural elements behind the development and blossoming of an entrepreneurial ecosystem (such as entrepreneurial culture and mindset, availability of entrepreneurial financing, legal, R&D and market infrastructure) also impact the attainment of unicorn status. The specific characteristics of a unicorn venture, including its business model, scalability and technological intellectual property (IP) determine the specific impact it can generate at the firm, industry, city, country and global level (country brand status, reshuffling of the industry competitive landscape, 'cloud fiefdom'). Figure 2.1 depicts the proposed framework and the chapters of this book address the aspects of the dynamic relationships of its components to distinct degrees of breadth and depth. The intention is to facilitate a conversation and search for common patterns, while acknowledging the great diversity of the unicorn phenomenon across emerging markets, not the least because of data availability. We also aim to allow for systematisation of the wide range of theoretical lenses for scholarly exploration.

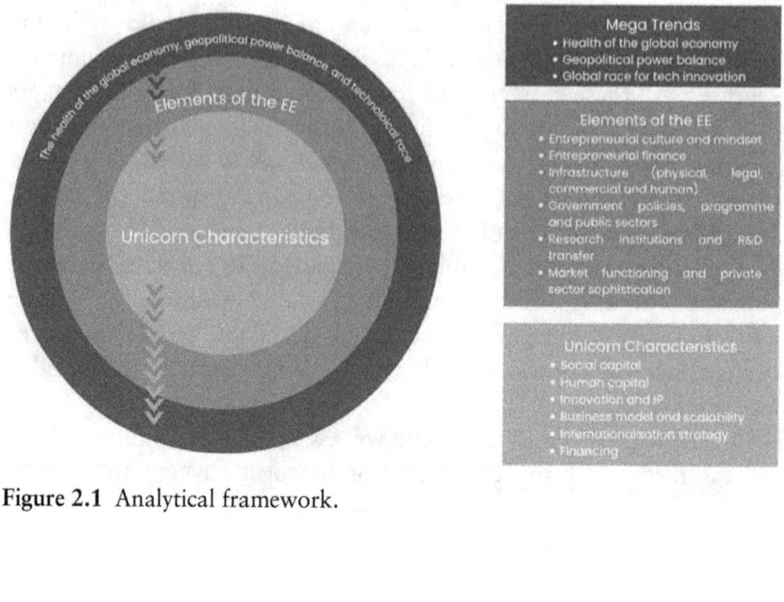

Figure 2.1 Analytical framework.

2.2 The Health of the Global Economy, Geopolitical Power Balance and the Race for Technological Superiority

Past studies have uncovered a correlation between the broader economic climate and the valuation levels of ventures, considering factors such as gross domestic product (GDP) growth, interest rates and the quantity of IPOs (Dias & Macedo, 2016). The significance of this lies in the tendency of venture capital funds to escalate the implied valuation of their investments during periods of increased capital inflow (Gompers & Lerner, 2000).

However, according to Yanis Varoufakis (2023), the world's economic system has been living through a profound transformation since the global financial crisis of 2008. Arguably, when the G7 central banks coalesced to keep the global financial system afloat by printing money in 2009, they made this an ongoing arrangement. Allegedly, the freshly printed financial resources found their way to private venture capital funds. These are significantly more profitable as they have the appetite for taking stakes in high-growth high-risk digital and technology ventures looking to get ahead in these winner-takes-all industry dynamics. As a result, the rise of unicorns has been stimulated by money printing globally. Many of them turned into digital platforms, such as Facebook and Amazon, changing the economy's private value generation mechanisms (Varoufakis, 2023). One could argue that the former system, which relied on traditional markets with oligopolistic corporate competitors, has been gradually replaced by digital platforms that function according to the logic of 'private fiefdoms or cloud estates'. These charge rent rather than seeking a market profit, emulating feudalist value generating mechanisms (Varoufakis, 2023). In such a world, platforms earn a controlling position, synonymous with being a dominant technology-based player, through their status or the quality of their algorithm. As a result, companies expect the race to unicorn status to be severe, with significant geopolitical implications in addition to economic ones. In such a system, the relatively abundant financial capital available to unicorns from emerging economies means they enjoy significant opportunities when compared to previous periods. They face lower barriers to knowledge and idea sharing due to digitalisation and better transportation technologies.

It is not a coincidence that the president of the Republic of China, Xi Jinping declared that 'with the rapid development of information technology and the emergence of disruptive technologies at any time, it is necessary to maintain a solid footing on the path of innovation and contribute to the realisation of high-level self-reliance in technology' (Reuters, 2023). At the same time, the president of the Russian Federation, Vladimir Putin, said that the West should not be allowed to develop a monopoly in the sphere of artificial intelligence and declared a much more ambitious Russian strategy for the development of AI (Faulconbridge, 2023). In parallel, the regional and global ambitions of India are clearly driven by its achievements in the information technology domain. The 111 Indian unicorns have a combined valuation of US$347 billion (Invest India, 2023) and are a testimony to the prime minister's claim that 'in the development of digital technology, India is behind no developed nation' (Modi, 2023). This statement comes at a time when India has been reiterating its claim to a seat on the United Nations security council, an entity meant to maintain the post-WWII geopolitical realities, which have now been reshuffled by the digitalisation and technological race. The evident emancipation of the nations of the Global South, exemplified by the founding nations of BRICS (Brazil, Russia, India, China and South Africa) and the newly accepted Ethiopia, Egypt, United Arab Emirates, Indonesia, Saudi Arabia and Iran has evolved against the backdrop of the USA's maintained leadership and the decoupling of the post-World War II geopolitical cloud of European Union countries and their less impressive performance in the unicorn race. Between 2008 and the second quarter of 2021, venture capitalists invested an average of €125 million per unicorn in the European Union, €138 million in the United States and €125 million in China. However, the large funding rounds in China enabled companies to achieve substantial valuations more quickly and with fewer rounds compared to their EU and US counterparts (Testa et al., 2022). The average age of both private and 'exited' unicorns is notably lower in China compared to the United States and European Union, indicating that unicorns in China tend to be considerably younger. One potential explanation for the rise in the average exit time in the EU and US may lie in the escalating costs associated with attaining a dominant (platform) position in established markets, particularly for software-based companies (Kenney & Zysman, 2019). Despite the reduced costs of launching software-based start-ups, which has led to increased competition, the time and effort related to achieving market dominance has significantly risen, especially in more mature markets. During the same period, the average investment in exited unicorns in the US and China surpassed that of the EU. This indicates a possible lower frequency of IPOs and merger and acquisition (M&A) transactions occurring in the EU (Testa et al., 2022). Regional disparities regarding the unicorn phenomenon are a prevalent pattern, with European unicorns exhibiting significant concentration in countries such as Germany, France and Sweden (see Chapter 3).

When examining the top 25 most valuable unicorns and their countries of origin, China leads the technological race with companies like ByteDance (first, artificial intelligence), SHEIN (third, e-commerce) and Xiaohongshu (twelfth, e-commerce) as tracked by the Global Innovation Index 2023. The United States follows closely, represented by companies such as SpaceX (second, space and telecommunications), Stripe (fourth, fintech) and Epic Games (seventh, video games). Other countries making appearances in the top 25 include Australia with Canva (fifth, graphic design and software) and Indonesia with J&T Express (13th, logistics and delivery). However, when unicorn valuation is analysed in conjunction with economic development scaled by GDP, patterns highlighting the role of emerging economies from the Global South emerge. Middle-income economies such as China, India and Brazil stand out due to their high concentration of unicorn companies relative to their level of development. Middle- and low-income economies that also host unicorn companies, albeit with comparatively lower valuations, include a large share of Latin America's economies, including Argentina, Chile, Colombia, Ecuador and Mexico. Notable unicorns from this region include Kavak (Mexico, e-commerce), Rappi (Colombia, supply chain) and Ualá (Argentina, fintech) (Global Innovation Index, 2023).

It is clear that the unicorn phenomenon has caused dynamic changes to the global competitive landscape and that a better understanding of the entrepreneurial ecosystems of the Global South is necessary to articulate the implications and expected outcomes. Unicorns from emerging and developing economies might shift the tectonic plates of path-dependent economic trajectories, offer leapfrogging opportunities based on thrifty innovation and generate optimism and hope for a brighter economic future to the young and entrepreneurial populations of the nations with such emerging economies (see Chapter 4). Looking at the specific parameters of their entrepreneurial ecosystems that shape the attainment of a unicorn status is an important next step.

2.3 Elements of Entrepreneurial Ecosystems in Emerging Economies

Entrepreneurial ecosystems facilitate the emergence of unicorns (Bock & Hackober, 2020). This section examines the key components, actors and interactions within the principal domains of entrepreneurial ecosystems, with a particular focus on the dynamics in emerging economies (Andonova et al., 2019). While entrepreneurial finance is rarely the most critical ingredient, it plays a vital role in enabling experimentation, scaling and the achievement of unicorn status. Government programmes and agencies contribute by protecting entrepreneurial activity from volatile market shifts, helping to stabilise and sustain the ecosystem. Academic and research institutions, along with R&D transfer capabilities, ensure a steady pipeline of innovations that progress through product–market fit to scaling. Market-supporting institutions and the sophistication of competitive strategies and business processes also complement unicorn development. The strategic vision of business leaders has proven instrumental in nurturing thriving entrepreneurial ecosystems (Zahra & Nambisan, 2012). These domains – together with infrastructure (physical, legal, and human) – form the foundational drivers of vibrant ecosystems. Ultimately, however, it is the entrepreneurial mindset, shaped by local culture, that animates new venture creation and fuels entrepreneurial ambition.

2.3.1 Entrepreneurial Culture and Mindset

In entrepreneurial ecosystems, entrepreneurs are the central actors, with the leading structuring role in entrepreneurial activity; we can only understand this from a holistic and systemic perspective (Borissenko & Boschma, 2016) given that different layers of context interact and shape their behaviour. This is because entrepreneurship takes place in a community of interdependent actors (Stam, 2015) who belong to the broader cultural environment within which entrepreneurial expectations are shaped (Schmutzler et al., 2019) and where entrepreneurial ventures are created and operate (Mason & Brown, 2014). For example, entrepreneurial mindset as an expression of the cognitive drivers that allow the attainment of unicorn status illustrates the role of the cognitive biases of founders and investors (Cristofaro et al., 2023).

It is well documented that the highest levels of early-stage entrepreneurial activity are observed in emerging economies. According to the Global Entrepreneurship Monitor 2022/2023, the top 5 countries for early-stage entrepreneurial drive are from Latin America and the Caribbean: Guatemala, Colombia, Panama, Chile and Uruguay. Moreover, reports show a negative association between the level of early-stage entrepreneurial activity and human capital development, as measured by the UN Human Development Index (HDI) (Global Entrepreneurship Monitor, 2022/2023). This lends evidence of a statistically significant correlation between stronger entrepreneurial predispositions and the emerging status of an economy, making such geographies especially prone to the development of an entrepreneurial mindset.

Within such a context, the widely circulated success stories of the first unicorns tend to inspire the founders of a new generation of local innovative start-ups (Gao & Guo, 2020). In China, for example, cultural values, including motivation for achievement, tolerance to failure, aptitude for problem-solving and the importance of social networks (*guanxi*) all play significant roles in shaping entrepreneurial behaviour (Ahlstrom & Ding, 2014). These specific cultural factors arguably contributed significantly to the growth and dynamism of the entrepreneurial landscape and the rise of unicorns in the country (Poon et al., 2023).

2.3.2 *Entrepreneurial Finance*

The availability of financial capital serves as a binding constraint on the growth of a new venture and significantly influences the extent to which start-ups can attain unicorn status (Somaya & You, 2024). Many venture capitalists adhere to a strategy of only investing in start-ups with the potential to achieve unicorn status (Zimmerman, 2016).

Historically, the majority of successful VC-backed companies went public within three to eight years of their initial VC funding (Gornall & Strebulaev, 2020). However, in the 2010s, many successful VC-backed companies have chosen to stay private for extended periods and have grown to significant sizes without pursuing a public offering, enjoying the privilege of limited regulation and information disclosure obligations. The impressive valuations of unicorns have stirred concerns about the degree of overvaluation derived from endemic information asymmetries among investors, as the value of unicorns and their shares is highly contingent on the contractual terms offered to investors. Arguably, while a select few privileged investors are privy to and have negotiated advantageous contractual terms, many other stakeholders lack easy access to this information and often struggle to comprehend its implications for valuation (Gornall & Strebulaev, 2020). Pointing to this important concern, both foreign VC firms and local VC entities have played a pivotal role in fuelling the growth of unicorns in emerging economies. Notably, many foreign VC firms operate in China and local VC firms are affiliated with China's tech giants such as Baidu, Alibaba and Tencent in an attempt to overcome information asymmetries (see Chapter 11).

In the case of Chinese unicorns, direct investments from overseas investors have been relatively modest, with only 13 per cent originating in the USA and minimal contributions from Europe (Albers-Schoenberg, 2019). However, many Chinese VC funds were connected to the Chinese diaspora and returnees, especially from the United States (Poon et al., 2023). Based on the number of unicorns in which they invested, half of the top 10 institutional investors in Chinese unicorns in 2021 were of Chinese origin (Hurun Research Institute, 2021).

Corporate venture capital investors play a uniquely positive role in increasing the likelihood of ventures becoming unicorns. In addition to their role as investors, corporate venture capital funds are recognised for their operational support, offering resources such as production facilities and market access rather than solely focusing on investment selection (Chesbrough, 2002; Narayanan et al., 2009; Chemmanur et al., 2014).

In parallel to VCs, governments have made large investments in start-up firms through federal, provincial and local investment programmes (see Chapter 6 for the case of India). In many countries there are dozens of direct and indirect programmes that provide resources to start-up companies. These have helped launch thousands of high-growth start-ups (He et al., 2018).

2.3.3 *Infrastructure and Human Capital*

A unicorn needs physical, legal and commercial infrastructure as well as human capital to scale its operation and grow. Many emerging economies' vast geographies and constrained public resources make it impossible to envisage large-scale improvements in physical infrastructure; however, high rates of urbanisation in hubs such as São Paulo, Beijing, Shenzhen and Bangalore guarantee access to state-of-the-art infrastructure and vibrant domestic markets for talent and services. It is no coincidence that these cities have consistently made the list of top 30 entrepreneurial ecosystem hubs (CBI Insights, 2023) and are the birthplaces of many unicorns. Yet, unpacking the impact of city, regional and national level infrastructure and human capital, particularly given the levels of migration and the rise of remote technologies, has been a significant challenge (see Chapter 8 for the case of Latin America).

Bureaucracy, complex labour, tax and environmental regulation and economic volatility are challenging for entrepreneurs and private equity and VC investors in many emerging economies; local, context-specific knowledge is required to overcome these obstacles. In emerging economies these specificities in entrepreneurial ecosystems occasionally become business opportunities. For example, a significant number of experienced managers in the Global South learned to successfully exploit inefficiencies and execute the traditional private equity model: In Brazil, the average private equity and VC gross internal rate of return in USD terms since 2010 has been 25 per cent and 21 per cent per annum, respectively (Minardi et al., 2020).

Human capital is crucial when developing an entrepreneurial ecosystem and nurturing start-ups to attain unicorn status. While there is an ongoing debate regarding the precise role of universities in entrepreneurial ecosystems (Fritsch, 2002; Kitagawa, 2004), regional universities are undisputedly central for producing talent with the requisite knowledge for the entrepreneurship sector, especially in the areas of high-technology and innovation (Steigertahl & Mauer, 2023). Additionally, universities often serve as articulating platforms for talent and other ecosystem stakeholders to interact, share experiences and discuss challenges. The quality of technical education in India and China has been credited with supporting these countries' status as rising technological powers and birthplaces of unicorns.

2.3.4 Research Institutions and R&D Transfer

The presence of highly educated individuals is crucial for the creation of innovative venture firms (Bock & Hackober, 2020). There is a positive correlation between proximity to universities and the establishment of innovative ventures (Calcagnini et al., 2016). Other spillover mechanisms from knowledge institutions to the broad entrepreneurial ecosystem include patents, collaboration agreements and university spin-offs, all of which are favourable for the establishment of new ventures (Ubeda et al., 2019).

A high intensity of technology and innovation present in a specific entrepreneurial ecosystem triggers a high density of VC investors, who provide essential funding for new ventures as they progress along their growth trajectories (Castilla, 2003). This, in turn, triggers a virtuous circle of entrepreneurial success. Such innovation-intensive ecosystems streamline access to funding, thereby accelerating the development speed of respective ventures and potentially elevating them to unicorn status (Inderst & Müller, 2004; Gaba & Meyer, 2008).

There are positive trends regarding innovation across the Global South (see Chapter 5 for an overview of the case of China). For example, according to the Global Innovation Index 2023 ranking, India consistently outperformed in innovation relative to its development for thirteen years straight. Meanwhile, the ranking showed that Indonesia, Uzbekistan and Pakistan had maintained their overperformer status since 2022, with Brazil also exceeding expectations in 2023 for the third consecutive year. Encouragingly, there were notable positive trends in innovation rankings across the Middle East in 2023, with the United Arab Emirates (UAE) nearing the top 30 (see Chapter 9). Additionally, Saudi Arabia, Qatar, Bahrain, Oman and other neighbouring countries have been moving up in the rankings. Mauritius and South Africa are among the leaders in Sub-Saharan Africa.

2.3.5 Market Functioning and Private Sector Sophistication

Well-functioning entrepreneurial ecosystems present new ventures with the opportunity to access large, competitive marketplaces early on (see Chapter 10 on the challenges African start-ups face in this regard). This is because the potential customers of new, innovative products also form part of the proximate environment, enabling faster feedback on product functionality (Gilbert et al., 2008). Consequently, new ventures grow, adapting their products more swiftly to customer needs and ultimately offering superior services or products. Such a dynamic has led some researchers to conclude that entrepreneurial ecosystems compel new ventures to be more competitive, given the heightened competition in these geographically-delimited regions

(Gilbert et al., 2008). Additionally, entrepreneurial ecosystems arguably facilitate differentiation behaviours, as entrepreneurs can identify gaps in existing products or services and fill them by providing new alternatives (Gilbert et al., 2008) and ultimately build a robust competitive advantage.

Corporations are among the most sophisticated market participants. Corporations can offer strong support for start-ups to achieve unicorn status through corporate venture capital. Supporting ventures in accessing complementary assets sets corporate investors apart from purely financial investors. They facilitate the commercialisation of new ventures' products and services (Paik & Woo, 2017; Röhm et al., 2018). Specifically, some authors pose that innovation levels and research intensity increase when corporate investors provide access to these complementary assets (Alvarez-Garrido & Dushnitsky, 2016). Arguably, innovation rates are markedly higher for ventures funded by corporate investors (Park & Steensma, 2013).

2.3.6 Government Programmes and Public Support for Unicorns

Politicians have increasingly shown interest in unicorn companies (Jinzhi & Carrick, 2019). They are drawn to the economic growth potential that unicorns offer, which are often associated with job creation and GDP growth (Wennekers & Thurik, 1999). Additionally, politicians appreciate the media attention that unicorn companies bring to their regions, particularly in countries like China where government officials take pride in having top companies within their jurisdictions (Chen et al., 2005). As a result, establishing strong relationships with the government is crucial for achieving robust growth in Chinese start-ups (see Chapter 5). Founders must prioritise building and nurturing these relationships to navigate regulatory environments effectively and access resources and support from government agencies (Jinzhi & Carrick, 2019).

Past research has highlighted that the political and regulatory environment directly influences the likelihood of unicorn births (Wright et al., 2005). However, this effect primarily refers to an inter-country level (Bock & Hackober, 2020) and government programmes have not been equally effective in fostering a bubbling entrepreneurial ecosystem across emerging economies. In Ethiopia, for example, frustration with the government's equal allocation of support led to a sense of resignation and disillusionment with the programme, which was perceived to favour ventures that had no ambitions or intentions of achieving unicorn status (Biru et al., 2020).

On the other hand, the development of entrepreneurial ecosystems within China began within the government, emphasising technological innovation and high-tech industrialisation to propel national economic growth. In 1999, the State Council issued their decision on strengthening technological innovation, developing high technology and realising its industrialization, initially targeting the public sector and state-owned enterprises (Poon et al., 2023). During the same year, the government established the Innovation Fund (Innofund), which provided grants or loans to technology-based small- and medium-sized enterprises (SMEs) to support early-stage commercialisation projects with innovative technology and promising market potential. The size of the Innofund grew significantly, expanding from US$30.3 million in 1999 to US$760.4 million in 2012 (ESCAP, 2018). Government policies in the late 1990s increasingly emphasised the promotion of market-led innovation in China. As a result, a wave of innovative start-ups emerged in China towards the end of the 1990s including Baidu, Alibaba and Tencent, which played a significant role in fostering the rapid growth of unicorns in the country (Poon et al., 2023).

2.4 Unicorn Characteristics

Entrepreneurial ecosystems in emerging markets are giving birth to unicorns at an increasing rate despite the salient shortcomings that set them apart, including delay in digital transformation, resource scarcities, structural gaps and institutional voids (Cao & Shi, 2021). In what follows, we highlight the essential elements of unicorns, paying special attention to those from the emerging economies. Namely, these elements refer to their ability to attract talent and develop human capital, generate innovation and proprietary IP, scale up, internationalise carefully and attract entrepreneurial finance, as well as their reliance on social capital.

2.4.1 Social Capital

Start-ups generally seek to employ their social capital for growth by adopting a few common tactics such as enhancing team knowledge, skills and contacts, building new alliances and expanding brand visibility. For example, the strong reliance on establishing trusting communities among their stakeholders led most Indian entrepreneurs to identify mentoring, networking and learning opportunities as their major challenges to growth, surpassing access to capital as their main concern (BL Mumbai Bureau, 2022). Forming focal points for building social capital around successful serial entrepreneurs and unicorn founders is not uncommon.

While there is limited data on migration patterns following post-successful exits, research indicates that entrepreneurs who have resided in a region for a longer duration and have stronger social connections there tend to achieve greater success than newcomers (Dahl & Sorenson, 2012). The depth of these social ties suggests that entrepreneurs are likely to remain in the region following a successful exit, ensuring that the capital, knowledge, networks and expertise cultivated by their venture stay within the ecosystem (Spigel & Harrison, 2017). This can occur through serial entrepreneurship or by providing mentorship and investment to newer generations of entrepreneurs. The strong network surrounding the Colombian unicorn Rappi was labelled 'the Rappi mafia'.

While financial capital is more mobile than human capital, it too may exhibit some degree of local embeddedness and, in this case, a link to emerging countries' contexts. Entrepreneurs and early employees who profit from a successful exit often reinvest in the local ecosystem as angel investors or join VC funds and/or company builders, thus capitalising on their expertise and social capital embedded within the entrepreneurial ecosystem. This is the case of Kaszek, a VC fund created by successful Argentine entrepreneurs to finance projects in Latin America. Such individuals often have complementary altruistic motivations and are driven by their desire to 'pay back' to the societies and communities in need that abound in the context of emerging economies.

The experience and skills of the investors directly impacts the performance of a VC-backed company (Bengtsson & Wang, 2010; Achleitner et al., 2013), as does the social capital they bring. The expertise of VC investors plays a crucial role, given that they typically offer more than just financial support by providing additional guidance and advice (Bonini et al., 2012; Jackson et al., 2012). Geography has impacted the focus of networking power, social capital and mentoring skills because the predominant lead investors for unicorns were initially situated in the United States. Nevertheless, as time progresses there is a noticeable upward trend in the involvement of investors located outside the USA, creating alternative loci of VC capital in emerging markets that go hand in hand with social capital building (see Chapter 7 for an overview of unicorn development in Southeast Asia, featuring the determinant role of Singapore and its finance and banking sectors).

2.4.2 *Human Capital and Talent*

Everywhere, early-stage technology start-ups heavily rely on skilled scientists and engineers to bring new technologies to market. However, start-up ventures face fierce competition from established technology firms for top talent. Arguably, variations in both worker abilities and preferences enable start-ups to attract talented individuals who are drawn to the start-up environment despite lower pay (Roach & Sauermann, 2023).

A study of 628 entrepreneurs from emerging economies concluded that 75 per cent of ventures that showed the potential to become unicorns or were rapidly growing identified lack of adequate talent as the biggest barrier to attaining unicorn status (Lazarow, 2020). As a result, many of these companies have assumed the responsibility of training their own employees, establishing a long-term view of the employer–employee relationship and providing a huge positive externality to the whole entrepreneurial ecosystem.

Additionally, the need to access the right level of talent, given local constraints, has been pushing high growth start-ups from the Global South to search internationally, leveraging social networks and national diasporas (Andonova et al., 2023). High-growth ventures from emerging economies have been particularly fearless in building distributed workforces as well as embracing fully remote working arrangements (Lazarow, 2020).

In addition to the talent a venture manages to attract, its quality and management team play a role in its probability of success (Maschke & zu Knyphausen-Aufseß, 2012). Although it is quite difficult to measure the quality of a venture, innovativeness seems to have a positive influence on the potential for success (Häussler et al., 2008; Block et al., 2015) and the innovation capabilities of unicorns from emerging economies have been increasingly recognised.

2.4.3 Innovation

In emerging markets, innovations are often perceived to be based on, therefore to have taken advantage of, existing technology, generally invented in developed economies and reshaping it to offer novel-to-the-market solutions rather than radically new technologies (Guede et al., 2021). Many unicorns are seen to be building technological platforms consisting of management analytical tools, desktop and mobile applications, hardware, ecosystems, algorithms and simple websites such as marketplaces, among others. This generalisation, pointing to a haphazard process rather than an intentional strategy, does not seem to appreciate the role that governments across the Global South give to innovations as pillars of their national competitiveness in the context of a knowledge-based global economy. The example of China is the most dramatic (Chapter 5).

There is a consensus that unicorns from emerging economies approach innovation differently from the way unicorns from developed countries do (Cuervo-Cazurra et al., 2018; Cahen et al., 2021) as these solutions are adapted to the voids and challenges of emerging markets, including contexts of war (Duque et al., 2021). To an extent, a potential opportunity for the creation of unicorn business models in emerging markets is to transfer and adapt technologies or business models from advanced economies. In emerging markets, relationships with consumers face the reality of economic informality and institutional weakness (Casanova et al., 2021). Thereby, adapting to local infrastructure and volatile business environments, along with other aspects of emerging contexts such as inequality and occasionally violence, offers unique challenges for emerging unicorns and shapes their innovation efforts.

Against this backdrop, the ascent of numerous middle-income and emerging economies in the Global Innovation Index standings in 2023 cannot be ignored: 21 nations surpassed expectations in innovation compared to their developmental stage (Andonova, 2021). Regarding innovation index rankings, Indonesia has experienced rapid growth, while the Philippines and Vietnam are making strides. This result goes in hand with the fact that Indonesia boasts the second-largest number of unicorns in ASEAN (Association of SE Asian Nations), only trailing behind Singapore with twenty-six unicorns.

With a total of fifteen unicorns, including two companies with valuations above US$10 billion (GoTo and J&T Express), the country's start-up ecosystem demonstrates remarkable growth and potential, matching its improvement in innovation capabilities (Siew Yean, 2023). In the same vein, both the Philippines and Vietnam's entrepreneurial ecosystems have given birth to unicorns in the finance, insurance, crypto trading, entertainment and e-commerce domains.

2.4.4 Business Model and Scalability

In general, unicorn valuations are mostly based on strong growth metrics and market share acquisition relying on digital channels and other innovations. The rise of unicorns is strongly correlated with the use of growth indicators of value, prioritising metrics such as user growth, engagement, customer acquisition, retention rates and revenue streams rather than profit (see Chapter 12 for an overview of scale-up drivers in Brazil). Such observations are consistent with the idea that in the eyes of investors, unicorns hold the promise of creating a monopoly market position and extract rents that could transform into significant capital gains. This makes them worth the higher risk of investment.

Unicorns from emerging economies appear to have a more balanced approach to growth and a better survival rate than those in the United States (Lazarow, 2020). Arguably, the Silicon Valley approach to building a business model geared for growth by rushing 'to develop a viable product, raise capital and lay waste' can be calibrated by a more balanced approach to growth that does not impede innovation or venture capital participation (Lazarow, 2020). Moreover, in most advanced economies unicorns develop business models for newly emerging needs. Therefore, they initially need to educate the market on the importance of their service or product. On the other hand, unicorns in emerging economies seek to solve pre-existing or basic needs that traditional means have failed to satisfy. Hence, unicorns in emerging markets focus on providing services that meet basic human needs in new ways and for this, consumers are willing to pay from the beginning (Lazarow, 2020).

This intense emphasis on growth is indicative of how the unicorns and their investors strive for market dominance, particularly when operating under a platform business model. The goal of unicorns is to outcompete incumbents and other new entrants by acquiring them

(Kenney & Zysman, 2019). It is argued that this new model of value extraction has transitioned away from traditional markets and onto the digital platforms of former unicorns such as Facebook and Amazon, which no longer function akin to oligopolistic corporations. Rather, they resemble private fiefdoms or estates, making themselves into the main actors of 'techno feudalism' (Varoufakis, 2023). Along a similar line, Stayton and Mangematin (2018) argue that being first to market in winner-takes-all market niches is a key success factor for new venture creation, as such a position guarantees a sustainable competitive advantage. Kaplan and Strömberg (2000) emphasise the importance of high growth potential, especially through acquisitions, in shaping investment decisions for investors. For example, 111 Indian unicorns led over 400-plus acquisitions between 2014 and 2023 (Inc42 Datalabs, 2023).

Seeking growth to assure market dominance, or 'private cloud fiefdom' (Varoufakis, 2023), offers benefits not only in terms of market share and sales but also from a cost perspective (Bock & Hackober, 2020). Acquisitions provide opportunities for the acquirer to leverage synergies and drive value in the combined businesses (Das & Kapil, 2015; Hammer et al., 2016) and allows access to technologies and assets possessed by the acquisition target. These can be utilised to consolidate the lock-in position of the acquirer (Borell & Heger, 2013).

2.4.5 *Internationalisation Strategy*

Globally, the most significant economic sectors boast the highest number of successful unicorns. Three sectors, each generating annual revenues exceeding US$5 trillion (technology, media and telecommunications; industrials; and healthcare), comprised nearly a third of the top 100 unicorns in 2022 (Berger-de-León et al., 2022). Therefore, participating in a large market enhances a venture's likelihood of achieving substantial success, and internationalisation boosts the total addressable market potential. Successful start-ups can also emerge from smaller markets or niche sectors, provided that the potential for global market disruption is significant in cases such as AI and big data (Berger-de-León et al., 2022). It is important to highlight that the activities of most unicorns differ from region to region. As shown in Chapter 3, internet software and services and fintech are the most recurrent areas of unicorn creation in Europe and North America while in emerging markets, e-commerce and direct to consumer activities are the most prominent domains. The areas of unicorn emergence are arguably related to both the resource abundance in different regions (knowledge and capital) as well as to diverse structural conditions. For instance, companies like Jumia in Africa and Mercado Libre in Latin America have thrived in the e-commerce business because they were able to adapt and innovate under infrastructure deficiencies and institutional voids (Casanova et al., 2021). Similarly, Chapter 7 illustrates how the Indonesian unicorn PrimaKu fills in the gaps in the health industry that local governments could not cover.

Start-ups originating from emerging economies often disproportionately depend on the entrepreneur's skills and vision for international expansion (Cahen et al., 2017) as well as on the social capital of the founders (Prashantham & Dhanaraj, 2010). This reliance serves to offset the resource and capability limitations commonly encountered within the business landscape of their home countries. Against this backdrop, high-growth start-ups from smaller economies tend to embark on an accelerated internationalisation, arguably because of their lean, early and fast market development processes (Neubert, 2017). Start-ups from large emerging economies seem to exhibit a different approach to international isation (Cahen, 2019). For example, Brazilian start-ups have a tendency to invest more time in developing the organisational capabilities necessary for their internationalisation efforts. Additionally, those with a longer tenure in the domestic market (over five years) tend to lean heavily on their innovation capabilities and prowess in international marketing throughout the internationalisation journey. Conversely, younger start-ups often forego reliance on organisational capabilities for their initial and rapid expansion into international markets (Cahen, 2019).

The international growth of unicorns also has geostrategic implications that should be recognised. For example, while the Asia-Pacific regions are traditionally a favourite international location for Chinese unicorn companies, the decision of the Indian government to ban hundreds of mobile apps, many of which are of Chinese origin, has removed India from the Chinese unicorn map of international expansion (*Global Times*, 2021).

2.4.6 *Funding Strategy*

In emerging economies, where the availability of capital and appetite for risk tend to be significantly lower than in developed countries, funding has been perceived as a constraint (see Chapter 10 for a discussion on the role of finance and other framework conditions of an entrepreneurial ecosystem). Start-ups that aspire to achieve unicorn status outside of globally renowned innovation and entrepreneurial ecosystems frequently follow a less aggressive approach to raising and burning capital and focus on solutions to fundamental problems and needs (Finchelstein, 2018; Lazarow, 2020). Such an approach results in a balance between growth and profitability, better resiliency and a longer-term outlook (Lazarow, 2020).

In addition to the capital of local investors, unicorns from emerging economies benefit greatly from attracting highly esteemed foreign investors. Prestigious VCs invest in superior ventures thus accelerating the achievement of unicorn status that can be very significant in the case of start-ups from unlikely places. Moreover, such VCs offer robust operational support for portfolio companies in the form of mentoring and financial assistance over the full growth trajectory, leading to successful venture development (Tykvová, 2018). Consequently, investors with a stronger reputation garner greater visibility and act as a good quality signal to other investors (Megginson & Weiss, 1991; Krishnan et al., 2011), attracting ventures of higher quality and thereby increasing the likelihood of achieving unicorn status. At the same time, investors, particularly successful VC firms, have the propensity of drawing in highly qualified fund managers and decision-makers (Cumming & Dai, 2011). They also maintain expansive networks within their industry (Alexy et al., 2012). This grants them an information advantage concerning valuable investment opportunities and heightens the probability of the VC firm receiving greater investments (Groh & von Liechtenstein, 2011) to support the path to unicorn status. In essence, investment support is comprehensive and includes business referrals, industry-bound mentoring and financial support (Breuer & Pinkwart, 2018). It frequently extends to recruiting executive managers and other team members (Hellmann & Puri, 2002).

Corporate venture funds also play an important role. By supporting innovation-driven high-growth start-ups, corporations create a technology endorsement effect, signalling their confidence in a particular technology or innovation outcome to markets. This serves as a compelling argument for other market participants to adopt these products or services (Paik & Woo, 2017). Given that many unicorns have developed disruptive and innovative products and services, the technology endorsement effect is particularly potent for this subset of ventures. It reduces market entry barriers and facilitates stronger sales growth (Bock & Hackober, 2020). Moreover, corporate venture capital investors exhibit greater patience regarding returns and exits compared to independent venture capitalists (Chesbrough, 2002), operating with longer time horizons for their investments (Paik & Woo, 2017). Corporate venture funds are willing to remain invested for extended periods, unlike independent VC funds with finite lifetimes. This enables high follow-on funding rounds rather than pushing for an exit through an IPO, granting unicorns the opportunity for continued growth and dominance (Wadhwa & Phelps, 2009; Guo et al., 2015). Past research has provided evidence suggesting that corporate VC investors can outperform independent VC investors, particularly when there is a strategic alignment between the venture and the investor (Morck, 2000), an aspect that is evident in the case of Chinese corporate VCs.

The role of VC investors differs across emerging markets. In Asia, VCs emerged earlier and have been more widely present in the region than in Latin America (see Chapter 8). Approximately 37,000 projects were funded by VCs in Asia between 2017 and 2021 while only 1,250 were funded in Latin America for the same period. As presented in Chapter 10, funding in Africa has been scarce; however, it has significantly grown, tripling between 2020 and 2021. The state has been an important source of financing in some Latin American countries through specific programmes such as Start-up Chile or those of Brazilian national agencies, although the state has been less active in Argentina. In several Asian countries, the role of state funding and aid has been crucial, with China being the most iconic, though not the only, example.

2.5 Feeding Back into the Loop

Unicorns from emerging markets are able to overcome many of the challenges presented by their contexts, creating value at a high speed and on a large scale. The growing number of start-ups founded and located in emerging markets represents a new mechanism for adding value to these economies. Changing the focus from commodity extraction to innovation-based technology and services can provide dynamism by spurring economic growth, broadening business opportunities, accelerating job creation and exports and facilitating new channels for interaction at the geopolitical level.

Unicorns also play a central role within entrepreneurial ecosystems, providing role models, improving the entrepreneurial culture, promoting the knowledge and technology transfer and triggering innovation. They have a direct positive effect on the regional economy. At the same time unicorns from emerging economies transform the local entrepreneurial ecosystems, influence the country's brand standing, shape the narrative about the nation's commitment to progress, competitiveness, and forward-thinking and profoundly disrupt the realities of industries and societal groups. Because of the speed and depth of the changes brought by the growing number of unicorns from the Global South, a large-scale transformation of the productive systems and rebalancing of societal equilibria are set in motion by these new types of economic players.

Optimists forecast that innovation- and technology-driven start-ups with the potential to aspire to unicorn status can bring solutions to pressing societal challenges, enhance human development and improve access to education, healthcare, banking and other services. In fact, as of 2023, internet software and services and e-commerce seem to be the industries most populated by unicorns, followed by fintech and healthcare. However, poor public oversight and deficient regulatory effectiveness in emerging economies shift enormous power to these technologically advanced giants. They occupy dominant positions in markets, often holding a monopoly, meaning they influence societal balances and political dynamics.

The unicorn phenomenon in the context of emerging markets is fascinating and at the same time difficult to address in a systematic manner. The following chapters allow us to highlight the interplay between mega trends and global conditions, local characteristics and the features of emerging economies with unicorn emergence and specific strategy. The collection of quantitative and qualitative studies as well as theoretical advancements based on observations from diverse geographical regions draws a rich canvas for future research. This promises to be as disruptive for the field of study as the impact of unicorns from emerging economies has been for the Global South and its standing on the world geopolitical and economic map.

References

Achleitner, A.-K., Engel, N., and Reiner, U. (2013). The performance of venture capital investments: Do investors overreact? *Review of Financial Economics* 22(1), 20–35.

Adhanan, E. (n.d). *What are the three stages of a startup?* Silicon Valley Bank. tinyurl.com/2ztpdm5t

Ahlstrom, D., and Ding, Z. (2014). Entrepreneurship in China: An overview. *International Small Business Journal 32*(6), 610–618. doi.org/10.1177/0266242613517913

Albers-Schoenberg, A. (2019, 10 August). *The year of the red unicorns.* MPE.

Alexy, O. T., Block, J. H., Sandner, P., and Ter Wal, A. L. J. (2012). Social capital of venture capitalists and start-up funding. *Small Business Economics 39*(4), 835–851.

Alvarez-Garrido, E., and Dushnitsky, G. (2016). Are entrepreneurial venture's innovation rates sensitive to investor complementary assets? Comparing biotech ventures backed by corporate and independent VCs. *Strategic Management Journal 37* (5), 819–834.

Andonova, V. (2021). Entrepreneurial ecosystems and innovation in the Balkans. In F. Cahen, L. Casanova, and A. Miroux, eds. *Innovation from Emerging Markets: From Copycats to Leaders.* Cambridge University Press, pp. 150–182.

Andonova, V., Gavrilova, S., Perez, J., Schmutzler, J., and Krusteff, M. (2023). Bulgaria: the relevance and impact of transnational diaspora in technology-driven entrepreneurship. In R. Sternberg, M. Elo, J. Levie, and J. Amorós, eds. *Research Handbook on Transnational Diaspora Entrepreneurship*. Edward Elgar Publishing, pp. 86–109.

Andonova, V., Nikolova, M., and Dimitrov, D. (2019). *Entrepreneurial Ecosystems in UnexpectedPplaces*. Palgrave MacMillan.

Bengtsson, O., and Wang, F. (2010). What matters in venture capital: Evidence from entrepreneurs stated preferences. *Financial Management 39*(4), 1367–1401.

Berger-de-León, M., Königsfeld, J., Leypoldt, L. and Vollhardt, K. (2022). *How to build a unicorn: Lessons from venture capitalists and start-ups.* McKinsey Digital. tinyurl.com/2kemz9ev

Biru, A., Gilbert, D., and Arenius, P. (2020). Unhelpful help: The state of support programmes and the dynamics of entrepreneurship ecosystems in Ethiopia. *Entrepreneurship & Regional Development 33*(1–2), 1–23. www.tandfonline.com/doi/full/10.1080/08985626.2020.1734267

BL Mumbai Bureau (2022). Hindu Business Line Homepage. www.thehindubusinessline.com/

Block, J. H., Fisch, C. O., Hahn, A., and Sandner, P. G. (2015). Why do SMEs file trademarks? Insights from firms in innovative industries. *Research Policy 44*(10), 1915–1930.

Bock, C., and Hackober, Ch. (2020). Unicorns—What drives multibillion-dollar valuations? *Business Research 13*, 949–984.

Bonini, S., Alkan, S., and Salvi, A. (2012). The effects of venture capitalists on the governance of firms. *Corporate Governance: An International Review* 20(1), 21–45.

Borell, M., and Heger, D. (2013). *Sources of value creation through private equity-backed mergers and acquisitions: The case of buy-and-build strategies.* ZEW Centre for European Economic Research Discussion Paper No.13-094.

Borissenko, Y., and Boschma, R. (2016). A critical review of entrepreneurial ecosystems towards a future research agenda. *Paper in Evolutionary Economic Geography* 16(30), 1–20.

Breuer, W., and Pinkwart, A. (2018). Venture capital and private equity finance as key determinants of economic development. *Journal of Business Economics* 88(3–4), 319–324.

Brown, K. C., and Wiles, K. W. (2015). In search of unicorns: Private IPOs and the changing markets for private equity investments and corporate control. *Journal of Applied Corporate Finance* 27(3), 34–48.

Cahen, F. R. (2019). Internationalization of Brazilian high-tech startups. In M. Oliveira Jr, F. Cahen, and F. Borini, eds. *Startups and Innovation Ecosystems in Emerging Markets.* Palgrave Macmillan, Cham. doi.org/10.1007/978-3-030-10865-6_3

Cahen, F., Casanova, L., and Miroux, A. (2021). *Innovation from Emerging Markets.* Cambridge University Press.

Cahen, F., Oliveira, M., and Borini, F. (2017). The internationalisation of new technology-based firms from emerging markets. *International Journal of Technology Management* 74(1), 23–44.

Calcagnini, G., Favaretto, I., Giombini, G., Perugini, F., and Rombaldoni, R. (2016). The role of universities in the location of innovative start-ups. *The Journal of Technology Transfer* 41(4), 670–693.

Cao, Z., and Shi, X. (2021). A systematic literature review of entrepreneurial ecosystems in advanced and emerging economies. *Small Bussiness Economics* 57, 75–110. doi.org/10.1007/s11187–020-00326-y

Casanova, L., and Miroux, A. (2023). *Emerging market multinational report 2023 risks and realignments.* Cornell S. C. Johnson College of Business, Emerging Markets Institute.

Casanova, L., Miroux, A., and Finchelstein, D. (2021). Digital companies driving business model innovation in emerging markets: The cases of Alibaba, Flipkart, Jumia and Mercado Libre. In F. Cahen, L. Casanova, and A. Miroux, eds. *From Copycat to Leaders: Innovation from Emerging Markets.* Cambridge University Press, pp. 122–149.

Castilla, E. J. (2003). Networks of venture capital firms in Silicon Valley. *International Journal of Technology Management* 25(1), 113–135.

CB Insights. (2023). www.cbinsights.com/

CFI Team. (2023, 16 May). *Emerging market economy*. Corporate Finance Institute. corporatefinanceinstitute.com/resources/economics/emerging-market-economy

Chemmanur, T., Loutskina, E., and Tian, X. (2014). Corporate venture capital, value creation, and innovation. *The Review of Financial Studies 27(*8), 2434–2473. doi.org/10.1093/rfs/hhu033

Chen, Y., Li, H., and Zhou, L.-A. (2005). Relative performance evaluation and the turnover of provincial leaders in China. *Economics Letters 88*(3), 421–25. www.sciencedirect.com/science/article/abs/pii/S0165176505001813

Chesbrough, H. W. (2002). Making sense of corporate venture capital. *Harvard Business Review 80*(3), 90–99.

Cristofaro, M., Giannetti, F., and Abatecola, G. (2023). The initial survival of the unicorns: A behavioral perspective of Snapchat. *Journal of Management History* 29(4), 456–480. doi.org/10.1108/JMH-11-2022-0066

Cuervo-Cazurra, A., Carneiro, J., Finchelstein, D., Duran, P., Gonzalez-Perez, M. A., Montoya, M. A., Borda Reyes, A., Fleury, M. T. L., and Newburry, W. (2018). Uncommoditizing strategies by emerging market firms. *Multinational Business Review 27*(2), 141–177.

Cumming, D., and Dai, N. (2011). Fund size, limited attention and valuation of venture capital backed firms. *Journal of Empirical Finance 18*(1), 2–15.

Dahl, M., and Sorenson, O. (2012). Home sweet home: Entrepreneurs' location choices and the performance of their ventures. *Management Science 58*(6), 1059–1071.

Das, A., and Kapil, S. (2015). Inorganic growth of technology sector firms in emerging markets: Influence of firm-specific factors in Indian firms' M&A activities. *International Journal of Emerging Markets 10*(1), 52–72.

Dias, R. D. S., and Macedo, M. A. D. S. (2016). Private equity and venture capital funds: What drives the demand and supply? *BAR Brazilian Administration Review 13*(2), 1–21.

Divan, D. (2016). What's the difference between a US$0 million and a US$0 billion company? *IEEE Power Electronics Magazine 3*(1), 69–70.

Duque, J. G., Andonova, V., and Correa, M. E. (2021). Innovation in war and peace: How Colombian conflict and postconflict triggered military and business model innovation. In F. Cahen, L. Casanova, and A. Miroux, eds. *Innovation from Emerging Markets: From Copycats to Leaders*. Cambridge University Press, pp. 325–348.

ESCAP. (2018). *Evolution of science, technology and innovation policies for sustainable development: The experiences of China, Japan, the Republic of Korea and Singapore*. Economic and Social Commission for Asia and the Pacific, United Nations. Flanders Investment and Trade.

Faulconbridge, G. (2023, 24 November). *Putin says West cannot have AI monopoly so Russia must up its game*. Reuters. tinyurl.com/2nw2nuje

Fenwick, M., and Vermeulen, E. P. M. (2015). The new firm: Staying relevant, unique and competitive. *European Business Organization Law Review 16*(4), 595–623.

Finchelstein, D. (2018).Social embedding of the corporation: Family conglomerates around the world. In A. Nölke and C. May, eds. *Handbook of the International Political Economy of the Corporation*. Eldgar Online, pp. 199–214.

Fritsch, M. (2002). Measuring the quality of regional innovation systems: A knowledge production function approach. *International Regional Science Review 25*(1), 86–101.

Gaba, V., and Meyer, A. D. (2008). Crossing the organizational species barrier: How venture capital practices infiltrated the information technology sector. *Academy of Management Journal 51*(5), 976–998.

Gao, J., and Guo, Y. (2020). *The new Chinese unicorns: Seizing opportunity in China's burgeoning economy*. PWC. www.pwccn.com/en/research-and-insights/pwc-chinese-unicorns.pdf

Gilbert, B. A., McDougall, P. P., and Audretsch, D. B. (2008). Clusters, knowledge spillovers and new venture performance: An empirical examination. *Journal of Business Venturing 23*(4), 405–422.

Global Entrepreneurship Monitor. (2022/2023). *Report*. www.gemconsortium.org/reports/latest-global-report

Global Innovation Index. (2023). *Innovation in the face of uncertainty*. www.wipo.int/global_innovation_index/en/2023/

Global Times. (2021). *PwC survey on Chinese unicorns showed most companies slowing overseas business plans for pandemic and geopolitics reasons, with India failing to attract a single firm*. www.globaltimes.cn/page/202102/1214839.shtml

Gompers, P., and Lerner, J. (2000). Money chasing deals? The impact of fund inflows on private equity valuations. *Journal of Financial Economics 55*, 281–325.

Gornall, W., and Strebulaev, I. A. (2020). Squaring venture capital valuations with reality. *Journal of Financial Economics* 135(1), 120–143. www.sciencedirect.com/science/article/abs/pii/S0304405X19301692

Groh, A. P., and von Liechtenstein, H. (2011). The first step of the capital flow from institutions to entrepreneurs: The criteria for sorting venture capital funds. *European Financial Management 17*(3), 532–559.

Guede, B., Cancino, C., and Lezana, B. (2021). *Características de emprendimientos unicornio en América Latína*. Presented at XIX Congreso

Asociación Latino-Iberoamericana de Gestión Tecnológica, Lima, Peru. tinyurl.com/ybpez9fa

Guo, B., Lou, Y., and Pérez-Castrillo, D. (2015). Investment, duration, and exit strategies for corporate and independent venture capital-backed start-ups. *Journal of Economics and Management Strategy* 24(2), 415–455.

Hammer, B., Hinrichs, H., and Schweizer, D. (2016). Buy and build strategies in private equity: Boost or transformation? *SSRN Electronic Journal*. http://dx.doi.org/10.2139/ssrn.2819995

Häussler, C., Harhoff, D., Müller, E. (2008). *To be financed or not – The role of patents for venture capital financing*. ZEW Centre for European Economic Research Discussion Paper No. 09-003.

He, C., Lu, J., and Qian, H. (2018). Entrepreneurship in China. *Small Business Economics* 1, 1–10.

Hellmann, T., and Puri, M. (2002). Venture capital and the professionalization of start-up firms: Empirical evidence. *The Journal of Finance* 57(1), 169–197.

Hurun Research Institute. (2021). *Hurun global unicorn index 2021. Hurun Research Institute. www.hurun.net/en-US/Info/Detail?num=R18H7AJUWBIX*

Inderst, R., and Müller, H. M. (2004). The effect of capital market characteristics on the value of start-up firms. *Journal of Financial Economics* 72(2), 319–356.

Inc 42 Datalabs. (2023). *Decoding India's unicorn club report*. tinyurl.com/2ntytaff

Invest India. (2023). *The Indian unicorn landscape*.

Jackson, W. E., Bates, T., and Bradford, W. D. (2012). Does venture capitalist activism improve investment performance? *Journal of Business Venturing* 27(3), 342–354.

Jinzhi, Z., and Carrick, J. (2019). The rise of the Chinese unicorn: An exploratory study of unicorn companies in China. *Emerging Markets Finance and Trade*, 1–15. doi:10.1080/1540496x.2019.1610

Kaplan, S. N., and Strömberg, P. (2000). *How do venture capitalists choose investments*. Working Paper, University of Chicago, 121, 55–93.

Kenney, M., and Zysman, J. (2019). Unicorns, Cheshire cats, and the new dilemmas of entrepreneurial finance. *Venture Capital* 21(1), 35–50.

Kitagawa, F. (2004). Universities and regional advantage: Higher education and innovation policies in English regions. *European Planning Studies* 12(6), 835–852.

Krishnan, C. N. V., Ivanov, V. I., Masulis, R. W., and Singh, A. K. (2011). Venture capital reputation, post IPO performance, and corporate governance. *The Journal of Financial and Quantitative Analysis* 46(5), 1295–1333.

Lazarow, A. (2020, March–April). Beyond Silicon Valley: How start-ups succeed in unlikely places. *Harvard Business Review*. hbr.org/2020/03/beyond-silicon-valley

Maschke, K., and zu Knyphausen-Aufseß, D. (2012). How the entrepreneurial top management team setup influences firm performance and the ability to raise capital: A literature review. *Business Research* 5(1), 83–123.

Mason, C. and Brown, R. (2014). *Entrepreneurial ecosystems and growth oriented entrepreneurship*. Final Report to OECD, Paris, 30, 77–102.

Megginson, W. L., and Weiss, K. A. (1991). Venture capitalist certification in initial public offerings. *The Journal of Finance* 46(3), 879–903.

Minardi, A. M. A. F., Kanitz, R., and Bassani, R. H. (2020). An overview of the private equity and venture capital industry in Brazil. In D. Klonowski, ed. *Entrepreneurial Finance in Emerging Markets*. Palgrave Macmillan, pp.145–160. doi.org/10.1007/978-3-030-46220-8_10

Modi, N. (2023, 27 October). *In the development of digital technology, India is behind no developed nation*. Narendra Modi. tinyurl.com/5ecszh2m

Morck, R. (ed). (2000). *Concentrated Corporate Ownership*. University of Chicago Press.

Narayanan, V., Yang, Y., and Zahra, S. (2009). Corporate venturing and value creation: A review and proposed framework. *Research Policy* *38*(1), 58–76. doi.org/10.1016/j.respol.2008.08.015

Neubert, M. (2017). Lean internationalization: How to globalize early and fast in a small economy. *Technology Innovation Management Review* 7(5). ssrn.com/abstract=3394512

Paik, Y., and Woo, H. (2017). The effects of corporate venture capital, founder incumbency, and their interaction on entrepreneurial firms' R&D investment strategies. *Organization Science* *28*(4), 670–689.

Park, H., and Steensma, H. (2013).The selection and nurturing effects of corporate investors on new venture innovativeness. *Strategic Entrepreneurship Journal* 7(4), 273–342.

Poon, T., Wu, Ch., and Liu, M. (2023). Developing entrepreneurial ecosystem: A case of unicorns in China and its innovation policy implications. *Asian Journal of Technology Innovation* *32*(1), 20–36. doi.org/10.1080/19761597.2022.2157849

Prashantham, S., and Dhanaraj, C. (2010). The dynamic influence of social capital on the international growth of new ventures. *Journal of Management Studies* 47(6), 967–994. doi.org/10.1111/j.1467-6486.2009.00904.x

Reuters. (2023, 7 July). *China's Xi urges greater innovation amid tech curbs from US*. www.reuters.com/world/china/chinas-xi-urges-greater-innovation-amid-tech-curbs-us-2023-07-07/

Roach, M., and Sauermann, H. (2023). Can technology startups hire talented early employees? Ability, preferences, and employee first job choice. *Management Science 70*(6), 3381–4165. doi.org/10.1287/mnsc.2023.4868

Röhm, P., Köhn, A., Kuckertz, A., and Dehnen, H. S. (2018). A world of difference? The impact of corporate venture capitalists' investment motivation on startup valuation. *Journal of Business Economics 88*(3–4), 531–557.

Schmutzler, J., Andonova, V., and Diaz-Serrano, L. (2019). How context shapes entrepreneurial self-efficacy as a driver of entrepreneurial intentions: A multilevel approach. *Entrepreneurship Theory and Practice 43*(5), 880–920.

Siew Yean. T. (2023). *Rise of Unicorns in Southeast Asia*. The University of Melbourne Asialink.

Spigel, B., and Harrison, R. (2017). Toward a process theory of entrepreneurial ecosystems. *Strategic Entrepreneurship Journal 12*(1), 151–168. sms.onlinelibrary.wiley.com/doi/abs/10.1002/sej.1268

Somaya, D., and You, J. (2024). Scalability, venture capital availability, and unicorns: Evidence from the valuation and timing of IPOs. *Journal of Business Venturing 39*(1), Article 106345. doi.org/10.1016/j.jbusvent.2023.106345

Stam, E. (2015). Entrepreneurial ecosystems and regional policy: A sympathetic critique. *European Planning Studies 23*(9), 1759–1769.

Stayton, J. and Mangematin, V. (2018). Seed accelerators and the speed of new venture creation. *Journal of Technology Transfer 44*, 1163–1187.

Steigertahl, L., and Mauer, R. (2023). Investigating the success factors of the Nordic entrepreneurial ecosystem – Talent transformation as a key process. *The International Journal of Entrepreneurship and Innovation 24*(1), 7–18. doi.org/10.1177/14657503211051217

Testa, G., Compañó, R., Correia, A., and Rückert, E. (2022). *In search of EU unicorns –What do we know about them?* JRC Technical Report.

Tykvová, T. 2018. Venture capital and private equity financing: An overview of recent literature and an agenda for future research. *Journal of Business Economics 88*(3–4), 325–362.

Ubeda, F., Ortiz-de-Urbina-Criado, M., and Mora-Valentín, E.-M. (2019). Do firms located in science and technology parks enhance innovation performance? The effect of absorptive capacity. *The Journal of Technology Transfer 44*(1), 21–48.

Varoufakis, Y. (2023). *Technofeudalism: What Killed Capitalism*. Penguin, Random House.

Wadhwa, A., and Phelps, C. (2009). An option to partner: A dyadic analysis of CVC relationships. *Academy of Management Proceedings 2009*(1), 1–6.

Wennekers, S., and Thurik, R. (1999). Linking entrepreneurship and economic growth. *Small Business Economics 13*(1), 27–56.

Wright, M., Pruthi, S., and Lockett, A. (2005). International venture capital research: From cross-country comparisons to crossing borders. *International Journal of Management Reviews* 7(3), 135–165.

Zahra, S. A., and Nambisan, S. (2012). Entrepreneurship and strategic thinking in business ecosystems. *Business Horizons 55*(3), 219–229.

Zimmerman, J. L. (2016). Private equity, the rise of unicorns, and the reincarnation of control-based accounting. *Journal of Applied Corporate Finance 28*(3), 56–67. onlinelibrary.wiley.com/doi/10.1111/jacf.12193

3 *Unicorns: From Silicon Valley to a Global Phenomenon?*

JAN JACOB VOGELAAR AND ERIK STAM

3.1 Introduction

Entrepreneurship is widely recognised as a driver of economic growth and transformation (Schumpeter, 1934). For this reason, it has been cherished by governments worldwide. Over the past decades, the entrepreneurship research and policy community has largely shifted its interest from a broad conception of entrepreneurship to a narrower focus on a limited set of high-growth firms that have been found to contribute disproportionately to economic, employment and productivity growth (Henrekson & Johansson, 2010; Du & Temouri, 2015; Haltiwanger et al., 2017). This has become even narrower with a focus on venture capital-backed high-growth technology firms. This combination of venture capital, frontier technology and entrepreneurship has become known as the 'Silicon Valley model for entrepreneurship' (Herrmann, 2019; Audretsch, 2021). Unicorns, defined as privately held companies worth US$1 billion or more, are perhaps the most mythical manifestation of Silicon Valley entrepreneurship and have drawn particular attention (Kuckertz et al., 2023).

The unicorn phenomenon is novel both in reality and in terminology. The term was coined by Aileen Lee (2013) in her TechCrunch article 'Welcome to the unicorn club: Learning from billion-dollar start-ups' in 2013. Before the 2000s, founders simply took their start-ups public by issuing common stock (an initial public offering, hereafter IPO) before reaching unicorn status, rather than granting special privileges to new investors to achieve unicorn valuation. Google (founded 1999, IPO 2004) and Facebook (founded 2004, IPO 2012) are probably the best-known unicorns *avant la lettre*. In the last decade, IPOs have become less attractive for the start-ups that eventually become unicorns. Davydova et al. (2022) explain the rise of unicorns in two parts. Firstly, funding has become increasingly available to unicorns, reducing the funding and liquidity advantages of an

IPO for these start-ups. Secondly, a new type of 'platform company' has emerged that relies more on organisational capital and network effects to create a winner-takes-all-dynamic and achieve market dominance (Parker et al., 2016; Srnicek, 2017). These companies can become highly valuable if they manage to capture the benefits associated with the organisational capital and network effects that are central to their business plan. The emergence of this new type of firm makes it optimal for firms with unicorn status to stay private as they build up their organisational capital and network. However, this would not be possible without the increased availability of funding in recent years.

The mystique around unicorns and their potential to disrupt industries and shape the future economy has resulted in a growing body of research on unicorns (see Giardino et al., 2023) and prompted many countries to adopt policy objectives aimed at increasing their number. The European Commission, for example, has set the objective to double its number of unicorns by 2030 (Mocanu & Thiemann, 2023). The appeal of unicorns goes beyond their potential economic impacts. Mocanu and Thiemann (2023) document how the European Commissions' unicorn ambition also reflects the belief that unicorns are essential for ensuring technological leadership and accelerating the green and digital transition. Emerging economies including Indonesia, Malaysia and Vietnam (Sittipoonaegkapat, 2023) have expressed the ambition to increase their number of unicorns as well, and multiple African cities have been declared the new African Silicon Valley in popular media (Nkontwana & Stam, 2023).

However desirable, entrepreneurship is a rather skewed phenomenon in terms of success. Many new firms fail, and few start-ups ever reach a substantial size, let alone unicorn status. The unlikely emergence of unicorns has also been compared to black swans, calling them black swan start-ups (Mahroum, 2016). Studies suggest that the geographical distribution of unicorns is also highly uneven. The United States, China and, to a lesser extent, the European Union have been found to dominate the unicorn statistics (Testa et al., 2022) and even within those regions the distribution of unicorns is highly uneven. For instance, Testa et al. (2022) report that California, New York and Massachusetts accounted for 75 per cent of all unicorns within the United States in the 2008–2021 period.

Few studies have looked at unicorns in the context of emerging economies. As our data show many emerging economies have only recently begun to partake in the global unicorn landscape, making it particularly timely to consider their role. The aim of this chapter is to understand how the global geography of unicorns has evolved over the past decade and to reflect critically on its implications for emerging economies. To this end, we examine the development of the absolute number of unicorns between 2016 and 2024 and relate the number of unicorns to population. Additionally, we explore in what industries unicorns are most prevalent and how this varies across regions.

We are especially interested in the role of emerging economies in the evolving global geography of unicorns. While a widely accepted definition is not available, definitions of emerging economies often consider the comparatively low level of economic development, high pace of economic growth and the orientation towards a free-market system (Arnold & Quelch, 1998). Because of this ambiguity, we choose to pragmatically define emerging economies in this chapter based on the World Bank's classification by country income. The World Bank distinguishes between low income, lower-middle income, upper-middle income and high-income countries. We consider all countries that are not classified as high-income countries to be emerging economies.[1] As China is classified as an upper-middle income country, we will treat China as an emerging economy. Nonetheless, we are aware that China may soon become a high-income country and that scholars have argued that China has developed beyond emerging economy status (Bruton et al., 2021).

The analysis reveals that unicorns are very unevenly distributed across countries. The United States, China and, to a lesser extent, the European Union dominate the unicorn population. Meanwhile, the data show that there is a 'second league' of countries that consistently have over ten unicorns, suggesting that unicorns have become more of a global phenomenon. The fact that the number of countries with one unicorn or more is widening over time reinforces this idea. However, when we relate the number of unicorns to the population of countries, a more nuanced picture appears. From this analysis, Singapore and Israel emerge as high-performing countries in terms of unicorn output. Finally, the data demonstrates that about 40 per cent of all unicorns worldwide are concentrated in two industries: 'fintech' and 'internet

[1] In 2022 the threshold for high-income economies was a gross national income of US$13,845 per capita.

software and services'. This picture changes when we look at different regions. Compared to the global distribution, unicorns in emerging markets are relatively concentrated in the 'e-commerce and direct-to-consumer' and 'fintech' industries. Building on these insights, we develop a research agenda and discuss whether targeting unicorns is sensible policy for emerging economies.

3.2 Data and Methods

For our analysis, we combined unicorn data from Fortune (2017) (see also Lehmann et al., 2019) and CB Insights (2024) (see also Davydova et al., 2022; Venâncio et al., 2023). Fortune reported the actual number of unicorns in 2016 in their online magazine in 2017, and CB Insights provides an online tracker of the actual number of unicorns for the 2018–2024 period.[2] These datasets contain unicorns defined as privately held companies worth US$1 billion or more. In contrast to some other studies (for example Testa et al., 2022), 'exited' unicorns are not included in the datasets. Attribution to countries is based on the location of the headquarters, which can change over time. Based on these sources, a unicorn dataset was constructed for 2016 and 2018–2024. The dataset covered all countries with one or more unicorns at any point in this period (fifty-seven countries in total). To get a sense of the geographical concentration of unicorns, we calculated location quotients for all countries across the entire period. Location quotients are straightforward descriptive measures of concentration that allow us to grasp the number of unicorns compared to what would be expected based on a specific denominator. As is common in other studies (Leendertse et al., 2022), we related the number of unicorns to country level population data, retrieved from the World Bank (2023). In this case, a location quotient above one suggests that a country has more unicorns than we would expect based on its number of inhabitants. Conversely, a country with a location quotient below unity (value of one) has fewer unicorns than we would expect based on its population. The formula for calculating location quotient was as follows:

$$LQ_{cy} = \frac{U_{cy}/P_{cy}}{U_{wy}/P_{wy}}$$

2 We downloaded the list in February of each year.

Where LQ_{cy} is the location quotient of a given country '*c*' in a given year '*y*'. U_{cy} and P_{cy} are the number of unicorns and the population of the same country, respectively. U_{wy} and P_{wy} are the number of unicorns and the population worldwide '*w*' in a given year, respectively.

The usage of location quotients for understanding the concentration of unicorns is not without limitations. As unicorns are rather exclusive phenomena, the number of data points remains limited. Several countries had at most one unicorn during the period studied. Especially in the first years when the total number of unicorns worldwide was still relatively low, one additional unicorn could have a considerable effect on a country's location quotient. This is even more true for countries with smaller populations. Location quotients should thus be interpreted with caution (Miller et al., 1991). Additionally, we also computed the number of unicorns per ten million inhabitants as a more intuitive measure of the density of unicorns per country.

To analyse the industry distribution of unicorns, we relied on the industry categorisations of CB Insights (we use the 2023 data, which is much more fine-grained than the 2024 data). Industry classifications differ between Fortune and CB Insights and have changed over the years, which makes longitudinal comparisons arduous. Therefore, we limit this analysis to the industry distribution for 2023.

3.3 Results

Over the past eight years, the number of unicorns worldwide has increased dramatically, from 174 unicorns in 2016 to 1,230 in 2024 (the number and share of unicorns per country are reported in Tables A3.1 and A3.2, included in the appendix). While our data is insufficient to provide a conclusive explanation for this stark increase, the supply of venture capital offers a potential explanation. Low interest rates driven by quantitative easing policies enabled the growth of private equity, with global venture capital investments increasing sharply from 2016 onwards and peaking in 2021 (CB Insights, 2024). The vast supply of venture capital may not just affect the number of high-growth firms; it also allows firms to remain private longer with the consequence of more firms reaching unicorn status. Overvaluation, perhaps driven by the desire of entrepreneurs and investors to reach unicorn status, provides another explanation for the growing number of unicorns (Gornall & Strebulaev, 2020).

The data show that in 2016 over two-thirds of all unicorns worldwide could be found in two countries: the United States (57 per cent) and China (21 per cent). The European Union, if considered as a whole, trails far behind with only 6 per cent of all unicorns. Only thirteen other countries had at least one unicorn in 2016. In the subsequent years, the United States maintained its leading position as the nursery for unicorns throughout the years and has, in absolute terms, significantly widened the gap with China. Only in 2019 was the United States nearly overtaken by China, with 125 and 119 unicorns, respectively. The gap between the United States and China and the European Union has widened in absolute terms (see Figure 3.1). In some respects, this picture has not changed much in 2024. While the total number of unicorns worldwide has increased to 1,230, the triad of the United States, China and the European Union remains intact. The United States is still responsible for the majority of unicorns (657 unicorns, 53 per cent), again followed by China, although with a smaller share (170 unicorns, 14 per cent), and the European Union retains its third position, accounting for 106 unicorns (9 per cent).

Although the United States, China and the European Union still lead in terms of unicorn output, the increase in unicorns worldwide has led

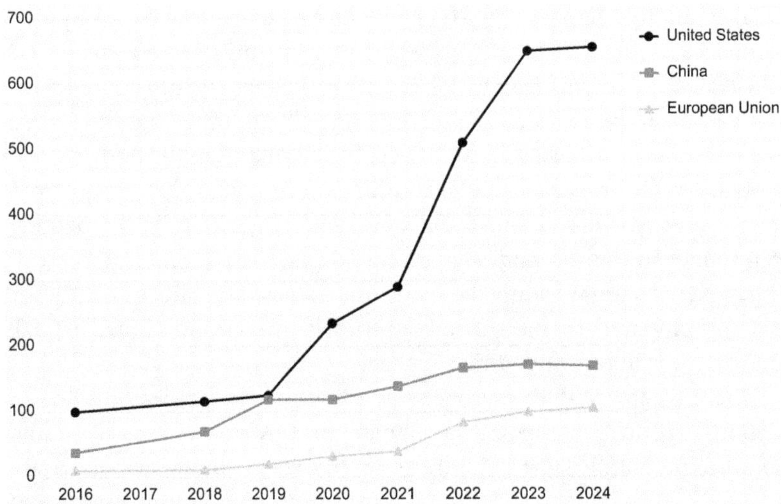

Figure 3.1 Number of unicorns in the United States, China and the European Union, 2016 and 2018–2024.

Source: Compiled by authors based on Fortune (2017) and CB Insights (2024).

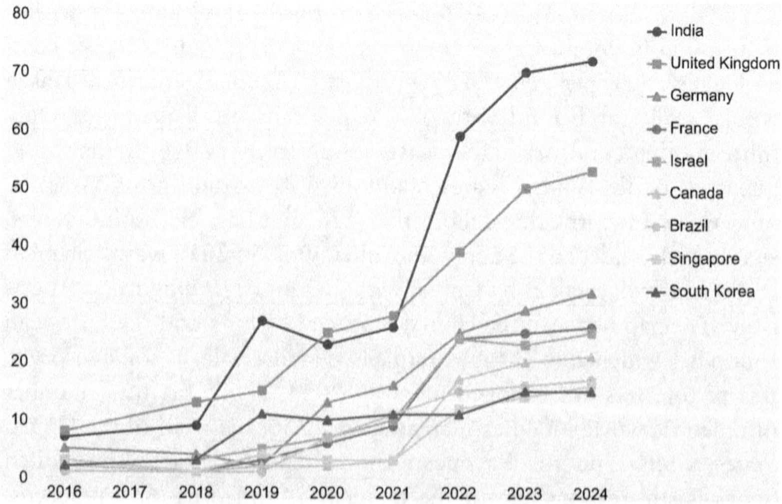

Figure 3.2 Number of unicorns in selected countries (all countries with >10 unicorns in 2024, excluding China and the United States), 2016 and 2018–2024.

Source: Compiled by authors based on Fortune (2017) and CB Insights (2024).

to meaningful changes. By 2024, unicorns can be found in fifty-two countries, compared to just sixteen countries in 2016. As Figure 3.2 illustrates, a 'second league' of countries has emerged, each consistently home to more than ten unicorns since 2020. India and the United Kingdom lead this league, followed by Germany and South Korea. Brazil, Israel, France, Canada and Singapore joined this group from 2021 onwards. Brazil and India stand out as the only two emerging economies in this 'second league'. India's case is particularly interesting, given its significantly lower gross domestic product (GDP) per capita compared to the other countries in this group (Brazil's GDP per capita is about three times higher).

There is remarkable heterogeneity among the (once) leading BRICS countries (Brazil, Russia, India, China, South Africa). China is leading in absolute number just behind the United States, Brazil and India are hosting a growing and substantial number of unicorns and Russia and South Africa are stagnating at best, with Russia having had only one unicorn in 2019. Indonesia and Mexico now appear to be better positioned than these two lagging BRICS members.

India and Brazil are the most prominent runners-up. In 2016, India launched its large-scale entrepreneurship policy 'Start-up India' (Tiwari et al., 2021; Khanna, 2022). Most of its unicorns (and venture capital) are concentrated in Mumbai, Bangalore and Delhi. Although India has taken important steps, its entrepreneurial ecosystem still suffers from serious issues (Tiwari et al., 2021; Khanna, 2022). The government has set up a fund-of-funds to tackle the severely constrained access to finance in India, which is not yet fulfilling its promise (Tiwari et al., 2021). Moreover, scholars have observed that investments are concentrated in relatively low-tech sectors as opposed to science-based start-ups, due to lack of access to knowledge (Khanna, 2022).

As Feferman (2022) documents, Brazil began its own large-scale entrepreneurship initiative in 2013 with 'Start-up Brasil'. Multiple accelerators, both for-profit and public, have been established and many venture capitalists have entered Brazil, especially since 2017. A notable characteristic of Brazilian start-ups is their focus on addressing issues specific to the Brazilian context, such as high transaction costs, information asymmetries, underdeveloped logistics and imperfect regulatory systems. These start-ups have managed to address and overcome these frictions and inefficiencies (also known as 'Brazil cost', which refers to the fact that many aspects of doing business are simply more expensive than in comparable countries) through technology. Interestingly, these 'institutional voids' may provide Brazilian start-ups with a competitive advantage over international competitors who lack a thorough understanding of such contextual conditions.

It is notable that many countries do not follow the global upward trend in unicorn numbers. Most countries had no unicorn at all during the period studied (2016, 2018–2024). Moreover, about half of all countries that did have at least one unicorn in the period studied never had more than two unicorns in any given year. This group includes countries from various continents, such as Argentina, Denmark and Senegal. It is perhaps no surprise that most emerging economies fall into this category. Figure 3.3 zooms in on emerging economies, showing how the number of unicorns has developed in those (excluding China) that had at least three unicorns in 2024. A final noteworthy observation is that within the group of countries with their first unicorn, many newcomers appeared in 2022, 2023 and 2024: in Europe (Austria, Denmark, Greece, Norway, Finland, Italy and Liechtenstein), but also in Africa (Egypt, Senegal, Seychelles), South America

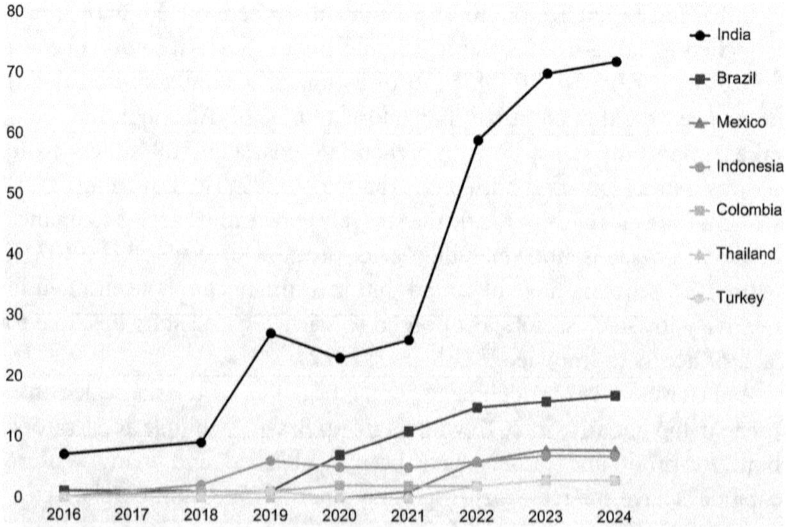

Figure 3.3 Number of unicorns in selected emerging economies (all emerging economies with >2 unicorns in 2024, excluding China), 2016 and 2018–2024.
Source: Compiled by authors based on Fortune (2017) and CB Insights (2024).

(Ecuador), Asia (Malaysia, Saudi Arabia, Thailand, Vietnam) and North America (Cayman Islands). This suggests that, even though the geographical distribution remains highly skewed, unicorns have become more of a global phenomenon, with a growing number of emerging economies now hosting at least one unicorn.

3.3.1 Unicorn Concentration

A more balanced, and arguably more policy-relevant, representation of the geographic distribution of unicorns is the number of unicorns per country relative to its population. Table 3.1 presents how the unicorn location quotients for a selected number of countries have changed over time. For a more comprehensive overview, Table A3.3 provides an overview of unicorn location quotients for all countries, while Table A3.4 reports the number of unicorns per 10 million inhabitants (both tables are included in the appendix).[3] Ranking the location quotients

[3] We also computed the location quotients based on GDP instead of population, but the results are not qualitatively different.

Table 3.1 ***Unicorn location quotients of selected countries ranked from high to low, 2016–2023***

	2016	2018	2019	2020	2021	2022	2023	2024
Singapore	23.03	5.66	15.29	8.40	7.33	16.93	16.39	18.73
Israel	10.07	10.78	12.04	12.10	14.22	19.97	15.88	17.26
United States	13.32	11.33	8.30	11.29	11.68	12.19	12.89	13.01
Estonia	0.00	0.00	16.44	11.98	10.01	11.79	9.78	9.78
Ireland	0.00	0.00	0.00	3.19	2.65	7.75	7.72	9.01
European Union	0.97	0.79	0.97	1.14	1.16	1.49	1.47	1.53
China	1.15	1.59	1.84	1.34	1.31	0.94	0.80	0.79
Brazil	0.21	0.15	0.10	0.52	0.68	0.55	0.49	0.52
India	0.23	0.21	0.43	0.26	0.25	0.33	0.33	0.34
South Africa	0.00	1.11	0.00	0.54	0.45	0.27	0.22	0.11
Indonesia	0.00	0.24	0.49	0.29	0.24	0.17	0.17	0.17

Note: For a full overview see Table A3.3 in the appendix.
Source: Compiled by authors based on CB Insights (2024), Fortune (2017) and the World Bank (2023).

from high to low reveals a picture that differs from the absolute ranking of unicorns per country. A first observation is that smaller economies outperform the United States, although it still has a location quotient well above unity in all years covered. In 2024, Singapore and Israel emerge as the top performing countries in terms of unicorns relative to their population, with location quotients of 18.73 and 17.26, respectively.[4] These figures suggest that these countries generate high numbers of unicorns despite their relatively small populations. Israel is widely regarded as an entrepreneurial powerhouse. Through dedicated government intervention, the Israeli government has successfully transformed its economy into a strong ecosystem for high-tech entrepreneurship (Breznitz, 2007). This transformation stands in stark contrast to its earlier characterisation as a country with extremely low levels of research and development (R&D) in the 1960s. Perhaps most notable are the country's efforts to build a thriving venture capital industry from scratch (Klingler-Vidra et al., 2016).

While fostering entrepreneurship has been central to Israel's economic strategy, economic policymaking in Singapore has historically revolved around attracting foreign multinational companies. More recently, Singapore has shifted its focus to entrepreneurship and innovation. At face value, a favourable interpretation of Singapore's unicorn location quotient development would be that this strategy bears fruit. This is particularly intriguing given that the active involvement of the Singaporean state has been critiqued for hindering entrepreneurship (Cheang, 2022; Audretsch & Fiedler, 2023). Audretsch and Fiedler (2023) propose an alternative explanation, namely that in 2021 all Singaporean unicorns were founded by foreign nationals. One such example is Moglix, a unicorn founded by the Indian entrepreneur Rahul Garg. While Moglix is headquartered in Singapore, it is a leading

[4] It should be noted that Bermuda, the Cayman Islands, Liechtenstein and the Seychelles also have location quotients higher than the United States and, as a matter of fact, higher than Israel and Singapore as well. Their high location quotients are explained by the presence of a single or two unicorn(s) in all four cases which, given their small populations, has resulted in extraordinarily high location quotients. As the presence of these single unicorns may be partly due to favourable tax conditions, we have decided not to include them in Table 3.1. These location quotients are reported in Table A3.3, included in the Appendix.

e-commerce company for industrial tools and equipment in India (Balachandran, 2021).

A comparison of China, the European Union and the United States reveals a stark difference between the United States and the other leading economic powers. In 2024, the United States had thirteen times more unicorns than we would expect based on its population. Only in 2019 did the country's location quotient drop below ten, reflecting a relatively stable performance over time. The sustained strong position of the United States is perhaps unsurprising. Investments in R&D and venture capital, two key inputs for unicorns, are significantly higher in the United States. Moreover, the country is characterised by formal and informal institutions that support high-growth entrepreneurship (Herrmann, 2019), such as flexible labour markets and a culture that fosters ambitious entrepreneurship (Herrmann, 2019; Stam, 2021).

The concentration of unicorns in China is considerably lower and has declined in recent years. Nevertheless, over the entire period studied, China's location quotient remained above unity in most years. This indicates that China's number of unicorns is largely in line with what would be expected based on its population. Given China's historical context, this is quite an achievement. Since its economic reforms in the 1980s, the Chinese government has been committed to private sector development, with investments in science and technology as a cornerstone of this strategy. More recently, the Chinese government has placed greater emphasis on creating an environment that is conducive to innovative entrepreneurship (Poon et al., 2023). This shift is also reflected in the Chinese government's commitment to developing the domestic venture capital market, which has grown steadily over the past decade and is now the second largest in the world (Malkin, 2021).

Similar to China, the European Union has a location quotient that has remained close to one throughout the years studied. In contrast to China, however, the trend is upward. This positive trend reflects the increased performance of some member states in the 2016–2024 period, including Estonia, France and Ireland. Mocanu and Thiemann (2023) analysed the European Union's ambition to double its number of unicorns by 2030. As noted earlier, their analysis highlights that this ambition is driven not only by the direct economic value associated with these extreme types of entrepreneurship. Instigated by geopolitical developments, policies to breed unicorns are also intended to secure technological sovereignty.

Turning the lens to emerging economies, it becomes clear that only a handful rank among the well-performing economies (i.e. economies with a location quotient above unity). Large emerging economies such as Brazil and India have location quotients well below one. Smaller emerging economies like South Africa and Uruguay have location quotients above one in some of the years studied but failed to maintain this position.

3.3.2 Industry Distribution

Tables A3.5, A3.6 and A3.7 (included in the appendix) report the distribution of unicorns across industries by global region in 2023. The data show that unicorns are more common in certain sectors. Around 40 per cent of all unicorns worldwide are concentrated in 'fintech' and 'internet software & services'. One potential explanation for the dominance of these industries is that software companies tend to scale faster than hardware companies (De la Tour et al., 2017). The distribution of North American unicorns over industries drives the global pattern. A relatively high number of the unicorns in Europe and South America belong to the 'fintech' sector, comprising 33 per cent and 44 per cent of the total, respectively. Given the low numbers of unicorns in Africa and Oceania, these industry distributions provide limited insights.

Asian unicorns are distributed more evenly across industries. The 'e-commerce and direct to consumer' industry stands out, with its share almost double that of North America (17 per cent vs. 9 per cent). When comparing Asia's unicorn profile to the rest of the world, it becomes clear that although 27 per cent of all unicorns are based in Asia, 50 per cent or more of the unicorns in 'automotive and transportation', 'e-commerce and direct to consumer', 'edtech', 'hardware', 'mobile and telecommunications' and 'travel' are headquartered on the continent. This reflects the greater prominence of hardware-based industries in Asia's unicorn profile. In contrast, North America's unicorn profile is more weighted towards software-based industries, with 83 per cent of 'cybersecurity' unicorns, 74 per cent of 'internet software and services' unicorns and 78 per cent of 'data management and analytics' unicorns headquartered in the region. This may reflect the relative strength of these regions in these specific industries.

Andonova et al. (2021) have demonstrated that unicorns in emerging economies tend to be concentrated in lower-tech, mass-market domains. A closer look at the industry distribution among all unicorns in emerging economies confirms this trend. The data indicates a relative concentration of emerging economy unicorns in the 'e-commerce and direct-to-consumer' and 'fintech' industries. Andonova et al. (2021) do not consider China an emerging economy. If we exclude China from our list of emerging economies, the concentration of unicorns in these industries increases even further. In the remaining emerging economies, 22 per cent of unicorns are in 'e-commerce and direct-to-consumer', while 32 per cent are in 'fintech'. Distinct opportunities in these sectors in emerging economies might explain this concentration. Emerging economies face specific challenges, such as high levels of unbanked individuals (Demirgüç-Kunt et al., 2015), which can present business opportunities for large scale, low-cost solutions to overcome these challenges (Andonova et al., 2021).

3.4 Conclusion and Discussion

Unicorns have become exclusive symbols of entrepreneurial success and hold extraordinary appeal to policymakers. The aim of this chapter was to gain insight into how the global geography of unicorns has evolved over the past decade, with a specific focus on the role of emerging economies. From the analysis, we can draw three main conclusions.

First of all, our analysis reveals a highly skewed distribution of unicorns across the globe. This is accentuated by the dominant position of the United States, China and, albeit to a lesser extent, the European Union. Their dominance holds over time, but the gap between the United States and the two other economic powers has widened since 2020. This is an important observation from a hegemonic perspective, as unicorns can have a significant impact on the global economy, as well as on societies. At the same time, a 'second league' of countries has emerged that consistently host more than ten unicorns. This suggests that unicorns have become a more global phenomenon. The finding that the number of countries with at least one unicorn is growing further supports this proposition. This expanding group also includes multiple emerging economies.

Secondly, relating the number of unicorns to population provides a more nuanced picture. The unicorn location quotient analysis reveals that Singapore and Israel were the best-performing countries in 2024. They are followed by the United States, which maintains a consistently high number of unicorns relative to its population. In contrast, China and the European Union have an average performance most years. Relating unicorn output to population is arguably more relevant from a policy perspective, as it can be indicative of the extent to which countries are living up to their potential. Accordingly, the performance of Singapore and Israel, along with other recent high performers such as Estonia and Ireland, is particularly intriguing. However, a deeper look reveals spatial concentration of unicorns within (especially large) economies. If California and Massachusetts in the United States and Shanghai and Beijing in China were counted as separate countries, their unicorn performance would surpass that of Singapore and Israel.

Whether the high number of unicorns in particular places is the result of coincidence or effective government intervention deserves further scrutiny. With few exceptions, emerging economies have fewer unicorns than expected based on their populations. This is perhaps unsurprising, as population alone is clearly an imperfect predictor of high-growth entrepreneurship. Instead, a set of factors that enable entrepreneurship, such as access to finance and talent, sufficient infrastructure and new knowledge creation, explain why certain localities produce more entrepreneurial output than others (Stam, 2015; Leendertse et al., 2022). These contextual factors may be less robust in emerging economies, where entrepreneurial ecosystems are not yet 'mature' (Kantis et al., 2020).

Thirdly, our analysis indicates that unicorns are distributed unevenly across industries. On a global level, around 40 per cent of unicorns are concentrated in the 'fintech' and 'internet software and services' industries. Industry distribution varies across regions, with Asian unicorns relatively more dispersed across different industries. A closer look at Asia and North America shows that Asia's unicorn profile is more hardware-based, whereas North America's unicorn profile is more software-based. This may reflect the relative strength of these economic powers in these respective industries. An examination of emerging economy unicorns reveals a concentration within the 'e-commerce and direct-to-consumer' and 'fintech' industries.

3.4.1 Implications for Future Research

The explorative analysis presented in this chapter raises various questions for future research and highlights the uneven distribution of unicorns across the globe. This raises the question: What conditions are necessary to nurture unicorns and what role can governments play in this process? The entrepreneurial ecosystem approach (Stam, 2015; Wurth et al., 2022) provides a useful starting point for explaining these differences. A recent study on European regions shows that the quality of entrepreneurial ecosystems is a strong predictor of the prevalence of unicorns (Leendertse et al., 2022). Building on this insight, future studies should investigate whether specific entrepreneurial ecosystem configurations are more conducive to unicorn creation than others (Venâncio et al., 2023; Schrijvers et al., 2024). Moreover, future studies should explore emerging economies more thoroughly, as much of the entrepreneurial ecosystem literature is based on insights generated in high-income economies.

How unicorns create value for their localities presents another relevant direction for future research. Although unicorns have been celebrated as symbols of entrepreneurial success, concerns have been raised about how they create value, at what cost and for whom. Scholars have emphasised that entrepreneurship has a direction: Financial valuation does not necessarily equate to social value creation (Mazzucato, 2018; Kuckertz et al., 2023). From this perspective, other types of entrepreneurship might better fit an inclusive economic growth paradigm (Herrmann, 2019; Audretsch, 2021; Breznitz, 2021). Although these concerns are well-documented, few studies have explored the impacts of unicorns on their communities in depth. Such studies could contribute to the discussion on more inclusive types of entrepreneurship and shed new light on prior studies that have utilised unicorn presence as a proxy for productive entrepreneurship (see for example Leendertse et al., 2022) or suggested that unicorn output reflects the maturity of entrepreneurial ecosystems (Andonova et al., 2021).

Studying value creation by unicorns is especially relevant in the context of emerging economies, because emerging markets may present opportunities for value creation that differ from those in high-income economies:

> We conjecture that the natural and endowed conditions of emerging economies such as large populations coupled with a lack of basic infrastructure and services offer excellent opportunities for unicorns, which can provide solutions and even boost technological leap-frogging in basic services such as banking or education. (Andonova et al., 2021: 181)

This also resembles Feferman's (2022) earlier point. He suggests that in Brazil, such 'institutional voids' may give Brazilian start-ups a competitive advantage over foreign firms that lack a deep understanding of the local institutional context. A similar point is made in Chapter 14 of this book, where the structural conditions of emerging markets are highlighted as a crucial point for the unique value proposition of unicorns from the Global South.

These arguments resemble the concept of market-creating innovations, which emphasises the importance of accessible and affordable innovations that reach large, underserved populations who previously had no access to the product or service (Christensen et al., 2018). The American unicorn Zipline is an interesting example in this regard. The company uses autonomous drones for precise delivery in areas where infrastructure, or the lack thereof, hinders the fast delivery of goods. Zipline was founded and is based in the United States but started its operations in Rwanda, initially delivering blood and medical products (Zipline, 2024). Exploring whether the success of unicorns in emerging economies can indeed be attributed to such market-creating innovations would be a valuable next step.

Investigating the relocation behaviour of unicorns presents a final avenue for future research. Like other multinational companies, unicorns are not necessarily tied to the locality in which they were founded. A recent study shows that forty out of 147 unicorns founded in the European Union between 2008 to 2021 relocated their headquarters elsewhere, primarily to the United States (Testa et al., 2022). The authors hypothesise that access to venture capital is a key explanation, but more research is needed to assess this hypothesis and identify other reasons why unicorns might be inclined to relocate. The case of Singapore is particularly intriguing. Many of the unicorns headquartered in the city-state were founded elsewhere (Audretsch & Fiedler, 2023) and/or had foreign-born founders (Lee et al., 2024). Whether this makes them more likely to relocate compared to ventures founded by local entrepreneurs warrants further analysis. As exemplified by the Moglix case, Singapore's situation highlights that the location of unicorns may not reflect the markets they serve and, therefore, where they create most value for consumers. Future studies should take this into consideration when evaluating the value of unicorns.

3.4.2 Policy Implications for Emerging Economies: Is Targeting Unicorns Sensible Policy?

One question that arises is whether targeting unicorns is sensible policy for emerging economies that currently lag in terms of unicorn output. Unicorns are exclusive phenomena that have been embraced by policy-makers seeking to promote economic development and enhance hegemony in a global economy tempered by geopolitical tensions (Mocanu & Thiemann, 2023). While there is a case to be made for targeting unicorns, their exclusivity also poses a challenge, making chasing unicorns tricky policy for both pragmatic and normative reasons.

An initial argument for caution is that scholars have extensively documented the difficulty in identifying high-growth firms, let alone unicorns (Stam & Bosma, 2015; Terjesen et al., 2016). For one thing, as Brown et al. (2017: 418) stress, high growth is a state rather than a characteristic of a firm, making high-growth firms 'effectively a "moving target"'. This challenge, combined with a lack of sound evidence supporting the effectiveness of policies intended to foster high-growth firms (Lerner, 2009; Mason & Brown, 2013), raises the question of whether targeting unicorns is effective policy. As previously noted, relocation behaviour poses a second concern. The risk of unicorns relocating away from the country where they were founded is perhaps a more significant risk for emerging economies, as their institutions, internal markets and venture capital markets tend to be less developed. From a policy perspective, this suggests that actively investing in the creation of unicorns may be insufficient to capture the value created by this exclusive subset of firms. Retaining unicorns is also necessary, yet unicorns' relocation behaviour and the underlying motivations remain understudied.

Moreover, while many countries have attempted to replicate Silicon Valley, a region that has proven to be fertile ground for unicorns, most efforts have failed. The varieties of capitalism framework proposed by Hall and Soskice (2001) and applied to entrepreneurship by others (Dilli et al., 2018; Herrmann, 2019) may offer cues for understanding these failed efforts. In essence, the argument is that institutions, defined as the formal and informal 'rules of the game', shape how resources critical for entrepreneurship (such as finance, talent and new knowledge) are allocated, how relationships are governed and how economic activities are coordinated. Different institutional contexts explain why liberal market economies like the United States are better suited to fostering typical

Silicon Valley entrepreneurship. In contrast, coordinated market economies, commonly illustrated by the case of Germany, are more conducive to medium-tech entrepreneurship characterised by incremental innovation. Following this logic, emerging economies should not blindly chase unicorns but instead focus on the types of entrepreneurship that best align with their local institutional contexts, embracing the idea of 'comparative institutional advantage' (Hall & Soskice, 2001).

Finally, there is a normative argument against adopting unicorns as the target of entrepreneurship policy. While Silicon Valley and Israel's start-up ecosystem are widely regarded as success stories of entrepreneurship and innovation, scholars have also identified a dark side to these stories. Both regions are characterised by high levels of inequality (Breznitz, 2021; Kwon & Sorenson, 2023), which is already a burning issue for many emerging economies. This resonates with studies on the micro-level stakeholder consequences of high-growth firms, which show that rapid growth may come at the cost of stakeholders of these firms (Kuratko et al., 2020; Schrijvers & Vogelaar, 2025). Moreover, a concentration of high-tech firms can have negative repercussions for other parts of the economy. It raises the costs of doing business as salaries and prices increase, while these firms attract human and financial capital at the expense of other industries. This could lead to a less diversified, and thus less resilient, economy in the long run (Kwon & Sorenson, 2023).

In conclusion, policymakers in emerging economies find themselves in a difficult position. While the appeal of unicorns is understandable, many emerging economies play a limited role in the global unicorn landscape thus far. Whether it is effective to attempt to alter this through entrepreneurship policy remains uncertain. The critical perspective presented here highlights that targeting unicorns is challenging, and their impact is unlikely to be unequivocally positive. Rather than blindly pursuing the Silicon Valley model, scholars have suggested that policymakers should foster types of entrepreneurship that better fit their local context (Herrmann, 2019; Audretsch, 2021; Breznitz, 2021), particularly in emerging economies (Nkontwana & Stam, 2023). Although whether the negatives outweigh the positives is an empirical question, the discussed repercussions of unicorns on localities underscore the need for a more nuanced perspective in emerging economies towards these mythical entrepreneurial creatures.

Appendix

Table A3.1 *Unicorns per country, 2016 and 2018–2024*

	2016	2018	2019	2020	2021	2022	2023	2024
Argentina	0	0	1	0	0	1	1	1
Australia	0	1	3	2	3	6	8	9
Austria	0	0	0	0	0	2	2	2
Belgium	0	0	2	0	1	3	3	3
Bermuda	0	0	0	0	1	1	1	1
Brazil	1	1	1	7	11	15	16	17
Canada	2	1	2	2	3	17	20	21
Cayman Islands	0	0	0	0	0	0	0	1
Chile	0	0	1	0	0	2	2	2
China	37	70	119	119	139	167	172	170
Colombia	0	1	1	2	2	2	3	3
Croatia	0	0	0	1	1	1	2	2
Czech Republic	1	1	0	0	0	1	1	1
Denmark	0	0	0	0	0	2	2	2
Ecuador	0	0	0	0	0	0	1	1
Egypt	0	0	0	0	0	0	0	1
Estonia	0	0	1	1	1	2	2	2
Finland	0	0	0	0	0	2	4	4
France	1	1	3	6	9	24	25	26
Germany	5	4	2	13	16	25	29	32
Greece	0	0	0	0	0	0	0	2

Hong Kong	0	0	4	5	4	7	7	6
India	7	9	27	23	26	59	70	72
Indonesia	0	2	6	5	5	6	7	7
Ireland	0	0	0	1	1	5	6	7
Israel	2	3	5	7	10	24	23	25
Italy	0	0	0	0	0	0	2	2
Japan	0	2	2	4	4	6	6	7
Liechtenstein	0	0	0	0	0	0	1	1
Lithuania	0	0	1	1	1	1	2	2
Luxembourg	0	1	2	1	1	1	1	1
Malaysia	0	0	0	0	0	1	1	1
Malta	0	1	0	0	0	0	0	0
Mexico	0	0	0	0	1	6	8	8
Netherlands	1	2	0	2	3	5	7	7
Nigeria	0	1	0	0	0	1	1	1
Norway	0	0	0	0	0	4	4	4
Philippines	0	0	0	1	1	2	2	1
Portugal	0	0	3	1	0	0	0	0
Russia	1	0	1	0	0	0	0	0
Saudi Arabia	0	0	0	0	0	0	0	1
Senegal	0	0	0	0	0	1	1	1
Seychelles	0	0	0	0	0	0	1	2
Singapore	3	1	4	3	3	12	14	16
South Africa	0	2	0	2	2	2	2	1
South Korea	2	3	11	10	11	11	15	15

Table A3.1 (*cont.*)

	2016	2018	2019	2020	2021	2022	2023	2024
Spain	0	0	2	2	2	4	5	5
Sweden	2	1	4	3	3	6	7	6
Switzerland	0	2	3	4	5	4	6	5
Thailand	0	0	0	0	0	2	3	3
Turkey	0	0	1	0	0	2	3	3
Ukraine	0	0	2	0	0	0	0	0
United Arab Emirates	1	1	1	2	2	3	3	5
United Kingdom	8	13	15	25	28	39	50	53
United States	100	116	125	235	291	511	651	657
Uruguay	0	0	0	1	1	0	0	0
Vietnam	0	0	0	0	0	2	2	2
World	174	240	355	491	592	1000	1205	1230

Source: The unicorn data was compiled by authors based on Fortune (2017) and CB Insights (2024).
Note: Countries that had no unicorn at any point in the period studied (2016, 2018–2023) are not included in this table.

Table A3.2 *Share of unicorns per country, 2016 and 2018–2024*

	2016 (%)	2018 (%)	2019 (%)	2020 (%)	2021 (%)	2022 (%)	2023 (%)	2024 (%)
Argentina	0.00	0.00	0.28	0.00	0.00	0.10	0.08	0.08
Australia	0.00	0.42	0.85	0.41	0.51	0.60	0.66	0.73
Austria	0.00	0.00	0.00	0.00	0.00	0.20	0.17	0.16
Belgium	0.00	0.00	0.56	0.00	0.17	0.30	0.25	0.24
Bermuda	0.00	0.00	0.00	0.00	0.17	0.10	0.08	0.08
Brazil	0.57	0.42	0.28	1.43	1.86	1.50	1.33	1.38
Canada	1.15	0.42	0.56	0.41	0.51	1.70	1.66	1.71
Cayman Islands	0.00	0.00	0.00	0.00	0.00	0.00	0.00	0.08
Chile	0.00	0.00	0.28	0.00	0.00	0.20	0.17	0.16
China	21.26	29.17	33.52	24.24	23.48	16.70	14.27	13.82
Colombia	0.00	0.42	0.28	0.41	0.34	0.20	0.25	0.24
Croatia	0.00	0.00	0.00	0.20	0.17	0.10	0.17	0.16
Czech Republic	0.57	0.42	0.00	0.00	0.00	0.10	0.08	0.08
Denmark	0.00	0.00	0.00	0.00	0.00	0.20	0.17	0.16
Ecuador	0.00	0.00	0.00	0.00	0.00	0.00	0.08	0.08
Egypt	0.00	0.00	0.00	0.00	0.00	0.00	0.00	0.08
Estonia	0.00	0.00	0.28	0.20	0.17	0.20	0.17	0.16
Finland	0.00	0.00	0.00	0.00	0.00	0.20	0.33	0.33
France	0.57	0.42	0.85	1.22	1.52	2.40	2.07	2.11
Germany	2.87	1.67	0.56	2.65	2.70	2.50	2.41	2.60
Greece	0.00	0.00	0.00	0.00	0.00	0.00	0.00	0.16

Table A3.2 (*cont.*)

	2016 (%)	2018 (%)	2019 (%)	2020 (%)	2021 (%)	2022 (%)	2023 (%)	2024 (%)
Hong Kong	0.00	0.00	1.13	1.02	0.68	0.70	0.58	0.49
India	4.02	3.75	7.61	4.68	4.39	5.90	5.81	5.85
Indonesia	0.00	0.83	1.69	1.02	0.84	0.60	0.58	0.57
Ireland	0.00	0.00	0.00	0.20	0.17	0.50	0.50	0.57
Israel	1.15	1.25	1.41	1.43	1.69	2.40	1.91	2.03
Italy	0.00	0.00	0.00	0.00	0.00	0.00	0.17	0.16
Japan	0.00	0.83	0.56	0.81	0.68	0.60	0.50	0.57
Liechtenstein	0.00	0.00	0.00	0.00	0.00	0.00	0.08	0.08
Lithuania	0.00	0.00	0.28	0.20	0.17	0.10	0.17	0.16
Luxembourg	0.00	0.42	0.56	0.20	0.17	0.10	0.08	0.08
Malaysia	0.00	0.00	0.00	0.00	0.00	0.10	0.08	0.08
Malta	0.00	0.42	0.00	0.00	0.00	0.00	0.00	0.00
Mexico	0.00	0.00	0.00	0.00	0.17	0.60	0.66	0.65
Netherlands	0.57	0.83	0.00	0.41	0.51	0.50	0.58	0.57
Nigeria	0.00	0.42	0.00	0.00	0.00	0.10	0.08	0.08
Norway	0.00	0.00	0.00	0.00	0.00	0.40	0.33	0.33
Philippines	0.00	0.00	0.00	0.20	0.17	0.20	0.17	0.08
Portugal	0.00	0.00	0.85	0.20	0.00	0.00	0.00	0.00
Russia	0.57	0.00	0.28	0.00	0.00	0.00	0.00	0.00
Saudi Arabia	0.00	0.00	0.00	0.00	0.00	0.00	0.00	0.08
Senegal	0.00	0.00	0.00	0.00	0.00	0.10	0.08	0.08
Seychelles	0.00	0.00	0.00	0.00	0.00	0.00	0.08	0.16
Singapore	1.72	0.42	1.13	0.61	0.51	1.20	1.16	1.30
South Africa	0.00	0.83	0.00	0.41	0.34	0.20	0.17	0.08
South Korea	1.15	1.25	3.10	2.04	1.86	1.10	1.24	1.22

Spain	0.00	0.00	0.56	0.41	0.34	0.40	0.41	0.41
Sweden	1.15	0.42	1.13	0.61	0.51	0.60	0.58	0.49
Switzerland	0.00	0.83	0.85	0.81	0.84	0.40	0.50	0.41
Thailand	0.00	0.00	0.00	0.00	0.00	0.20	0.25	0.24
Turkey	0.00	0.00	0.28	0.00	0.00	0.20	0.25	0.24
Ukraine	0.00	0.00	0.56	0.00	0.00	0.00	0.00	0.00
United Arab Emirates	0.57	0.42	0.28	0.41	0.34	0.30	0.25	0.41
United Kingdom	4.60	5.42	4.23	5.09	4.73	3.90	4.15	4.31
United States	57.47	48.33	35.21	47.86	49.16	51.10	54.02	53.41
Uruguay	0.00	0.00	0.00	0.20	0.17	0.00	0.00	0.00
Vietnam	0.00	0.00	0.00	0.00	0.00	0.20	0.17	0.16
World	100.00	100.00	100.00	100.00	100.00	100.00	100.00	100.00

Source: The unicorn data was compiled by authors based on Fortune (2017) and CB Insights (2024).

Note: Countries that had no unicorn at any point in the period studied (2016, 2018–2023) are not included in this table.

Table A3.3 *Unicorn location quotients per country, 2016 and 2018–2024*

	2016	2018	2019	2020	2021	2022	2023	2024
Argentina	0.00	0.00	0.49	0.00	0.00	0.17	0.14	0.14
Australia	0.00	1.28	2.58	1.24	1.56	1.83	2.03	2.28
Austria	0.00	0.00	0.00	0.00	0.00	1.76	1.46	1.46
Belgium	0.00	0.00	3.80	0.00	1.15	2.04	1.69	1.69
Bermuda	0.00	0.00	0.00	0.00	208.97	125.15	103.86	103.86
Brazil	0.21	0.15	0.10	0.52	0.68	0.55	0.49	0.52
Canada	2.38	0.86	1.16	0.84	1.05	3.47	3.39	3.56
Cayman Islands	0.00	0.00	0.00	0.00	0.00	0.00	0.00	96.04
Chile	0.00	0.00	1.15	0.00	0.00	0.81	0.67	0.67
China	1.15	1.59	1.84	1.34	1.31	0.94	0.80	0.79
Colombia	0.00	0.65	0.43	0.63	0.52	0.31	0.38	0.38
Croatia	0.00	0.00	0.00	3.93	3.44	2.06	3.42	3.42
Czech Republic	4.07	3.00	0.00	0.00	0.00	0.75	0.62	0.62
Denmark	0.00	0.00	0.00	0.00	0.00	2.69	2.24	2.24
Ecuador	0.00	0.00	0.00	0.00	0.00	0.00	0.37	0.37
Egypt	0.00	0.00	0.00	0.00	0.00	0.00	0.00	0.06
Estonia	0.00	0.00	16.44	11.98	10.01	11.79	9.78	9.78
Finland	0.00	0.00	0.00	0.00	0.00	2.86	4.75	4.75
France	0.65	0.48	0.97	1.41	1.77	2.81	2.43	2.52
Germany	2.61	1.54	0.52	2.49	2.56	2.37	2.28	2.52
Greece	0.00	0.00	0.00	0.00	0.00	0.00	0.00	1.27

Hong Kong	0.00	0.00	11.62	10.65	7.19	7.58	6.29	5.39
India	0.23	0.21	0.43	0.26	0.25	0.33	0.33	0.34
Indonesia	0.00	0.24	0.49	0.29	0.24	0.17	0.17	0.17
Ireland	0.00	0.00	0.00	3.19	2.65	7.75	7.72	9.01
Israel	10.07	10.78	12.04	12.10	14.22	19.97	15.88	17.26
Italy	0.00	0.00	0.00	0.00	0.00	0.00	0.22	0.22
Japan	0.00	0.50	0.34	0.50	0.42	0.38	0.32	0.37
Liechtenstein	0.00	0.00	0.00	0.00	0.00	0.00	167.78	167.78
Lithuania	0.00	0.00	7.80	5.70	4.76	2.81	4.66	4.66
Luxembourg	0.00	52.50	70.35	25.26	20.82	12.17	10.10	10.10
Malaysia	0.00	0.00	0.00	0.00	0.00	0.23	0.19	0.19
Malta	0.00	65.86	0.00	0.00	0.00	0.00	0.00	0.00
Mexico	0.00	0.00	0.00	0.00	0.11	0.37	0.41	0.41
Netherlands	2.53	3.70	0.00	1.83	2.28	2.25	2.61	2.61
Nigeria	0.00	0.16	0.00	0.00	0.00	0.04	0.03	0.03
Norway	0.00	0.00	0.00	0.00	0.00	5.83	4.84	4.84
Philippines	0.00	0.00	0.00	0.14	0.12	0.14	0.11	0.06
Portugal	0.00	0.00	6.36	1.55	0.00	0.00	0.00	0.00
Russia	0.30	0.00	0.15	0.00	0.00	0.00	0.00	0.00
Saudi Arabia	0.00	0.00	0.00	0.00	0.00	0.00	0.00	0.18
Senegal	0.00	0.00	0.00	0.00	0.00	0.46	0.38	0.38
Seychelles	0.00	0.00	0.00	0.00	0.00	0.00	55.04	110.08
Singapore	23.03	5.66	15.29	8.40	7.33	16.93	16.39	18.73
South Africa	0.00	1.11	0.00	0.54	0.45	0.27	0.22	0.11
South Korea	1.68	1.86	4.63	3.07	2.83	1.69	1.92	1.92

Table A3.3 (*cont.*)

	2016	2018	2019	2020	2021	2022	2023	2024
Spain	0.00	0.00	0.93	0.67	0.56	0.67	0.69	0.69
Sweden	8.68	3.14	8.49	4.62	3.84	4.55	4.40	3.78
Switzerland	0.00	7.50	7.63	7.38	7.65	3.62	4.51	3.76
Thailand	0.00	0.00	0.00	0.00	0.00	0.22	0.28	0.28
Turkey	0.00	0.00	0.26	0.00	0.00	0.19	0.23	0.23
Ukraine	0.00	0.00	0.98	0.00	0.00	0.00	0.00	0.00
United Arab Emirates	4.79	3.49	2.37	3.43	2.85	2.53	2.10	3.49
United Kingdom	5.25	6.24	4.89	5.94	5.57	4.63	4.93	5.22
United States	13.32	11.33	8.30	11.29	11.68	12.19	12.89	13.01
Uruguay	0.00	0.00	0.00	4.64	3.89	0.00	0.00	0.00
Vietnam	0.00	0.00	0.00	0.00	0.00	0.16	0.13	0.13
World	1.00	1.00	1.00	1.00	1.00	1.00	1.00	1.00

Source: The unicorn data was compiled by authors based on Fortune (2017) and CB Insights (2024).

Note: Countries that had no unicorn at any point in the period studied (2016, 2018–2023) are not included in this table. As population data for 2023 were not yet released at the time of writing, the location quotients for 2023 are calculated based on the 2022 population data.

Table A3.4 *Unicorns per ten million inhabitants per country, 2016 and 2018–2024*

	2016	2018	2019	2020	2021	2022	2023	2024
Argentina	0.00	0.00	0.22	0.00	0.00	0.22	0.22	0.22
Australia	0.00	0.40	1.18	0.78	1.17	2.31	3.08	3.46
Austria	0.00	0.00	0.00	0.00	0.00	2.21	2.21	2.21
Belgium	0.00	0.00	1.74	0.00	0.86	2.57	2.57	2.57
Bermuda	0.00	0.00	0.00	0.00	156.83	157.40	157.40	157.40
Brazil	0.05	0.05	0.05	0.33	0.51	0.70	0.74	0.79
Canada	0.55	0.27	0.53	0.53	0.78	4.37	5.14	5.39
Cayman Islands	0.00	0.00	0.00	0.00	0.00	0.00	0.00	145.55
Chile	0.00	0.00	0.53	0.00	0.00	1.02	1.02	1.02
China	0.27	0.50	0.85	0.84	0.98	1.18	1.22	1.20
Colombia	0.00	0.20	0.20	0.39	0.39	0.39	0.58	0.58
Croatia	0.00	0.00	0.00	2.47	2.58	2.59	5.19	5.19
Czech Republic	0.95	0.94	0.00	0.00	0.00	0.94	0.94	0.94
Denmark	0.00	0.00	0.00	0.00	0.00	3.39	3.39	3.39
Ecuador	0.00	0.00	0.00	0.00	0.00	0.00	0.56	0.56
Egypt	0.00	0.00	0.00	0.00	0.00	0.00	0.00	0.09
Estonia	0.00	0.00	7.54	7.52	7.51	14.83	14.83	14.83
Finland	0.00	0.00	0.00	0.00	0.00	3.60	7.20	7.20
France	0.15	0.15	0.45	0.89	1.33	3.53	3.68	3.83
Germany	0.61	0.48	0.24	1.56	1.92	2.98	3.46	3.82
Greece	0.00	0.00	0.00	0.00	0.00	0.00	0.00	1.92

Table A3.4 (*cont.*)

	2016	2018	2019	2020	2021	2022	2023	2024
Hong Kong	0.00	0.00	5.33	6.68	5.40	9.53	9.53	8.17
India	0.05	0.07	0.20	0.16	0.18	0.42	0.49	0.51
Indonesia	0.00	0.07	0.22	0.18	0.18	0.22	0.25	0.25
Ireland	0.00	0.00	0.00	2.01	1.99	9.75	11.70	13.65
Israel	2.34	3.38	5.52	7.60	10.67	25.11	24.06	26.16
Italy	0.00	0.00	0.00	0.00	0.00	0.00	0.34	0.34
Japan	0.00	0.16	0.16	0.32	0.32	0.48	0.48	0.56
Liechtenstein	0.00	0.00	0.00	0.00	0.00	0.00	254.28	254.28
Lithuania	0.00	0.00	3.58	3.58	3.57	3.53	7.06	7.06
Luxembourg	0.00	16.45	32.26	15.86	15.62	15.31	15.31	15.31
Malaysia	0.00	0.00	0.00	0.00	0.00	0.29	0.29	0.29
Malta	0.00	20.63	0.00	0.00	0.00	0.00	0.00	0.00
Mexico	0.00	0.00	0.00	0.00	0.08	0.47	0.63	0.63
Netherlands	0.59	1.16	0.00	1.15	1.71	2.82	3.95	3.95
Nigeria	0.00	0.05	0.00	0.00	0.00	0.05	0.05	0.05
Norway	0.00	0.00	0.00	0.00	0.00	7.33	7.33	7.33
Philippines	0.00	0.00	0.00	0.09	0.09	0.17	0.17	0.09
Portugal	0.00	0.00	2.92	0.97	0.00	0.00	0.00	0.00
Russia	0.07	0.00	0.07	0.00	0.00	0.00	0.00	0.00
Saudi Arabia	0.00	0.00	0.00	0.00	0.00	0.00	0.00	0.27
Senegal	0.00	0.00	0.00	0.00	0.00	0.58	0.58	0.58
Seychelles	0.00	0.00	0.00	0.00	0.00	0.00	83.42	166.84
Singapore	5.35	1.77	7.01	5.28	5.50	21.29	24.84	28.38
South Africa	0.00	0.35	0.00	0.34	0.34	0.33	0.33	0.17

South Korea	0.39	0.58	2.12	1.93	2.13	2.13	2.91	2.91
Spain	0.00	0.00	0.42	0.42	0.42	0.84	1.05	1.05
Sweden	2.02	0.98	3.89	2.90	2.88	5.72	6.67	5.72
Switzerland	0.00	2.35	3.50	4.63	5.74	4.56	6.84	5.70
Thailand	0.00	0.00	0.00	0.00	0.00	0.28	0.42	0.42
Turkey	0.00	0.00	0.12	0.00	0.00	0.24	0.35	0.35
Ukraine	0.00	0.00	0.45	0.00	0.00	0.00	0.00	0.00
United Arab Emirates	1.11	1.09	1.09	2.15	2.14	3.18	3.18	5.30
United Kingdom	1.22	1.96	2.24	3.73	4.18	5.82	7.47	7.91
United States	3.10	3.55	3.81	7.09	8.76	15.33	19.53	19.71
Uruguay	0.00	0.00	0.00	2.92	2.92	0.00	0.00	0.00
Vietnam	0.00	0.00	0.00	0.00	0.00	0.20	0.20	0.20
World	0,23	0,31	0,46	0,63	0,75	1,26	1,52	1,55

Source: The unicorn data was gathered from Fortune (2017) and CB Insights (2024).

Table A3.5 *Unicorn distribution over industries per region (absolute numbers), 2023*

Industry	World	Africa	Asia	Oceania	Europe	Latin America and Caribbean	USA and Canada	*Emerging economies*	*Emerging economies (excluding China)*
Artificial intelligence	90	0	25	0	7	3	55	20	1
Auto & transportation	37	0	19	0	8	0	10	19	2
Consumer & retail	31	1	12	0	3	1	14	11	3
Cybersecurity	58	0	8	0	2	0	48	1	0
Data management & analytics	45	0	4	0	6	0	35	3	1
E-commerce & direct-to-consumer	109	0	57	1	16	7	28	56	27
Edtech	32	0	20	0	2	0	10	19	7
Fintech	252	3	43	2	53	14	137	46	39
Hardware	40	0	20	0	5	0	15	18	0
Health	96	0	14	0	9	0	73	12	2
Internet software & services	228	0	36	5	19	0	168	29	14
Mobile & telecommunications	40	1	21	0	4	1	13	18	5
Other	66	0	14	0	14	2	36	10	4
Supply chain, logistics, & delivery	67	0	28	0	8	4	27	26	14
Travel	14	0	7	0	5	0	2	5	2
Total	1205	5	328	8	161	32	671	293	121

Source: The unicorn industry data was gathered from CB Insights (2024).

Table A3.6 *Unicorn distribution over industries per region (percentages), 2023*

Industry	World	Africa	Asia	Oceania	Europe	Latin America and Caribbean	USA and Canada	*Emerging economies*	*Emerging economies (excluding China)*
Artificial intelligence	7.5%	0.0%	7.6%	0.0%	4.3%	9.4%	8.2%	6.8%	0.8%
Auto & transportation	3.1%	0.0%	5.8%	0.0%	5.0%	0.0%	1.5%	6.5%	1.7%
Consumer & retail	2.6%	20.0%	3.7%	0.0%	1.9%	3.1%	2.1%	3.8%	2.5%
Cybersecurity	4.8%	0.0%	2.4%	0.0%	1.2%	0.0%	7.2%	0.3%	0.0%
Data management & analytics	3.7%	0.0%	1.2%	0.0%	3.7%	0.0%	5.2%	1.0%	0.8%
E-commerce & direct-to-consumer	9.0%	0.0%	17.4%	12.5%	9.9%	21.9%	4.2%	19.1%	22.3%
Edtech	2.7%	0.0%	6.1%	0.0%	1.2%	0.0%	1.5%	6.5%	5.8%
Fintech	20.9%	60.0%	13.1%	25.0%	32.9%	43.8%	20.4%	15.7%	32.2%
Hardware	3.3%	0.0%	6.1%	0.0%	3.1%	0.0%	2.2%	6.1%	0.0%
Health	8.0%	0.0%	4.3%	0.0%	5.6%	0.0%	10.9%	4.1%	1.7%
Internet software & services	18.9%	0.0%	11.0%	62.5%	11.8%	0.0%	25.0%	9.9%	11.6%
Mobile & telecommunications	3.3%	20.0%	6.4%	0.0%	2.5%	3.1%	1.9%	6.1%	4.1%
Other	5.5%	0.0%	4.3%	0.0%	8.7%	6.3%	5.4%	3.4%	3.3%
Supply chain. logistics. & delivery	5.6%	0.0%	8.5%	0.0%	5.0%	12.5%	4.0%	8.9%	11.6%
Travel	1.2%	0.0%	2.1%	0.0%	3.1%	0.0%	0.3%	1.7%	1.7%

Source: The unicorn industry data was gathered from CB Insights (2024).

Table A3.7 *Share of worldwide unicorn population per industry and region, 2023*

Industry	Africa	Asia	Oceania	Europe	Latin America and Caribbean	USA and Canada	*Emerging economies*	*Emerging economies (excluding China)*
Artificial intelligence	0.0%	27.8%	0.0%	7.8%	3.3%	61.1%	22.2%	1.1%
Auto & transportation	0.0%	51.4%	0.0%	21.6%	0.0%	27.0%	51.4%	5.4%
Consumer & retail	3.2%	38.7%	0.0%	9.7%	3.2%	45.2%	35.5%	9.7%
Cybersecurity	0.0%	13.8%	0.0%	3.4%	0.0%	82.8%	1.7%	0.0%
Data management & analytics	0.0%	8.9%	0.0%	13.3%	0.0%	77.8%	6.7%	2.2%
E-commerce & direct-to-consumer	0.0%	52.3%	0.9%	14.7%	6.4%	25.7%	51.4%	24.8%
Edtech	0.0%	62.5%	0.0%	6.3%	0.0%	31.3%	59.4%	21.9%
Fintech	1.2%	17.1%	0.8%	21.0%	5.6%	54.4%	18.3%	15.5%
Hardware	0.0%	50.0%	0.0%	12.5%	0.0%	37.5%	45.0%	0.0%
Health	0.0%	14.6%	0.0%	9.4%	0.0%	76.0%	12.5%	2.1%
Internet software & services	0.0%	15.8%	2.2%	8.3%	0.0%	73.7%	12.7%	6.1%
Mobile & telecommunications	2.5%	52.5%	0.0%	10.0%	2.5%	32.5%	45.0%	12.5%
Other	0.0%	21.2%	0.0%	21.2%	3.0%	54.5%	15.2%	6.1%
Supply chain. logistics. & delivery	0.0%	41.8%	0.0%	11.9%	6.0%	40.3%	38.8%	20.9%
Travel	0.0%	50.0%	0.0%	35.7%	0.0%	14.3%	35.7%	14.3%
Total	0.4%	27.2%	0.7%	13.4%	2.7%	55.7%	24.3%	10.0%

Source: The unicorn industry data was gathered from CB Insights (2024).

References

Andonova, V., García, J., and Andrés, G. A. (2021). What unicorns say about emerging markets and the respective entrepreneurial ecosystems: Three cases from Latin America. In L. Casanova and A. Miroux, eds. *Emerging Market Multinationals Report 2020: 10 Years That Changed Emerging Markets.* Cornell University, pp. 155–163.

Arnold, D. J., and Quelch, J. A. (1998). *New strategies in emerging markets.* MIT Sloan Management Review. sloanreview.mit.edu/article/new-strategies-in-emerging-markets/

Audretsch, D. B. (2021). Have we oversold the Silicon Valley model of entrepreneurship? *Small Business Economics 56*(2), 849–856.

Audretsch, D. B., and Fiedler, A. (2023). Does the entrepreneurial state crowd out entrepreneurship? *Small Business Economics 60*(2), 573–589.

Balachandran, M. (2021, 7 June). *Moglix: How Rahul Garg built an unexpected unicorn.* Forbes India. tinyurl.com/3yu3hsjw

Breznitz, D. (2007). *Innovation and the State: Political Choice and Strategies for Growth in Israel, Taiwan, and Ireland.* Yale University Press.

(2021). *Innovation in Real Places: Strategies for Prosperity in an Unforgiving World.* Oxford University Press.

Brown, R., Mawson, S., and Mason, C. (2017). Myth-busting and entrepreneurship policy: The case of high growth firms. *Entrepreneurship & Regional Development 29*(5–6), 414–443.

Bruton, G. D., Ahlstrom, D., and Chen, J. (2021). China has emerged as an aspirant economy. *Asia Pacific Journal of Management 38*(1), 1–15.

CB Insights. (2023). *The complete list of unicorn companies.* www.cbinsights.com/research-unicorn-companies

(2024). *The complete list of unicorn companies.* www.cbinsights.com/research-unicorn-companies

Cheang, B. (2022). *What can industrial policy do? Evidence from Singapore.* The Review of Austrian Economics.

Christensen, C. M., Ojomo, E., Gay, G. D., and Auerswald, P. E. (2018). The third answer: How market-creating innovation drives economic growth and development. *Innovations: Technology, Governance, Globalization 12*(3–4), 10–26. doi.org/10.1162/inov_a_00272

Davydova, D., Fahlenbrach, R., Sanz, L., and Stulz, R. M. (2022). *The unicorn puzzle.* Working Paper No. 30604. National Bureau of Economic Research. doi.org/10.3386/w30604

De la Tour, A., Soussan, P., Harlé, N., Chevalier, R., and Duportet, X. (2017). *From Tech to Deep Tech. Fostering Collaboration between*

Corporates and Startups. Boston Consulting Group & Hello Tomorrow.

Demirgüç-Kunt, A., Klapper, L. F., Singer, D., and Van Oudheusden, P. (2015). *The global findex database 2014: Measuring financial inclusion around the world*. SSRN Scholarly Paper No. 2594973. papers.ssrn.com/abstract=2594973

Dilli, S., Elert, N., and Herrmann, A. M. (2018). Varieties of entrepreneurship: Exploring the institutional foundations of different entrepreneurship types through 'Varieties-of-Capitalism' arguments. *Small Business Economics 51*, 293–320.

Du, J., and Temouri, Y. (2015). High-growth firms and productivity: Evidence from the United Kingdom. *Small Business Economics 44*(1), 123–143.

Feferman, F. (2022). The Brazilian innovation ecosystem takes off. In J. S. Engel, ed. *Clusters of Innovation in the Age of Disruption*. Edward Elgar Publishing, pp. 374–418.

Fortune. (2017). *The unicorn list ranking (2016)*. http://fortune.com/unicorns/

Giardino, P. L., Delladio, S., Baiocco, S., and Caputo, A. (2023). Beyond myth: A systematic literature review on the emergence of unicorn firms. *Journal of Small Business and Enterprise Development 30*(6), 1156–1177.

Gornall, W., and Strebulaev, I. A. (2020). Squaring venture capital valuations with reality. *Journal of Financial Economics 135*(1), 120–143. doi.org/10.1016/j.jfineco.2018.04.015

Hall, P. A., and Soskice, D. (2001). *Varieties of Capitalism: The Institutional Foundations of Comparative Advantage*. Oxford University Press.

Haltiwanger, J., Jarmin, R. S., Kulick, R., and Miranda, J. (2017). High growth young firms: Contribution to job growth, revenue growth and productivity. In J. Haltiwanger, E. Hurst, J. Miranda, and A. Schoar, eds. *Measuring Entrepreneurial Businesses: Current Knowledge and Challenges*. University of Chicago Press.

Henrekson, M., and Johansson, D. (2010). Gazelles as job creators: A survey and interpretation of the evidence. *Small Business Economics 35*(2), 227–244.

Herrmann, A. M. (2019). A plea for varieties of entrepreneurship. *Small Business Economics 52*(2), 331–343. doi.org/10.1007/s11187–018-0093-6

Kantis, H. D., Federico, J. S., and García, S. I. (2020). Entrepreneurship policy and systemic conditions: Evidence-based implications and recommendations for emerging countries. *Socio-Economic Planning Sciences* 72, 100872.

Khanna, T. (2022). *Science-based entrepreneurship in India: A policy glass (as yet) quarter-full.* tinyurl.com/4kc9ayth

Klingler-Vidra, R., Kenney, M., and Breznitz, D. (2016). Policies for financing entrepreneurship through venture capital: Learning from the successes of Israel and Taiwan. *International Journal of Innovation and Regional Development* 7(3), 203. doi.org/10.1504/IJIRD.2016.079462

Kuckertz, A., Scheu, M., and Davidsson, P. (2023). Chasing mythical creatures – A (not-so-sympathetic) critique of entrepreneurship's obsession with unicorn startups. *Journal of Business Venturing Insights 19*, e00365. doi.org/10.1016/j.jbvi.2022.e00365

Kuratko, D. F., Holt, H. L., and Neubert, E. (2020). Blitzscaling: The good, the bad, and the ugly. *Business Horizons 63*(1), 109–119. doi.org/10.1016/j.bushor.2019.10.002

Kwon, D., and Sorenson, O. (2023). The Silicon Valley syndrome. *Entrepreneurship Theory and Practice 47*(2), 344–368. doi.org/10.1177/10422587211050892

Lee, A. (2013, 2 November). *Welcome to the unicorn club: Learning from billion-dollar startups.* TechCrunch. techcrunch.com/2013/11/02/welcome-to-the-unicorn-club/

Lee, N., Ni, M., and Boey, A. (2024). *The scale-up state: Singapore's industrial policy for the digital economy.* LSE Southeast Asia Working Paper Series, 11.

Leendertse, J., Schrijvers, M., and Stam, E. (2022). Measure twice, cut once: Entrepreneurial ecosystem metrics. *Research Policy 51*(9), 104336. doi.org/10.1016/j.respol.2021.104336

Lehmann, E. E., Schenkenhofer, J., and Wirsching, K. (2019). Hidden champions and unicorns: A question of the context of human capital investment. *Small Business Economics 52*(2), 359–374.

Lerner, J. (2009). *Boulevard of Broken Dreams: Why Public Efforts to Boost Entrepreneurship and Venture Capital Have Failed and What To Do about It.* Princeton University Press.

Mahroum, S. (2016). *Black Swan Start-Ups: Understanding the Rise of Successful Technology Business in Unlikely Places.* Palgrave MacMillan.

Malkin, A. (2021). *China's experience in building a venture capital sector: Four lessons for policy makers.* CIGI Papers No. 248, pp. i–20. Centre for International Governance Innovation. www.jstor.org/s8/resrep28842.1

Mason, C. M., and Brown, R. (2013). Creating good public policy to support high-growth firms. *Small Business Economics 40*(2), 211–225.

Mazzucato, M. (2018). *The Value of Everything: Making and Taking in the Global Economy.* Hachette UK.

Miller, M. M., Gibson, L. J., and Wright, N. G. (1991). Location quotient: A basic tool for economic development analysis. *Economic Development Review* 9(2), 65–68.

Mocanu, D., and Thiemann, M. (2023). Breeding 'unicorns': Tracing the rise of the European investor state in the European venture capital market. *Competition & Change* 28(3–4), 10245294231204984. doi.org/10.1177/10245294231204984

Nkontwana, P., and Stam, E. (2023). Entrepreneurial ecosystems for the Africa we want. *USE Working Papers Series* 23(5). www.uu.nl/sites/default/files/LEG_USE_WP_23-05.pdf

Parker, G. G., Alstyne, M. W. V., and Choudary, S. P. (2016). *Platform Revolution: How Networked Markets Are Transforming the Economy and How To Make Them Work for You*. W. W. Norton & Company.

Poon, T. S.-C., Wu, C.-H., and Liu, M.-C. (2023). Developing entrepreneurial ecosystem: A case of unicorns in China and its innovation policy implications. *Asian Journal of Technology Innovation* 32(1), 1–17. doi.org/10.1080/19761597.2022.2157849

Schrijvers, M., Stam, E., and Bosma, N. (2024). Figuring it out: Configurations of high-performing entrepreneurial ecosystems in Europe. *Regional Studies* 58(5), 1096–1110. doi.org/10.1080/00343404.2023.2226727

Schrijvers, M., and Vogelaar, J. J. (2025). Grow, grow, grow? Stakeholder value creation by high-growth firms. *Small Business Economics (2025)*. doi.org/10.1007/s11187-025-01095-2

Schumpeter, J. A. (1934). *The Theory of Economic Development*. Harvard University Press.

Sittipoonaegkapat, K. (2023, 6 October). *Rise of unicorns in Southeast Asia*. Asialink. asialink.unimelb.edu.au/diplomacy/article/rise-unicorns-southeast-asia/

Srnicek, N. (2017). *Platform Capitalism*. John Wiley & Sons.

Stam, E. (2015). Entrepreneurial ecosystems and regional policy: A sympathetic critique. *European Planning Studies* 23(9), 1759–1769. doi.org/10.1080/09654313.2015.1061484

(2021). *A culture of ambitious entrepreneurship*. USE Working Paper Series, *21*(12). www.uu.nl/sites/default/files/LEG_USE_WP_21-12.pdf

Stam, E., and Bosma, N. (2015). Local policies for high-growth firms. In D. Audretsch, A. Link, and A. Walshok, eds. *The Oxford Handbook of Local Competitiveness*. Oxford University Press. pp. 286–305.

Terjesen, S., Bosma, N., and Stam, E. (2016). Advancing public policy for high-growth, female, and social entrepreneurs. *Public Administration Review* 76(2), 230–239. doi.org/10.1111/puar.12472

Testa, G., Compañó, R., Correia, A., and Rückert, E. (2022). *In search of EU unicorns: What do we know about them?* Joint Research Centre.

Tiwari, A., Hogan, T., and O'Gorman, C. (2021). The good, the bad, and the ugly of 'Startup India'—A review of India's entrepreneurship policy. *Economic & Political Weekly (EPW) 56*(50), Article 50.

Venâncio, A., Picoto, W., and Pinto, I. (2023). Time-to-unicorn and digital entrepreneurial ecosystems. *Technological Forecasting and Social Change 190*, 122425. doi.org/10.1016/j.techfore.2023.122425

The World Bank. (2023). *World development indicators. Population, total* [dataset]. data.worldbank.org/indicator/SP.POP.TOTL

Wurth, B., Stam, E., and Spigel, B. (2022). Toward an entrepreneurial ecosystem research program. *Entrepreneurship Theory & Practice* 46(3), 729–778. doi.org/10.1177/1042258721998948

Zipline. (2024). *About | Zipline drone delivery & logistics*. Zipline. www.flyzipline.com/about/

4 *Finding the Unicorns: A National Entrepreneurship Ecosystem Approach*

JOSÉ ERNESTO AMORÓS EDUARDO AVANCCI DIONISIO EDMUNDO INÁCIO JÚNIOR CRISTIANO MORINI LILIANE OLIVEIRA GUIMARÃES

4.1 Introduction

Entrepreneurship has garnered increasing attention from policymakers and researchers alike (Ács et al., 2016; Egan, 2021) due to its potential socioeconomic benefits, which include job creation (Henrekson & Johansson, 2010; Decker et al., 2014; Rey-Martí et al., 2016), reducing inequalities (Bruton et al., 2021) and driving innovation (Huesig et al., 2014; Pinkse et al., 2014; Si et al., 2020). In general, promoting productive entrepreneurship generates positive economic effects (Lucas & Fuller, 2017; Nicotra et al., 2018; Aeeni et al., 2019; Trubnikov, 2021). The entrepreneurial ecosystems (EEs) approach has gained prominence for understanding how new ventures are created and how the entrepreneurial context impacts on their performance (Stam, 2015; Ács et al., 2017). Interest in unicorns as high-growth, high-value ventures has been growing within this broad context.

An EE can be defined as a network of interconnected actors and environmental factors that facilitate entrepreneurship and influence the outcomes of new ventures (Carayannis et al., 2016; Mack & Mayer, 2016; Karami & Read, 2021; Shi & Shi, 2022). Governmental and non-governmental organisations, venture capitalists and market intelligence companies are keen on measuring entrepreneurial ecosystems. Institutions such as the World Bank, Organisation for Economic Cooperation and Development (OECD), Global Entrepreneurship Monitor (GEM) consortium and Startup Genome projects have developed indicators for capturing entrepreneurship conditions and classify entrepreneurial ecosystems (Ács et al., 2014; OECD, 2017; GEM, 2020; Startup Genome, 2020; World Bank, 2020).

Despite the widespread use of these indicators, particularly those from GEM, for comparing EEs' performance at a national level as well as their use in research that seeks to combine framework indicators with output variables, there are still few studies that assess whether GEM entrepreneurial framework conditions (EFCs) are necessary for different entrepreneurial outputs (Nicotra et al., 2018; Torres & Godinho, 2021). Necessary conditions are those in the absence of which the entrepreneurial output does not take place. As highlighted by various researchers (Stam, 2015; Alvedalen & Boschma, 2017; Stam & van de Ven, 2021), the literature on entrepreneurial ecosystems has largely overlooked testing whether the conditions measured by these indicators are necessary for entrepreneurship to occur. Studies typically rely on methods such as cluster analysis and utilise effort or input indicators, rarely combining them with output indicators (Kantis et al., 2020; Xie et al., 2021).

To address this gap, we propose applying a necessary condition analysis (NCA), a novel technique (Dul, 2016) that differs significantly from the previously applied qualitative comparative analysis (QCA) (Ragin, 1989), to allow us to answer the following research question: What are the necessary conditions inherent in EEs and to what extent do they affect the achievement of specific levels of entrepreneurial productive output, including the emergence of unicorn companies?

In this study, we focus on whether the indicators used by GEM represent necessary conditions for entrepreneurship. The choice of GEM indicators is motivated by the GEM status as the most relevant longitudinal and systemic study of the entrepreneurial context indicators, making them widely used in entrepreneurship research (Györfy & Madaras, 2019; Vyas & Vyas, 2019; Qin, 2021; Torres & Godinho, 2021).

In addition, we explore variations in entrepreneurial ecosystems between developed and emerging economies. This analysis sheds light on patterns, differences and innovation rates within each category. Such an analysis is crucial for understanding the nuances of entrepreneurial environments across different economic contexts. We have integrated this into our methodological approach to explore the necessary conditions and their critical levels for each desired output measure.

We use data from multiple sources, drawing from the EFCs provided by the GEM's national expert survey (NES) for measuring input entrepreneurial conditions, to output measures such as the proportion of early-stage start-ups (total early-stage entrepreneurial activity, or TEA), established businesses ownership (EBO) and high-expectation (HE) jobs TEA (HE-TEA) from the GEM adult population survey (APS). Additionally, private intelligence platforms such as Crunchbase, CB Insights, and Dealroom.co were used to create proxies for EE outputs such as funded start-ups (F-firms) and unicorn companies (unicorns).

We have organised the remainder of the chapter in the following way. In Section 4.2 we review literature related to entrepreneurial ecosystems in the context of developed and emerging economies. Section 4.3 describes the methodological approach, and Section 4.4 contains the results of the analysis. In Section 4.5 we discuss the implications of our findings and, finally, we provide concluding remarks and avenues for future research in Section 4.6.

4.2 Conceptualisation

4.2.1 Entrepreneurial Ecosystems as Providers of Entrepreneurial Conditions

Entrepreneurial ecosystems as a repository of resources and interactions are drivers for entrepreneurial development, but they can occasionally provide only the necessary (not the sufficient) conditions (Miller & le Breton-Miller, 2021) for entrepreneurs to explore economic opportunities through the creation of new ventures (Ács et al., 2017). We refer to the conditions that enable entrepreneurship and may include the availability of tangible or intangible assets that can affect entrepreneurial performance and its outcomes, such as knowledge (Qian et al., 2012; Qian & Ács, 2013; Zhang & Wang, 2022) embedded in local human capital (Spigel & Vinodrai, 2020). Although human capital is thought to be a necessary condition for companies to incorporate new technologies and/or develop new products and/or services (AlQershi et al., 2021; Hu, 2021), there are aspects that firms cannot obtain through formal economic exchanges; rather they affect the creation and development of new ventures (Bendig et al., 2018; Thompson et al., 2018). These conditions are provided by actors grouped in entrepreneurial ecosystems, such as venture capitalists and angel investors who contribute the necessary financial resources for the different stages of businesses (Dutta & Meierrieks, 2021) as well as formal and informal institutions (Pitelis, 2012), which provide political and cultural support for the creation of innovative businesses (Autio & Rannikko, 2016; Bogatyreva et al., 2019). A well-functioning EE, therefore, provides entrepreneurs with the conditions necessary to create and grow their businesses (Ács et al., 2017; Autio et al., 2018; Leendertse et al., 2022). Moreover, many latent actors such as individuals with entrepreneurial intentions, mentors, business angels, venture capitalists and small- and medium-sized enterprises (SMEs) settle within the spatial boundaries of an EE to access its conditions, thus strengthening the region through a process of accumulation and resource recycling. This results in the improvement of an EEs' existing conditions (Spigel, 2017; Spigel & Vinodrai, 2020), thus enabling a virtuous cycle of upgrading the ecosystem conditions.

There are two lines of research that deal with the conditions that a specially delimited entrepreneurial ecosystem can offer potential entrepreneurs and early-stage entrepreneurs. The first line of research proposes the specific conditions that could drive the creation of new ventures (Isenberg, 2011; Feld, 2012; Stam, 2015; Brown & Manson, 2017). Spigel (2017) highlights that EEs have three attributes: material attributes that include policies, universities, infrastructure, markets and support services; social attributes that address the networks, talent, mentors and role models and investment capital; and finally cultural attributes that include the supportive culture and stories of entrepreneurship. The existence and proper functioning of these attributes could provide potential entrepreneurs with the conditions for them to explore economic opportunities through the creation of new businesses. For example, in addition to providing qualified human capital proximity to universities and higher education and research institutions can also train new entrepreneurs and create knowledge spillovers (Huynh et al., 2017; Fuster et al., 2019). Furthermore, universities can provide the necessary infrastructure for the development of new ventures (Astebro et al., 2012).

The second line of research deals with empirically identifying the optimal set of conditions for driving entrepreneurship output levels through multivariate analysis methods, such as regression and/or fuzzy set/qualitative comparative analysis (fs/QCA). For example, Alves et al. (2021) used a fs/QCA approach to identify that in the case of São Paulo State in Brazil, knowledge-intensive entrepreneurial activity is more intense in cities that offer a combination of sufficient conditions for entrepreneurship, namely urban agglomeration, infrastructure, human capital and knowledge-intensive businesses services. Other researchers have approached EEs from an evolutionary perspective (Mack & Mayer, 2016), identifying that an EE's elements offer different conditions for boosting entrepreneurs during economic cycles (Auerswald & Dani, 2017). Furthermore, some EEs enjoy specific conditions that are more relevant to late-stage than early-stage start-ups (Vedula & Fitza, 2019).

In general, most studies associated with this second line of research focus on elements that produce outputs, while neglecting drivers that enable outputs – those necessary to obtain an outcome (van der Valk et al., 2016). Enabling drivers are necessary conditions because 'a necessary condition is a condition that must be present to enable a certain outcome; without the condition, the outcome will be absent' (van der Valk et al., 2016: 268). For example, a country's capacity to create and disseminate knowledge is a necessary condition for the emergence of digitally enabled unicorns. In absence of access to technological knowledge infrastructure, this form of digital entrepreneurship does not take place (Torres & Godinho, 2021). The literature on necessary conditions presupposes causality since the exclusion of an antecedent will prevent the output from occurring. Thus, a necessary condition is seen as a bottleneck that prevents a result from being achieved (Dul, 2016).

Statements that reflect this necessity are very common in entrepreneurship studies. For example, although they focus on sufficient conditions rather than necessary conditions, Xie et al. (2021) suggest that internet infrastructure and knowledge flows are conditions that produce high-quality entrepreneurship outputs, meaning those that provide sufficient conditions for obtaining an outcome. However, 'enabling' necessary conditions that must be present to achieve this outcome have not been tested, and such tests are rarely present in research on entrepreneurship. Studies that adequately test the necessary conditions in the context of EEs only emerged in 2016, through the introduction of NCA proposed by Dul (2016). Both sufficient conditions and necessary conditions have presumed causality; X is necessary and correlated with Y. However, the approaches are substantially different. In the context of an EE's policies, recognition of sufficient conditions suggests that policymakers should allocate efforts to the cause to increase outcomes (such as whether financing is a cause of the rise of venture capital (VC)-funded start-ups, or increasing the number of financial resources boosts entrepreneurial activity).

Meanwhile, recognition of a necessary condition requires policymakers to ensure a minimal necessary level for a given cause for an output to occur. For example, if knowledge flows are a cause of the emergence of disruptive entrepreneurial firms, policymakers must ensure that knowledge transfer occurs. However, in the absence of this cause, the result will not occur, and it will not be possible to compensate for its absence with other factors.

4.2.2 *Entrepreneurial Ecosystems Outputs and Outcomes*

A well-functioning entrepreneurial ecosystem generates entrepreneurship outputs and produces outcomes that translate into the creation of added value in the form of new products and/or services and contributions to employment levels, among other positive impacts. To measure both outputs and outcomes, studies have been based on the definition of productive entrepreneurship, which refers to 'any entrepreneurial activity that contributes directly or indirectly to net output of the economy or to the capacity to produce additional output' (Baumol, 1993: 30).

A typical measure of EE performance is an EEs' prevalent output of early-stage businesses such as start-ups or university spin-offs. Start-ups are often associated with disruptive ventures with the potential to transform themselves into SMEs, which can in turn contribute to a region's economic resilience and growth through the creation of jobs. On the other hand, the prevalence of SMEs in an ecosystem is a representative measure of the EE's capacity to provide the necessary conditions for start-ups to successfully cross the 'valley of death' and become established businesses. Studies on EE performance often use the GEM's TEA as an output measure. The GEM database provides information on the prevalence of innovative and technology-based entrepreneurs and expected employment level growth, among other factors. Typical entrepreneurship output often measures routine business, which can be classified as low- or high-impact entrepreneurship (HIE). However, when seeking to assess the quality of EEs in providing the conditions for entrepreneurial innovation, the prevalence of disruptive ventures is more appropriate as an output proxy than HIE measures.

Studies that assess the performance of EEs from a high-quality perspective often use extreme outputs associated with Schumpeterian entrepreneurship, such as venture capital funded by initial public offerings (IPO) and unicorns (Henrekson & Sanandaji, 2019; Leendertse et al., 2022). A VC-funded IPO refers to a company that, due to its capability or propensity to engage in disruptive innovation activities, attracts large amounts of VC funding. Unicorns refer to a rare type of young company that achieves at least a billion dollars in valuation in a short period of time after its founding (Jinzhi & Carrick, 2019). These companies are characterised by disruptive business models (Henrekson & Sanandaji, 2019). Thus, they are a relevant output for measuring the quality of an entrepreneurial ecosystem (Ács et al., 2017) and are at the centre of this chapter.

Despite these companies' propensity for disruptive innovation, some of the new ventures remain small, as the introduction of breakthrough innovations does not guarantee the achievement of increasing returns to scale in the form of profit or market share (Audretsch & Ács, 1988; Messeni Petruzzelli et al., 2018). Furthermore, highly innovative activities may not translate into the growth of innovators (Christensen, 1997). There are entrepreneurs who intend to remain small to maintain levels of flexibility in their business models (Lin et al., 2019; Stock et al., 2002). Meanwhile, other entrepreneurs operate in delimited market segments that cap growth. In this sense, the size or growth rate of a young company is no guarantee that it will be innovative. Despite these considerations, overall Schumpeterian entrepreneurial firms are more likely to grow than non-innovative organisations (Henrekson & Sanandaji, 2019).

Based on a neo-Schumpeterian approach, indirect impacts regarding the outcomes relate to national innovation system conceptualisation (Lundvall, 1992; Nelson, 1993). Drawing on the insights of the Oslo manual (OECD, 2018), World Bank (Gertler et al., 2016; Gomes et al., 2022) and studies such as those associated with the Bureau Economies Théorique et Appliquée methodology (Bach et al., 1995), many researchers also follow frameworks that guide our understanding of entrepreneurial ecosystems outcomes. We proceed to empirically test these ideas in the following section.

4.3 Research Design

4.3.1 Sample

We classify countries using the World Bank Atlas method from 2020, which relies on the 2019 gross national income per capita to give rise to four groups of countries. Hence, countries classified as high-income are labelled as 'developed', while those falling into the low-income, lower middle-income, and upper middle-income categories are labelled as 'emerging'.

To construct our final sample of countries, we considered regional balance and distribution between the two economic groups. Additionally, we considered the availability of both GEM surveys; the APS and NES. The input indicators, the EFCs, come from the NES, while the output indicators come from the APS. There are instances where countries respond to one survey but not the other, in which case they were excluded. We used the most recent available data, encompassing all countries that took part in the GEM 2020 research report, intentionally selecting data from before the onset of the COVID-19 pandemic. However, as shown in Table 4.1, this approach resulted in an unbalanced sample, with two-thirds classified as developed (twenty-four countries) and one-third as emerging (thirteen countries), because of the restricted coverage of APS data.

To address the limitation of data availability and sample size, we included all countries from the GEM 2018 and 2019 data that were not included in 2020. This added twenty-three more countries, resulting in a final sample of sixty. The discrepancy in the total number of countries per economic group arises because data from the input (NES) and output (APS) indicators for six countries were collected in different years: Bulgaria (2019, 2018), Canada (2019, 2020), Japan (2020, 2019), Mexico (2020, 2019), Puerto Rico (2020, 2019) and Thailand (2019, 2018). The numbers in parentheses denote the years of the NES and APS surveys, respectively.

Table 4.1 ***Composition of sample according to GEM reports by economic group***

	National expert survey (NES)			Adult population survey (APS)		
Reports	Total	Developed	Emerging	Total	Developed	Emerging
GEM 2018	6	1	5	8	1	7
GEM 2019	15	4	11	15	5	10
GEM 2020	39	25	14	37	24	13
Total	**60**	**30**	**30**	**60**	**30**	**30**

Source: Created by authors using GEM (2018, 2019, 2020).

Table 4.2 *Distribution of sample according to regions by economic group*

Regions	Total	Economic group: Developed	Economic group: Emerging
East Asia & Pacific	6	3	3
Europe & Central Asia	24	17	7
Latin America & Caribbean	10	3	7
Middle East & North Africa	10	5	5
North America	2	2	
South Asia	2		2
Sub-Saharan Africa	6		6
Total	60	30	30

Source: Created by authors using GEM (2018, 2019, 2020).

Ultimately, we achieved a balanced sample, with 50 per cent representation for each economic group, by excluding six countries. This was done while maintaining proportionality in terms of total number of countries by region and their indicators to capture the overall trends. As stated in the introduction, our focus is on observing broad patterns rather than the specificities of individual countries, akin to looking at the forest rather than individual trees.

Three of the eliminated countries were from Europe and Central Asia (Slovenia, Slovakia and Latvia), one was from the Middle East and North Africa (Oman), one from Latin America and the Caribbean (Panama) and one from East Asia and the Pacific (Taiwan). Table 4.2 contains the distribution of regions by economic group, while Figure 4.1 provides a geographic depiction of countries divided by each economic group, along with their names and alpha2-ISO codes.

4.3.2 Input Data

Data regarding EE conditions are sourced from the GEM NES. This survey offers harmonised and internationally comparable data focusing on the entrepreneurial conditions within ecosystems at the country level. Experts were interviewed annually and asked to complete an NES questionnaire. Unlike other indices such as the World Economic Forum's Global Competitiveness Index and the World Bank's Doing Businesses report, which focus on general economic conditions, the

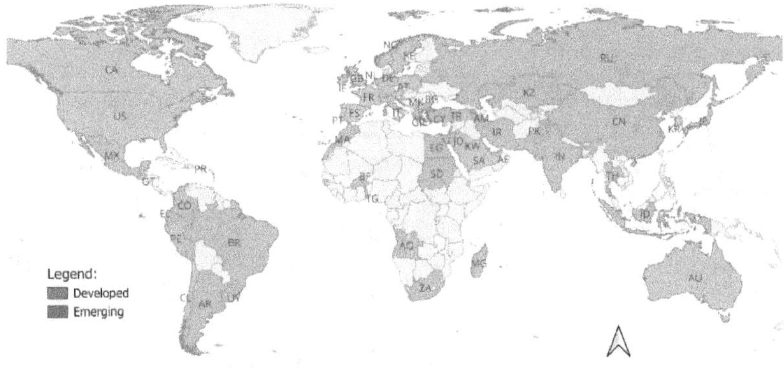

Code	Name	Code	Name	Code	Name	Code	Name
AE	United Arab Emirates	IT	Italy	AM	Armenia	JO	Jordan
AT	Austria	JP	Japan	AO	Angola	KZ	Kazakhstan
AU	Australia	KR	South Korea	AR	Argentina	LB	Lebanon
CA	Canada	KW	Kuwait	BF	Burkina Faso	MA	Morocco
CH	Switzerland	LU	Luxembourg	BG	Bulgaria	MG	Madagascar
CL	Chile	NL	Netherlands	BR	Brazil	MK	North Macedonia
CY	Cyprus	NO	Norway	BY	Belarus	MX	Mexico
DE	Germany	PL	Poland	CN	China	PE	Peru
ES	Spain	PR	Puerto Rico	CO	Colombia	PK	Pakistan
FR	France	PT	Portugal	EC	Ecuador	RU	Russia
GB	United Kingdom	QA	Qatar	EG	Egypt	SD	Sudan
GR	Greece	SA	Saudi Arabia	GT	Guatemala	TG	Togo
HR	Croatia	SE	Sweden	ID	Indonesia	TH	Thailand
IE	Ireland	US	United States	IN	India	TR	Turkey
IL	Israel	UY	Uruguay	IR	Iran	ZA	South Africa

Figure 4.1 Geographical distribution of GEM 2020 participating countries by group.

Source: Created by authors using QGIS and GEM (2020).

Note: Countries are listed in alphabetical order by alpha2-ISO code, beginning with a developed country.

GEM specifically focuses on entrepreneurial ecosystems. Table 4.3 presents the GEM's twelve indicators of EE conditions.

4.3.3 Output Data

Productive entrepreneurship is considered a key output of a well-functioning EE. Studies assessing EE performance often rely on data regarding the share of 'gazelles' (high-growth firms) as a measure for productive entrepreneurship. Relying solely on these measures to evaluate ecosystem performance does not adequately reflect the

Table 4.3 ***GEM'S NES entrepreneurial framework conditions: EFCs***

Indicators and description	Code
1. Access to entrepreneurial finance It measures the availability of financial resources for new ventures.	Financing
2. Government policy: Support and relevance It is the extent to which public policies support entrepreneurship.	Policy
3. Government policy: Taxes and bureaucracy It is the extent to which business taxes and fees are affordable to new business.	Taxation
4. Government entrepreneurship programs It refers to the presence and quality of programs directly assisting new ventures.	Programs
5. Entrepreneurial education at school It refers to the presence and quality of programs directly assisting new ventures.	Education
6. Entrepreneurial education post-school Is the extent to which training in creating or managing SMEs incorporated within the education and training system in higher education, such as vocational, college, business school, among others.	H-education
7. Research and development transfer It is the extent to which national research and development will lead to new commercial opportunities and is available to SMEs.	R&D
8. Commercial and professional infrastructure It refers to the presence of property rights, commercial, accounting and other legal and assessment services and institutions that support or promote SMEs.	Commercial
9. Ease of entry: Market dynamics It refers to the existence of free, open and growing markets where no large business controls entry or prices.	M-dynamics
10. Ease of entry: Market burdens and regulations It is the extent to which regulations facilitate rather than restrict the entry of new businesses in markets.	M-openness
11. Physical infrastructure It concerns to the ease of access to physical resources (e.g. roads), internet and physical spaces at a price that does not discriminate against new ventures.	Infrastructure

Table 4.3 (*cont.*)

Indicators and description	Code
12. Social and cultural norms It is the extent to which social and cultural norms encourage or allow action leading to new business methods or activities that can potentially increase personal wealth and income.	Culture

Source: Created by authors using GEM (2018, 2019, 2020).
Note: Descriptions are based on GEM consortium definitions, available at gemconsortium.org/wiki/1154.

capacity to foster innovative ventures. They can yield skewed results, as many companies engaged in disruptive activities may remain small despite their innovative impact in their respective sectors and markets.

Similarly, evaluating EE performance exclusively based on the prevalence of highly innovative companies does not fully capture the ecosystems' ability to generate diverse outputs and outcomes, as breakthrough ventures typically create few jobs. To address these limitations and avoid misleading results, we have selected five entrepreneurship outputs for analysis.

The first three variables (as shown in Table 4.4) are derived from data on entrepreneurship available by the GEM's APS. We have chosen TEA to characterise the entry of new entrepreneurs into the EE. The proportion of EBO serves as a proxy for the EE's ability to facilitate the survival and growth of entrepreneurs, leading them to establish sustainable businesses or SMEs. Additionally, we have selected HE-TEA to represent the EE's performance in creating conditions conducive to fostering businesses with high expected levels of job creation.

The fourth and fifth indicators are collected directly from three private organisations: Crunchbase, Dealroom.co and CB Insights. The F-firms variable collected from Crunchbase pertains to the number of new businesses that have received any kind of funding, such as seed, Series A, or other private equity investment.

The fifth indicator, unicorns, was collected from CB Insights and Dealroom.co. Both sources maintain an up-to-date list of companies classified as unicorns. We enhanced our dataset by cross-referencing countries from these sources, as we always selected the highest reported number.

Table 4.4 *Variable definitions and data source on entrepreneurship outputs*

Variable	Description	Source
TEA	Total early-stage entrepreneurial activity: percentage of 18–64 population who are either a starting a business or running a new business (within the first 42 months of starting), but has not yet paid salaries, wages or made any other payments to the owners for more than three months.	GEM
EBO	Established business ownership: percentage of 18–64 population who are currently an owner-manager of an established business, that has paid salaries, wages or any other payments to the owners for more than 42 months.	GEM
HE-TEA	High-expectation TEA: percentage of those involved in TEA who expected to create six or more jobs in five years.	GEM
F-firms	Number of firms (log 10 base) funding by any kind of venture capital, such as seed, Series A or private equity, in the last three years (from 2018 to 2020), the same from GEM research.	Crunchbase
Unicorns	Number of unicorns (log 10 base), that is, firms that attained a one-billion-dollar market value in the last three years (from 2018 to 2020), the same from GEM research.	CB Insights Dealroom.co

Source: Created by authors using GEM (2018, 2019, 2020), CB Insights (2018–2020), available at www.cbinsights.com/research-unicorn-companies; Crunchbase (2018–2020), available at www.crunchbase.com; Dealroom.co (2018–2020), available at dealroom.co. GEM descriptions are based GEM Consortium definitions available at gemconsortium.org/wiki/1154.

Even though unicorns are rare, they are one of the most relevant productive entrepreneurship outputs, as they enjoy significant market shares (or have created new markets) and valuations (Ács et al., 2017; Jinzhi & Carrick, 2019). Additionally, unicorns are often associated with platform business models that can impact the country-wide, regional and even global socioeconomic context and traditional businesses (Evans & Schmalensee, 2016). All three sources of output data, Crunchbase (Dalle et al., 2017; Nylund & Cohen, 2017), Dealroom.co (van Meeteren et al., 2022; Smachylo et al., 2023) and CB Insights (Lee & Lin, 2020; Andonova et al., 2023), have been utilised in recent studies of EE, providing empirical support for their inclusion in our research effort.

The analysis relies on data from between 2018 and 2020 for both the year of foundation (for F-firms and unicorns) and year of funding (only F-firms). The three-year period ensures that we select firms at similar growth stages. Furthermore, this period allows us to focus solely on innovative start-ups and aligns with the timeframe covered by GEM's NES and APS surveys.

4.3.4 Normalization of Indicators

Given that we utilised data from diverse sources and in varied formats (for instance, GEM's NES EFCs are assessed on a 7-point Likert scale, while GEM's APS entrepreneurial activity indicators are presented as percentages of the population, and Schumpeterian entrepreneurship indicators pertain to the total number of companies) we deemed standardisation necessary to facilitate readers' comprehension. To achieve this, we employed the min–max method ($x' = \frac{[x - min(x)]}{[max(x) - min(x)]}$), where x is an original value and x′ is the scaling value, to scale them from 0 to 100. In the indicators F-firms and unicorns, we also applied a logarithm base 10 transformation, due to their positive skewness, after which the min–max scaling was applied. Additionally, outliers were verified using the 2.5 x interquartile interval method; however, there was no need to act. Table 4.5 exhibits the main descriptive and distributional statistics and testing for normality for the selected input–output set. Although four indicators do not exhibit a close to normal distribution, the difference between means using the analysis of variance (ANOVA) is not a problem for our type of analysis, as heteroscedasticity is corrected for with the Welch ANOVA.

4.3.5 The Method of Analysis: Necessary Condition Analysis (NCA)

NCA, pioneered by Dul and colleagues (Dul, 2016; Vis & Dul, 2018), represents an advancement in determining necessary conditions

Table 4.5 ***Descriptive and distributional statistics, and testing for normality for the selected input–output set***

Variables	Mean	Median	Standard deviation	Test of normality Kolmogorov-Smirnov[1]	
				Statistic	Significance
Inputs					
Financing	55.3	53.9	23.31		
Policy	48.5	48.0	24.04	0.078	> 0.150
Taxation	50.9	49.5	25.66	0.074	> 0.150
Programs	51.0	46.3	26.10	0.109	0.077
Education	27.1	21.3	21.60	0.116	0.043
H-education	40.0	36.8	22.76	0.176	< 0.010
R&D	40.4	40.8	23.08	0.099	0.144
Commercial	57.6	56.2	21.49	0.123	0.023
M-dynamics	43.7	41.5	23.03	0.077	> 0.150
M-openness	44.1	45.6	23.30	0.085	> 0.150
Infrastructure	61.4	64.4	21.48	0.072	> 0.150
Culture	45.3	44.7	26.49	0.096	> 0.150
				0.075	> 0.150
Outputs					
TEA	25.5	19.9	19.23		
TEE	33.4	27.0	22.59	0.146	< 0.010
HE-TEA	35.4	32.4	21.42	0.148	< 0.010
F-Firms	42.8	44.5	23.18	0.099	> 0.150
Unicorns	100.0	15.0	0.00	0.061	> 0.150

Source: Created by authors using data from GEM (2018, 2019, 2020), CB Insights (2020), Crunchbase (2020) and Dealroom.co (2020).

[1] Lilliefors Significance Correction.

compared to the existing QCA methodology developed by Ragin and colleagues (Ragin, 1989; Rihoux & Ragin, 2009). A necessary condition is a fundamental factor driving an output, without which the output cannot be achieved. For example, placing a bet is a necessary condition for winning the lottery, and no other critical factors can compensate for its absence. However, the presence of a necessary condition does not guarantee the output, as is the case with a sufficient condition. Mathematically, necessary conditions can be expressed in various forms, with two common formulations: if Y = 1, then X = 1, or if not X, then not Y. The other formulation employs the symbol '~' for negation, indicating if ~X, then ~Y. When X = 1, then Y = 1 or Y = 0.

4.4 Findings

4.4.1 Descriptive Analyses of Indicators

4.4.1.1 Input Indicators

Comparing EFCs between developed and emerging economies reveals significant disparities, as shown in Figure 4.2. Developed economies excel in all but one indicator – market dynamics (M-dynamics). These higher scores suggest a more supportive environment for entrepreneurship, with better access to financial resources, adequate policies and robust infrastructure.

Conversely, emerging economies lag in all indicators but one (market dynamics) in comparison to developed economies, indicating challenges mainly in education, R&D and market openness. Notably, emerging economies surpass developed economies in market dynamics as free, open and growing markets foster entrepreneurial activities.

Shifting the focus to strengths and weaknesses in EFCs, the data displayed in Figure 4.2 reveals nuanced patterns between developed

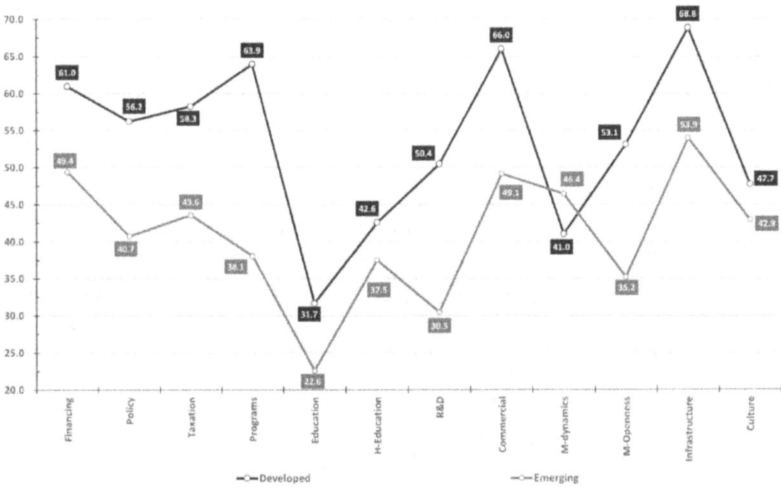

Figure 4.2 Entrepreneurship framework conditions (EFCs) by group.

Source: Created by authors using data from GEM (2018, 2019, 2020), CB Insights (2020), Crunchbase (2020) and Dealroom.co (2020).

and emerging economies: the indicators in which both economic groups show higher scores are not always the same. Developed economies exhibit strengths in four: access to entrepreneurial finance, government entrepreneurship programmes, commercial and professional infrastructure and physical infrastructure. Emerging economies demonstrate a strength in only one: market dynamics. However, developed and emerging economies both show weaknesses in the same three indicators: entrepreneurial education at school, entrepreneurial education post-school, and social and cultural norms, which are crucial for fostering entrepreneurship. Addressing these weaknesses could unlock significant potential for fostering entrepreneurship and economic development in emerging economies, ensuring sustainable growth and prosperity.

In conclusion, developed economies have higher scores in all but one indicator compared to emerging economies. However, these patterns are group-specific, as the highest and lowest scores are not consistent across both groups. Therefore, the crucial observation, mainly for emerging economies, is that the elements of EFCs that shape a vibrant entrepreneurial ecosystem are very context specific, and public policies based on 'follow the leader' have great potential to undermine their success. Instead, it is more suitable to build policies collectively with the support of evidence-based success stories and data. Unfortunately, emerging economies often follow the economic trajectory of mimicking what has 'gone well' for developed economies elsewhere, the result of the fundamental and myopic bias of policymakers who lack courage and expertise.

4.4.1.2 Output Indicators

In this subsection we focus on analysing the output indicators of a dynamic entrepreneurial ecosystem, considering both developed and emerging economies. Comparing the output indicators reveals notable disparities. Developed economies generally exhibit lower values in TEA and EBO, indicating lower levels of early-stage entrepreneurial activity compared to emerging economies. However, developed economies tend to have higher levels of HE-TEA and F-firms and presence of unicorns. This suggests a greater proportion of Schumpeterian entrepreneurial activity (see Figure 4.3).

The lower values of TEA and EBO in developed economies can be attributed to several factors. Firstly, developed economies often have

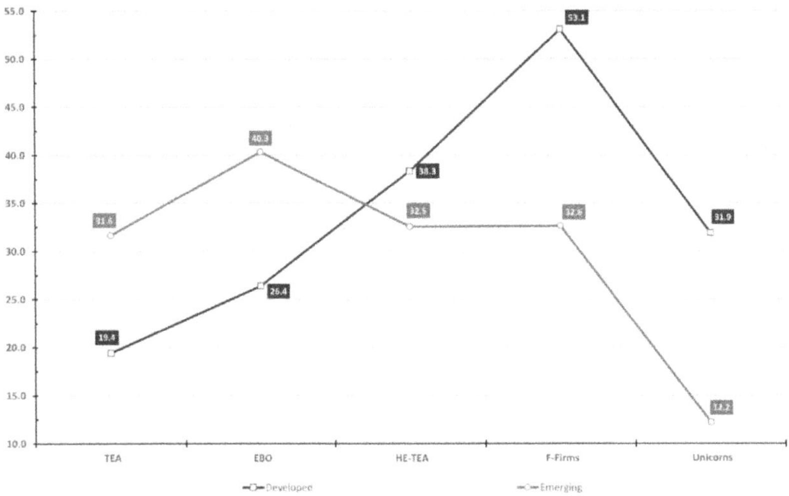

Figure 4.3 Entrepreneurial output indicators by group.
Source: Created by authors using data from GEM (2018, 2019, 2020), CB Insights (2020), Crunchbase (2020) and Dealroom.co (2020).

more established industries and established businesses, resulting in fewer opportunities for new entrepreneurs to enter the market. Secondly, stringent regulatory frameworks and higher entry barriers in developed economies may deter individuals from starting new businesses or transitioning from wage employment to entrepreneurship. Moreover, the availability of alternative career paths, such as stable employment opportunities in established companies, may reduce the incentive for individuals to pursue entrepreneurship in developed economies. These factors collectively contribute to the lower levels of TEA and EBO observed in developed economies.

4.4.2 Necessary Condition Analysis

Table 4.6 shows the results of the multivariate NCA. TEA showed d-values ranging from not significant (for four input indicators) to medium (for five indicators). The permutation test (p) for these eight indicators with small and medium effects showed non-significant values, suggesting the existence of spurious association. This means the conditions are present when entrepreneurship output occurs, but these conditions have no influence on the result. Thus, TEA cannot be

Table 4.6 *Results of multivariate necessary condition analysis and permutation test (p-value)*

	TEA		EBO		HE-TEA		F-Firms		Unicorns	
Conditions	d^1	p^2	d^1	p^2	d^1	p^2	d^1	p^2	d^1	p^2
Financing	.18 ··	.87 +	.20 ··	.54 +	.32 ···	.040 *	.30 ··	.00 *	.37 ···	.13 +
Policy	.17 ··	.76 +	.09 ·	.86 +	.29 ··	.017 *	.24 ··	.10 +	.31 ···	.13 +
Taxation	.15 ··	.86 +	.21 ··	.27 +	.30 ··	.030 *	.25 ··	.15 +	.35 ···	.12 +
Programs	.08 ·	.97 +	.09 ·	.90 +	.28 ··	.061 +	.31 ···	.02 **	.39 ···	.05 *
Education	.06 ·	.78 +	.03 ·	.77 +	.20 ··	.002 *	.14 ··	.10 +	.21 ··	.06 +
H-education	.00 +	1.00 +	.13 ··	.36 +	.20 ··	.063 +	.23 ··	.03 *	.34 ···	.01 *
R&D	.00 +	1.00 +	.08 ·	.77 +	.19 ··	.089 +	.22 ··	.04 *	.33 ···	.02 *
Commercial	.00 +	1.00 +	.19 ··	.77 +	.29 ··	.245 +	.39 ···	.01 *	.51 ····	.01 *
M-dynamics	.18 ··	.65 +	.11 ··	.67 +	.26 ··	.016 *	.21 ··	.14 +	.28 ··	.14 +
M-openness	.06 ·	.98 +	.09 ·	.82 +	.24 ··	.053 +	.29 ··	.01 *	.38 ···	.01 *
Infrastructure	.00 +	1.00 +	.05 +	.97 +	.31 ···	.193 +	.40 ···	.00 *	.56 ····	.00 *
Culture	.17 ··	.62 +	.15 ··	.28 +	.27 ··	.012 *	.29 ··	.00 *	.48 ···	.00 **

Source Author-generated based on data from GEM (2018, 2019, 2020), CB Insights (2020), Crunchbase (2020) and Dealroom.co (2020).

Note:

1 Effect size calculated using ceiling envelopment-free disposal hull (CE-FDH) algorithm.

2 Number of permutations = 10,000

Effect size (*d*)

+ not significant (d = 0.0)

· small effect (0 < d < 0.1)

·· medium effect (0.1 ≤ d < 0.3)

··· large effect (0.3 ≤ d < 0.5)

···· very large effect (d ≥ 0.5)

Permutation test (*p*)

+ not significant

* significant at 5% (p < 0.05)

** significant at .1% (p < 0.001)

considered a necessary condition for a dynamic EE. EBO presents similar results, varying from small to medium d-values, but none of them showed statistical significance in the permutation test (p). Therefore, these conditions can also not be considered necessary conditions for a dynamic EE.

In terms of Schumpeterian entrepreneurship, our results revealed that for HE-TEA, F-firms and unicorns' conditions exhibited effect sizes ranging from medium to very large. However, the permutation test (p) indicated that six, eight and seven conditions, respectively, are necessary for entrepreneurship. Our findings show that the necessary conditions for each output are not the same. Only one condition, culture, is revealed to be necessary for all three output indicators.

4.4.2.1 Bottleneck Analysis

After conducting the multivariate analysis of the NCA, we performed the bottleneck analysis, which provides insight into the minimum required values of necessary conditions to achieve specific levels of output. The results are presented in Table 4.7, where the first column comprises the output variables (proxies for entrepreneurship) and the second column displays the desired output levels on a scale from 0 to 100 per cent. Starting from the third column, the necessity levels for each input to attain the desired output level are reported. For instance, for a low output level of F-firms (10 per cent), the programmes requirement level is 17.1 per cent.

In the case of HE-TEA, we found that six necessary conditions (financing, policy, taxation, education, M-dynamics and infrastructure) are required to achieve high levels of output (from 80 per cent to 100 per cent). These conditions remain essential even at medium output levels, such as 50 per cent. For F-firms, we found that eight necessary conditions (financing, programmes, H-education, R&D, commercial, M-openness, infrastructure and culture) are required to achieve high levels of output (from 80 per cent to 100 per cent). Table 4.7 also presents the requirement levels for unicorns. The results indicate that seven conditions are necessary to stimulate the emergence of unicorns, the same as for F-firms but with the exclusion of financing. As expected, there is an upward trend in the requirement levels for these conditions, indicating that as output levels increase, so too does the necessity level for each condition. Additionally, there is a tipping point effect, as the scores jump abruptly above a certain level of desired

Table 4.7 *Bottleneck analysis*

Output level (Y) in %		Entrepreneurial framework conditions (Inputs: X)											
		Financing	Policy	Taxation	Programs	Education	H-education	R&D	Commercial	M-dynamics	M-openness	Infrastructure	Culture
HE-TEA	0	NN	NN	NN		NN				NN			NN
	10	NN	NN	NN		NN				NN			NN
	20	10.9	NN	NN		NN				NN			NN
	30	24.5	NN	NN		NN				NN			NN
	40	25.2	21.8	16.0		6.8				15.4			8.3
	50	25.2	21.8	16.0		10.0				23.2			13.9
	60	34.2	21.8	27.7		10.0				38.5			13.9
	70	36.4	28.8	33.1		18.4				38.5			57.0
	80	72.7	74.9	88.0		69.8				55.9			63.6
	90	72.7	74.9	88.0		69.8				55.9			63.6
	100	73.0	100.0	95.5		69.8				62.8			93.4
F-Firms	0	NN			NN		NN	NN	NN		NN	NN	NN
	10	NN			17.1		4.5	5.1	20.9		9.6	8.1	NN
	20	NN			17.1		4.5	5.1	20.9		9.6	8.1	NN
	30	NN			17.1		4.5	5.1	25.4		16.0	8.1	NN
	40	NN			18.6		4.5	5.1	25.4		16.0	33.1	NN
	50	25.2			24.6		8.9	5.1	25.4		16.7	42.3	13.9
	60	38.2			41.6		24.1	21.0	25.4		24.1	51.2	19.9
	70	38.2			44.0		24.1	45.9	25.4		54.3	57.7	19.9
	80	80.6			47.6		36.1	48.6	72.0		54.3	57.7	60.3
	90	80.6			47.6		62.2	48.6	80.2		54.3	73.5	100.0
	100	80.6			47.6		62.2	48.6	80.2		54.3	73.5	100.0

Unicorns	0		NN		NN	NN	NN		NN	NN	NN
	10		24.6		8.9	5.1	25.4		16.7	42.3	13.9
	20		29.9		8.9	21.0	25.4		24.1	42.3	13.9
	30		36.5		8.9	21.0	25.4		24.1	43.6	19.9
	40		36.5		30.2	21.0	40.3		24.1	51.2	33.8
	50		47.6		36.1	45.9	64.6		24.1	57.7	33.8
	60		47.6		36.1	48.6	65.7		54.3	57.7	60.3
	70		47.6		62.2	48.6	65.7		54.3	73.5	86.8
	80		47.6		62.2	48.6	65.7		54.3	73.5	86.8
	90		47.6		62.2	48.6	80.2		54.3	73.5	100.0
	100		47.6		62.2	48.6	80.2		54.3	73.5	100.0

Source: Created by authors.

Note: NN = not necessary. The grey-coloured cells correspond to unreported indicators as they are not necessary conditions.

output. This is akin to the concept of decreasing marginal returns, like those associated with cleaning a dirty versus already organised house: A dirty and disorganised house will experience a significant benefit and impact from a quick and simple cleaning process. In a house that is already extremely organised, improving performance by a few more per cent will require enormous effort.

Finally, the striking similarity between the necessary conditions for F-firms and unicorns, as opposed to HE-TEA, underscores the distinct nature of entrepreneurial endeavours in different sectors. While F-firms and unicorns primarily focus on high-technology entrepreneurship and innovation, HE-TEA encompasses a broader spectrum of entrepreneurial ventures, including both technological (but not necessarily scalable) and non-technological innovations. This broader scope necessitates a more diverse set of conditions, covering policy, taxation, basic education and the existence of growing markets (M-dynamics). Moreover, the convergence of necessary conditions between F-firms and unicorns highlights the interconnectedness of various technological entrepreneurial activities, demanding well-trained entrepreneurs (H-education), R&D public funds, commercial and open-market services, providers with specific programmes to compensate or alleviate market burdens and regulations and very good technological infrastructure. These findings underscore the importance of tailoring policy interventions and support mechanisms to the unique needs and characteristics of different entrepreneurial ecosystems, fostering a conducive environment for diverse forms of entrepreneurship to thrive, given the transformational potential of unicorns. Figure 4.4 illustrates how bottleneck analysis can help policymakers to reduce gaps and enhance conditions to generate entrepreneurship outcomes.

4.5 Discussion

Given that HE-TEA encompasses a broad spectrum of nascent SMEs and generally includes more traditional ventures, its necessary conditions are expected to differ from those of F-firms and unicorns. Therefore, for HE-TEA, conditions such as government policy (support and relevance, and taxes and bureaucracy), entrepreneurial education at school and ease of entry (market dynamics) are expected to appear as strong necessary conditions. These conditions are essential for fostering an environment conducive to the growth and

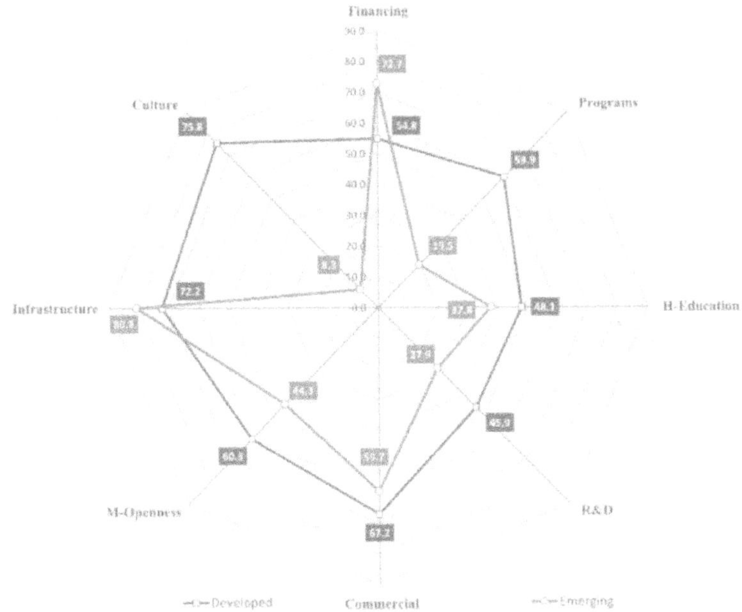

Indicators that are necessary conditions	Maximum value from Table 5 (1)	Required minimum level necessary for 80% for F-Firms: From Table 7 (2)	Required minimum level necessary for 80% for F-Firms: (1) x (2)	Country from: Developed	Country from: Emerging
Financing	100.0	80.6	80.6	54.8	72.7
Programs	100.0	47.6	47.6	59.9	19.5
H-Education	100.0	36.1	36.1	48.1	37.8
R&D	100.0	48.6	48.6	45.9	27.9
Commercial	100.0	72.0	72.0	67.2	59.7
M-openness	100.0	54.3	54.3	60.3	44.3
Infrastructure	100.0	57.7	57.7	72.2	80.8
Culture	100.0	60.3	60.3	75.8	8.3

Figure 4.4 Practical example of how to use bottleneck analysis to public policy guidance.

Source: Created by authors.

Note: Shaded cells are the ultimate necessary conditions to be prioritised in public policies.

sustainability of traditional SMEs, which often operate within different regulatory and market dynamics compared to high-growth ventures backed by venture capital or private equity funding (Loader, 2005; de Jong & Marsili, 2006; Tsai & Kuo, 2011).

In contrast, all but one necessary condition is the same for F-firms and unicorns. Specifically, for F-firms, financing also emerged as a necessary condition. These firms are characterised by a high degree of novelty in their products or services as well as their business models (Lee, 2020; Yeganegi et al., 2021). Consequently, they operate within an environment rife with uncertainties regarding technological paths, high risks and few guarantees of success associated with their innovative ventures. Traditional financing avenues, such as bank loans, are often inaccessible to them, prompting reliance on venture capitalists who typically finance such start-ups with the expectation of high returns (Gu et al., 2018).

Unicorns are viewed as having exceptional market potential, necessitating specialised support services such as legal and accounting expertise to facilitate their growth trajectory (Stam & van de Ven, 2021). Additionally, infrastructure plays a crucial role in supporting entrepreneurship by enabling seamless connections between businesses and consumers (Audretsch & Belitski, 2017; Xie et al., 2021).

R&D and higher education on entrepreneurship were also necessary conditions for both F-firms and unicorns, but not for HE-TEA, as the former tend to engage in innovative activities to a much greater extent (de Jong & Marsili, 2006). Knowledge transfer, especially from R&D, represents a critical factor for innovative entrepreneurship. EEs characterised by high performance in knowledge creation and dissemination tend to stimulate more innovative ventures compared to ecosystems with low knowledge flows (Tavassoli et al., 2021). A high education level is a relevant condition for entrepreneurship. Prior studies show that entrepreneurial education programmes in universities improve the ability of individuals to recognise opportunities as potential entrepreneurs (Costa et al., 2018) as well as increase entrepreneurial intentions (Sukavejworakit et al., 2018) and develop an entrepreneurial mindset and the propensity to take risks (Cui et al., 2021).

Finally, the presence of entrepreneurial culture and social norms that endorse and support entrepreneurship are vital for nurturing the existence of entrepreneurs themselves and maintaining stocks of entrepreneurial human capital (Bogatyreva et al., 2019; Neumeyer et al., 2019). This is the only necessary condition common for all tree EE outputs. To boost Schumpeterian entrepreneurship in the form of F-firms or unicorns, it is not necessary to uniformly allocate resources to all necessary conditions. The conditions (financing, programmes, high education, R&D, commercial, market openness, infrastructure and culture) must be prioritised in the decision-making process for resource allocation. These conditions are the ones that showed the highest level of relevance for obtaining entrepreneurial outputs, that is, impacts greater than 50 per cent. However, although the conditions are the same, their required levels are different for F-firms and unicorns. For stimulating unicorn creation at 50 per cent, the levels of these conditions range from 24.1 per cent to 64.6 per cent, while for F-firms the variation is between 5.1 per cent and 42.3 per cent.

4.6 Concluding Remarks

As we have shown, our research aims to assess the level of necessity of EFCs for productive entrepreneurship, considering different measures of entrepreneurial activity. The findings indicate that while framework conditions play a crucial role in producing high-quality entrepreneurial outputs like F-firms and unicorns, not all conditions are equally necessary for traditional outputs such as TEA and EBO. This distinction underscores the importance of contextual factors and the specific type of entrepreneurial activity in assessing the effectiveness of entrepreneurial ecosystem conditions and performance.

From an academic standpoint, our findings contribute to existing research on the causal relationships between entrepreneurial conditions and activity, clarifying the varying levels of necessity among elements of the entrepreneurial ecosystem and entrepreneurial outputs (Nicotra et al., 2018; Andonova et al., 2019; Muñoz et al., 2020). Furthermore, our results fuel the debate around the necessary elements in entrepreneurial ecosystems. We argue that the necessary conditions for EFCs are best suited to stimulating outputs from a Schumpeterian entrepreneurship perspective than any other form of entrepreneurship (Torres & Godinho, 2021). Thus, the fact that a condition is necessary for entrepreneurship does not automatically imply that it must show high scores; different conditions have different levels of relevance that vary according to the level of need for different types of entrepreneurial activity.

From a policymaker's perspective, our findings offer insights which are often overlooked in studies of entrepreneurial ecosystems, particularly regarding the level of necessity of each condition. Policymakers should consider allocating resources to conditions that maximise entrepreneurial outputs. Additionally, high-quality entrepreneurship measures such as F-firms and unicorns could be prioritised as indicators of ecosystem performance, surpassing traditional measures like the prevalence of start-ups or established businesses. Due to their significant innovation requirements, they need more of the elements of entrepreneurial ecosystems, therefore stimulating more ambitious developmental goals for the case of emerging economies.

However, this study has limitations that pave the way for future research. Firstly, it focuses on assessing the causes of entrepreneurial activity without specifically delving into the realm of digital entrepreneurship. Future studies could include digital economy indicators or digital entrepreneurial ecosystems as special cases. Secondly, while this research examines indicators related to context and entrepreneurial activity, future studies could evaluate entrepreneurial ecosystems' efficiency using data envelopment analysis or stochastic frontier analysis. This would enable a more comprehensive evaluation of entrepreneurial ecosystem performance, considering the weights associated with the necessary level of each condition to achieve a specific entrepreneurship output.

References

Ács, Z. J., Åstebro, T., Audretsch, D., and Robinson, D. T. (2016). Public policy to promote entrepreneurship: A call to arms. *Small Business Economics 47*(1), 35–51. doi.org/10.1007/s11187–016-9712-2

Ács, Z. J., Autio, E., and Szerb, L. (2014). National systems of entrepreneurship: Measurement issues and policy implications. *Research Policy 43*(3), 476–494. tinyurl.com/5ejwj2cn

Ács, Z. J., Stam, E., Audretsch, D. B., and O'Connor, A. (2017). The lineages of the entrepreneurial ecosystem approach. *Small Business Economics 49*(1). doi.org/10.1007/s11187-017-9864-8

Aeeni, Z., Motavaseli, M., Sakhdari, K., and Dehkordi, A. M. (2019). Baumol's theory of entrepreneurial allocation: A systematic review and research agenda. *European Research on Management and Business Economics 25*(1), 30–37. doi.org/10.1016/j.iedeen.2018.09.001

AlQershi, N., Mokhtar, S. S. M., and Abas, Z. (2021). The relationship between strategic innovations, human capital and performance: An empirical investigation. *Sustainable Futures 3*. doi.org/10.1016/j.sftr.2021.100056

Alvedalen, J., and Boschma, R. (2017). A critical review of entrepreneurial ecosystems research: Towards a future research agenda. *European*

Planning Studies 25(6), 887–903. doi.org/10.1080/09654313.2017.1299694

Alves, A. C., Fischer, B. B., and Vonortas, N. S. (2021). Ecosystems of entrepreneurship: Configurations and critical dimensions. *The Annals of Regional Science* 67(1). doi.org/10.1007/s00168-020-01041-y

Andonova, V., Casanova, L., Finchelstein, D., and Garcia Duque, J. (2023). The rise of digital entrepreneurship in Latin America. *Internext 18*(1), 104–110. doi.org/10.18568/internext.v18i1.735

Andonova, V., Nikolova, M. S., and Dimitrov, D. (2019). *Entrepreneurial Ecosystems in Unexpected Places*. Palgrave Macmillan. doi.org/10.1007/978-3-319-98219-9

Astebro, T., Bazzazian, N., and Braguinsky, S. (2012). Startups by recent university graduates and their faculty: Implications for university entrepreneurship policy. *Research Policy 41*(4), 663–677. doi.org/10.1016/j.respol.2012.01.004

Audretsch, D. B., and Ács, Z. J. (1988). Innovation in large and small firms – An empirical analysis. *American Economic Review 78*, 109–112.

Audretsch, D. B., and Belitski, M. (2017). Entrepreneurial ecosystems in cities: Establishing the framework conditions. *The Journal of Technology Transfer 42*(5), 1030–1051. doi.org/10.1007/s10961-016-9473-8

Auerswald, P. E., and Dani, L. (2017). The adaptive life cycle of entrepreneurial ecosystems: The biotechnology cluster. *Small Business Economics 49*(1), 97–117.

Autio, E., Nambisan, S., Thomas, L. D. W., and Wright, M. (2018). Digital affordances, spatial affordances, and the genesis of entrepreneurial ecosystems. *Strategic Entrepreneurship Journal 12*(1). doi.org/10.1002/sej.1266

Autio, E., and Rannikko, H. (2016). Retaining winners: Can policy boost high-growth entrepreneurship? *Research Policy 45*(1), 42–55. doi.org/10.1016/j.respol.2015.06.002

Bach, L., Conde-Molist, N., Ledoux, M.-J., Matt, M., and Schaeffer, V. (1995). Evaluation of the economic effects of Brite-Euram programmes on the European industry. *Scientometrics 34*(3), 325–349. doi.org/10.1007/BF02018003

Baumol, W. J. (1993). *Entrepreneurship, Management and the Structure of Payoffs*. MIT Press.

Bendig, D., Strese, S., Flatten, T. C., da Costa, M. E. S., and Brettel, M. (2018). On micro-foundations of dynamic capabilities: A multi-level perspective based on CEO personality and knowledge-based capital. *Long Range Planning 51*(6). doi.org/10.1016/j.lrp.2017.08.002

Bogatyreva, K., Edelman, L. F., Manolova, T. S., Osiyevskyy, O., and Shirokova, G. (2019). When do entrepreneurial intentions lead to actions? The role of national culture. *Journal of Business Research 96*, 309–321. doi.org/10.1016/j.jbusres.2018.11.034

Brown, R., and Mason, C. (2017). Looking inside the spiky bits: A critical review and conceptualisation of entrepreneurial ecosystems. *Small Business Economics 49*(1). doi.org/10.1007/s11187-017-9865-7

Bruton, G., Sutter, C., and Lenz, A.-K. (2021). Economic inequality – Is entrepreneurship the cause or the solution? A review and research agenda for emerging economies. *Journal of Business Venturing 36*(3), 106095. doi.org/10.1016/j.jbusvent.2021.106095

Carayannis, E. G., Provance, M., and Grigoroudis, E. (2016). Entrepreneurship ecosystems: An agent-based simulation approach. *The Journal of Technology Transfer 41*(3), 631–653. doi.org/10.1007/s10961-016-9466-7

Christensen, C. (1997). *The innovator's dilemma: When new technologies cause great firms to fail. Harvard Business Review Press.*

Costa, S. F., Santos, S. C., Wach, D., and Caetano, A. (2018). Recognizing opportunities across campus: The effects of cognitive training and entrepreneurial passion on the business opportunity prototype. *Journal of Small Business Management 56*(1). doi.org/10.1111/jsbm.12348

Cui, J., Sun, J., and Bell, R. (2021). The impact of entrepreneurship education on the entrepreneurial mindset of college students in China: The mediating role of inspiration and the role of educational attributes. *The International Journal of Management Education 19*(1). doi.org/10.1016/j.ijme.2019.04.001

Dalle, J.-M., den Besten, M., and Menon, C. (2017). *Using Crunchbase for economic and managerial research.* OECD Science, Technology and Industry Working Paper No. 2017/08, OECD Publishing. doi.org/10.1787/6c418d60-en

Decker, R., Haltiwanger, J., Jarmin, R., Miranda, J., Decker, R., Haltiwanger, J., and Jarmin, R. (2014). The role of entrepreneurship in US job creation and economic dynamism. *The Journal of Economic Perspectives 28*(3), 3–24.

Dul, J. (2016). Identifying single necessary conditions with NCA and fsQCA. *Journal of Business Research 69*(4), 1516–1523 doi.org/10.1016/j.jbusres.2015.10.134

Dutta, N., and Meierrieks, D. (2021). Financial development and entrepreneurship. *International Review of Economics & Finance 73*, 114–126. doi.org/10.1016/j.iref.2021.01.002

Egan, E. J. (2021). A framework for assessing municipal high-growth high-technology entrepreneurship policy. *Research Policy 51*(9), 104292. doi.org/10.1016/j.respol.2021.104292

Evans, D. S., and Schmalensee, R. (2016). *Matchmakers: The new economics of multisided platforms. Harvard Business Review Press.*

Feld, B. (2012). *Startup Communities: Building an Entrepreneurial Ecosystem in Your City.* John Wiley & Sons.

Fuster, E., Padilla-Meléndez, A., Lockett, N., and Del-Águila-Obra, A. R. (2019). The emerging role of university spin-off companies in developing regional entrepreneurial university ecosystems: The case of Andalusia. *Technological Forecasting and Social Change 141*, 219–231. doi.org/10.1016/j.techfore.2018.10.020

GEM. (2020). *Global entrepreneurship monitor 2019/2020.* Global Entrepreneurship Research Association, London Business School. www.gemconsortium.org/data

Gertler, P. J., Martinez, S., Premand, P., Rawlings, L. B., and Vermeersch, C. M. J. (2016). *Impact Evaluation in Practice* (2nd ed.). Inter-American Development Bank and World Bank. doi.org/10.1596/978-1-4648-0779-4

Gomes, S., Ferreira, J., Lopes, J. M., and Farinha, L. (2022). The impacts of the entrepreneurial conditions on economic growth: Evidence from OECD countries. *Economies 10*(7), 163. doi.org/10.3390/economies10070163

Gu, W., Qian, X., and Lu, J. (2018). Venture capital and entrepreneurship: A conceptual model and research suggestions. *International Entrepreneurship and Management Journal 14*(1). doi.org/10.1007/s11365-017-0463-6

Györfy, L., and Madaras, S. (2019). The influence of self-employment on early-stage entrepreneurship in Romania. A global entrepreneurship monitor-based analysis. *Acta Universitatis Sapientiae, Economics and Business* 7(1), 23–35. doi.org/10.1515/auseb-2019-0002

Henrekson, M., and Johansson, D. (2010). Gazelles as job creators: A survey and interpretation of the evidence. *Small Business Economics 35*(2), 227–244. doi.org/10.1007/s11187-009-9172-z

Henrekson, M., and Sanandaji, T. (2019). Measuring entrepreneurship: Do established metrics capture Schumpeterian entrepreneurship? *Entrepreneurship Theory and Practice 44*(4), 733–760. doi.org/10.1177/1042258719844500

Hu, G.-G. (2021). Is knowledge spillover from human capital investment a catalyst for technological innovation? The curious case of the fourth industrial revolution in BRICS economies. *Technological Forecasting and Social Change 162*. doi.org/10.1016/j.techfore.2020.120327

Huesig, S., Timar, K., and Doblinger, C. (2014). The influence of regulation and disruptive potential on incumbents' submarket entry decision and success in the context of a network industry. *Journal of Product Innovation Management 31*(5), 1039–1056. doi.org/10.1111/jpim.12143

Huynh, T., Patton, D., Arias-Aranda, D., and Molina-Fernández, L. M. (2017). University spin-off's performance: Capabilities and networks of founding teams at creation phase. *Journal of Business Research 78*, 10–22. doi.org/10.1016/j.jbusres.2017.04.015

Isenberg, D. J. (2011). *The Entrepreneurship Ecosystem Strategy as a New Paradigm for Economic Policy: Principles for Cultivating Entrepreneurship*. Babson College.

Jinzhi, Z., and Carrick, J. (2019). The rise of the Chinese unicorn: An exploratory study of unicorn companies in China. *Emerging Markets Finance and Trade 55*(15). doi.org/10.1080/1540496X.2019.1610877

de Jong, J. P. J., and Marsili, O. (2006). The fruit flies of innovations: A taxonomy of innovative small firms. *Research Policy 35*(2), 213–229. doi.org/10.1016/j.respol.2005.09.007

Kantis, H., Federico, J. S., and García, S. I. (2020). Entrepreneurship policy and systemic conditions: Evidence-based implications and recommendations for emerging countries. *Socio-Economic Planning Sciences 72*. doi.org/10.1016/j.seps.2020.100872

Karami, M., and Read, S. (2021). Co-creative entrepreneurship. *Journal of Business Venturing 36*(4), 106125. doi.org/10.1016/j.jbusvent.2021.106125

Lee, D., and Lin, K.-C. (2020). How to transform sustainable energy technology into a unicorn start-up: Technology review and case study. *Sustainability 12*(7), 3018. doi.org/10.3390/su12073018

Lee, Y.-C. (2020). Does staying private longer affect innovation of VC-backed IPOs and outcomes of VC investments? *Journal of International Financial Markets, Institutions and Money 66*. doi.org/10.1016/j.intfin.2020.101205

Leendertse, J., Schrijvers, M., and Stam, E. (2022, November). Measure twice, cut once: Entrepreneurial ecosystem metrics. *Research Policy 51*(9), 104336. doi.org/10.1016/j.respol.2021.104336

Lin, W.-L., Cheah, J.-H., Azali, M., Ho, J. A., and Yip, N. (2019). Does firm size matter? Evidence on the impact of the green innovation strategy on corporate financial performance in the automotive sector. *Journal of Cleaner Production 229*. doi.org/10.1016/j.jclepro.2019.04.214

Loader, K. (2005). Supporting SMEs through government purchasing activity. *The International Journal of Entrepreneurship and Innovation 6*(1), 17–26. doi.org/10.5367/0000000053026383

Lucas, D. S., and Fuller, C. S. (2017). Entrepreneurship: Productive, unproductive, and destructive—Relative to what? *Journal of Business Venturing Insights 7*, 45–49. doi.org/10.1016/j.jbvi.2017.03.001

Lundvall, B. Å. (1992). *National Systems of Innovation: Towards a Theory of Innovation and Interactive Learning* (1st ed.). Pinter Publishers.

Mack, E., and Mayer, H. (2016). The evolutionary dynamics of entrepreneurial ecosystems. *Urban Studies 53*(10), 2118–2133. doi.org/10.1177/0042098015586547

van Meeteren, M., Trincado-Munoz, F., Rubin, T. H., and Vorley, T. (2022). Rethinking the digital transformation in knowledge-intensive services: A technology space analysis. *Technological Forecasting and Social Change 179*, 121631. doi.org/10.1016/j.techfore.2022.121631

Messeni Petruzzelli, A., Ardito, L., and Savino, T. (2018). Maturity of knowledge inputs and innovation value: The moderating effect of firm age and size. *Journal of Business Research 86*. doi.org/10.1016/j.jbusres.2018.02.009

Miller, D., and le Breton-Miller, I. (2021). Paradoxical resource trajectories: When strength leads to weakness and weakness leads to strength. *Journal of Management 47*(7). doi.org/10.1177/0149206320977901

Muñoz, P., Kibler, E., Mandakovic, V., and Amorós, J. E. (2020). Local entrepreneurial ecosystems as configural narratives: A new way of seeing and evaluating antecedents and outcomes. *Research Policy 51*(9),104065. doi.org/10.1016/j.respol.2020.104065

Nelson, R. R. (1993). *National Innovation System*. Oxford University Press.

Neumeyer, X., Santos, S. C., and Morris, M. H. (2019). Who is left out: Exploring social boundaries in entrepreneurial ecosystems. *Journal of Technology Transfer 44*(2), 462–484. doi.org/10.1007/s10961-018-9694-0

Nicotra, M., Romano, M., Del Giudice, M., and Schillaci, C. E. (2018). The causal relation between entrepreneurial ecosystem and productive entrepreneurship: A measurement framework. *The Journal of Technology Transfer 43*(3), 640–673.

Nylund, P. A., and Cohen, B. (2017). Collision density: Driving growth in urban entrepreneurial ecosystems. *International Entrepreneurship and Management Journal 13*(3). doi.org/10.1007/s11365-016-0424-5

OECD. (2017). *Entrepreneurship at a Glance 2017*. OECD Publishing. doi.org/10.1787/entrepreneur_aag-2017-en

OECD. (2018). *Oslo Manual 2018: The Measurement of Scientific, Technological and Innovation Activities* (4th ed.). OECD Eurostat. doi.org/10.1787/9789264304604-en

Pinkse, J., Bohnsack, R., and Kolk, A. (2014). The role of public and private protection in disruptive innovation: The automotive industry and the emergence of low-emission vehicles. *Journal of Product Innovation Management 31*(1), 43–60. doi.org/10.1111/jpim.12079

Pitelis, C. (2012). Clusters, entrepreneurial ecosystem co-creation, and appropriability: A conceptual framework. *Industrial and Corporate Change 21*(6). doi.org/10.1093/icc/dts008

Qian, H., and Ács, Z. J. (2013). An absorptive capacity theory of knowledge spillover entrepreneurship. *Small Business Economics 40*(2), 185–197. doi.org/10.1007/s11187-011-9368-x

Qian, H., Ács, Z. J., and Stough, R. R. (2012). Regional systems of entrepreneurship: the nexus of human capital, knowledge and new firm formation. *Journal of Economic Geography 13*(4), 559–587. doi.org/10.1093/jeg/lbs009

Qin, S. (2021). Perceptual enablers of global nascent entrepreneurs: A quantitative investigation based on global entrepreneurship monitor data. *International Journal of Entrepreneurial Knowledge 9*(1), 112–126. doi.org/10.37335/ijek.v9i1.132

Ragin, C. C. (1989). *The comparative Method: Moving Beyond Qualitative and Quantitative Strategies*. University of California Press.

Rey-Martí, A., Ribeiro-Soriano, D., and Sánchez-García, J. L. (2016). Giving back to society: Job creation through social entrepreneurship. *Journal of Business Research 69*(6). doi.org/10.1016/j.jbusres.2015.12.010

Rihoux, B., and Ragin, C. C. (2009). Configurational Comparative Methods: Qualitative Comparative Analysis (QCA) and Related Techniques (Vols. 1–51). SAGE. doi.org/10.4135/9781452226569

Shi, X., and Shi, Y. (2022, November). Unpacking the process of resource allocation within an entrepreneurial ecosystem. *Research Policy* 51(9), 104378. doi.org/10.1016/j.respol.2021.104378

Si, S., Zahra, S. A., Wu, X., and Jeng, D. J.-F. (2020). Disruptive innovation and entrepreneurship in emerging economics. *Journal of Engineering and Technology Management 58*, 101601. doi.org/10.1016/j.jengtecman.2020.101601

Smachylo, V. V, Sliusareva, L. V, Bozhydai, I. I., and Kulinich, O. V. (2023). The modeling of startup ecosystems in Central and Eastern Europe based on socio-economic indicators. *Akademichnyĭ Ohli͡ad 2*(59), 310–324. doi.org/10.32342/2074-5354-2023-2-59-21

Spigel, B. (2017). The relational organization of entrepreneurial ecosystems. *Entrepreneurship: Theory and Practice 41*(1), 49–72. doi.org/10.1111/etap.12167

Spigel, B., and Vinodrai, T. (2020). Meeting its Waterloo? Recycling in entrepreneurial ecosystems after anchor firm collapse. *Entrepreneurship & Regional Developmen. 33*(7–8), 599–620. doi.org/10.1080/08985626.2020.1734262

Stam, E. (2015). Entrepreneurial ecosystems and regional policy: A sympathetic critique. *European Planning Studies 23*(9), 1759–1769. doi.org/10.1080/09654313.2015.1061484

Stam, E., and van de Ven, A. (2021). Entrepreneurial ecosystem elements. *Small Business Economics 56*(2), 809–832. doi.org/10.1007/s11187-019-00270-6

Startup Genome. (2020). *Global startup ecosystem report 2020.* startupgenome.com/report/gser2020

Stock, G. N., Greis, N. P., and Fischer, W. A. (2002). Firm size and dynamic technological innovation. *Technovation 22*(9), 537–549.

Sukavejworakit, K., Promsiri, T., and Virasa, T. (2018). Oetel: An innovative teaching model for entrepreneurship education. *Journal of Entrepreneurship Education 21*(2), 1–15.

Tavassoli, S., Obschonka, M., and Audretsch, D. B. (2021). Entrepreneurship in cities. *Research Policy 50*(7), 104255. doi.org/10.1016/j.respol.2021.104255

Thompson, T. A., Purdy, J. M., and Ventresca, M. J. (2018). How entrepreneurial ecosystems take form: Evidence from social impact initiatives in Seattle. *Strategic Entrepreneurship Journal 12*(1). doi.org/10.1002/sej.1285

Torres, P., and Godinho, P. (2021). Levels of necessity of entrepreneurial ecosystems elements. *Small Business Economics 59*, 29–45. doi.org/10.1007/s11187-021-00515-3

Trubnikov, D. (2021). What entrepreneurship is really 'productive'? An alternative view on Baumol's typology. *Journal of Business Venturing Insights 16*, e00258. doi.org/10.1016/j.jbvi.2021.e00258

Tsai, W.-H., and Kuo, H.-C. (2011). Entrepreneurship policy evaluation and decision analysis for SMEs. *Expert Systems with Applications 38*(7). doi.org/10.1016/j.eswa.2011.01.022

van der Valk, W., Sumo, R., Dul, J., and Schroeder, R. G. (2016). When are contracts and trust necessary for innovation in buyer-supplier relationships? A necessary condition analysis. *Journal of Purchasing and Supply Management 22*(4). doi.org/10.1016/j.pursup.2016.06.005

Vedula, S., and Fitza, M. (2019). Regional recipes: A configurational analysis of the regional entrepreneurial ecosystem for U.S. venture capital-backed startups. *Strategy Science 4*(1). doi.org/10.1287/stsc.2019.0076

Vis, B., and Dul, J. (2018). Analyzing relationships of necessity not just in kind but also in degree: Complementing fsQCA with NCA. *Sociological Methods & Research 47*(4), 872–899.

Vyas, V., and Vyas, R. (2019). Human capital, its constituents and entrepreneurial innovation: A multi-level modeling of global entrepreneurship monitor data. *Technology Innovation Management Review 9*(8), 5–17. doi.org/10.22215/timreview/1257

World Bank. (2020). *Doing business 2020.* World Bank Group.

Xie, Z., Wang, X., Xie, L., and Duan, K. (2021). Entrepreneurial ecosystem and the quality and quantity of regional entrepreneurship: A configurational approach. *Journal of Business Research 128*, 499–509. doi.org/10.1016/j.jbusres.2021.02.015

Yeganegi, S., Laplume, A. O., and Dass, P. (2021). The role of information availability: A longitudinal analysis of technology entrepreneurship. *Technological Forecasting and Social Change 170*, 120910. doi.org/10.1016/j.techfore.2021.120910

Zhang, S., and Wang, X. (2022). Does innovative city construction improve the industry–university–research knowledge flow in urban China? *Technological Forecasting and Social Change 174*, 121200. doi.org/10.1016/j.techfore.2021.121200

5 Where Unicorns Are Born: Innovation Hubs in China

LOURDES CASANOVA, ANNE MIROUX AND XINGQI YE*

5.1 Introduction

China is increasingly positioning itself as a world leader in technology and innovation. It has become a leader in a variety of domains, including critical technologies such as energy, space, artificial intelligence, robotics, quantum computing, biotech and green transition. This remarkable achievement is illustrated through technology and innovation indexes such as the Global Innovation Index (GII) which in 2023 ranked China as the 12th most innovative economy out of 132 countries (WIPO, 2023). This represented significant progress compared to its rank (34th) ten years before. As the only middle-income country within the top 30, China's innovation performance not only tops emerging markets but exceeds a large group of developed economies, including Japan, Canada, Australia, Italy and many more. It notably outperforms on innovation relative to its development, holding a position high above the trend line predicting innovation performance of countries based on GDP per capita (Table 5.1). A country's innovation activities can also be measured in the number of patents filed in both local and foreign jurisdictions. China led in patents in 2022 with 1.58 million; followed by the United States with 505,539; Japan with 405,361; the Republic of Korea with 272,315 and Germany with 155,896 (WIPO, 2023). China also exhibits impressive performance in other common innovation indicators, such as high-tech manufacturing (48.5 per cent of manufacturing output in 2018), scholarly output (H-index of 1,112 in 2021) and intangible asset intensity (78.4 per cent in 2021), along with having global tech leaders such as Huawei, Tencent and Alibaba, to name just a few (Scimago Journal & Country Rank, 2022).

* The contribution of Noel Liu, Cornell Class of 2025 and research assistant at the Emerging Markets Institute (EMI), Cornell University, is gratefully acknowledged as well as the Management Library support.

Table 5.1 *Summary of China's Global Innovation Index*

Total Rank	Output/Input rank	Income	Region	Population (mn)	GDP, PPP$ (bn)	GDP per capita, PPP$
12	8/21	Upper middle	SEAO	1,444.2	27,072.0	19,090.0
Pillar			**Score**			**Rank**
Institutions			64.8			42
Human capital and research			53.1			20
Infrastructure			57.5			25
Market sophistication			56.0			12
Business sophistication			55.9			12
Knowledge and tech outputs			56.8			6
Creative outputs			49.3			11

Source: Authors' work based on WIPO (2022).

The GII (WIPO, 2022) breaks down innovation performance into seven pillars of capabilities. China registers a strong performance across diverse dimensions, ranking 12th overall and 6th in knowledge and tech outputs. China's weakest categories fit into in two areas: human capital and research (especially education) and institutions (especially political and regulatory environments).

China's lead in technology and innovation is the product of a deliberate policy and long-term planning that began more than forty years ago. This chapter highlights the recent evolution of such policies in the face of mounting international tensions and the concept of the 'innovation chain' that China's leadership has embraced. It then focuses on the key role of technology hubs and the increased participation of Chinese enterprises (especially tech firms) in China's transformation into a technology and innovation powerhouse, as well as the birthplace of unicorns – privately held technology companies with valuations above US$1 billion.

5.2 Looking Back: The History of China's Innovation Policies

To better understand China's emergence in the global innovation landscape, it is important to look at China's innovation policies over time. This section summarises the different phases of China's innovation policy, building upon the four phases analysed by Casanova and Miroux (2019) (see Table 5.2).

The Experimental Phase (1978–1985) – With a relatively weak economic foundation and a low level of research and development (R&D) activities at the time, China started to depart from the original Soviet-type model for innovation by facilitating the spin-off and privatisation of state-owned enterprises. While central planning remained strong, the push towards greater enterprise autonomy (including greater flexibility in organisational appointment, more freedom in producing and selling at prices beyond state price to meet market demands and make profits, and less restricted labour market policies, among others) drove more innovation activities (Yusuf et al., 2005). The removal of organisational bottlenecks led to the creation and establishment of some of the most successful tech companies in today's China, including Lenovo Group Ltd, a spin-off from the Computing Institute of the Academy of Sciences, and Founder Group Co. Ltd, a spin-off from Peking University. In addition, national initiatives were

Table 5.2 *China's innovation phases*

Innovation phase	Key features
The Experimental Phase (1978–1985)	Departure from the Soviet model by privatising state owned enterprises (SOEs) and fostering enterprise autonomy
Systemic Reform Phase (1985–1995)	Passed Science and Technology System Reform Act to connect research institutes with industries
Deepening Reform (1996–2006)	Strategy for rejuvenating the economy with science and education; continued push for technology commercialisation and major investments into research infrastructure
Long-Term Plan and Policy (2006–now)	Ambition to become a top innovative nation; indigenous innovation; adoption of the 2006 Medium- and Long-Term Science and Technology (S&T) Development Plan; launch of the 'Made in China 2025' strategy; reducing dependency on foreign technology and closing the gaps throughout the innovation chain

Source: Authors.

in place to incentivise research activities through merit-based funding allocation.

Systemic Reform Phase (1985–1995) – The Science and Technology System Reform Act of 1985 further narrowed the technological gap. The reform aimed to build strong ties between industries and research institutes and facilitate the conversion of scientific findings into business value and market competitiveness. A remarkable part of the reform was the establishment of the National Natural Science Foundation of China for providing financial support for basic research as well as applied and translational research. Moreover, China also started to strengthen the legal foundation for innovation during this period. In 1985, China acceded to the Paris Convention for the Protection of Industrial Property and first implemented the national patent law to improve the incentive mechanism for innovators (China National Intellectual Public Administration, 2013). In an effort to accumulate high-quality human capital needed for sustainable innovation performance, the 211 Project was instituted in 1993, which allocated specialised budgets to selected universities to elevate the academic standards of higher education in the country. The Hundred Talents Programme of the Chinese Academy of Sciences was also introduced to attract Chinese scholars living abroad back to their homeland.

Deepening Reform (1996–2006) – With the 9th five-year national budget plan and the outline of the 2010 national target, the Chinese government established a national strategy for revitalizing the national economy through science and education. The Promoting Commercialisation of S&T Discoveries and Inventions Act helped companies become innovators and facilitated the commercialisation of academic research output. The infrastructure needed for innovation was also strengthened by the launch of the 985 Project to further optimise research funding allocation, the implementation of the Knowledge Innovation Initiative from the Chinese Academy of Sciences to encourage more advanced scientific research and the introduction of the Yangtze River Scholars Programme to improve universities' ability to recruit and retain top faculty members.

Long-Term Plan and Policy Optimisation (2006–2020) – In the mid-2000s, China established its ambition to become a 'top innovative nation' by 2020, and 'Indigenous innovation' has been at the core of policies since then, starting with the 2006 Medium- and Long-Term Science and Technology (S&T) Development Plan (2006–2020). The plan outlines four major pillars for science and technology development in the country. These are i) nurturing independent innovation; ii) fostering the capacity to leapfrog in key technology areas; iii) building major infrastructure and iv) developing future global leadership. The 18th Communist Party National Congress later set more specific goals including improving entrepreneurship, fostering industry-led innovation and establishing more efficient technology transfer mechanisms to bridge the gap between academia and industry. Examples of these include, among others, the granting of rights to universities to license patents generated with public funding, the adoption of an action plan for further implementation of the National Intellectual Property Strategy to enhance lawful protection of innovation and encourage IP creation and the launch of the National Equities Exchange and Quotations, an over-the-counter market for non-publicly listed companies, to help innovative small- and medium-sized enterprises raise capital. China's long-term plan was built around an innovation-led growth strategy, aiming to achieve sustainable economic growth through more efficient innovation networks and a more entrepreneurship-friendly capital market.

Another important milestone during this final period was the launch of the 'Made in China 2025' strategy in 2015 aimed at reducing China's dependence on foreign technology and transforming China into a high-end manufacturing economy. This strategy signalled a shift in China's focus from pure research and invention towards market outcomes and commercialisation along the innovation chain. In the subsequent years, China's leadership increasingly embraced the concept of the innovation chain. The goal was to ensure successful coverage for all the steps along the chain, from basic research to commercialisation. The concept was embodied in the 2016 Innovation-Driven Development Strategy, and several steps were taken to encourage the shift. For instance, new guidelines on the evaluation of research were issued in 2020, placing less emphasis on Science Citation Index publications. Commercialisation became a more important criterion for obtaining grant funding from the state, and an increasing number of key state laboratories have been transformed into commercial enterprises (Groenewegen-Lau & Laha, 2023).

Besides making China, still an emerging market, an innovation leader in many sectors, these policies have also spurred the creation of an innovation ecosystem. This ecosystem has allowed the organic creation of technology start-ups and unicorns that have disrupted sectors domestically and globally.

5.3 Key Actors in China's Innovation Eco-System: The Government, Knowledge Institutions and Enterprises

Unlike world innovation leaders such as the United States, Europe or Japan, the government plays a key role in China's innovation ecosystem across all industries. As a result, the Chinese ecosystem is more centralised and coordinated among the different actors. Regarding financing, government *and* corporate venture capital have played a more important role in the emergence of unicorns than in the West. What follows examines these actors and their relationship in more detail.

5.3.1 Government as an Innovation Driver

The Chinese government is a major actor in China's transformation into an innovation-driven and knowledge-based economy, and the creation of an internationally competitive innovation ecosystem in the country. Its efforts span from basic science research to value capture with innovation, and it usually takes the following three forms: financial support, industry development or the creation of 'innovation laboratories' at the industry/city level.

A key player in the financing of innovation in China is the Natural Science Foundation of China, founded in 1986, in affiliation with China's State Council. The foundation manages the National Natural Science Fund to finance research projects in China. It has a department that specialises in funding biomedical and public health research, similar in role to the National Institute of Health in the United States. The new National Key Research & Development Projects programme was launched in 2016 to support R&D in key areas related to social welfare such as agriculture, energy and health. It became the most active national funding programme in China, investing over US$7 billion (RMB 50 billion) during the first year to support nearly 2,300 projects across academia, public organisations and private entities (China Innovation Funding, 2022). Science and Technology Megaprojects is one of the most important public research initiatives established in recent years. Its investments are focused on projects considered as 'China's most important' for the country's medium- and long-term development.[1]

Besides facilitating the generation of research and technology output, funds are also allocated to accelerate the commercialisation of scientific knowledge and the formation of new high-tech industries. An example of this effort is the financial and infrastructure support provided to establish nearly 200 National Engineering Research Centres (NERCs) that bridge applied research and domestic industrial companies. NERCs cover diverse areas such as clean energy, electric vehicles, information technology in agriculture and human stem cells. Many NERCs reside within top Chinese universities while involving active collaboration with companies (Tsinghua University, 2023a).

Finally, the Chinese government also established several innovation zones to enable efficient technology and help innovators scale their pilot projects at the national level. China has built 173 high-tech

[1] This refers to projects dealing with the production of large domestic aircrafts, space stations, space robots, vaccines, genetically modified plants and more recently artificial intelligence (AI). Megaprojects also include military projects.

industrial development zones since 1988, with the plan to build some fifty more by 2030, to boost technology entrepreneurship and the formation of knowledge-driven industrial clusters. These high-tech zones are tasked with creating value-added tech products. While occupying fewer than 0.1 per cent of the country's territory, they contribute to about 13 per cent of China's GDP (Lanzhou High Tech Zone, 2023). For example, the Chengdu High-Tech Industrial Development Zone, initiated in 1998, includes a pilot free-trade zone that facilitates foreign investments and international trade. A life-sciences hub named 'Tianfu Bio-town' brings together pharmaceutical and biotech companies, chemical product manufacturers, medical device developers and digital health services. A final example is a 'software park' comprising a close-connected network of incubators, digital entrepreneurs and tech giants. In addition, the local government also involves international partners, jointly developing the Singapore-Sichuan High-Tech Innovation Park that focuses on the development of 5G, cybersecurity, AI and big data analytics. Furthermore, more specialised pilot zones have been built in recent years to reduce China's import reliance in core technology sectors like AI and robotics. To expand China's AI industry, the Chinese government has set up twenty National New Generation Artificial Intelligence Innovation and Development Pilot Zones where firms receive financial support and less regulatory constraints in R&D and business operations. China's 14th Five-Year Plan for the Development of The Robotics Industry (2021–2025) outlined the plan to build between three and five robotics clusters in the country by 2025 (Macquarie, 2022). The main goal was the expansion of industries where robots can be applied, such as healthcare and construction. Local governments offer funding in these clusters to promote cooperation between local universities, public research institutes and companies engaged in robotics and smart manufacturing (Groenewegen-Lau & Laha, 2023). The United States has notably begun to implement a similar strategy with thirty-one regional innovation hubs through the CHIPS Act (United States Congress, 2022).

5.3.2 The Role of Enterprises as Innovation Drivers and Venture Capitalists

Private-sector companies are a growing driver of innovation in China. Since the turn of the century, Chinese firms have been gradually changing from copycats to innovators, shifting towards value-added activities and actively expanding in global markets (see Chapter 11 for detailed examples of innovative firms such as Huawei, Tencent, Alibaba and a few young Chinese unicorns).

Enterprises contribute to China's innovation ecosystem in many ways. While Chinese firms have traditionally been described as 'copycats', taking advantage of the weak intellectual property system and directly adopting and localising products and business models from the West, there is evidence that they are gradually building internal innovative capabilities and becoming tech leaders. For instance, Chinese Huawei spent over US$20 billion on R&D in 2021. In 2022 the company received a record number of 2,770 patents in the United States and ranked among the top 5 companies obtaining the most US patents (Bloomberg, 2022). As one of the 'top patent holders in 5G technology' Huawei continues to be a dominant 5G network supplier despite US sanctions. Similarly, the Chinese automobile company Geely set an R&D budget of US$23 billion in 2021 to attain its 2025 goal of boosting its autonomous driving capability (Ren, 2021).

Firstly, the government plays an important role in enterprise-led R&D in China. For example, in the R&D-intensive biopharmaceutical industry, the Chinese government invests billions in biotech companies each year to support their R&D programmes and creates data-sharing initiatives and industry platforms to facilitate knowledge diffusion and research collaboration. It funds basic science projects to feed firms with new academic findings, improves intellectual property (IP) protection to incentivise new drug development, restructures healthcare reimbursement schemes to increase market access and builds a more favourable regulatory environment to encourage the entry of international players.

Secondly, technology entrepreneurship brings technology from lab to market. The past decade has seen a host of technology-based enterprises from China flourishing in both the domestic and global markets. The increasing number of Chinese unicorns is just one example of the trend. As of 2021 China had 301 unicorns, or 28 per cent of the world total, ranking second after the United States (46 per cent) and far ahead of the next country on the list (Asia Nikkei, 2021). According to a Forbes report, China added seventy-four unicorns in 2022, 70 per cent of which came from what the country considered to be the 'core technology sectors' of clean technology, healthcare, smart logistics and renewable energy (Shen, 2023), and included ten semiconductor start-ups. Two prime examples of Chinese unicorns are ByteDance and DJI Innovations. The former built an AI-powered social media algorithm company that underlies all its major products, including TikTok, the social media platform with over 1 billion monthly active users, nearly double that of X, formerly Twitter (Statista, 2023a). The latter is a leading commercial drone company focused on aerial photography and videography (see Chapter 10).

Thirdly, innovations by firms can often have spillover effects that help other innovators. A firm can offer infrastructure that enhances R&D efficiency, helping other companies' research projects and allowing for new entrepreneurial technology firms. Huawei's 5G network is an example of one innovation acting as the infrastructure for many other innovations. Internet of things (IoT) technology, AI, virtual reality and autonomous vehicles can all be improved with reduced latency, which gives opportunities to innovators in those areas to leverage the 5G capacities to boost their own technology. In addition, many platform-based innovation ecosystems were formed as China's digital economy exploded and digital platforms acted as infrastructure for facilitating knowledge exchange and collaboration between innovation entities. In particular, several companies have joined China's National Open Platform for Next Generation AI (set up in 2017), with each of them establishing an innovation platform in a specific area. These include YITU Technology for vision computing, MININGLAMP Technology for marketing intelligence, Huawei for software and hardware infrastructures, Ping An for inclusive finance, Hikvision for video sensing, JD.com for intelligent supply chains, MEGVII for image sensing, Qihoo 360 for cybersecurity, TA for smart education, Xiaomi for smart homes, Baidu for autonomous driving, Tencent for medical imaging and Alibaba for smart cities (EqualOcean, 2019). Moreover, many large companies are backing new start-ups, offering financial and technical support for the growth of next-generation tech leaders. For instance, seven of the ten largest institutional investors in Chinese unicorns are venture capitalists and investment banks and three are technology companies themselves: Tencent, Alibaba and Baidu (Gao & Guo, 2018). Tencent is well known for funding start-ups that it then acquires.

5.3.3 Knowledge Institutions

Universities and research centres are another key driver of innovation. Unlike in other countries there is more centralisation and coordination within the innovation ecosystem in China. As Chinese universities have improved their position in global rankings for research productivity over the past ten years, they have also played a crucial role in the emergence and growth of the technological innovation ecosystem in China. Academia–industry collaboration has been a key catalyst in technology-driven entrepreneurship, especially during the early stages of economic liberalisation. Since it is not possible to separate universities from the government in China, given the public nature of most Chinese universities, our analysis partially adopts a policy perspective with a focus on industry–university–government collaborations.

Universities have four main roles in the Chinese innovation system. Firstly, they directly act as innovators. Secondly, they facilitate knowledge and technology creation and transfer through direct linkages with the industry. Thirdly, they supply high-quality human capital to knowledge-driven industries, and finally, they incubate spin-offs and drive the clustering of high-tech companies, many of which grow to attain unicorn status.

Universities are active innovators, dominating basic and applied research in China's science and technology ecosystem. As of 2019, they performed about 59 per cent of China's basic research (Fedasiuk et al., 2022). The University of Science and Technology of China topped the list of basic research spenders, investing nearly US$2 billion in disclosed basic R&D projects, followed far behind by Tsinghua University, which invested US$0.32 billion, then Peking University at US$0.25 billion, and Zhejiang University with an investment of US$0.17 billion. As a comparison, Stanford spent US$1.2 billion on R&D in 2020 (Statista, 2022). Findings generated from Chinese universities' basic research are publicly accessible and can be acquired by industrial firms to expand their knowledge base and stimulate applied innovation. Universities also directly engage in applied research and, increasingly, technology development. Chinese universities were granted 308,000 patents in total in 2021 (China National Intellectual Property Administration, 2022), more than three times the figure of 2012 (69,000). It is interesting to note that universities generally monetise their patents through licensing, sales or spin-offs.

A well-known example of a university-driven innovation ecosystem is Zhongguancun, China's Silicon Valley. Designated as an educational district at the birth of the Republic of China in 1949, Zhongguancun is home to many universities and research institutes, including Tsinghua University and Peking University, the country's best universities. A turning point for the district to transition into a technology hub was the implementation of the Open-Door Policy, which drove a series of economic reforms that encouraged technological development and high-tech entrepreneurship from the late 1970s to the late 1980s. During this period the first Chinese patent application was filed, the first Chinese-foreign joint venture for technology-driven business was established and the first private Chinese technology company was formed, all in Zhongguancun (Dong et al., 2018). Several technology business incubators and many successful technology companies were born, including the Stone Group, Founder Group and Lenovo Group. Universities played a key role in the birth of those firms. The Founder Group, for instance, was a spin-off from Peking University and was first led by Wang Xuan, both a graduate of Peking University and a professor there. The company started as an effort to commercialise Peking University faculty patents and later grew and diversified into one of the largest technology conglomerates in China. The Zhongguancun district became the 'Beijing High-Technology Development Experimental Zone' In 1988. Since then, Zhongguancun has continued to assist local entrepreneurs and has attracted top talents back from overseas. Tsinghua graduate Charles Zhang, for example, returned to Beijing after obtaining his PhD from MIT and started the first Chinese online search engine, Soho.com, in Zhongguancun. As a National Innovation Demonstration Zone, Zhongguancun hosts several science and technology parks and acts as a major innovation hub in the country.

Universities not only act as a pool of external knowledge for industries, but they also actively build and expand innovation networks, thereby facilitating the diffusion of knowledge and technology and the conversion of academic insights into business value. Tsinghua is a good example. The university has a wholly owned subsidiary, Tsinghua Holdings, that engages in the commercialisation of the university's academic innovation. It has built many start-up incubation centres on and outside the campus. Besides direct incubation of, and investments in, university-based start-ups and R&D collaborations between university labs and industry scientists, the university also engages in facility sharing, informal knowledge exchange and supply chain partnerships (including undertaking R&D contracts) with companies.

Furthermore, universities mediate knowledge transfer across countries to expand domestic companies' access to knowledge generated in more developed economies. For instance, Tsinghua has built numerous ties with universities overseas as well as with global firms, such as joint research centres built with the University of Chicago, a large-scale research collaboration agreement with the University of Cambridge, Imperial College London and Tokyo University (among others) signed in 2021 (Tsinghua University, 2023b), and multiple R&D contracts with firms such as the one with Bristol Myers Squibb to conduct structural biology research to assist in new drug discovery.

In recent years, universities have undergone reforms. The introduction of the Double First-Class University Plan is one. The new plan replaced the 211 Project and 985 Project, where universities were classified based on the research output and strategic position in China's innovation ecosystem of the whole institution. Instead, it redesigned the measurement of universities' innovation performance, considering each discipline individually. Being a 'first-class' department means being in the top 5 per cent of all Chinese university departments in the discipline and implies government financial support (Peters & Besley, 2018). The goal of this reform was to create a group of 'world-class disciplines' and a group of 'world-class universities' at the same time, to structure the innovation strategy around the core technologies of national interests and boost emerging disciplines, including those important in the digital age. Overall, the initiative has created new incentives for all universities, not just the top ones (those which previously held 985 or 211 titles), to innovate. There are incentives to push the boundary for technology breakthroughs and expand support mechanisms to tailor resources to specific academic disciplines and universities.

Another interesting development is the founding of Westlake University in 2018, the first private research university in China described by the media as the similar to the American Caltech (Yan, 2018). The first president of the university is Shi Yigong, a biologist who used to serve as dean of Tsinghua University's School of Life Sciences. The university places a great emphasis on biomedicine and engineering. While it is hard to predict the future of Westlake

University at such an early stage, the university offers a new model for experimenting with schemes that drive innovation in a presumably more autonomous environment with less government intervention.

Besides government policies and university-driven ecosystem formation, China's innovation system is also characterised by the strong position of public research centres and massive research consortia formed within and beyond academia. China's public research system follows a strict hierarchical structure with the state council's science and technology group as the highest decision-making body, which sets the overarching goals and formulates the Science and Technology (S&T) policies. Key leading institutes include the Chinese Academy of Sciences, the Chinese Academy of Engineering and the National Natural Science Foundation of China, all of which play a key role in managing the allocation of funding among diverse public and private research institutes, universities and enterprises. Using the Chinese Academy of Sciences (CAS) as an example, it has hired around 56,000 professional researchers in its 104 research institutes across twenty-three provinces, is home to 'dozens of' national key labs and engineering centres and owns over thirty large-scale science facilities including the Beijing Electron Positron Collider, the Shanghai Synchrotron Radiation Facility and a data storage facility that can store 150 TB of scientific data. CAS hosts a number of research networks, publishes 267 research journals and has set up many collaborations with international partners. As the most important scientific think-tank and governing body in China, CAS generates many innovations and draws strategic roadmaps that guide the future direction of China's S&T development.

There is an increasing hierarchy among research labs in China which allows more centralised control (Groenewegen-Lau & Laha, 2023). For instance, public research labs and research centres are divided into 'national labs and research centres', 'state key labs', 'provincial/ministerial co-constructed state key labs', 'CAS key labs', 'provincial key labs' and 'ministry of education key labs', among many others. To some degree, the overall structure was like that of the US system of national laboratories, federally funded R&D centres and university research centres. Most 'State Key Labs' (SKLs) are public, affiliated with either universities or CAS; for the area of chemistry alone, CAS administers twelve SKLs, while universities manage fourteen SKLs in total. Meanwhile, there are also enterprise-operated SKLs. For

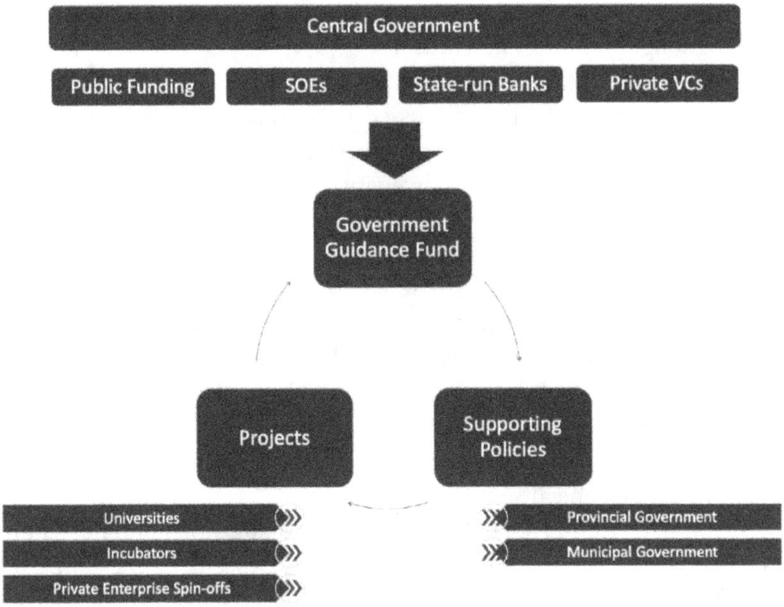

Figure 5.1 Actors of Chinese national eco-systems of innovation.
Source: Authors and Noel Liu, research assistant at the Emerging Markets Institute.
Note: Government guidance funds refer to those funds meant for innovation, policy focus areas and projects and start-ups.

instance, Trina Solar Co. Ltd, a Chinese company that engages in R&D and manufacturing of photovoltaic products, operates the State Key Laboratory of Photovoltaic Science and Technology.

This evolving ecosystem has played an important role in regional innovation clusters that foster innovation and are home to technology start-ups and unicorns. The distinguishing feature of these Chinese clusters is that they are better organised and coordinated within themselves because the different actors work together to reinforce each other's roles (Figure 5.1).

5.4 Regional Innovation Clusters

Regional innovation clusters are important components of the Chinese national innovation ecosystem. A few city clusters act as major innovation hubs, notably Jing-jin-ji (Beijing, Tianjin, Hebei), the Yangtze

River Delta (Shanghai, Zhejiang, Jiangsu) and the Greater Bay Area (Guangdong, Hong Kong, Macau).

Beijing remains the most innovative Chinese city (WIPO, 2022). Its Zhongguancun subdistrict, discussed in Section 5.3, offers an exemplary case of how China innovates. There are ninety-one universities in Beijing, notably Tsinghua University, Peking University, Renmin University of China, Beihang University and many others well represented in global university rankings, especially in STEM (science, technology, engineering and mathematics) disciplines. Many of the largest Chinese tech companies are based in Beijing, such as Baidu, JD.com and Soho. As of February 2023, there are a total of 1,011 software firms in Beijing (Crunchbase, 2023). According to Statista (2023b), around 1.4 million people were employed by the information technology (IT) sector of Beijing in 2021 and one million worked in the scientific and technical services sector.

In Southern China, Shanghai, Shenzhen, Guangzhou and Hangzhou are important innovation hubs. Shanghai is expected to be home to 1,000 high-tech companies by 2025 (Jing, 2022). Its Lin-Gang Special Area of China, a pilot free-trade zone established in 2019, saw expanding industrial clusters specialising in diverse high-tech areas such as information science, AI, biomedicine and smart manufacturing. Hangzhou, the city where Alibaba has its headquarters, has been focusing on innovation in the digital and life sciences industries.

The Framework Agreement on Deepening Guangdong-Hong Kong-Macau Cooperation in the Development of the Bay Area was signed in July 2017, followed by a series of initiatives to eliminate hurdles in the flow of knowledge and financial resources and facilitate collaboration in the Greater Bay Area of China. Measures to spur innovation collaboration in the area include subsidies and tax incentives, new partnership platforms and numerous regulatory changes. Measures, including the construction of a 36-km-long bridge that links Hong Kong to Macau and a high-speed rail that connects Hong Kong to Shenzhen and Guangzhou, also improved labour mobility.

The Greater Bay Area connects eleven cities – Hong Kong, Guangzhou, Shenzhen, Macau, and seven other cities in Guangdong – into an economic hub. It was the second-best science and technology cluster in the world in 2022 (behind Tokyo–Yokohama) according to patent-filing and scientific article publication metrics (WIPO, 2022). The Greater Bay Area is unique in its size, structural balance and integrated nature. This involves the presence of diverse industries, the strong linkage between tech innovators and financial capital and the coordination of different tax and legal systems. Referred to by many as 'the Silicon Valley of China' (Deng, 2021), Shenzhen has grown into a major tech hub in the country. Long seen as the 'world's hardware factory' (90 per cent of the world's electronics are manufactured there (Zhang, 2018)), Shenzhen is home to tech giants such as Huawei, Tencent and BYD as well as emerging unicorns such as the leading drone company DJI Innovations, the augmented reality company Royole Co. and e-commerce platform SHEIN (see Chapter 10 for more on the subject). In recent years, the city has built a larger pool of unicorns in core areas including life sciences, semiconductors, robotics, new energy and others, thanks to investments and reduced administrative barriers to entrepreneurship and stock listings. Hong Kong, on the other hand, is one of the world's largest financial centres and a major gateway for international investments and trade to and from mainland China. While similar cities exist in other geographies, such as New York and the actual Silicon Valley in the United States, the Greater Bay Area is different in its proximity to tech and finance hubs within the region. For instance, the shortest air travel distance between New York and San Francisco is 4,139 km (2,572 miles), while that between Hong Kong and Shenzhen is only 50 km (31 miles). The proximity and complementarity of the two cities have historically boosted the area's growth (Wu, 1997) and have been used to create new sources of connectivity for innovation and economic development. Specifically, technology enterprises can enjoy greater access to the international financial market and a looser regulatory burden in Hong Kong. At the same time, Hong Kong's advantage in basic research and education – a highly concentrated cluster of top universities with strong STEM research capabilities – can be utilised to create new business opportunities using Guangdong region's technological infrastructure and to provide talents to the tech companies in the region. Just like Stanford and UC Berkeley relate to San Francisco and Tokyo University to the Tokyo–Yokohama corridor, universities in Hong Kong help the Greater Bay Area to acquire the knowledge at the frontier of human understanding and attract the right talent. The Greater Bay Area and Hong Kong are home to four of the world's top 50 universities for AI and computer science, giving it a pool for knowledge and human capital needed for industrial AI development across the region. An example of collaboration between Hong Kong and Shenzhen is the establishment of the Hong Kong-Shenzhen Innovation Technology Park, which aims to facilitate research partnerships between universities in both cities and enhance industry-academia collaboration across geographical boundaries.

Besides the four main cities, there are also seven 'supporting cities' in Guangdong province, each of which has different characteristics. For instance, Zhuhai is a life sciences hub, while Zhongshan is home to several equipment-manufacturing and electronic information clusters. According to Guangdong Bureau's Market Environment for Innovation Index, which considers the number of R&D firms, R&D manpower, the investment in R&D and R&D output, the innovation output of mainland cities in the Greater Bay Area tripled from 2013 to 2018 (EY Greater China, 2021).

The Greater Bay Area, however, faces the challenge of administrative barriers. The different legal and regulatory systems between Mainland China, Hong Kong and Macau as well as cultural differences (Hong Kong is generally considered more 'Westernised' than the other two) creates friction in collaboration. While Hong Kong's autonomy has been diminishing over the last decade, there are still gaps between the markets. For instance, Hong Kong has separate taxation and finance policies and uses different currencies (the HK dollar instead of the Chinese yuan). Compared to the Mainland, it has free trade and fewer market restrictions on foreign and domestic firms. Efforts have been put into aligning the two systems, by collaboratively designing, synergistically developing, and collectively celebrating policy achievements (Hua, 2022). However, changes are going to take time.

5.5 Moving Forward: Focusing on Self-Sufficiency and Moving Ahead on the Innovation Chain

Geopolitical tensions, including the lingering US–China trade war and the conflict in Ukraine, have reinforced China's decision to pursue self-reliance and master all the steps of the innovation process, giving further impetus to the concept of the innovation chain. President Xi Jingping's report to the 20th CCP Congress in 2022 emphasised that it is important for China to gain supremacy in critical technologies (Groenewegen-Lau & Laha, 2023). Technological self-sufficiency was a key theme of the report, and the re-centralisation of technology investment was another. Government policies implemented since 2020 have reflected China's renewed strategy toward self-reliance in technology. These include the creation of new incentives for basic science research and technology transfer, greater central control for innovation projects, stricter regulations over laboratories and development zones to shift from quantity to quality and reduced openness and narrower international collaboration networks. At the same time, China is paying increased attention to the commercialisation of research output, in line with the innovation chain concept (such as the linkage of diverse entities to optimise innovation outcomes, monetise knowledge and create more market-ready technologies) that the 20th CCP Congress highlighted.

From the implementation of the Science and Technology System Reform Act in the 1980s to the introduction of the innovation chain concept in recent years, China has always tried to boost its growth with science and technology. To this end, the Chinese government has guided the country's science and technology trajectory through a series of strategic plans and targeted policies over the past four decades. 'Made in China 2025', for instance, has played an important role in the process, emphasising heavier investments in high-tech manufacturing and focusing on increasing the quantity and quality of domestically produced 'core materials' to move away from labour-intensive manufacturing and enhance Chinese firms' competitiveness. While VCs in Silicon Valley may attribute their success to being far from regulators, China's technology and innovation leadership has evolved differently, with the government frequently facilitating and driving innovation.

Admittedly, there are still challenges to be solved such as those related to the implementation of intellectual property rights protection systems (Mercator Institute for China Studies, 2021). Nonetheless, the multiplicity of actors in the Chinese innovation ecosystem and the emergence of many clusters fostering innovative companies and unicorns illustrate the successful transformation of China into a technology and innovation powerhouse. Unicorns are the pride of a country – major disruptors and innovation leaders. China is one of the two leading nations by number of unicorns; the other is the United States. Both countries have very different histories and ways of stimulating innovation. For instance, China has achieved impressive progress under the supervision of central and local governments with the coordinated help of universities, research centres and companies. Innovation hubs created around cities or universities with the support of local and central authorities have fostered collaborative partnerships among firms and between firms and academia, facilitated knowledge transfer, fostered synergies among enterprises and, as a result, played a key role in the remarkable rise of innovative start-ups and unicorns in China. However, faced with mounting geopolitical and economic tensions (such as the US–China trade war), China is increasingly focusing on self-sufficiency, prioritising AI, robotics and semiconductors. At the same time, it wants to expand its technological influence within its zone of influence. This may lead to different international standards and, perhaps, networks. It remains to be seen how this situation will affect start-ups and unicorns in China, and the further rise of China as a global innovation leader.

References

Asia Nikkei. (2021). *China trails U.S. in creating unicorns, Hurun ranking shows.* asia.nikkei.com/Business/Startups/China-trails-U.S.-in-creating-unicorns-Hurun-ranking-shows

Bloomberg. (2022). *Huawei ranks no. 5 in U.S., patents in sign of Chinese growth.* www.bloomberg.com/news/articles/2022-01-11/huawei-ranks-no-5-in-u-s-patents-in-sign-of-chinese-growth#xj4y7vzkg

Casanova, L., and Miroux, A. (2019). *The Era of Chinese Multinationals.* Elsevier Science & Technology. tinyurl.com/u7yd34e6

China Innovation Funding. (2022). *National key R&D programmes.*

China National Intellectual Property Administration. (2013). *General introduction to the Third Revision of the Patent Law of the People's Republic of China and its implementing regulations.* english.cnipa.gov.cn/art/2013/7/17/art_1349_81674.html

(2022). *Patent commercialization activities at Chinese universities skyrocket in past decade.* english.cnipa.gov.cn/art/2022/8/3/art_2829_176992.html

Crunchbase. (2023). *Beijing software companies.* www.crunchbase.com/hub/beijing-software-companies

Deng, I. (2021). *China's tech hub Shenzhen, home to Huawei and Tencent, wants to become a 'unicorn' paradise.* MyNews. tinyurl.com/dcuce2z4

Dong, X., Hu, Y., Yin, W., and Kuo, E. (2018). The history of Zhongguancun: Building a park and establishing a benchmark. *Zhongguancun Model: Driving the Dual Engines of Science & Technology and Capital*, 1–16. doi.org/10.1007/978-981-13-2267-9_1

EqualOcean. (2019). *10 companies join China's national open platform for next generation AI*. equalocean.com/news/2019082911628

EY Greater China. (2021). *Strategy for a tech-driven Greater Bay Area*. www.ey.com/en_cn/china-opportunities/strategy-for-a-tech-driven-greater-bay-area

Fedasiuk, R., Omar Loera Martinez, A., and Puglisi, A. (2022). *A competitive era for China's universities: How increased funding is paving the way*. Data Brief. Center for Security and Emerging Technology. tinyurl.com/mu2abpsw

Gao, J., and Guo, Y. (2018). *The new Chinese unicorns: Seizing opportunity in China's burgeoning economy*. PwC. www.pwc.com/gx/en/technology/publications/assets/pwc-chinese-unicorns.pdf

Groenewegen-Lau, J., and Laha, M. (2023). *Controlling the innovation chain: China's strategy to become a science & technology superpower*. Merics | Mercator Institute for China Studies Report.

Hua, C. (2022). *Clearing cross-border partnership barriers*. China Daily. www.chinadaily.com.cn/a/202211/04/WS6364c55da3105ca1f227417a.html

Jing, S. (2022). *Shanghai zone to be home of 1,000 high-tech firms by 2025*. China Daily. www.chinadaily.com.cn/a/202208/23/WS63043112a310fd2b29e73ba8.html

Lanzhou High Tech Zone. (2023). *Lanzhou high tech industrial development zone*. lanzhou-hightechzone.com

Macquarie. (2022). *Why China is focused on a robotic future*. www.macquarie.com/au/en/perspectives/why-china-is-focused-on-a-robotic-future.html

Mercator Institute for China Studies. (2021, December). *China essentials*. tinyurl.com/3fkfyakw

Peters, M., and Besley, T. (2018). China's double first-class university strategy: 双一流. *Educational Philosophy and Theory 50*(12), 1075–1079. www.tandfonline.com/doi/full/10.1080/00131857.2018.1438822

Ren, D. (2021). *China's Geely puts US$23.4 billion research budget behind 2025 goal for electric cars to make up 40 per cent of its production*. South China Morning Post. tinyurl.com/2bk7t2uu

Scimago Journal and Country Rank. (2022). *Country rankings*. www.scimagojr.com/countryrank.php

Shen, X. (2023). *China added 74 unicorns in 2022, maintaining steady pace of growth despite fundraising crunch*. South China Morning Post. tinyurl.com/yc8fee8m

Statista. (2022). *R&D expenditures of Stanford University from 2006 to 2020*. www.statista.com/statistics/697602/rnd-expenditure-stanford-university/

(2023a). *Most popular social networks worldwide as of January 2023, ranked by number of monthly active users*. tinyurl.com/5n7sp3yc

(2023b). *Number of employees in Beijing, China in 2021, by industry.* tinyurl.com/mrevje8a

Tsinghua University. (2023a). *National Engineering Research Center.* tinyurl.com/3tf3auyn

(2023b). *Overseas partnerships.* tinyurl.com/3ctpmxmw

United States Congress. (2022). *H.R.4346 – CHIPS and Science Act, 117th Congress (2021–2022).* www.congress.gov/bill/117th-congress/house-bill/4346

WIPO. (2022). *Global innovation index: What is the future of innovation-driven growth?* www.wipo.int/global_innovation_index/en/2022/

(2023) *Global innovation index: Innovation in the face of uncertainty.* www.wipo.int/global_innovation_index/en/2023/

The World Bank. (2013). *China 2030: Building a modern, harmonious, and creative society.* www.worldbank.org/content/dam/Worldbank/document/China-2030-complete.pdf

Wu, W. (1997). Proximity and complementarity in Hong Kong-Shenzhen industrialization. *Asian Survey 37*(8), 771–793. doi.org/10.2307/2645449

Yan, A. (2018). *China is setting up its own version of America's Caltech to rival US in innovation.* South China Morning Post. www.scmp.com/?module=masthead&pgtype=article

Yusuf, S., Nabeshima, K., and Perkins, D. H. (2005). *Under new ownership: privatizing China's state-owned enterprises.* The World Bank.

Zhang, E. (2018). *Shenzhen: The tech capital of the world.* Medium. medium.com/wonk-bridge/shenzhen-the-tech-capital-of-the-world-7b1a0469c39f

6 A Supply–Demand Model of Indian Start-Ups and Unicorns

RAVI RAMAMURTI

6.1 Introduction

India is developing a vibrant start-up ecosystem. By December 2022, it had spawned 108 unicorns, the third highest number in the world behind China (316) and the United States (666), and ahead of fourth-ranking Israel (85). In this chapter we explore why this has happened, and whether it is sustainable or just a passing phase. While it might be surprising that a country with a per-capita income of only US$2,500 could produce so many start-ups and unicorns, a closer look reveals that important drivers of the demand for and supply of start-ups, particularly in digital businesses, have come together in the last decade. This has resulted in a significant increase in the number of start-ups, with risk capital running into billions of dollars from early- and late-stage investors. Start-up fever has reached most parts of India, but three city-clusters dominate the landscape: Bengaluru, Mumbai and Delhi. On the demand side, India's large and fast-growing market, coupled with 'leapfrogging advantages' (Ramamurti & Hillemann, 2018), have encouraged start-ups in many digital businesses. On the supply side, India's abundant and affordable technical talent, nurtured by the country's information technology (IT)/software companies and the research and development (R&D) centres of foreign multinationals, have combined with a surge in angel investors, incubators, accelerators and local and foreign venture capitalists (VCs). Government policies have reinforced both demand-side and supply-side factors, as have global developments such as the COVID-19 pandemic and geopolitical tensions involving China. Despite setbacks and inevitable corrections in 2022–2023, the fundamental supply and demand features of the Indian ecosystem have been strong. Therefore, India will continue to be an important source of digital start-ups and unicorns.

6.2 India's Unicorn Landscape

According to Start-up India, the government's nodal agency for the promotion of entrepreneurship, the number of start-ups recognized by the Government of in India grew from around 500 when the agency was created in 2016 to almost 116,000 by January 2025 (Ministry of Commerce & Industry, 2025). Inc42, a consultancy focused on tech start-ups, reports that the cumulative number of start-ups rose from 37,000 in 2015 to over 58,000 in 2022, an increase of 54 per cent over a seven-year period (see Figure 6.1). The amount of venture capital invested in Indian start-ups grew more than seven-fold in roughly the same period, from US$5.3 billion in 2014 to a high of US$41.8 billion in 2021 (Figure 6.2). Not surprisingly, the number of new unicorns created follows a similar pattern, rising from just one in 2010 to twenty-one in 2022 (Kashyap, 2022; Statista, 2024a). The cumulative number of unicorns had risen to 111 by November 2023, with a total market valuation exceeding US$345 billion (Sil, 2022).

India produced the second highest number of unicorns in the world in 2022 but lagged behind the United States by a very large margin. China had a strong run of unicorns until 2020, when COVID hit and the Chinese government also clamped down on the tech sector, took stern measures against legendary companies such as Ant Financial and

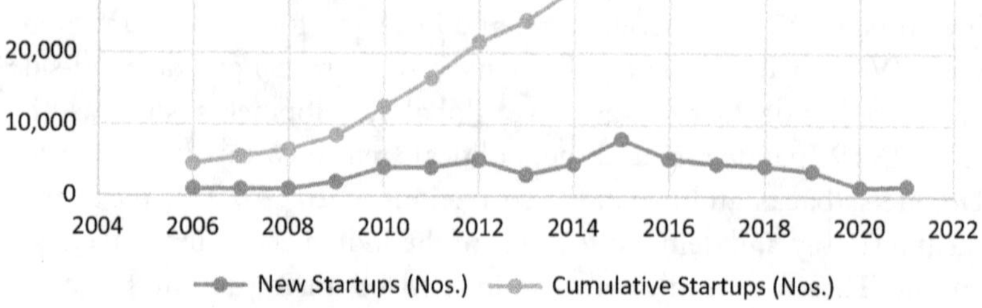

Figure 6.1 Start-ups in India 2006–2021.
Source: Created by the author using data in Inc42 (2022).

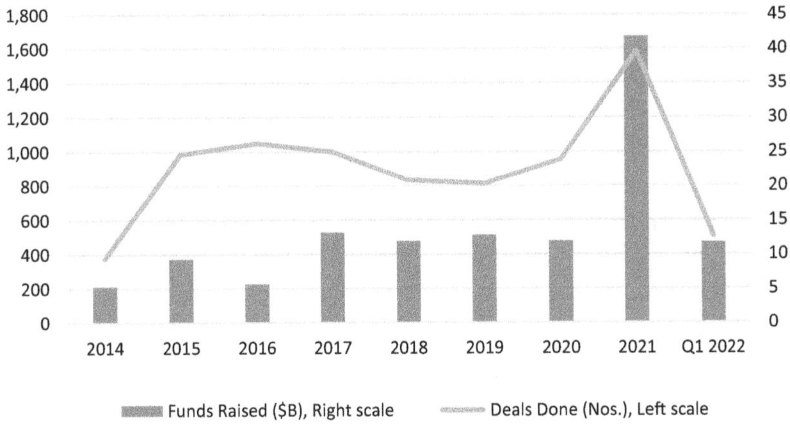

Figure 6.2 Funds raised, deals done by Indian start-ups, 2014–2022.
Source: Created by the author using data in Inc42 (2022).

Tencent and shut down several edtech start-ups overnight. However, in terms of cumulative funds raised for start-ups, India's total until 2022 was US$136 billion, compared to US$837 billion in China and US$2,700 billion in the United States (Kashyap, 2022). All the same, India's upward trend in this area is impressive. Yet, two questions are worth asking: Why did India experience such a dramatic surge in start-ups and unicorns in the last decade? Is it the beginning of a sustainable, secular trend or merely a passing phase? We explore these questions in this chapter.

Indian start-ups cover the gamut from e-commerce, fintech, consumer services and enterprisetech, to edtech, healthtech, transport-tech and media and entertainment. In terms of sectoral distribution, a good number of Indian start-ups follow the international pattern of focusing on e-commerce, fintech, and consumer services. However, India stands out for having the greatest number of start-ups (nearly 7,500) in the enterprisetech space, which had cumulatively attracted US$11.7 billion in funding by 2022. India's participation in enterprisetech was arguably driven by its legacy in B2B (business to business) digital businesses during the rise of India's IT and software companies (Tata Consultancy Services, Infosys, Wipro, etc.). In terms of funding amount, though, e-commerce and fintech dwarf the funds raised by the other sectors. This was particularly evident in 2021 when their funding level was twice that of other sectors (Agarwal, 2022). The sectoral

Table 6.1 *Sector and location of India's first 100 unicorns*

Unicorns by sector		Unicorns by city cluster	
E-commerce	23	Bengaluru	39
Fintech	21	Delhi National Capital Region	32
Entreprisetech	19	Mumbai	16
Consumer services	9	Pune	6
Media/Entertainment	7	Chennai	5
Edtech	6	Hyderabad	2
Logistics	5	**Total**	**100**
Healthtech	4		
Traveltech	2		
Transport tech	2		
Cleantech	1		
Real estate tech	1		
Total	**100**		

Source: Inc42, 2022: 18, 23.

distribution of India's first 100 unicorns (see Table 6.1) shows that e-commerce and fintech led the pack with over twenty each, followed by enterprisetech (nineteen) and consumer services (nine). By way of illustration, we include short profiles of three Indian unicorns in consumer services (Zomato), fintech (Paytm), and ecommerce (Snapdeal) in Tables 6.2, 6.3, and 6.4, respectively.

Start-up activity in India is concentrated in India's big cities, led by Bengaluru, New Delhi and Mumbai, in that order (Table 6.1). These cities also housed some of India's leading IT, software and business process outsourcing companies. These three cities accounted for 85 per cent of all start-ups in 2022, and their share of funds invested in start-ups was also about 85 per cent (Sarkar, 2023). Nevertheless, many other cities including Chennai, Hyderabad and Pune were also important centres for digital start-ups.

Almost all Indian unicorns are digital businesses. Of the top 10 companies in terms of funds raised, only one (Renew Power, a leading player in solar power generation) was not a digital business. In other words, the rise of Indian unicorns is a direct result of the rise of the digital economy in India. Therefore, to explain India's start-up and unicorn boom, one must understand why digital start-ups took off during the last decade.

Table 6.2 *Zomato – A consumer-tech unicorn*

Founding year	2008
Founders' background	Two graduates of the Indian Institute of Technology-Delhi who met while working at Bain & Company started Foodiebay, which was later renamed Zomato. The app allowed customers to get information on local restaurants, menus and reviews and place orders which would be delivered quickly at their homes or offices (Saju & Mohandas, 2020).
Strategy or business model	Zomato was one of the pioneers, globally, in the hyperlocal food delivery business. It was founded two years before China's Meituan, five years before Doordash and six years before both Uber Eats and Zomato's main Indian rival, Swiggy. Zomato started in Delhi and the National Capital Region, then expanded nationally and by 2012 started expanding internationally (eventually to more than twenty countries, including the US). By 2023, as pressures mounted to attain profitability, Zomato scaled back its services to just India and the UAE. Zomato's revenues came from commission on food orders from both restaurants and customers, ad revenue on its site by restaurants, commissions on referrals and reservations for dining in (Govindarajan & Srivastava, 2021). Upfront costs were high because of high customer acquisition costs, restaurant enrolment costs and brand-building, all funded by fresh investments by large, international VCs. Zomato also has subsidiaries for restaurant services (Hyperpure) and quick commerce (BlinkIt).
Investors	Info Edge, a local early-stage investor founded by a successful entrepreneur (Sanjeev Bikchandani) invested US$1 million in Zomato to help scale up its operations. Later, its investors included foreign VCs such as Tiger Global, China's Ant Financial, Singapore's Temasek, Mirae, etc. Total capital raised US$2.6 billion
Exit strategy	IPO on Indian stock markets (NSE and BSE) in July 2021

Table 6.2 (*cont.*)

Market results	By 2023, the food delivery industry's total revenues were US$33 billion, including US$22 billion in grocery and US$11 billion in food (gross merchandise value, or GMV), with a CAGR (compound annual growth rate) of 20 per cent (Statista, 2023b). A fraction of the GMV is earned by delivery firms such as Zomato. Total number of users of meal delivery services was estimated at 346 million. Zomato's share was estimated at 56 per cent and Swiggy's at 46 per cent (Agarwal, 2023).
Financial results	In FY2022–2023, Zomato's sales were INR 78 billion (US$937 million) and its net loss margin fell from -29.2 per cent to -17.7 per cent. In Q1 of FY 2023–2024, Zomato is reported to have turned a profit on its food delivery business.
Market cap, December 2023	US$13.7 billion (vs. US$12 billion at IPO in July 2021)

Source: Compiled by author using sources cited as indicated.

Table 6.3 *Paytm – A fintech unicorn*

Founding year	2010
Founders' background	Vijay Shekhar Sharma, an alumnus of Delhi College of Engineering, founded Paytm. He previously ran a content management service (CMS) service and sold it for US$500,000. After this, he started One97, Paytm's parent company, which was a telecom value-added services provider (Gupta et al., 2019). Following the introduction of the App Store and Google Play Store, he anticipated the growth of mobile-first financial services in the untapped Indian market.
Strategy or business model	Paytm started as a mobile recharge platform and expanded into a comprehensive digital payment ecosystem, pioneering QR code payments in India. It capitalised on demonetisation to promote digital wallets, created Paytm Mall (e-commerce) and ventured into financial services with Paytm Payments Bank. Innovations like Paytm Soundbox enhanced transactional confirmations, and Paytm pursued lending products (Center for Emerging Markets,

Table 6.3 (*cont.*)

	2023b). However, Paytm Mall faced significant competition and operational challenges, leading to a strategic re-evaluation.
Investors	Some of the notable investors in Paytm include: Alibaba Group, SoftBank, Ant Financial Services Group, Berkshire Hathaway, Ratan Tata, Saif Partners, Intel Partners and Mountain Capital. Total capital raised US$8 billion
Exit strategy	IPO on Indian stock markets (NSE and BSE) in November 2021
Market results	In 2023, monthly UPI (Unified Payment Interface) crossed 10 billion monthly transactions, out of which 56.1 per cent of transactions are from peer-to-merchants, with this share projected to increase to 75 per cent by 2025 (Aggarwal, 2023). Paytm Bank's merchant acquiring model made it a leader in this targeted category, which has also made it profitable due to better lending capabilities developed from the target merchant client base (Zeebiz, 2023). Overall, Paytm ranks 3rd in processing payments by processing roughly 14.66 per cent of UPI transactions and 10.79 per cent of total transaction monthly (Zeebiz, 2023).
Financial results	In FY2022–2023, Paytm's revenues aggregated to INR 79.90 billion (US$960 million), and its net loss margin fell from -14.2 per cent to -11.87 per cent (PayTM, 2023). In Q3 of FY 2022–2023, Paytm achieved operating profitability.
Market cap, December 2023	US$5.3 billion (vs. US$18.7 billion at IPO in November 2021)

Source: Compiled by author using sources cited as indicated.

Table 6.4 *Snapdeal – An e-commerce unicorn*

Founding year	2010
Founders' background	Kunal Bahl and Rohit Bansal, an alumnus of the Wharton School and IIT Delhi, respectively, started Snapdeal with a vision to create a significant impact in the online retail space after working in companies like Microsoft (Center for Emerging Markets, 2023a).

Table 6.4 (*cont.*)

Strategy or business model	Snapdeal's evolution in the e-commerce space has been marked by strategic pivots driven by market dynamics and competition. Initially a coupon and deals platform, it shifted to a marketplace model to expand its product offerings. Recognising the stiff competition from giants like Amazon and Flipkart, Snapdeal reoriented its focus towards value e-commerce, targeting the burgeoning segment of price-sensitive consumers in India's tier 2+ cities. This strategic shift to value e-commerce, known as 'Snapdeal 2.0', aimed to carve out a unique market position by offering affordable yet quality products, tapping into the growing aspirations of the middle-income demographic. Snapdeal's journey also involved significant mergers and acquisitions, including Freecharge, Voonik and Zayple (Nair, 2017). These moves were strategically aimed to diversify and strengthen Snapdeal's market position. However, these initiatives faced executional challenges, which impacted their success.
Investors	Investments came from: Nexus Venture Partners, Indo-US Venture Partners, Bessemer Venture Partners, eBay, Intel Capital, BlackRock, Temasek Holdings, Premji Invest, Alibaba Group, Foxconn, Ratan Tata, Peak XV Partners and SoftBank. Total capital raised US$2.07 billion
Exit strategy	The company was engaged in acquisition talks with Flipkart for US$950M in 2017, but the acquisition was cancelled. Later, it filed for an IPO in December 2021 for US$150M, but the plan for the IPO was later cancelled.
Market results	As per Snapdeal's CEO, Himanshu Chakrawarti, "the value (lifestyle retail) market in India is growing significantly, from US$88 billion to US$175 billion. Also, along with this, the e-commerce portion will increase from 8 per cent to 22 per cent … [Snapdeal is] largely focused on our journey because this opportunity size is huge" (Business Standard, 2023). Snapdeal believes it will have a 'decent slice' in the space, as it currently sees 75 per cent of business coming from repeat customers.

Table 6.4 (*cont.*)

Financial results	In FY2022–2023, Snapdeal's parent entity AceVector generated US$45 million, and its net loss margin narrowed by 44.7 per cent (Rudra, 2024).
Market cap, December 2023	The private company had last raised an unknown amount of money at an unknown valuation in 2021.

Source: Compiled by author using sources cited as indicated.

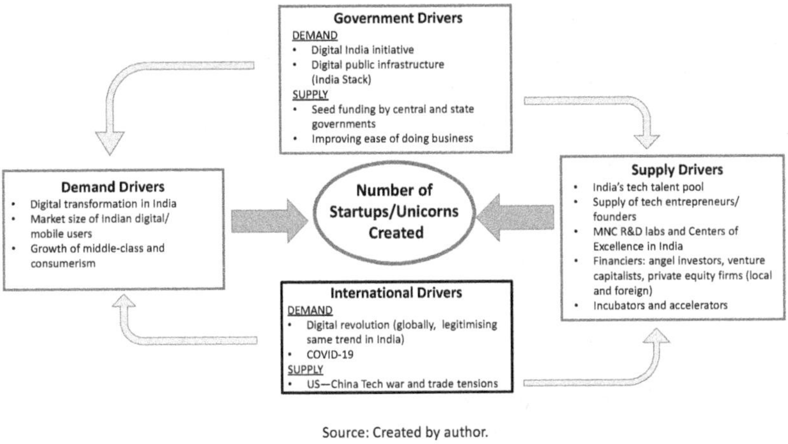

Figure 6.3 A supply–demand model of start-ups in India.
Source: Author.

6.3 Explaining the Rise of Indian Start-Ups and Unicorns

It can be argued that unless a country produces a lot of resilient start-ups, it is unlikely to produce a lot of unicorns, which are start-ups with a private valuation exceeding US$1 billion. Only about 0.2 per cent of Indian start-ups turn into unicorns. To explain the rise of unicorns at a country level we must therefore explain a country's propensity to spawn successful start-ups with scalable business models. Figure 6.3 demonstrates this propensity for the case of India by the coming together of a set of supply and demand factors such as a 'demand' for new digital start-ups that is matched by a local capability to 'supply' such firms.

6.3.1 Demand-Side Drivers

There are two important drivers on the demand side. The first is the rise of digital technology that has helped to disrupt many industries globally; India has been no exception. The last decade has seen the rise of digital technology-based business models that have disrupted banking, payments, retailing, education, healthcare and so on through the creation of new start-ups. These have been unencumbered by legacy investments in old technologies and business models. Thus, mobile payments have flourished under disruptive start-ups rather than incumbent financial institutions. The pioneering firm in India was PayTM, founded in 2010. Similarly, online education blossomed under new players, such as Byju's, Physicswallah and UpGrad, rather than under established education providers. Local start-ups often satisfied the demand for digital services that leapfrogged traditional models, rather than digital firms from developed countries. This was arguably because they required a high degree of local adaptation and optimisation, which was the forte of local firms. Moreover, digital businesses took off in emerging economies within a few years of doing so in developed countries, leaving less time for firms in developed countries to expand internationally. Even when US firms like Amazon or eBay expanded into countries like Brazil or China, they were not able to completely adapt their business models quickly enough to effectively compete in those countries. This gave local competitors the opportunity to build strong businesses and introduce well-adapted local innovations. As Jack Ma famously said, 'eBay is a shark in the ocean. We are a crocodile in the Yangtze River. If we fight in the ocean, we will lose. But if we fight in the river, we will win' (Zafar, 2017). Unlike China, India was quite open to foreign digital giants such as Google, Amazon, Twitter, Whatsapp or Instagram until recently (Ramamurti, 2022). That strategic treatment of home-grown digital players may explain why China was so far ahead of India in digital businesses despite India's head start with its foray into IT services in the 1980s.

A second driver on the demand side, which is important in the Indian case, was the size and growth of the local market. India had 834 million people with internet connections and 600 million smartphone users by 2022, making it the second largest market in the world, after China, and more than twice as big as the US market (Anand, 2022; Statista, 2023a; Statista, 2024b). As in China, many internet users in India were digital natives who connected to the internet mostly through their phones (rather than desktops or laptops), which accelerated the adoption of mobile-based digital solutions. To be sure, the purchasing power of Indians was much less than that of North Americans or even the Chinese. Therefore, the dollar value of e-commerce was much higher in the United States and China, but India had headroom for growth because internet and smartphone penetration in 2023 were still only 59 per cent and 42 per cent, respectively. Digital businesses could potentially leapfrog over traditional brick-and-mortar business models to serve millions of unserved or underserved customers, fuelling the growth of B2C (business to consumer) digital businesses. Even with growth rates of 9.26 per cent during 2015–2022, e-commerce accounted for only 18.5 per cent of retail sales, and traditional retail accounted for the rest. The size of the Indian market and the prospects for growth motivated many entrepreneurs to start new digital ventures (India Retailing, 2022).

6.3.2 *Demand-Side Government Policies*

As shown in Figure 6.1, the government has also played an important catalytic role in promoting digital start-ups through its Digital India initiative. India's prime minister Narendra Modi pushed for digitisation in the public sphere almost from the beginning of his term in 2014. The Modi government saw digital technology as an important way to promote inclusive growth because digital technology could put products and services within reach of the poor. It was also seen as a vehicle for improving government services, or e-government, and reducing corruption by making transactions more transparent. These proactive measures by the Indian government laid the foundation for the accelerated growth of digital start-ups.

The Digital India initiative encompassed many elements, including the ambitious programme known as Aadhar, which gave each Indian a unique biometric ID based on their iris scan and ten fingerprints. This would make it easier for them to participate in economic transactions. The congress government launched this programme in 2009, and it was continued by the Bharatiya Janata Party government under Prime Minister Modi. With Aadhar, every citizen would be able to prove his or her identity using their unique biometric data. Building on Aadhar, the government encouraged the unbanked to open bank accounts into which government social welfare payments could be deposited directly, cutting out the intermediaries who often syphoned off payments meant for the poor. In a matter of months, almost 400 million new bank accounts were opened, using Aadhar for identification over a mobile phone platform. This became known as the Jan Dhan-Aadhar-Mobile (JAM) system of banking (Narayan, 2022). Based on historic patterns across countries, the Bank of International Settlements estimates that an average country would have taken forty-two years to bring as many unbanked into the banking system as India did in seven years (D'Silva et al., 2019). As more people switched to smartphones and companies could take advantage of big data, the range of digital services they could access increased. This simple but inexpensive and universally accessible payments platform was developed by a non-profit organisation called iSpirt, run by volunteers. Any firm, big or small, could use the Unified Payments Interface (UPI) to deliver mobile payment services.

Aadhar and UPI became the foundations of what came to be known in India as the 'digital public infrastructure'. The next layer gave consumers (not firms) ownership of all their data, which they could store in a 'digilocker' and share with private providers of credit, investment options or loan products that were previously beyond their reach if they wished (NPCI, 2023). The digilocker would also be used to store citizens' health and education records, possibly alongside other kinds of personal data in the future. In 2023, India added an e-commerce platform called Open Network for Digital Commerce to its digital public infrastructure, which any consumer or merchant, however small, could join. This layered system of public digital platforms was sometimes referred to as the 'India Stack'. The public infrastructure India created for digital services was unique and very different from systems that evolved in China or the United States. It democratised financial access and democratised market entry for new players who may have been precluded by oligopolistic control of channels by companies such as Apple Pay, Google Pay or Amazon in the United States, and Alipay, WeChat Pay or Alibaba and Tencent in China. These measures added greatly to the demand for digital services such as payments, borrowing and e-commerce, while also facilitating entry by new providers piggybacking on the open-access digital public infrastructure.

6.3.3 Supply-Side Drivers

In India's case, key elements of the entrepreneurial ecosystem have fallen into place over the years to stimulate the rise of digital start-ups. One key element is the supply of human capital to sustain start-ups. India is one of the largest providers of STEM (science, technology, engineering and mathematics) graduates in the world. In 2022, India graduated hundreds of thousands of engineers, scientists, mathematicians, biologists, IT specialists and so on. India ranked 2nd in the world in the absolute number of STEM graduates each year, only behind China. Available data suggests that 34 per cent of Indian students pick STEM as their undergraduate majors. There were significantly fewer PhD graduates from India than from North America or even China, but data shows an upward trend (Timesnow, 2022). The quality of graduates from top schools such as the Indian Institute of Technology (IIT) and regional engineering colleges is first-rate while that of lower-tiered schools is sometimes below the standard of excellence. Companies often must hire fresh graduate students before they are fully trained and knowledgeable. Even so, India has a large supply of raw talent that is employable at internationally competitive prices and can be moulded and nurtured by start-ups.

Perhaps more important is the presence of technically seasoned talent that leads the effort to create new products or services. Here, India's decades-long experience in creating globally competitive software and IT firms is instrumental for the flourishing of a vibrant entrepreneurial ecosystem. Years of working for IT and software companies in India or abroad (as employees of Indian IT companies) have created a vast pool of technical talent that start-ups could draw on.

The Indian IT cluster includes many leading multinationals that have opened product development or R&D centres locally. Over 1,000 multinational firms had established R&D centres and centres of excellence in India by 2022 (Sujit, 2013). In these, Indian managers, engineers and scientists are exposed to global technologies and markets. Many collaborate closely with research teams based in the United States or Europe and receive training in said countries. Such collaborative dynamics driven by globalisation have elevated the human capital preparation in India.

India also has a growing supply of start-up founders. Many of these went to top Indian universities, such as the Indian Institutes of

Technology and the regional engineering colleges, and have cut their teeth in the Indian operations of multinational corporations (MNCs). In another ongoing research project, I found that 60.4 per cent of the founders of fifty Indian unicorns had previously worked for the Indian subsidiary of a foreign MNC. The supply of Indian start-up founders was also bolstered by the hundreds of Indians who had gone to study in the United States but then returned after a few years to start new companies in India, for example, Snapdeal or Upstox.

Finally, a strong start-up ecosystem also needs a pool of financiers, angel investors, incubators and mentors. Karthik Reddy, founder of Indian VC firm Blume Ventures, notes that when he began his career as an investor India had only 400 angel investors, while by 2023 it had over 10,000 (Center for Emerging Markets, 2023a). Among these angel investors are high net worth individuals and successful entrepreneurs who want to invest their newfound wealth in the next generation of entrepreneurs. The co-founder of Flipkart, for instance, sold his e-commerce firm to WalMart for US$16 billion, and took his share of the proceeds to fund almost twenty other start-ups, including the unicorn Ola (Russell, 2019). The VC category includes both Indian firms and, in the last few years, foreign firms, such as Softbank, Accel, Tiger Global, Sequoia and Temasek, which have dominated funding for growth-stage start-ups. According to Sumer Juneja, Softbank's managing partner, 'our thesis in India is that we will invest in companies at US$1–2 billion valuation and exit at the US$5–6 billion valuation mark' (Raghavan, 2023). Foreign VCs like Softbank came to India in search of start-ups that could replicate the high returns they had earned in China, through investments in firms like Alibaba, Tencent or Meituan (Russell, 2015; Yap, 2015). By 2015, foreign VCs had poured US$231 billion into ventures in China, and India was seen as the next big source of unicorns (Oster & Chen, 2016).

A growing number of Indian VCs, such as Blume Ventures, Innoven Capital, and Trifecta Capital joined foreign VCs (Inc42, 2022). The Indian ecosystem also includes over 650+ incubators, including leading US firms such as Y Combinator and Venture Catalysts. By 2021, India was flush with talent, ideas and money to promote hundreds of start-ups. Indian start-ups received US$42 billion in venture investment that year, and the country produced forty-four unicorns – three times the number produced by China, whose numbers were adversely affected by its zero-COVID policy.

6.3.4 Supply-Side Government Policies

Just as government policies have helped on the demand side, they also played a positive role on the supply side. The government launched its Start-Up India campaign in 2016 aiming to 'catalyse start-up culture and build a strong and inclusive ecosystem for innovation and entrepreneurship in India' (Startup India, 2024). Its hope was to turn India from a country of job seekers into a country of job creators. To encourage start-ups, the Indian government implemented a plethora of policies, launched state-led venture incubators and created two funds at the central government level targeted at start-ups. One was the Start-Up India Seed Fund Scheme under the Department for Promotion of Industry and Internal Trade that had a corpus of approximately US$115 million to be spent over four years (2021–2025). In addition, the government created a Fund of Funds for Start-Ups with a corpus of about US$1.2 billion that would be distributed through the Small Industry Development Bank of India (Startup India, 2024).

At the same time, the government also aimed to increase ease of doing business by reducing red tape and increasing access to funds. The government pursued these objectives by fast-tracking applications for intellectual property claims, relaxing public procurement norms, providing access to a new Start-Up India Seed Fund scheme, creating a Fund of Funds for start-ups and providing tax concessions to investors in start-ups.

The efforts of the central government have been augmented by incentives offered by individual states, similar to those in China, although on a smaller scale. State and provincial governments realised that start-ups could create economic growth and high paying jobs within their provinces. For example, the state of Karnataka government announced a US$12 million start-up policy to add 10,000 more start-ups to their ecosystem between 2022 and 2027 (Cyrill, 2022). Meanwhile, Delhi-NCR, India's second largest start-up hub, has introduced a Delhi Start-Up Policy, which would provide companies with more tax incentives and interest free loans to add 15,000 start-ups by 2030 (Malhotra, 2022).

At the time of writing, it was unclear how much money was actually distributed by the central or state governments under various schemes.

6.3.5 *International Drivers of Demand and Supply*

The international context has also provided a tailwind to the Indian start-up scene over the last few years, mostly on the supply side but also on the demand side.

One important factor on the demand side was the COVID-19 pandemic which, according to one report, has dramatically increased opportunities for digital businesses in India. This has specifically been the case in the areas of e-commerce, financial services, online education and food delivery (Gerson Lehman Group, 2021). Estimates suggest that globally COVID-19 may have compressed a decade's worth of digital growth into a short two- to three-year period. India was no exception to this trend, which boosted demand for digital start-ups after mid-2020. One example is Zomato, a hyperlocal food delivery business, which is profiled in Table 6.2.

Two international drivers had a significant positive impact on the supply side. One was the tech boom in the United States and China, which saw a big increase in the number of successful digital start-ups with high valuations. This created a more positive outlook for new digital ventures in many countries, including India, as foreign VCs began to pour money into the search for India's version of such unicorns. The other important driver was the brewing tech war between China and the United States and China's abrupt tech clampdown in 2021, when the government retracted Alibaba's IPO days before it was scheduled, clamped down on other big digital start-ups such as Tencent, Bytedance, Meituan and Didi and abruptly barred for-profit edtech tutoring companies. US companies that became wary of investing in R&D centres in China saw India as a safer bet, and foreign VCs seemed to feel that property rights were also more secure in India than in China. US venture capital investment in China fell to a 10-year low in 2022 at US$1.3 billion, versus the peak of US$14.4 billion in 2018 (Goujon et al., 2023). The combined effect of these international events improved India's relative attractiveness as a place for digital start-ups, and foreign VC investments boomed in India in 2021, providing the base for subsequent optimism.

6.4 Future Outlook and Conclusions

The venture capital industry entered a 'winter season' in many countries around the world including emerging economies after

March 2022, when the US Federal Reserve started raising interest rates to fight off rising inflation. This reduced the appetite for risk-taking and the climate for initial public offerings, both of which resulted in a sharp fall in the funds available to VCs. India was not spared these developments. Its start-up scene also reversed course in the second half of 2022, after an exemplary year in 2021, when VC investment in start-ups peaked at US$35 billion, with US$3.7 billion in March 2022 alone. By December 2022, fresh VC investment was only US$900 million. There were other worrying signs as well. The stock prices of companies that went public in 2021 fell by more than 50 per cent in 2022, even as the Indian stock market held up well. One study found that only three of the forty start-ups that filed their financial results for 2022 were profitable (*The Economist*, 2023). In 2023, optimism gave way to pessimism about the long-run profitability of start-ups. As funding tightened from both domestic and foreign sources, their prospects dimmed. A handful were accused of financial impropriety including exaggeration of sales or other kinds of fraud. US-based short-seller Hindenburg Research's charges of massive fraud against one of India's largest business conglomerates, the Adani Group, could not have helped. They brought into question the quality of corporate governance and financial reporting by Indian companies including start-ups (Hindenburg Research, 2023). The Indian government's decision in early 2023 to tax funds provided by angel investors as regular income rather than investment, unless the start-ups could prove otherwise, was another blow to the outlook of Indian start-ups (*The Economist*, 2023).

However, these setbacks are unlikely to undermine the fundamental supply and demand factors driving the Indian start-up ecosystem. The digital revolution is still in the early innings in India, and the start-up ecosystem still has many strengths that will endure. As we noted earlier, India still has many upsides, in terms of the potential growth in internet connections, smartphone usage, e-commerce and financial services. The outlook for India's macro growth is also quite positive, as it has taken on the mantle of world's fastest growing major economy. Similarly, the strengthening of US–India technological relationships is boosting MNC investments in R&D centres in India, which will continue to boost the supply-side factors in terms of knowledge spillovers and human capital development. The output of STEM graduates is also expected to grow in the coming decades. In other words, the fundamental elements of the supply–demand factors in Figure 6.3 are likely to endure. The reversals or slowdown of 2022–2023 are arguably better understood as corrections for the 'irrational exuberance' of 2021.

Going forward, investors and founders need to be more selective in their pursuits and more focused on not just the number of customers or the top line growth, but also the bottom line. Some consolidation is likely, as are some bankruptcies. However, the firms that survive will do well, and they are likely to be joined by more disciplined early-stage start-ups. Indeed, even as VCs pulled back on their aggregate investment in Indian start-ups in 2023, the big cuts were in funding for growth-stage firms, while funding for seed-stage and early-stage firms grew. Kunal Bahl, co-founder of Snapdeal and Titan Capital, makes two predictions about the next phase of Indian start-ups and IPOs. The first is that smaller IPOs in the US$300-million range will become more common, rather than multibillion-dollar IPOs such as Paytm or Zomato. Secondly, start-ups shall focus more on profitability in sharply defined niches, rather than just top-line growth with giant 'total addressable markets', Mamaearth stands out as an example from Titan Capital's portfolio. The maker of natural skincare products for babies' market cap at the time of listing was about US$1.2 billion (Center for Emerging Markets, 2023a). As the Zomato and Paytm profiles (Tables 6.2 and 6.3) show, in 2023 both firms made a determined push towards profitability. In other words, Indian start-ups may be entering a new, more mature phase in which the euphoria of the last few years gives way to a more hard-nosed, focused approach to growth and value creation. This is likely to lead to better investments by angel investors and VCs and more disciplined strategies and operations by founders in the long run, leading to a healthier start-up ecosystem in India.

References

Agarwal, M. (2022). *\$25 bn funding, 21 unicorns: Decoding Indian startup funding landscape.* Inc42.

(2023). *The 2023 face-off: How Zomato powered past Swiggy in the food delivery race.* Inc42. tinyurl.com/2haza9hb

Aggarwal, R. (2023). *P2M transactions to make 75% of all UPI transactions by 2025: Report.* Business Standard. tinyurl.com/ykjfd57y

Anand, S. (2022). *India has over 1.2 bn mobile phone users: I&B ministry.* Mint. tinyurl.com/mrydr23y

Business Standard. (2023). *Snapdeal eyeing major share in value lifestyle growth in next 5-10 yrs: CEO.* tinyurl.com/tc35amz7

Center for Emerging Markets. (2023a). *Prof. Ramamurti interviews Kunal Bahl - Center for Emerging Markets' summit on "India—The next start-up nation?".* YouTube. Northeastern University, October 28, 2023. www.youtube.com/watch?v=WZMwY1kJ5vw

(2023b). *PayTM Vijay Shekar Sharma – Center for Emerging Markets' summit on "India—The Next Start-up Nation?"* YouTube. Northeastern University, October 28, 2023. www.youtube.com/watch?v=VchM08T_yPA

Cyrill, M., (2022). *Karnataka announces new start-up policy, provision of INR 1 billion vc fund.* India Briefing. tinyurl.com/mhru7v3c

D'Silva, D., Filkova Z., Packer F., and Tiwari, S. (2019). *The design of digital financial infrastructure: Lessons from India.* Bank of International Settlements No. 106 (Monetary and Economic Department), p. 4.

The Economist. (2023). *Indian startups: The painful development of India's startups.* (21 January 2023, p. 57). www.economist.com/business/2023/01/19/the-painful-development-of-indias-startups

Gerson Lehman Group. (2021). *COVID-19's impact on digital transformation in India.* tinyurl.com/bdz79ur9

Goujon, R., Vest, C., and Hanemann, T. (2023). *Big strides in a small yard: The New US outbound investment screening regime.* Rhodium Group. tinyurl.com/5y5xdxtc

Govindarajan V., and Srivastava A. (2021). What Zomato's $12 billion IPO says about tech companies today. *Harvard Business Review*, online.

Gupta S, Narayandas D, and Tahilyani R. (2019). *Paytm: Building a payments network.* Harvard Business School 9-517-091. Harvard Business Publishing Service.

Hindenburg Research. (2023). *Adani group: How the World's Third Richest Man is Pulling the Largest Con in Corporate History.* hindenburgresearch.com/adani/

Inc42. (2022). *Decoding India's 100 unicorns. Report 2022.* issuu.com/inc42/docs/inc42_s_100_unicorns_report_2022

India Retailing. (2022). *Online share in India's retailing jumps to 6.5% while organized players account 18.5% of India's annual retail market.* India Retailing. tinyurl.com/mrxtzkcm

Kashyap, H. (2022). *India minted 3X more unicorns than China in 2022.* Inc42. inc42.com/buzz/india-minted-4x-more-unicorns-china-2022/

Malhotra, T. (2022). *CM Arvind Kejriwal announces new startup policies for Delhi-NCR*. yourstory.com/2022/05/new-delhi-cm-arvind-kejriwal-government-startup-policy-ecosystem

Ministry of Commerce & Industry. (2025). *Nine years of Startup India* (Press release). Government of India. tinyurl.com/2uanrzhx

Nair, A. (2017). *The seven sins of Snapdeal: How and where they lost their way*. Yourstory. tinyurl.com/4u7tuv9t

Narayan, A. (2022). *What is the 'Jan Dhan Account-Aadhaar-Mobile' trinity & has it aided India's war on poverty?* The Print. tinyurl.com/37wrnafp

NPCI (2023). *What is UPI Circle?* www.npci.org.in/what-we-do/upi/product-overview

PayTM (2023). *Disclosure under Regulation 34 of the SEBI (Listing Obligations and Disclosure Requirements) Regulations, 2015 – Notice of 23rd Annual General Meeting and Annual Report for the Financial Year 2022–23*. tinyurl.com/t5hb7f7

Oster, S., and Chen, L. (2016). *Inside China's historic $ 338 billion tech startup experiment*. Bloomberg. tinyurl.com/2wa88bnh

Raghavan, R. (2023). *Softbank India scores over $5.5 billion exits since 2018*. Mint. tinyurl.com/3axt5bnd

Ramamurti, R. (2022). *Why India is a critical market for digital*. Rotman Magazine (Winter). pp. 112–114.

Ramamurti, R., and Hillemann, J. (2018). What is "Chinese" about Chinese multinationals? *Journal of International Business Studies* 49(1), 34–48.

Rudra, T. (2024). *Snapdeal's FY23 loss narrows to INR 282.2 cr, sales drop 31% YoY*. Inc42. inc42.com/buzz/snapdeals-fy23-loss-narrows-to-inr-282-2-cr-sales-drop-31-yoy/

Russell, J. (2015). *SoftBank leads $100m investment in India-Based budget hotel network OYO rooms*. Techcrunch. techcrunch.com/2015/08/03/softbank-oyo-rooms/

(2019). *Flipkart co-founder Sachin Bansal invests $92M in Ola*. Techcrunch. techcrunch.com/2019/02/19/flipkart-sachin-bansal-invests-92m-ola/

Saju, B., and Mohandas, P. (2020). *Zomato: Hyperlocal Battle for Online Food Delivery. Ivey Case Publishing W20365*. Harvard Business Publishing Service.

Sarkar, G. (2023). *Startup funding in Bengaluru tanked 48% YoY in 2022*. Inc42. inc42.com/features/startup-funding-in-bengaluru-tanked-48-yoy-in-2022/

Sil, D. (2022). *Decoding India's unicorn club of 2022 — 50% decline in new $1 bn startups, women founders' share goes up*. Inc42. tinyurl.com/4jj3xa3j

Startup India. (2024). Information retrieved from opening paragraph of webpage. www.startupindia.gov.in/content/sih/en/about_us/about-us.html

Statista. (2023a). *Number of internet connections in rural and urban areas of India from financial year 2015 to 2024*. tinyurl.com/3zp4x743

(2023b). *Online food delivery – India*. tinyurl.com/yn9tp29u

(2024a). *Number of start-ups becoming unicorns in India from 2015 to 2023*. www.statista.com/statistics/1238534/number-of-new-unicorns-2020/?locale=en

(2024b). *Countries with the largest digital populations in the world as of January 2023*. www.statista.com/statistics/262966/number-of-internet-users-in-selected-countries/

Sujit, J. (2013). *25 global companies set up R&D centres in India in last 18 months*. The Times of India. tinyurl.com/mr9ucj3a

Timesnow. (2022). *The future of research: Less than 2 per cent of world has PhD; India ranks 4th in doctoral graduates produced*. tinyurl.com/5n96vjpn

Yap, S. (2015). *2Q 2015 sees India account for 4% of Temasek portfolio*. Deal Street Asia. tinyurl.com/ymvycaxn

Zafar, S. (2017). *The crocodile in the Yangtze – The MoneyGram acquisition*. Fineextra. tinyurl.com/2sedfb7n

Zeebiz. (2023). *Paytm Payments Bank tops with almost 40% market share among merchant acquiring banks*. tinyurl.com/548r3p76

7 Entrepreneurial Ecosystems and Unicorns in Southeast Asia

JOHN R. MCINTYRE AND JAMES HOADLEY

7.1 Turmoil and Innovation Coexist in Southeast Asia

Joseph Schumpeter argued that 'economic progress, in capitalist society, means turmoil' (Rollert, 2018). One could argue that turmoil is endemic in Southeast Asia. The region is one of the most at-risk areas due to global warming trends and extreme weather events. All Association of SE Asian Nations (ASEAN) economies have been signatories to the Paris Agreements and have understandably committed to national targets for carbon footprint reduction (Denmark, 2021; Rahman, 2023). Institutional stability in the region is anticipated to continue to exhibit weakness, as events in Myanmar, the Philippines and Thailand have recently illustrated (Kurlantzick, 2022). Reducing corruption also represents a significant governance challenge for these relatively new democracies where high economic growth has coexisted with patterns of insufficient institutional transparency (Pepinski et al., 2022). Geopolitical events have further divided the ASEAN region, which comprises divergent regime types. There is evidence of significant polarisation driven by China's place in maritime Southeast Asia and the advent of what some foresee as the emergence of a *Pax Sinica* (Pongsudhirak, 2022).

Against this overall background of turmoil, the Asian Development Bank (ABD) reported 4.7 per cent growth for Southeast Asia in 2023, benchmarking it against a global average growth of 2.7 per cent for the same reference period (ADB, 2023a). In part, this positive outlook is propelled by twin forces: a rise in the middle class from 24 per cent in 2010 to some 65 per cent expected in 2030; and the advent of the Regional Comprehensive Economic Partnership (RCEP) free trade agreement which encompasses the majority of ASEAN economies. The analysis of the Asian Development Bank suggests that Southeast Asia will become the world's fourth single market area, after the European Union, United States and China, by 2030. Furthermore, the same analysis suggests the region will source some 8 per cent of global exports and receive 10 per cent of global inbound foreign direct investment (FDI), on par with mainland China (Rahman, 2023). The overall trend towards innovation-driven entrepreneurship has grown in the region. There were thirty-eight firms recognised as unicorns by February 2024, and a few had reached the level of decacorns (those with a valuation of US$10 billion or more) (Chaudry, 2024). However, the distribution of unicorn start-ups in Southeast Asia has not been uniform. Three quarters of firms that have attained this status are from Singapore and Indonesia, the region's innovation hubs.

7.2 Overview of the Entrepreneurial Ecosystem in Southeast Asia

Innovation driven entrepreneurship and economic growth in the Southeast Asia region are heavily driven by the agglomeration effects (economies of agglomeration) of rapid urbanisation in seven megalopolises: Jakarta, Manila, Yangon, Ho Chi Minh City, Bangkok, Kuala Lumpur and Singapore. Under certain conditions, these growth nodes and innovation hubs could have the potential to become the cities of the future, hosting sustainable liveable communities in compliance with the UN Sustainable Development Goals (McKinsey Global Institute, 2018). In parallel with rapid urbanisation are numerous digital transformation initiatives. These growth nodes foster innovation-driven entrepreneurship by establishing the essential conditions for clusters to arise and mobilise resources. Following the framework presented in Chapter 2, this section highlights the significant elements that foster the development of vibrant entrepreneurial ecosystems.

Strong financial sectors with resource availability, funding capacity and investment opportunities attract and promote entrepreneurship in Southeast Asian countries (Luc, 2018). Entrepreneurs' skills and opportunities to build networks and interact with other like-minded individuals and organisations such as accelerators and incubators appear to boost to the entrepreneurial process (Letaifa & Rabeau, 2013). This, along with a favourable regulatory environment, fosters entrepreneurship. Tax incentives and simplified permit procedures facilitate new business creation (Adomako & Danso, 2014; Chen et al., 2014), while affordable housing, public transportation and cultural amenities attract and retain talented individuals willing to engage in high-growth entrepreneurial ventures (Pennings, 1982). In addition, the diverse and competent workforces of megacities can help entrepreneurs succeed. Even while quality might lag behind quantity, certain emerging economies are investing heavily in education (see China's high-school graduation rates) (Papademetriou & Sumption, 2013). The positive effects of such efforts are visible in megacities where research and development facilities, technology transfer offices and incubators stimulate technology deployment through entrepreneurship. In parallel, incumbent companies use innovation platforms to maximise and coordinate their access to knowledge and information and become key participants in the ecosystems where new ventures are born (Zahra & Nambisan, 2011). Southeast Asian countries generally exhibit a correlation between research and development (R&D) intensity and income levels, with Singapore's expenditure nearing the OECD (Organisation for Economic Cooperation and Development) average of over 2 per cent. This is in contrast to most other countries in the region where it typically ranges between 0.05–0.2 per cent of the gross domestic product (GDP). In Singapore, Malaysia and the Philippines, the business sector dominates R&D spending and most Southeast Asian countries lag behind in needed reforms and commitment for public sector driven R&D (OECD, 2013).

A combination of these factors contributes to the creation of a bubbling entrepreneurial ecosystem. In megacities such as those in Southeast Asia, economies of agglomeration can act as an additional booster for entrepreneurial growth. By providing the resources and support that entrepreneurs need to start and grow their businesses, megacities can foster a culture of innovation and entrepreneurship that can drive economic growth, create new job opportunities and enhance overall productivity. Despite these advantages, Southeast Asian countries and those in the Global South tend to face significant challenges.

Political, legal and regulatory shortcomings can affect entrepreneurship. Entrepreneurs sometimes encounter excessive bureaucracy and face extreme uncertainty, which can limit scale-up ambitions and outcomes (Tracey & Phillips, 2011). Institutions in Southeast Asia play a crucial role in shaping the strategic decisions of economic actors and regional growth. Southeast Asian economies have idiosyncrasies that produce significant influence in relation to inter nationalisation and economic development (Hoskisson et al., 2012), and there are marked differences specific to Islamic Asian countries (Dewanti et al., 2022). Notably, financial institutions play a significant role in driving economic growth in the ASEAN (Haini, 2019).

Emerging markets, especially small- and medium-sized enterprises (SMEs), have insufficient capital due to a lack of established banking institutions, excessive borrowing rates and no collateral (Yiu & Lau, 2008). The structure of the financial market, regional financial integration and the impact of investments on economic growth influence the constraints on capital in Southeast Asia. Islamic banking has a noted influence on economic growth in Southeast Asia, which highlights the significance of financial market structure (Lebdaoui & Wild, 2016). Additionally, the integration between East and Southeast Asian capital markets has implications for monetary policies in ASEAN+3 (Association of Southeast Asian Nations and China, Japan and the Republic of South Korea) countries, indicating the impact of regional financial integration on capital constraints (Arsyad, 2015). Investments, particularly gross fixed capital formation, have been found to have a positive effect on economic growth in Southeast Asia, underscoring their importance in overcoming capital constraints (Ledhem & Mekidiche, 2021). The rise of China and its increasing investment in Southeast Asia have also affected capital flow in the region, presenting both opportunities and challenges (Samphantharak, 2011; Tan, 2021). Additionally, the high savings rates of Southeast Asian countries are identified as a factor that contributes to outstanding GDP growth in the region. This indicates the role of savings in addressing capital constraints. Overall, these factors collectively contribute to shaping the constraints on capital in Southeast Asia, reflecting the complex interplay of financial market structure, regional integration, investments and some external influences.

Entrepreneurs need well-trained and readily available talent. These entrepreneurs sometimes lack formal education, which makes business start-up and growth more difficult (Marvel et al., 2016). Overall, the availability of trained talent in Southeast Asia is influenced by labour migration, workforce characteristics, education and the influence of foreign investment. Labour migration from Southeast Asia to other regions such as Taiwan has been a significant aspect, impacting the supply of human capital and raising issues related to public response and future development (Deng et al., 2020). The impact of FDI on the technology gap in ASEAN countries has implications for the development and supply of human capital, particularly in the context of trade and investment dynamics (Du & King, 2022).

The ASEAN countries are actively intensifying the digitisation of financial services, particularly through the widespread use of digital payment apps such as e-banking and e-wallets. There is a notable desire for further digitalisation, especially among active users, entrepreneurs and those who are already well-banked (Lee & Sathirathai, 2022). This interest stimulates a very large market for digital skills. Finally, the growing focus on knowledge-intensive processes and innovation have led to the rise of firms with significant innovation capacity that need well-trained talent (Kumar et al., 2013).

Entrepreneurs benefit significantly from social networks and business partnerships. Private information travels across social networks, and knowledge is shared through partnerships. Network positions affect access to valuable information. Entrepreneurial success depends, to a significant extent, on access to private information. Therefore, an entrepreneurs' network position can be explained from the diversity of access they have to the knowledge they need for identifying promising new companies (Stuart & Sorenson, 2005). Business networks and partnerships are conduits of information that influence firms' non-predictive tactics and affordable losses principle (Bai et al., 2021). Within the framework of effectuation, networking is more significant than the network (Sarasvathy & Dew, 2003; Sarasvathy et al., 2014). Furthermore, social networking mediates effective internationalisation. All these factors play a critical role for entrepreneurial success in Southeast Asia, and such dynamics are embedded in deep cultural specificities.

The states that govern the former colonies in Southeast Asia promote a shared style of nationalism, claiming strength even with limited governmental capacity. They are characterised by the significant role of large business groups and the Chinese minority. In this part of the world, varieties of capitalism with a differential approach to state capacity and state-guided economic progress have emerged. Some analysts have challenged the traditional views of indigenous Southeast Asian businesspeople and nations, labelling them as lacking in entrepreneurial skills. Instead, they have suggested that historical structures have hindered successful large-scale entrepreneurial activity in the region (Tipton, 2009).

Tables 7.1 and 7.2 contain the IPO (initial public offering) market performance in Southeast Asia between 2016 and 2022, as well as the

Table 7.1 *Southeast Asia IPO market performance*

	2016	2017	2018	2019	2020	2021	2022
No. of IPOs	113	178	151	161	114	152	163
IPO funds raised (in billion USD)	5.6	10.4	9.5	7.3	7.0	13.3	7.6
IPO market cap (in billion USD)	18.6	33.2	46.1	25.2	29.1	50.9	56.1

Source: Authors' own work based on Deloitte (2022).

Table 7.2 *IPO statistics by country in Southeast Asia (in million USD)*

	Indonesia	Malaysia	Philippines	Singapore	Thailand	Vietnam	Total
2016	922	366	921	1,662	1,502	195	5,568
2017	1,024	2,219	473	3,492	2,912	304	10,424
2018	1,132	166	153	551	2,850	4,667	9,519
2019	1,052	447	407	2,263	2,996	172	7,337
2020	377	490	809	968	4,356	9	7,009
2021	4,502	337	2,889	1,217	4,377	16	13,338
2022	2,358	801	352	428	3,596	71	7,606

Source: Authors' own work based on Deloitte (2022).

specific performance of six countries. Indonesia generated US$3.6 billion with seventy-nine IPOs in 2023, primarily in the technology, telecommunications and media, and energy and resources sectors. In the same year, Thailand raised US$1.3 billion in consumer goods and financial services with forty IPOs. Overall, Southeast Asia IPO performance has a strong underlying trend, while specific deals produce significant deviations from the average deal flow. Indonesia and Thailand are catching up with Singapore and challenging its traditional leadership, while Malaysia, the Philippines and Vietnam follow at a larger distance. This positive and geographically spread-out entrepreneurial performance seems to be shared across different countries in the region, rather than extremely concentrated. Still, local entrepreneurial ecosystems are still in their growth and development stage and have not fully capitalised on the vast population and improving education levels.

7.3 Asean: Regional Economic Integration and Innovation

ASEAN has achieved success over the past fifty years due to its unique approach to regional governance and cooperation, the ASEAN way and 'open regionalism'. Economic growth has doubled in the past decade, poverty has fallen and prosperity is expected to keep rising. ASEAN established the ASEAN Economic Community (AEC) in 2015, which ushered in enhanced economic integration (Menon & Fink, 2019). The stages among member states are as follows: zero integration, bilateral treaties or limited scope, free trade association, customs union, common market and economic union. These stages exist in a continuum, rather than as discrete and exclusive stages. Arguably, the welfare gains of economic integration may be broken down into two effects: the production effect and the consumption effect. The production effect means that resources can be expended more efficiently using mechanisms such as specialisation and the importation of lower cost goods. The reduction of the cost of goods in the importation market demonstrates the consumption effect; the lower price of goods allows for a consumer surplus (Lohn et al., 1979).

The member nations of ASEAN are Brunei Darussalam, Cambodia, Indonesia, Lao PDR, Malaysia, Myanmar, the Philippines, Singapore, Thailand and Vietnam. Taken as a whole, ASEAN has the 3rd largest population in the world, at 662 million people. They have a GDP of US$3.2 trillion. The region is the 3rd fastest growing Indo-Pacific economy of the past decade after China and India. ASEAN seeks to promote economic growth and regional stability among its members through consultation, consensus and cooperation, based on the Treaty of Amity and Cooperation. Projections show that ASEAN's economy will grow at 5.5 per cent per year and become the 4th largest economy in the world by 2030. The United States is a strategic partner of ASEAN. The US–Singapore Free Trade Agreement (FTA) was America's first FTA in the Indo-Pacific, and the country currently has a trade surplus with Singapore. The United States exported more than US$122 billion in goods and services to ASEAN in 2022, ranking 4th after Canada, Mexico and China. The United States was the 2nd largest trading partner (imports plus exports) for ASEAN.

According to projections, ASEAN's digital economy will exceed US$300 billion by 2025, with 400 million active internet connections (Brophy et al., 2021). Nineteen US states have more than 10,000 jobs that rely on exports to ASEAN. In thirteen US states, ASEAN accounts for more than 20 per cent of export-dependent jobs to the Indo-Pacific. Visitors from ASEAN add nearly US$8 billion to the US economy each year. ASEAN students contribute more than US$2 billion to the US economy, and 7.6 million Asian Americans identify with an ASEAN ethnicity. By 2022, ASEAN had received more than US$338 billion in total US FDI, making it the number one destination for US investment in the Indo-Pacific region. Infrastructure development is one of the top priorities for member states.

ASEAN economies are embracing digital technologies and leveraging them for economic and social advancement. The uptake and use of the internet increased significantly between 2000 and 2015, with more than 80 per cent of individuals using the internet in Singapore, Malaysia and Brunei. However, there are wide gaps between ASEAN members and regional Asian neighbours. Additionally, there is a gap between small and large firms in terms of the use of the internet. To harness the promise of digital technologies, ASEAN must boost uptake and ensure people have the skills to make the best use of them. The association must put the right infrastructure and macroeconomic and regulatory conditions in place. ASEAN strategy documents seek to position the group in advance of a transition towards a digital economy (Box & Lopez-Gonzalez, 2017).

The AEC Blueprint 2025 specifically focuses on e-commerce, including harmonised consumer rights and protection laws, a harmonised legal framework for online dispute resolution, inter-operable e-identification and authorisation schemes and a coherent and comprehensive framework for personal data protection. The fourth industrial revolution has the potential to significantly alter the ways private and public domains function in ASEAN countries, providing huge value for individuals not captured by traditional measures. This could be a powerful force for economic inclusion, creating new ways for citizens to connect to each other, trade with each other and access services that are currently not available. It could also reduce the opportunities for corruption and rent-seeking activities, making it a more efficient and fair way of recruiting personnel. It could improve public accountability, reduce deadweight losses associated with corruption and increase the collection of government taxes and other sources of revenue. SMEs are the backbone of ASEAN economies. However, they lack access to finance, business services and information. The innovative solutions

Table 7.3 *IPO funds raised in USD (millions)*

	Indonesia	Malaysia	Philippines	Singapore	Thailand	Vietnam	Total
2016	4,348	942	3,911	3,228	4,497	1,704	**18,630**
2017	3,249	3,939	2,470	6,219	13,537	3,830	**33,244**
2018	5,998	683	763	2,168	5,355	31,103	**46,070**
2019	5,071	1,954	1,337	3,176	12,685	939	**25,162**
2020	2,484	2,900	3,045	2,835	17,590	285	**29,139**
2021	23,130	2,072	7,108	2,388	14,509	1,653	**50,860**
2022	37,001	2,549	1,299	629	14,061	537	**56,076**

Source: Authors' own work based on Deloitte (2022).

brought by the fourth industrial revolution could overcome these obstacles (Menon & Fink, 2019).

The ASEAN integration monitoring directorate has identified five dimensions of readiness for the changes brought by the fourth industrial revolution, namely innovation and technology, human capital, regulatory frameworks, infrastructure connectivity and inclusive sustainable growth. There are still deficiencies in the areas of infrastructure, regulatory frameworks and engagement. It is also important to address skill gaps. Lifelong learning should be available to those who wish to acquire skills and knowledge at any stage of their lives. The expected positive effects for ASEAN nations include increased wealth, economic inclusion and improved environmental management, while the risks include job losses, inequality, political instability and cyberattacks (Smith, 2021). Specifically, digital marketplaces and online services can empower SMEs to trade in new ways, and blockchain can revolutionise payments and logistics. By moving swiftly through these spaces of opportunity, ASEAN countries can leapfrog traditional industrial nations in domains such as mobile banking or drones. These domains can help deliver lightweight, high-value goods to remote regions with poor transport infrastructure across the region (Menon & Fink, 2019). Table 7.3 demonstrates the value of IPO funds raised across the major nations of Southeast Asia.

7.4 Country Profiles

This section contains profiles of four countries from the ASEAN region: Thailand, Indonesia, the Philippines and Singapore. For each country, we examine the key factors which influence the respective entrepreneurial ecosystem and feature a successful unicorn or soon-icorn venture.[1]

Singapore is home to twenty-seven unicorns (as of 2024). This is impressive, but also consistent with many other pro-business economic factors present in Singapore. Singapore has great access to capital. The government encourages the development of firms from the earliest stages to the cusp of an IPO. Singapore's government encourages FDI and the inward migration of entrepreneurs, which benefit the entrepreneurial climate. Indonesia, on the other hand, is a bit of an outlier. Access to capital is more likely to come from within families than from venture capitalists or crowdfunding. Indonesia has the largest population in the ASEAN region, however, it is a middle-income country on a per-capita GDP basis, even when adjusted for purchasing power parity (PPP). Thailand has a higher GDP per capita than Indonesia, while the Philippines has a lower GDP per capita in comparison. However, Indonesia boasts sixteen unicorn start-ups compared to three in Thailand and three in the Philippines.

It is clear from the data that many of the fundamental ecosystem drivers for robust entrepreneurial success are abundant in Singapore. Meanwhile, the same drivers are in early to moderate stages in Indonesia, Thailand and the Philippines. Indonesia seems to be 'punching above its weight' with regard to unicorn creation. GoTo, born out of the merger of unicorns Gojek and Tokopedia, accounted for nearly 2 per cent of Indonesia's GDP in 2021.

7.4.1 Thailand

Thailand has a growing entrepreneurial ecosystem with a mix of both traditional and innovation-driven businesses. The government has made significant efforts to promote entrepreneurship and innovation, with various initiatives and policies aimed at supporting start-ups and SMEs (Lekmat & Chelliah, 2014). Government programmes and

[1] The choice was informed by the insights shared during the conference organised by the Georgia Tech Center for International Business Education & Research and the University of San Francisco's Center for Business Studies and Innovation in Asia-Pacific, held on 3 November 2022, entitled 'Unicorn Strategies in Southeast Asia: Implications for the US and Asian Collaborative Innovation', in which each of the four case studies' executive teams presented their growth trajectory.

actions supporting entrepreneurship relate to tax incentives, grants and funding opportunities. The Board of Investment offers a range of incentives for businesses in key industries, such as technology and innovation, under the Investment Promotion Act of 1977. These incentives include both tax exemptions and non-tax incentives (PWCa, 2023).

Thailand has a growing start-up ecosystem, particularly in the technology and innovation sectors. Bangkok, the capital city, is a hub for tech start-ups, with a range of incubators, accelerators and co-working spaces. The start-up sector in Thailand began to emerge in the 2000s with clusters of small software firms. In 2011, Advanced Info Service (AIS) organised the AIS Start-up Weekend to promote the idea of start-ups in Thailand and identify business partners for digital innovation. By the mid-2010s, the government began to recognise the importance of start-ups and the contribution they can make to the economy. The Ministry of Digital Economy and Society (MDES) was created in 2016, and the National Start-up Committee was established to generate ideas for improving the ecosystem. A new Digital Economy Promotion Agency was created under MDES with a mandate to support start-ups (Langeland & Nitithanprapas, 2022).

Some observers argue that weak internal market demand limits the emergence of more innovation-driven start-ups. They say this is because low-income households in rural and peri-urban areas and poor farmers lack the resources and willingness to adopt new innovations in agritech. Thailand is home to the first dedicated edtech accelerator in Southeast Asia: Space-F, and the Global Cleantech Innovation Programme. Analysts argue that the government has created a supportive policy environment, but some policies have been questioned and expected to be revised. For example, as of 2024 start-ups could not issue convertible bonds, set up employee stock option plans or use public procurement procedures. There are few examples of deeptech innovation and a number of spin-offs from the country's good technology and science-based universities and research institutes. This venue for development could be further stimulated as it is seen as a path for scaling up businesses to unicorn status (Juraskil & Vandenberg, 2022).

Thailand's capital markets are seen as a strong driver of the country's growth, development and innovation. They are among Asia's deepest and most liquid, with strong bond and equity penetration, as well as growing offerings in alternative asset classes. The Stock Exchange of Thailand (SET) has been the main engine behind the development of an equity market in Thailand. It has seen strong long-term growth, deep liquidity and an increasing focus on environmental, social and governance (ESG)-related investment opportunities (McKinsey & Company, 2022). It has also hosted more than 100 IPOs since 2019 and is a popular destination for SMEs to raise funds. Ideally, Thailand's capital markets have the potential to serve the country under four pillars: funding a sustainable future for Thailand, fuelling economic growth and innovation, expanding access and knowledge around wealth creation and fostering long-term capital deployment. A supportive regulatory backdrop and a focus on innovation and de-risking can enabled these aspects. Thailand's capital markets have the potential to expand their services, increase investor participation and build new opportunities for collaboration in private equity, venture capital and beyond. Some of the bold new growth-focused initiatives include fostering sustainable finance to help Thailand move towards net-zero carbon emissions, providing opportunities for pension funds to create the capital required to support an aging population, nurturing SMEs/start-ups with capital and capability support, expanding digital assets, improving financial literacy, simplifying retail investors' journeys, attracting long-term foreign institutional capital, deepening domestic institutional investors, unlocking data analytics and attracting and nurturing talent (McKinsey & Company, 2022).

Thailand has a relatively well-educated and skilled workforce, particularly in the technology and engineering fields. However, the availability of skilled workers varies by region. Thailand can focus on expanding the availability of skills and increasing the share of top-performing students. The 2015 Program for International Student Assessment (PISA) results show that around half of Thai students performed below the basic proficiency level in science, reading and mathematics. At the other end of the spectrum, 30 per cent of students or more from Singapore and Vietnam attained level 4 or higher in science and mathematics. Equipping the workforce with the skills necessary for jobs today and in the future is critical for Thailand's economy. Focusing on eliminating functional illiteracy and/or innumeracy should be a priority (Lathapipat & Sondergaard, 2017).

Thailand can accelerate its economic transformation by leveraging spill overs from FDI inflows, accelerating the implementation of large infrastructure megaprojects and investing in its innovation ecosystem. The government has launched several initiatives to encourage this process. They include focusing on ten industries as 'new engines of growth' (or 'S-curve industries'), investing in the Eastern Economic Corridor Development Project and launching a major push for the creation of an electronic payment system. For these initiatives to reap their full potential, they require more investments in R&D and more graduates with sophisticated problem-solving, analytical-reasoning and STEM (science, technology, engineering and mathematics) skills. In relative terms, Thailand has fallen behind its ASEAN+3 peers in R&D spending despite the understanding that such investments offer high returns, especially if they give rise to unicorn companies such as Bitkub.

Bitkub is a Thai unicorn operating in the cryptocurrency space. It was founded in February 2018 as a next generation exchange platform for trading digital assets (Bitkub, 2023). It became the first Thai fintech firm to reach unicorn status after Siam Commercial Bank announced its willingness to acquire a 51 per cent stake for Bt17.8 billion (about US$500 million). The deal did not materialise for alleged regulatory issues. Topp Jirayut Srupsrisopa, Bitkub's founder and chief executive officer, announced plans to turn the country's largest cryptocurrency firm into a dominant crypto exchange platform in Southeast Asia. This expansion was seen as the logical next stage after its success in Thailand, where it commanded a near-monopoly 92 per cent market share, with revenue growing at more than 1,000 per cent annually since its creation in 2018 (Thai PBS World Business Desk, 2021).

Topp Jirayut Srupsrisopa highlighted at a November 2022 conference that Bitkub was the only fintech unicorn start-up in Thailand and that the first stage of the company development was concentrated on consolidating the digital asset exchange in Thailand. Bitkub offers their own bespoke coin, as well as an NFT (non-fungible token) marketplace, educational services and an investment firm. They have crypto mutual funds and joint ventures with large, family-owned firms in Thailand including the largest local retailer. They also offer blockchain as a service. As of 2023, Bitkub was the most profitable start-up in Thai history. Bitkub had no VC involvement as of 2023 and had relied on angel investors. They operate in a local monopoly model (Hoadley, 2022) but hope to enter the Southeast Asia market through an IPO, bringing the company to the status of regional champion.

7.4.2 Indonesia

Indonesia has a vibrant and dynamic entrepreneurial ecosystem with a growing number of start-ups and a supportive culture. It has the greatest number of unicorns in Southeast Asia after Singapore. The COVID-19 crisis has accelerated the shift to e-commerce and digital adoption, benefiting fintech and logistics start-ups. Indonesia has invested in entrepreneurship development programmes to tap into its youthful population's full potential. The Ministry of Education, Culture, Research and Technology prepared a medium-term investment plan for higher education for 2020–2024 promoting entrepreneurship at top universities and aiming to accelerate innovation and the development of new technologies. A study by the ADB echoes these efforts, showcasing best practices in nurturing the country's start-ups and acknowledging efforts to further strengthen entrepreneurship education and the replication of successful business models (BIMP-EAGA, 2021). For example, IncuBie of IPB University offers a three-year incubation programme that provides access to training, mentorship, networking and finance. The Directorate of Business Innovation and Incubation of the University of Indonesia provides six months of pre-incubation support and post-incubation acceleration. PENS Sky Venture of Surabaya State Electronics Polytechnic offers a three-year incubation programme for students and those sponsored by the Ministry of Education, Culture, Research and Technology. The Asia Entrepreneurship Training Programme is a start-up accelerator programme open to Indonesian and Swiss start-ups that want to venture into the international market. These examples have enjoyed relative success, particularly the Directorate of Business Innovation and Incubation, which boasts of a 100 per cent graduation rate; some of its graduates have received local and international recognition for their innovations (BIMP-EAGA, 2021).

The Medium-Term National Development Plan for 2020–2024 aims to encourage the emergence of three new unicorns. By 2022, nine unicorns had emerged, in addition to the five that existed in 2019 (Rayda, 2022). These unicorns belong to sectors that rely on vast consumer markets such as e-commerce, marketplaces, ride-hailing, logistics and fintech. Only a very limited number of tech start-ups with a direct impact on human and sustainable development, such as agritech (agriculture), edtech (education), cleantech (environment) and healthtech, have successfully initiated scaling up. At the time of writing, none have reached unicorn status. Nonetheless, the latter market segments have enormous transformational potential for a country with a population close to 300 million, as they improve human life (education and health), assist the rural poor (agriculture) and aid climate change mitigation and adaptation (Bachtiar et al., 2022).

There is a close relationship between growth of start-ups and venture capital (VC) financing. With 129 local VC funds as of 2021, Indonesia has the second largest VC market in Southeast Asia. Notable VC growth spurts include AC Ventures and Alpha JWC. Local VCs are leveraging their familiarity with the market to gain an edge when it comes to investing domestically. However, Indonesia lacks a deep VC base with experience in closing late-stage funding. There is also a regulatory squeeze on smaller funds that focus on pre-seed rounds. The US$3.4 million minimum capital requirement mandated by the Financial Services Authority (Otoritas Jasa Keuangan or OJK as it is locally known) in 2021 puts half of all existing Indonesian VCs at risk of failing to comply. As a result, Indonesian start-ups find themselves in a difficult position when sourcing local venture funds (Mackender et al., 2022).

Overall, Indonesia's entrepreneurial ecosystem supports the emergence of a growing number of start-ups and a number of unicorns. Most of these emulate the business models that have proven successful elsewhere and rely on the vast untapped internal market. Among them are Gojek, ride-hailing services for urban mobility founded in 2010; Bukalapak, an e-commerce platform that made history with its IPO in the Indonesia Stock Exchange in 2021; Tokopedia, another e-commerce platform that received investment from Alibaba in 2017; Akulaku, Ajaib and Kredivo in fintech; Ovo in digital payments; Kopi Kenangan, the first start-up company in the food and beverages domain to become a unicorn in Southeast Asia; Traveloka, offering online booking services; J&T Express in parcel delivery services and eFishery providing technology driven solutions in aquaculture. As the country continues to develop, it presents significant opportunities for entrepreneurs to innovate and create value. There is a large group of potential would-be unicorns solving the critical problems of the Global South, one of which is PrimaKu.

PrimaKu is a paediatric health platform that monitors children's growth and development. Immunisation schedules, child development tracking, growth charts and medical information are made readily available (Crunchbase, 2023). PrimaKu collaborates with the Indonesian Pediatrician Association and the Indonesian Ministry of Health (PrimaKu, 2024). According to its founder Muhammad 'Didit' Aditriya Indraputra, the start-up was created to help first-time parents to access and develop a community-based parenting network. It also helps healthcare providers access and monitor the widely spread population of the Indonesian archipelago. PrimaKu intends to fill in the gaps to which the government cannot currently effectively attend alone; PrimaKu receives support from a range of governmental agencies, international actors and health-related firms. It has a local focus; however, given that it addresses burning problems related to health service provisions across the Global South, the start-up has experienced some organic international growth (Hoadley, 2022).

7.4.3 The Philippines

The Philippine's rapidly developing entrepreneurial ecosystem is characterised by a growing number of start-ups and an expanding pool of actors, with both the number of start-ups and the amount of venture capital funding rising in recent years. According to the 2015 Global Entrepreneurship Monitor (GEM) report, the Philippines had the highest societal acceptance of entrepreneurship as a good career choice and the strongest positive media attention among Southeast Asian countries. GEM defines societal perception as the importance a society places on entrepreneurship. This perception is expected to produce an impact on entrepreneurial intentions. In the Philippines, 73 per cent of the participants in a representative national survey rated entrepreneurship as a good career choice. The positive media coverage of entrepreneurship was also identified as a component of a positive national culture regarding entrepreneurship (Velasco et al., 2017).

The country is home to several successful start-ups, including the unicorns PayMaya (Voyager Innovations), Mynt and Kalibrr. The majority of start-ups in the Philippines are focused on technology, particularly fintech, e-commerce and software development. The Philippines currently accounts for nearly 20 per cent of the population of Southeast Asia, yet it receives only 9 per cent of venture capital funding (Foxmont Capital Partners, 2022). The Philippines lag behind its Southeast Asian neighbours despite its advantageous location and a population of almost 120 million. For example, in 2018 the country's ventures attracted US$31.8 million in investments, a 10th of Indonesia's and a third of the amount Vietnam and Thailand received (Woo, 2022). This trend has proven hard to reverse despite some positive developments in 2021 and 2022 regarding IPO dynamics (see Table 7.2).

Entrepreneurial education in the Philippines is mandated by law and offered as bachelor's and master's degrees. Business incubator programmes offer training in opportunity identification, business plan development and elevator pitches for attracting venture capitalists and angel investors. The large Filipino diaspora has a high entrepreneurial propensity, and there is affordable, local access to resources which is open to all levels and types of business (Velasco et al., 2017). Mentorship helps start-ups succeed by providing entrepreneurs with knowledge and new connections. Most start-ups are co-founded with innovators. Entrepreneurs usually congregate in mentorship seminars in global hubs such as Silicon Valley to discuss business models and look for co-founding opportunities (Akehira et al., 2022).

High tech start-ups have the potential to address structural problems in the Philippines, particularly in the context of economic development and innovation. The Philippines is known for its rich biodiversity and marine species, making it a highly threatened centre of endemism (Carpenter & Springer, 2005). On top of such environmental considerations related to industrial growth, the country has faced challenges from external constraints and internal motivations in relation to technology and innovation driven entrepreneurship (Batalla, 2010). Global trends which have limited investment capital to high-tech start-ups in various European countries have highlighted the need for innovative financing solutions for start-ups in countries such as the Philippines (Yang et al., 2022). While raising capital is one of the top priorities for Filipino entrepreneurs, 48 per cent have walked away from a potential partnership or investment, or terminated an existing partnership, due to a lack of a shared vision. Low valuation was also among the top five reasons for closing a firm (PWC, 2020). In 2021, the Department of Trade and Industry launched the Philippine Start-up Venture Fund with 250 million Philippine Pesos (approximately US$4.3 million) to be invested in two years, in accordance with the Innovative Startup Act of 2019 (Desiderio, 2021).

There is a link between innovation performance and establishing a middle management layer in start-ups. This emphasises the importance of organisational design choices for high-tech start-ups and shows that the country very much needs such management talent (Grimpe et al., 2019). Most Filipino entrepreneurs and local investors still think start-ups are like any other business. Arguably, such attitudes lead to low investor confidence, ineffective start-up decision making and fewer investors, generating a vicious circle. Paul Rivera, CEO of skill-matching employment marketplace start-up Kalibrr, said they raised US$9 million, mostly from overseas investors, who have a better understanding of start-up building and scaling. Local start-ups could be more successful if local investors and the government became more proficient (Akehira et al., 2022).

Furthermore, the Philippines' policy towards emergent China and control over the South China Sea reflects the country's strategic balancing and sovereignty concerns among global powers (Castro, 2016). Therefore, there are high hopes for technology-driven start-ups that can play a crucial role in addressing economic, environmental and geopolitical challenges in the Philippines and contribute to sustainable development and innovation. Maya, formerly PayMaya, is an example of such a venture. Another example is Smart Money, powered by Smart e-Money Inc., which is a financial services and digital payments company based in Manila (Maya, 2024) that addresses the needs of advanced financial products and services to shares of the population with limited access to traditional financial services. The Philippines is a significantly underbanked market. Due to its unique archipelago geography, which is not conducive to physical bank branches, and its stage of development, the country is especially receptive to online lenders. Half of the adult population remains unbanked and roughly the same proportion of adults lack savings. Among those who do save, half do so through informal means. Additionally, only one third of adults have loans and just 18 per cent of these loans are from banks.

In partnership with 1st e-Bank (previously PDCP Bank; now BDO Unibank) and Mastercard, Smart Money was introduced in December 2000. It was the world's first card linked to a wireless phone. In the first quarter of 2016, PayMaya processed US$1 billion worth of transactions. The service was relaunched as PayMaya in January of the same year. By the end of 2021, PayMaya reached forty-four million registered users (Smart Money, 2024). In April 2022, PLDT and Smart

Communications, the two businesses that control PayMaya's parent firm, Voyager Innovations, announced that PayMaya would be revamped and renamed Maya to coincide with the debut of Maya Bank. The aforementioned rebranding was completed on 2 May 2022 (Abadilla, 2022). The Maya app is powered by Maya Philippines, Inc. for its digital payment services and Maya Bank, Inc. for its digital banking services. Maya is touted as the only end-to-end digital financial service in the country. Due to strong cooperation between the two organisations, Maya's consumers can perform both payments and digital banking through a unified money platform (Maya, n.d.). Mitch Padua, Maya's group chief product officer, highlighted the market opportunity in the fintech space, driven by the expected growth of the country's economy. This growth has been driven by young, tech-savvy users. Filipinos have traditionally had limited access to advanced financial products and services; however, through the use of an easy-to-use app, Maya aspired to bring these financial services to a larger percentage of the Philippines' digital economy (Hoadley, 2022).

7.4.4 Singapore

Historically, Singapore's culture has not embraced entrepreneurship. Fear of failure could explain low entrepreneurial intent among young Singaporean adults (Chua & Bedford, 2015). Singapore has become one of the richest sovereign nations in the world due to FDI, education and innovation. This has enabled it to invest in increasingly complex products, creating higher-value jobs for Singaporeans (Christensen et al., 2019). Le and Le's study explored the relationship between FDI and economic growth in Singapore from 1970 to 2018 and found that FDI and trade are the main drivers of long-term growth. This suggests that Singapore's 'economic miracle' can be attributed to effective strategies for managing FDI and promoting trade activities (Le & Le, 2020). In parallel, Singapore's science, technology and innovation policy aimed to create a knowledge hub to help local firms catch up firms from more advanced countries. The two research universities, the National University of Singapore and the Nanyang Technological University, were expected to become central players in the global knowledge network and generate returns on their intellectual property rights over their research outcomes. Unfortunately, they have failed to capture the associated intellectual rent, while foreign corporations garnered most of the rent generated by this knowledge hub (Rikap & Flacher, 2020).

The Singaporean government has worked to boost R&D, which can be an important part of commercialising new technologies and firms. The government implemented four science & technology (S&T) five-year plans between 1991 and 2010, resulting in an increase in R&D expenditure from US$760 million in 1991 to US$6.04 billion in 2009. Singapore has developed a unique spectrum of deep capabilities across the fields of biomedical sciences, physical sciences and engineering, creating a robust knowledge-based economy. In 2013, Singapore was the seventh most innovative country in the world (Narasimhalu, 2016).

Singapore has rapidly become one of the most dynamic and innovative economies in the world, with a thriving entrepreneurial ecosystem. The government set aside SGD 300 million (US$225 million) for the Start-up SG Equity Initiative in 2020 to co-invest in deeptech sectors, encourage entrepreneurship and mobilise private investment in technology-driven ventures. This policy is part of the government's push to integrate deeptech and innovative solutions into its digital and brick-and-mortar industries. Creating innovative deeptech processes requires longer incubation periods and a larger investment capacity (Thompson, 2021), and government support is instrumental.

Access to capital in Singapore is varied but there is a robust funding infrastructure that includes crowdfunding. Singapore's crowdfunding industry has grown rapidly due to its higher GDP per capita, financial sector development and greater availability of venture capital (Tan et al., 2021). More importantly, Singapore has achieved its status as a financial centre in the Asia-Pacific region and a top destination for venture capital funds. Public funds also complement the availability of private investments.

The Enterprise Financing Scheme was created in October 2019 to support start-ups and enterprises along various stages of growth. It engages in risk-sharing for loans of 50 per cent and up to 70 per cent for young companies. Venture debt loans are designed to support the growth of 'innovative enterprises' and are suited to high growth start-ups that do not have significant assets to use as collateral. This policy is an example of best practice of how to create solutions to specifically cater to start-ups (Thompson, 2021). The Global Ready Talent Program is a state-sponsored programme that encourages young talent to enter the start-up scene. It combines the SME Talent Program, Young Talent Program and Go Southeast Asia Award to send Singaporean talent to take up job postings abroad in key markets. The goal is to foster an entrepreneurial mindset with international exposure (Thompson, 2021).

Enterprise Singapore launched the Start-up SG Founder scheme in 2017 to nurture Singapore's start-up scene by providing mentorship and grants to first-time entrepreneurs. In 2019, seventy-four start-ups received mentoring, and the scheme awarded grants amounting to SGD 2.22 million. Subsequently, the government announced an additional SGD 150 million to enhance the scheme, including introducing a new Train path and increasing the pre-seed grant amount from SGD 30,000 to SGD 50,000. Individuals applying for the Train path must be citizens or permanent residents of Singapore, while applicant companies under the Start path must have a minimum of three Singaporean employees (including co-founders). Existing criteria for the Start path include minimum Singapore shareholding thresholds of 51 per cent, co-matching capital of at least SGD 10,000 and the start-up having been incorporated for less than six months at the date of application. These stimuli were expected to encourage more Singaporeans to explore entrepreneurial career paths (Huang & Wenrui, 2020). Such proactive state support has received criticism. Coordinated policies that prioritise capital, knowledge and human capital accumulation in specific industries, sectors, technologies and firms have created a societal knowledge barrier that can arguably impede endogenous entrepreneurial activity. Singapore's entrepreneurial state imposes its vision by making strong assumptions about the core entrepreneurial values of opportunity recognition, discovery and action, which can arguably slow down the transition to an entrepreneurial society (Audretsch & Fiedler, 2022).

Singapore's entrepreneurial ecosystem has flourished thanks to the city-state's government support, talent pool, location and connectivity, availability of funding and culture of innovation. As Singapore continues to attract start-ups from around the world, it is likely that the city-state will remain a key player in the regional and global start-up landscape. The result is that, as of 2024, the list of Singaporean unicorns increased to twenty-seven. Among them are HyalRoute, which provides a multi-fibre universal connection point; Moglix, an online marketplace for business supplies and industrial equipment; Coda Payments, which helps digital content providers to monetise their products and services; AIG, that provides Al-led technology for use in data-centric platforms; Trax, a provider of marketing solutions; Insider, an AI algorithm provider to predict behaviour and personalise cross-channel experiences for marketeers; Carousell, a platform for buying and selling pre-owned things; Matrixport, a fintech for crypto assets; Nium, a global payments platform; PatSnap, a marketplace and platform for anonymous innovation intelligence; ONE, a global sports media platform; Carro, an online used automobile marketplace; Ninja Van, a tech-enabled express delivery serving businesses across Southeast Asia and Bolttech, an insurtech firm building an artificial intelligence-powered point-of-sale insurance platform.

Bolttech is an international insurance technology firm which connects insurers, distributors and customers through an insurance exchange. It does business in thirty markets with three tech hubs and four regional offices. It started in 2020, and in 2024 it serves clients in North America, Asia and Europe. It has gone through Series B funding and is a unicorn with over 1,000 employees worldwide. Bolttech owns over US$52 billion in annual quoted premiums and has taken its focus on ESG, something unusual for an insurance exchange. It has undertaken unique initiatives. For example, as Bolttech provides insurance for cell phones, and it can easily support phone recycling. The firm does this as a way of reducing e-waste (PWCa, 2023).

Rob Schimek, Bolttech's group chief executive officer, describes the venture as one of the world's largest firms in the embedded insurance space but also as an insurance exchange between insurers, distributors and customers. They connect 800+ insurance distribution partners with 200+ insurance providers globally, offering 6,000+ ways for customers to purchase insurance around the world. Now, in 2024, they are the largest insurance marketplace in the world. Their Series A investors included venture capital firms from the United States, Europe and Singapore, and their Series B investors include Japanese firm Tokio Marine (Hoadley, 2022).

7.5 Discussion

ASEAN nations promote start-up growth and unicorn creation to varying degrees, and their entrepreneurial ecosystems are at varying stages of development. Singapore clearly leads, followed by Indonesia, then other nations like Thailand, the Philippines and Vietnam follow at some distance, undertaking ambitious efforts to catch up. Singapore is a truly unique case within the region, but Indonesia's success can act as a model for other ASEAN nations to emulate because its challenges are very much representative of those of most countries in the Global South. However, the true entrepreneurial potential of the ASEAN region can only be reached when local unicorns can move across regional borders more easily. This requires a level of economic integration that ASEAN has yet to achieve.

ASEAN has the potential to become one of the world's top five digital economies by 2025. With Indonesia, Malaysia, the Philippines, Singapore, Thailand and Vietnam in the lead, it exemplifies inherent trade-offs. For example, AI has the potential to transform the manner in which governments provide public services. Indonesia, Thailand, Singapore and Malaysia are the ASEAN nations that are most reliant on AI. Robotic automation poses a threat to unskilled workers, and there may be significant growth opportunities for knowledge-based businesses in ASEAN. While the COVID-19 pandemic accelerated digital transformation, ASEAN lacks the necessary cybersecurity measures to prevent and reduce the risk of external threats, especially in the context of geopolitical tensions in the South China Sea. There is no evident path leading to solutions for the region's many complex tensions and problems, so businesses and governments must collaborate to harness the transformational power of unicorns.

Finally, ASEAN is still an incomplete regional economic integration endeavour. It is more akin to a free trade association and customs union as it has not yet seen the benefits of a common market or an economic union. Boundaries matter, despite the potential for making connections and reducing transaction costs brought by digitalisation and innovation. The fundamental challenge of closer regional integration within the ASEAN holds the promise of enhanced prosperity, innovation success, knowledge creation and lifestyles better harmonised with the environment. These objectives no longer seem impossible to achieve on the wings of ASEAN unicorns against the backdrop of tighter regional integration.

References

Abadilla, E. V. (2022, 2 May). *PayMaya rebrands as Maya*. Manila Bulletin. mb.com.ph/2022/05/02/paymaya-rebrands-as-maya/

Adomako, S., and Danso, A. (2014). Regulatory environment, environmental dynamism, political ties, and performance: Study of entrepreneurial firms in a developing economy. *Journal of Small Business and Enterprise Development 21*(2), 212–230. doi.org/10.1108/JSBED-01-2014-0004

Akehira, S. P., Alcantara, E., and Laforga Jr, A. (2022). Competition and innovation: The rise of startups and its effects towards the Philippines economy. *Journal of Economics, Finance and Accounting Studies 4*(1), 383–411. doi.org/10.32996/jefas.2022.4.1.24

Arsyad, N. (2015). Integration between East and Southeast Asian equity markets. *Journal of Financial Economic Policy 7*(2), 104–121. doi.org/10.1108/jfep-02-2014-0012

Asian Development Bank (ABD). (2023a, 4 April). *ADB forecasts 4.8% growth for Asia and Pacific in 2023 and 2024.* tinyurl.com/bdbv8bdk

(2023b, 19 October). *How the Philippines is helping tech startups.* SEADS.

Audretsch, D. B., and Fiedler, A. (2022, 23 February). Does the entrepreneurial state crowd out entrepreneurship? *Small Business Economics 60*, 573–589 (2023). link.springer.com/article/10.1007/s11187-022-00604-x

Bachtiar, P. P., Vandenberg, P., and Sawiji, H. W. (2022, November). *City-level tech startup ecosystems and talent development in Indonesia.* ADB Briefs. tinyurl.com/5a43vc5s

Bai, W., Johanson, M., Oliveira, L., and Ratajczak-Mrozek, M. (2021). The role of business and social networks in the effectual internationalization: Insights from emerging market SMEs. *Journal of Business Research 129*, 96–109. doi.org/10.1016/j.jbusres.2021.02.042

Batalla, E. (2010). Entrepreneurship and Philippine development. *Canadian Journal of Development Studies/Revue Canadienne D Études Du Développement 31*(3–4), 341–365. doi.org/10.1080/02255189.2010.3673724

BIMP-EAGA. (2021, 15 December). *How Indonesia is creating a new generation of entrepreneurs.* BIMP. bimp-eaga.asia/article/how-indonesia-creating-new-generation-entrepreneurs

Bitkub. (2023). Bitkub. www.bitkub.com/

Box, S., and Lopez-Gonzalez, J. (2017). *The future of technology: Opportunities for ASEAN in the digital economy. Global megatrends: Implications for the ASEAN economic community*, pp. 37–60.

Brophy, C., Reyes, M. H., Baskin, B., and Seah, S. (2021). *ASEAN Matters for America/ America Matters For ASEAN.* East-West Center.

Carpenter, K., and Springer, V. (2005). The center of the center of marine shore fish biodiversity: The Philippine islands. *Journal of Applied Phycology 72*(4), 467–480. doi.org/10.1007/s10641-004-3154-4

Castro, R. (2016). Twenty-first century Philippines' policy toward an emergent China: From equi-balancing to strategic balancing. *Asian Politics & Policy* 8(2), 305–328. doi.org/10.1111/aspp.12249

Chaudry, L. (2024, 25 February). *Unicorn watch: Keeping up with SEA's startup stars*. Tech in Asia. www.techinasia.com/unicorn-watch-keeping-seas-startup-stars

Chen, Q., Hou, W., Li, W., Wilson, C., and Wu, Z. (2014). Family control, regulatory environment, and the growth of entrepreneurial firms: International evidence. *Corporate Governance: An International Review* 22(2), 132–144.

Christensen, C. M., Ojomo, E., and Dillon, K. (2019, 6 February). *How investment made Singapore an innovation hub*. Barron's. www.barrons.com/articles/how-investment-made-singapore-an-innovation-hub-51549458040

Chua, H. S., and Bedford, O. (2015). A qualitative exploration of fear of failure and entrepreneurial intent in Singapore. *Journal of Career Development* 43(4), 319–334. doi.org/10.1177/0894845315599255

Crunchbase Inc. (2023). *Primaku – Crunchbase company profile & funding*. www.crunchbase.com/organization/primaku

Deloitte. (2022). *Southeast Asia IPO Capital Market*. tinyurl.com/mp4z9h9c

Deng, J., Wahyuni, H., and Yulianto, V. (2020). Labor migration from Southeast Asia to Taiwan: Issues, public responses and future development. *Asian Education and Development Studies* 10(1), 69–81. doi.org/10.1108/aeds-02-2019-0043

Denmark, A. (2021, 6 April). *The climate crisis and Southeast Asia geopolitics*. Wilson Center Blog. www.wilsoncenter.org/blog-post/climate-crisis-and-southeast-asian-geopolitics

Desiderio, L. (2021, 18 November). *Government rolling out P250 million fund for startups*. Philstar.com. tinyurl.com/bdvbc58b

Dewanti, L., Rusmita, S., and Samad, K. (2022). Sensitivity Islamic stock return in Asia: The effect of exchange rate volatility. *Jurnal Ekonomi Dan Bisnis Islam (Journal of Islamic Economics and Business)* 8(2), 302–317. doi.org/10.20473/jebis.v8i2.39018

Du, H., and King, R. B. (2022). What predicts perceived economic inequality? The roles of actual inequality, system justification, and fairness considerations. *British Journal of Social Psychology* 61(1), 19–36.

Foxmont Capital Partners. (2022). *Philippine venture capital report 2022*. Foxmontcapital.com. www.foxmontcapital.com/_files/ugd/bf4602_9e8f86bec6814d2ebf80a39488e9ff5c.pdf

Grimpe, C., Murmann, M., and Sofka, W. (2019). Organizational design choices of high-tech startups: How middle management drives innovation performance. *Strategic Entrepreneurship Journal* 13(3), 359–378. doi.org/10.1002/sej.1330

Haini, H. (2019). Examining the relationship between finance, institutions and economic growth: Evidence from the ASEAN economies. *Economic Change and Restructuring 53*(4), 519–542. doi.org/10.1007/s10644-019-09257-5

Hoadley, J. (2022). *SE Asian unicorns Part 2 – Practitioners' panel.* YouTube. Georgia Tech Center for International Business Education and Research. youtu.be/29TK_yQkqYQ?si=qm3n1SE8EympEz4H

Hoskisson, R., Wright, M., Filatotchev, I., and Peng, M. (2012). Emerging multinationals from mid-range economies: The influence of institutions and factor markets. *Journal of Management Studies 50*(7), 1295–1321. doi.org/10.1111/j.1467-6486.2012.01085.x

Huang, S., and Wenrui, C. (2020, 24 August). *Singapore enhances scheme to encourage entrepreneurship.* Osborne Clarke. www.osborneclarke .com/insights/singapore-enhances-scheme-encourage-entrepreneurship

Kumar, V., Mudambi, R., and Gray, S. (2013). Internationalization, innovation and institutions: The 3 I's underpinning the competitiveness of emerging market firms. *Journal of International Management 19*(3), 203–206. doi.org/10.1016/j.intman.2013.03.005

Kurlantzick, J. (2022). *Why democracy in Southeast Asia will worsen in 2023.* Council on Foreign Relations. www.cfr.org/blog/why-democ racy-southeast-asia-will-worsen-2023

Langeland, T., and Nitithanprapas, R. (2022, 20 September). *Thailand's tech startups developing rapidly.* Asian Development Bank. www.adb .org/news/thailand-s-tech-startups-developing-rapidly

Lathapipat, D., and Sondergaard, L. (2017, 17 February). *Skilled workforce and strong R&D keys to Thailand 4.0 success.* World Bank Blogs. tinyurl.com/yey3sxfj

Le, H.-C., and Le, T.-H. (2020). Foreign direct investment inflows and economic growth in Singapore: An empirical approach. *Economics Bulletin 40*, 3256–3273.

Lebdaoui, H., and Wild, J. (2016). Islamic banking presence and economic growth in Southeast Asia. *International Journal of Islamic and Middle Eastern Finance and Management 9*(4), 551–569. doi.org/10.1108/ imefm-03-2015-0037

Ledhem, M., and Mekidiche, M. (2021). Islamic finance and economic growth nexus: An empirical evidence from Southeast Asia using dynamic panel one-step system GMM analysis. *Journal of Islamic Accounting and Business Research 12*(8), 1165–1180. doi.org/10.1108/jiabr-03-2021-0107

Lee, J.-O., and Sathirathai, S. (eds.). (2022, December). *ASEAN digital generation report: Digital financial inclusion.* tinyurl.com/58dhekay

Lekmat, L., and Chelliah, J. (2014). What are the antecedents to creating sustainable corporate entrepreneurship in Thailand? *Contemporary Management Research 10*(3). doi.org/10.7903/cmr.11741

Letaifa, S. B., and Rabeau, Y. (2013). Too close to collaborate? How geographic proximity could impede entrepreneurship and innovation. *Journal of Business Research* 66(10), 2071–2078. doi.org/10.1016/j.jbusres.2013.02.033

Lohn, D. R., Kilgore, E., Chang, J., McIntyre, J. R., and Robinson, R. (1979). Issue Brief. In F. W. Huszagh, ed. *Comparative Facts on Canada, Mexico, and the United States: A Foundation for Selective Integration and Trilateral Cooperation.* University of Georgia, pp. 12–17.

Luc, P. T. (2018). The relationship between perceived access to finance and social entrepreneurship intentions among university students in Vietnam. *The Journal of Asian Finance, Economics and Business* 5(1), 63–72.

Mackender, R., Yan, T. S., and Shawn Kit, C. (2022, 23 February). *Indonesia's innovative startups are the catalyst for increasing investment.* KrASIA. tinyurl.com/y9xysyfn

Marvel, M. R., Davis, J. L., and Sproul, C. R. (2016). Human capital and entrepreneurship research: A critical review and future directions. *Entrepreneurship Theory and Practice* 40(3), 599–626.

Maya. (2024). Maya brand story. Maya Philippines. www.maya.ph/maya-story

McKinsey & Company. (2022, 16 November). *Improving Thailand's capital market competitiveness and efficiency.* tinyurl.com/bdz4wx7r

McKinsey Global Institute. (2018, July). *Smart cities in Southeast Asia.* tinyurl.com/4pnp9kdw

Menon, J., and Fink, A. (2019). The fourth industrial revolution and its implications for regional economic integration in ASEAN. *Journal of Asian Economic Integration* 1(1), 32–47. doi.org/10.1177/2631684618821566

Narasimhalu, D. A. (2016, 23 September). *Thinking bigger: Pushing Singaporean entrepreneurship to the next level.* Asian Management Insights. cmp.smu.edu.sg/ami/article/20161116/thinking-bigger

OECD. (2013). *Innovation In Southeast Asia, OECD Reviews of Innovation Policy.* OECD Publishing. doi.org/10.1787/9789264128712-en

Papademetriou, D. G., and Sumption, M. (2013). Attracting and selecting from the global talent pool– Policy challenges. *Migration Policy Institute 16.* www.migrationpolicy.org/sites/default/files/publications/GlobalTalent-Selection.pdf

Pennings, J. M. (1982). The urban quality of life and entrepreneurship. *Academy of Management Journal* 25(1), 63–79. journals.aom.org/doi/abs/10.5465/256024

Pepinski, T.,Hutchinson, F., Atienza, M., Kwon, H. (2022). *Corruption and Democracy in Asia*. Brookings Institution. www.brookings.edu/research/corruption-and-democracy-in-asia/

Pongsudhirak, T. (2022, 12 October). *Geopolitical upheavals divide Southeast Asia*. GIS Reports. www.gisreportsonline.com/r/southeast-asia-divides-upheaval/

PrimaKu (2024). *Pelopor aplikasi Tumbuh Kembang Anak di Indonesia*. primaku.com/

PWC. (2020). *Charging ahead – 2020 Philippine startup survey*. tinyurl.com/yaraesuy

Thailand. Corporate – Tax credits and incentives. taxsummaries.pwc.com/thailand/corporate/tax-credits-and-incentives

Bolttech CEO on finding balance in a high-growth stage.

Rahman, S. (2023, 31 January). *Southeast Asia in 2023: Economic resurgence with climate change uncertainty: Climate change is the biggest threat*. Heinrich-Böll-Stiftung. tinyurl.com/3n9ze645

Rayda, N. (2022). *Pushing the boundaries of innovation: How 9 Indonesia start-ups become unicorns during the pandemic*. Channel News Asia. tinyurl.com/mry5cfvf

Rikap, C., and Flacher, D. (2020). Who collects intellectual rents from knowledge and innovation hubs? Questioning the sustainability of the Singapore model. *Structural Change and Economic Dynamics 55*, 59–73. doi.org/10.1016/j.strueco.2020.06.004

Rollert, J. P. (2018, 16 November). *Something's happening to the spirit of capitalism*. The University of Chicago Booth School of Business. www.chicagobooth.edu/review/somethings-happening-spirit-capitalism

Samphantharak, K. (2011). The rise of China and foreign direct investment from Southeast Asia. *Journal of Current Southeast Asian Affairs 30(*2), 65–75. doi.org/10.1177/186810341103000204

Sarasvathy, S. D., and Dew, N. (2005). New market creation through transformation. *Journal of Evolutionary Economics* 15(5), 533–565.

Sarasvathy, S., Kumar, K., York, J. G., and Bhagavatula, S. (2014). An effectual approach to international entrepreneurship: Overlaps, challenges, and provocative possibilities. *Entrepreneurship Theory and Practice* 38(1), 71–93.

Smart Money. Company website. (2024). smart.com.ph/About/profile/innovations-and-awards/smart-money

Smith, R. B. (2021). How can the least developed member countries of ASEAN benefit from the 4th industrial revolution? *Walailak Journal of Science and Technology (WJST) 18*(1), 1–12. doi.org/10.48048/wjst.2021.6502

Stuart, T. E., and Sorenson, O. (2005). Social networks and entrepreneurship. In S. Alvarez, R. Agarwal, and O. Sorensen, eds. *Handbook of*

Entrepreneurship Research: Interdisciplinary Perspectives. Springer, pp. 233–252.

Tan, S. L., Tok, Y. W., and Thitipat, C. (2021, August). *Financing Singapore financing Singapore's SMEs and the crowdfunding industry in Singapore*. ink.library.smu.edu.sg/cgi/viewcontent.cgi?article=3510&; context=soe_research

Tan, Y. (2021). *China's rise to changes in Southeast Asia's political landscape*. Proceedings of the 2021 3rd International Conference on Economic Management and Cultural Industry (ICEMCI).

Thai PBS World Business Desk. (2021, 6 December). *From troublemaker to Thailand's first fintech unicorn – Tracking Jirayut SRUPSRISOPA's crypto journey*.

Thompson, H. D. (2021, 29 March). *Startup policies in Singapore*. Enpact. enpact.org/news-archive/empower-singapore-policies/

Tipton, F.B. (2009). Southeast Asian capitalism: History, institutions, states, and firms. *Asia Pacific Journal of Management* 26, 401–434.

Tracey, P., and Phillips, N. (2011). Entrepreneurship in emerging markets: strategies for new venture creation in uncertain institutional contexts. *Management International Review 51*, 23–39.

Velasco, A. L., Castillo, P. J., Conchada, M. I. P., Gozun, B. C., Largoza, G. L., Perez, J. A., and Sarreal, E. D. (2017). *Philippine Entrepreneurship Report* (pp. 37–41). De La Salle University Publishing House.

Woo, M. (2022, 5 October). *Philippine startups lag behind Southeast Asian counterparts in 2018 funding, but 2019 looks rosy*. KrASIA. tinyurl .com/4cjxprdj

Yang, L., Qing, Z., Li, B., Ma, L., and Ordieres-Meré, J. (2022). Anticipating financial distress of high-tech startups in the European Union: A machine learning approach for imbalanced samples. *Journal of Forecasting 41*(6), 1131–1155. doi.org/10.1002/for.2852

Yiu, D. W., and Lau, C. (2008). Corporate entrepreneurship as resource capital configuration in emerging market firms. *Entrepreneurship Theory and Practice* 32(1), 37–57. doi.org/10.1111/j.1540-6520.2007 .00215.x

Zahra, S. A., and Nambisan, S. (2011). Entrepreneurship in global innovation ecosystems. *AMS Review 1*(1), 4–17. http://dx.doi.org/10.1007/ s13162-011-0004-3

8 Latin American Unicorn Firms: Transcending Entrepreneurial Hubs

ARMANDO BORDA, RICARDO BUITRAGO, FERNANDA CAHENAND MICHEL HERMANS

8.1 Introduction

Similar to other emerging markets (EM) contexts and following early successes such as Mercado Libre, Totus and Despegar, the number of unicorn firms in Latin America has substantially increased since the mid-2010s. While some early unicorns have issued their initial public offering and others have been acquired, as of 2025 CB Insights (2025) reported a total of thirty-three privately held firms valued at more than US$1 billion. Their distribution is concentrated in only six countries: Brazil (eighteen), Mexico (nine) , Colombia (three), Chile (two), and Argentina (one). The region has a history of intense political and economic swings and continues to pose challenges of many types. At the same time, it also boasts a vibrant technology-based entrepreneurship scene, a growing number of venture capital (VC) backed high-tech start-ups (Latitude, 2023) and a budding community of founders and managers able to articulate strategies that drive their firms' growth.

This chapter focuses on the emergence of unicorns in Latin America (LATAM). We argue that this process results from the interplay between local entrepreneurial ecosystems and the strategies these firms have pursued to become unicorns that transcend their local context.

To understand the specific dynamics within Latin America, we analyse how national and local institutions in Argentina, Brazil, Colombia, Mexico and Peru enable and constrain the emergence of unicorns in this region. Within these contexts, we identify strategies entrepreneurs have implemented to exploit available resources, compensate for those that are lacking, and overcome local contextual obstacles.

We draw on the entrepreneurial ecosystem (EE) approach (Acs et al., 2017), which has emerged as a helpful framework for investigating the growth of unicorns within entrepreneurial tech hubs in EMs (Andonova et al., 2019). The ecosystem concept has been essential in exploring three separate dimensions: i) innovation, ii) economic growth and iii) development since the late 1980s and has emerged in entrepreneurship research (Malecki, 2018). It is traditionally understood as a complex set of relationships between institutional entities such as universities, companies, VC firms, research institutes, business assistance organisations, funding agencies, policymakers, et cetera that allow for the exchange and combination of resources such as information, ideas, funding, technology and human capital. Informed by institutions at the national level, EEs are often understood to take place in localities or, at most, regions (Malecki, 2018). Unicorns have emerged from the EEs of large LATAM cities such as São Paulo in Brazil, Buenos Aires in Argentina, Mexico City in Mexico and Bogotá in Colombia.

However, focusing solely on the national or local EE is insufficient to develop a complete understanding of the emergence of unicorns. As knowledge- and technology-intensive companies with digital business models that allow them to expand beyond the geographical boundaries of an EE, the strategies that these firms pursue (Parker et al., 2017; Nambisan et al., 2019; Cahen & Borini, 2020) are a necessary complement as they create and develop their digital ecosystems. Digital ecosystems include all digital relationships (such as electronic data interchange, shared virtual sales and other electronic linkages) that allow for connecting with potential partners, complementors and end users within a company's digital assets (Bohnsack et al., 2024). To the extent that unicorns can scale, their complex relationships between 'tangible' agents and 'intangible' digital assets may become an engine for further development of the business and technological environments from which they emerged (Andonova et al., 2019).

Within this chapter, we highlight the interrelatedness of these two dimensions. On the one hand, local EEs provide resources such as a pool of skilled professionals, improved access to capital and supportive government initiatives that foster innovation and entrepreneurship. On the other hand, unicorns' strategies play an important role in articulating the available resources in their digital and EEs. Furthermore, we stress the importance of entrepreneurial agency in responding to environmental challenges and circumventing resource constraints to develop a global or regional position.

8.2 Bridging Entrepreneurial and Digital Ecosystems

In business, ecosystems are understood as interdependencies, networks and partnerships between agents and institutions (Brown & Mason,

2017). Emerging in the late 1980s, ecosystem studies initially concentrated on the influence of national contexts on innovation, as highlighted in research on innovation ecosystems, also known as national innovation systems (Edquist, 1997; Buitrago R. & Barbosa Camargo, 2021). Later, the focus shifted towards EEs as business environments, networks and cultures that support entrepreneurs in a particular location.

EEs can be analysed at the national or local level. However, while there is a degree of national impact on innovation and entrepreneurship activities (Malecki, 2018), the impact has been conceptualised as occurring primarily within a local context. This involves leveraging local resources, institutions and networks to develop and support entrepreneurial activities within a particular location. In this sense, the EE is a familiar concept for most companies as they manage interdependencies and strategic partnerships within their local business environment for their production process, supply chains or distribution networks (Malecki, 2018). The EE approach emphasises complex relationships involving human capital and institutions such as universities, companies and venture capitalists (Andonova et al., 2019). This approach has been crucial in studying the emergence of unicorns and tech hubs in EMs.

Because of the emphasis on conventional business relationships, which require face-to-face, tangible interactions between individual entrepreneurs and between organisations in the physical space (Banalieva & Dhanaraj, 2019), the EE approach is centred on the locus of entrepreneurial activities. However, digital technology has transformed the business landscape and how entrepreneurs and organisations relate (Nambisan et al., 2019). Whereas location played an important role in shaping interdependencies in traditional partnerships, value chains and industry structures, the rise of digital technologies and digital business models has expanded the geographical scope and nature of interactions (Sussan & Acs, 2017).

Digital companies simplify their technology by breaking it into software blocks designed to support dynamic websites, internet applications and web services that communicate through standardised interfaces, a concept known as modularity (Banalieva & Dhanaraj, 2019). This approach, facilitated by application programming interfaces enables easy integration with other digital applications, speeding up international digital distribution, facilitating digital interconnection with agents (Monaghan et al., 2020) and expanding networks beyond traditional business relationships. Consequently, digital companies can expand their networks beyond traditional and predominantly local business relationships, engaging directly with other companies that provide complementary assets, content producers, venture capitalists and end-users, fostering a broad, dynamic and less location-bound digital ecosystem (Sussan & Acs, 2017).

Digital ecosystems can involve multi-sided platforms (Bohnsack et al., 2024). A digital platform is an internet-based infrastructure connecting buyers and suppliers, facilitating interactions in multi-sided markets and serving as a hub in an ecosystem to enhance productivity and profitability (Teece, 2017). Typically, these ecosystems revolve around one or a few central platforms hubs that connect two or more groups – such as complementors, partners, and users – through interfaces across different platform layers. Focal platforms operate in an environment marked by market failure, with imperfect information about choices and their outcomes, allowing entrepreneurial agency to overcome such difficulties. Digital ecosystems include all a company's connected activities, such as electronic data interchange, shared virtual sales, pooled virtual-based user support and other electronic linkages (Cahen et al., 2022) to establish connections with many potential partners, complementors and end-users. A focal firm's positioning within its digital ecosystem is a key driver of its ability to scale, create and appropriate value, given that constellations involve numerous agents (actors) with diverse characteristics and goals. Hence, digital ecosystems pave the way to entrepreneurial agency and promote mechanisms for escaping constrained environments in a context of high levels of uncertainty.

Taken together, we argue that the EE approach should be complemented by the digital ecosystems concept (Nambisan et al., 2019) to develop a more comprehensive explanation of the emergence of unicorns. Figure 8.1 depicts the underlying logic of this chapter. The marked differences in entrepreneurial activity in general and, more specifically, in the number of unicorns that have emerged from particular cities suggest that national and local characteristics of the EE play an important role in unicorn emergence. Contextual characteristics enable and constrain entrepreneurial behaviour and will be most relevant in the early stages of new venture formation when start-ups are more vulnerable to contextual influence. However, because of the nature of digital business, entrepreneurs' agency, as reflected in

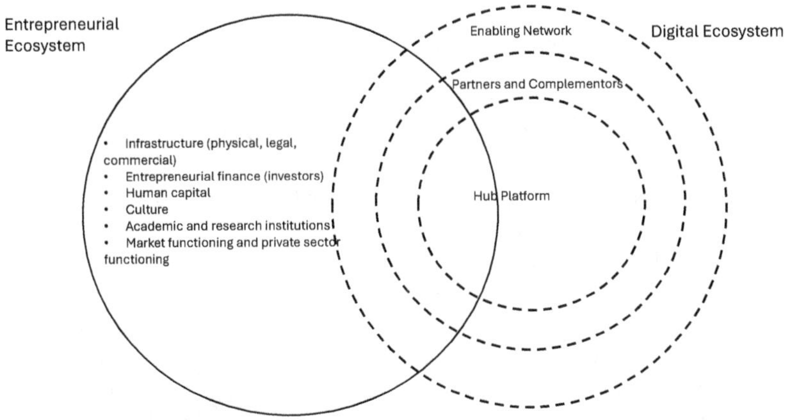

Figure 8.1 Digital entrepreneurial ecosystem.
Source: Author generated from Brown and Mason (2017), Sussan and Acs (2017) and Nambisan et al. (2019).

business models and organisational strategies, allows for interactions with actors beyond the local entrepreneurial system. To the extent that digital start-up firms can broaden their digital ecosystem and enhance their positioning within it, they will transcend the local EE and increase the likelihood of becoming a unicorn.

Accordingly, we organise the following sections of the chapter by illustrating the remarkable progress of entrepreneurial technology hubs in Latin America from which unicorns are likely to emerge. We combine country and city-level analyses to explain how the country's macro conditions relate to the development of EEs and the appearance of unicorns in specific locations. We highlight the evolution of VC investment in the last decade to understand the level and commitment of international funds to nurturing and developing local start-ups. Then, we identify characteristics of unicorns' strategies to identify how start-ups make use of available resources while dealing with the resource gaps they encounter as they pursue strategies for the creation and development of their digital ecosystem. Finally, we conclude this chapter with reflections on the conditions that favour high-tech entrepreneurship and innovation in local LATAM ecosystems and the capacity of these hubs to create the next generation of unicorns.

Vignette 8.1 iFood

iFood pioneered the digitisation of food delivery offerings in Latin America. The brand emerged in 2011 when online orders reached 42 per cent of the revenue of the original company (DiskCook), which handled food orders via telephone. iFood's focal user ecosystem comprises restaurants, customers and meal delivery drivers (see Figure 8.1a). Users access the platform application, choose from numerous restaurants and dishes, pay and track orders digitally. Restaurants offer their menus and receive online orders and payment, and drivers offer delivery services and are paid and tipped through the application. Since 2014, iFood's focus has been on growing and digitalising its ecosystem by enhancing the services of its focal ecosystem, bringing and growing new partners and complementors in and out of the food delivery value chain.

The initial ecosystem growth strategy involved market-seeking expansion through acquisitions and mergers with competitors having a similar business model, establishing itself as a market leader in Brazil and having a presence in Latin America. Later, acquisitions were used to grow the portfolio through digital services out of the food value chain. See Table 8.1b.

Although iFood initially had a digital offering, its platform started as an on-premises system (in the company's information technology (IT) environment). It migrated its operations to the cloud in 2016, which was crucial to digitalisation and enhanced the scalability of its overall business model. From there, the company started to digitalise and expand its ecosystem partners, broadening its digital solutions portfolio. It moved beyond its core activity into groceries, logistics, financial solutions and credit for establishments on its platform.

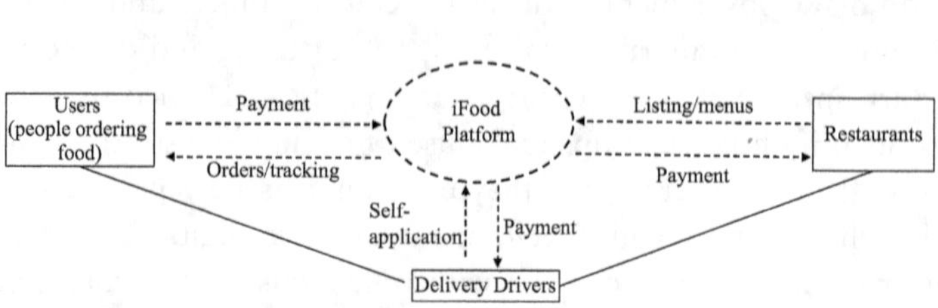

Figure 8.1a iFood focal ecosystem.

Source: Authors' elaboration based on AWS (2018), Pooler (2022), iFood (2023) and Mova (2023).

Vignette 8.1 *(cont.)*

Table 8.1b ***iFood's ecosystem expansion through acquisitions***

Invested companies	Investment type	Deal date	Industry invested company	Country of the invested company
Rapicarc	Seed VC	2020	Supply chain & logistics software (digital health)	Brazil
SinDelantal.Mx	Corporate minority	2016	Food delivery	Mexico
SpoonRocket	Acquisition	2016	Food delivery	United States
SiteMercado	Acquisition	2020	e-Commerce	Brazil
eComanda	Acquisition	2020	Internet software & services	Brazil
Domicilios	Corporate majority	2015	food delivery	Colombia
Hekima	Corporate majority	2020	Business intelligence, analytics & performance mgmt software	Brazil
PedidosJa	Acquisition	2018	e-Commerce (Food delivery)	Brazil
Rapiddo	Acquisition	2018	Mobile commerce	Brazil
Hellofood - Brazil	Acquisition	2016	Food delivery	Germany (Brazilian operation)
SpoonRocket	Acquisition	2016	Food delivery	United States
Netcook	Acquisition	2018	Food delivery	Brazil
A Deliveria	Acquisition	2015	Food delivery	Brazil
Apetitar	Acquisition	2015	Food delivery	Brazil
Papa Rango	Acquisition	2014	Food delivery	Brazil
Alakarte	Acquisition	2014	Food delivery	Brazil
RestauranteWeb	Acquisition	2014	Food delivery	Brazil
Central do Delivery	Acquisition	2014	Food delivery	Brazil

Source: Compiled by authors based on CrunchBase (2022) and CB Insights (2023).

The platform digitally connected restaurants with food and packaging suppliers. It introduced supermarkets, pharmacies, pet stores and general shopping delivery for end users, bringing new actors into the

Vignette 8.1 *(cont.)*

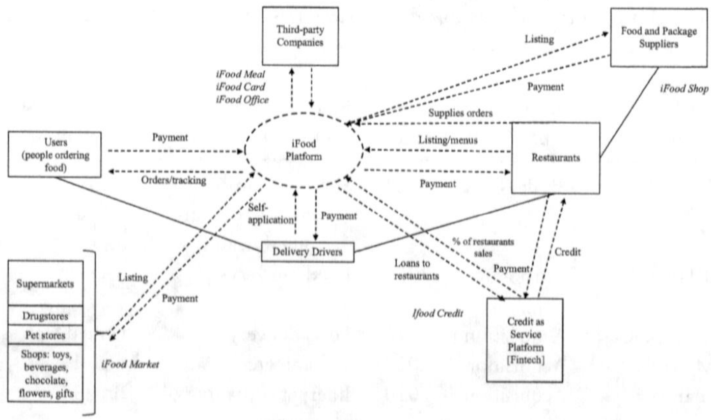

Figure 8.1c Evolution of iFood's ecosystem.
Source: Compiled by authors based on AWS (2018), Pooler (2022), iFood (2023) and Mova (2023).

ecosystem. Capitalising on opportunities from its platform users and transaction data, iFood added another actor to the ecosystem (third-party companies) by providing simplified reimbursement services for meals, digital meal vouchers and a 'gift card' for food. In 2018, it launched solutions beyond delivery, where the user collects the digital order at the restaurant or places an order inside the restaurant, minimising contact between consumers and restaurant staff.

In 2020, iFood began investing in restaurant management tools, financial solutions and loans. It acquired a company specialising in sales management systems, cash flow and restaurant inventory control. In 2021, it launched digital account services and prepaid cards for partner restaurants. Collaborating with the credit-as-a-service fintech Mova, iFood made credit lines available to restaurants, delivery drivers and partner establishments. Furthermore, iFood's expansion into various sectors beyond traditional food delivery, such as groceries and logistics, contributes to the economic dynamism of its ecosystem. By embracing cloud technology and continually advancing its digital capabilities, iFood differentiates itself and signals technological sophistication, further enticing investors. See Figure 8.1c.

8.3 Entrepreneurial Ecosystems in Latin America

Analysing entrepreneurial ecosystems requires acknowledging their complex nature with systemic conditions forming the core. These conditions encompass interconnected networks of entrepreneurs, leadership, financial resources, talent, knowledge and support services (Stam, 2018). The intricate interactions among these elements significantly shape the ecosystem's innovation capacity and potential success (Daniel et al., 2018; Cavallo et al., 2019; Stam & van de Ven, 2021). In this section, we explore institutional trajectories to understand whether and how national level dimensions influence resource availability and capacity development at the country and city levels, to understand the advantages and complementarities that may catalyse the growth of start-up ecosystems in Latin America and their role in the emergence of unicorn firms.

8.3.1 Entrepreneurial Hubs: National Level Dimensions

Many LATAM countries have followed a similar institutional development trajectory (Buitrago R. et al., 2023). The diverse systems developed by the region's native peoples were generally replaced under the colonial rule of the Spanish and Portuguese conquistadors. LATAM's economic growth was based mainly on exports of natural resources, complemented by industrial development to substitute imports. In the late 1980s and early 1990s, the region embraced pro-market reforms, as expressed in the principles established in the Washington Consensus (Cuervo-Cazurra & Dau, 2009). While several LATAM governments have reversed their commitment to neo-liberal policies (Cuervo-Cazurra & Dau, 2009), they actively seek to develop environments that support business creation and development. Amorós et al. (2021) and Martins et al. (2021) mention that economic and political reforms in countries such as Brazil, Mexico, Colombia and Chile had created favourable conditions for entrepreneurship and private capital. These countries have undertaken financial liberalisation, privatisation and other pro-market reforms that have spurred business formation and expanded access to financing.

We draw on the Global Innovation Index (GII) (WIPO, 2023) to compare the current state of LATAM EEs at the national level. The GII provides a perspective on a country's innovation capacity by evaluating input and output dimensions of innovation to capture an ecosystem's systemic nature. Concerning the innovation input dimensions, the GII considers five pillars: the quality of institutions, considering factors such as the quality of the institutional environment, regulatory environment and business environment; human capital and research, including education, tertiary education and research and development; infrastructure, encompassing information and communication technologies, general infrastructure, and ecological sustainability; market sophistication, examining credit, investment, trade, diversification and market scale; and business sophistication, analysing the knowledge of workers, innovation linkages and knowledge absorption.

An initial comparison of national-level GII indicators suggests that the aggregated input dimensions for innovation do not differentiate EEs in which unicorns are more likely to emerge from those that do not. For example, Table 8.1 shows that Peru achieves favourable scores across all input dimensions of innovation, consistently securing a position among the top 3 relative to countries with a higher likelihood of unicorns' emergence. While these input conditions suggest a potential for generating positive outcomes in the future, they do not inherently guarantee immediate or short-term desirable results.

However, certain input sub-indices may be more relevant to explaining the emergence of unicorns in Latin America. The potential impact of these sub-indices is hidden when we concentrate on analysing the aggregated dimensions. The first concerns the correlation between research and development (R&D), innovation links and knowledge absorption and the number of unicorns produced by countries in the region. These sub-indices are associated with knowledge production, the existing capacity to understand the knowledge available and incorporated into everyday lives and the ability to integrate the knowledge produced within industry clusters. When considered together, these input sub-indices may explain the development of entrepreneurs' networks that attract financial resources, develop human talent and support services that generate start-ups and high-potential new ventures. Peru exhibits a comparative delay in those sub-indices as a country that has yet to witness its first unicorn.

Concerning innovation output, the GII considers the quality of knowledge and technological outputs, including factors such as knowledge creation, knowledge impact and knowledge diffusion (see Table 8.2). It also evaluates creative outputs, analysing intangible assets, creative goods and services and online creativity. These general

Table 8.1 *Global Innovation Index: Input dimensions*

	Input dimensions				
	Argentina	Brazil	Colombia	Mexico	Peru
Institutions	**30.90**	**38.50**	**46.70**	**34.80**	**45.90**
Institutional environment	36.00	34.90	39.00	30.00	34.90
Regulatory environment	40.90	60.30	60.00	49.20	63.80
Business environment	15.80	20.20	41.00	25.00	38.90
Human capital and research	**30.00**	**33.50**	**27.00**	**31.70**	**34.70**
Education	43.70	50.00	43.80	42.80	43.50
Tertiary education	29.60	19.80	26.50	26.20	52.60
Research and development	16.50	30.80	10.70	26.10	8.00
Infrastructure	**39.90**	**43.50**	**43.10**	**40.40**	**41.40**
Information and communication technologies	74.80	81.00	71.50	73.20	69.90
General infrastructure	21.10	25.60	19.30	21.30	23.80
Ecological sustainability	23.60	23.90	38.50	26.60	30.50
Market sophistication	**25.20**	**38.10**	**33.40**	**37.20**	**37.90**
Credit	14.70	24.10	23.80	20.80	44.80
Investment	4.20	16.90	12.80	8.80	4.90
Trade diversification and market scale	56.80	73.30	63.50	81.90	64.00
Business sophistication	**30.80**	**37.60**	**37.30**	**25.40**	**31.00**
Knowledge workers	34.30	44.90	48.10	21.20	48.40
Innovation linkages	15.40	23.30	19.90	19.00	11.60
Knowledge absorption	41.10	44.70	43.90	35.80	32.90

Source: Compiled by authors based on data from WIPO (2023).

output dimensions indeed serve to differentiate between entrepreneurial hubs that generate unicorns in the region and those that do not. Notably, Peru exhibits the poorest performance in most dimensions considered.

Some output dimensions, such as patents granted, labour productivity growth, high-tech manufacturing and the export complexity of an economy, correspond with a unicorn's emergence. In particular, the

Table 8.2 *Global Innovation Index: Output dimensions*

	Output dimensions				
	Argentina	Brazil	Colombia	Mexico	Peru
Knowledge and technology outputs	**19.20**	**26.80**	**23.70**	**24.70**	**13.60**
Knowledge creation	13.00	21.20	9.70	11.20	8.10
Knowledge impact	23.80	37.40	37.30	31.30	21.60
Knowledge diffusion	20.90	22.00	24.00	31.50	11.10
Creative outputs	**30.30**	**31.20**	**19.10**	**31.70**	**20.90**
Intangible assets	39.70	47.40	23.00	38.20	31.30
Creative goods and services	18.20	5.60	5.80	31.70	31.00
Online creativity	23.40	24.60	24.70	18.90	17.80

Source: Compiled by authors based on data from WIPO (2023).

scores on the dimensions of knowledge creation (such as patent generation) and intangible assets (trademarks) are closely related to the number of unicorns that emerged in a country. Therefore, output dimensions represent valuable assets and resources that can be swiftly transferred to markets, fostering dynamism. However, these dimensions are not uniformly distributed within countries. Especially in Latin America, where populations and economic activity are concentrated in large cities, unicorn emergence may occur in specific pockets or subnational regions that concentrate the most available resources. The following section examines the most significant characteristics of cities in the above-mentioned countries.

8.3.2 *Entrepreneurial Ecosystems: City-level Characteristics*

National-level characteristics are instrumental to understanding a country's innovation potential and resource availability. However, the capacity of various stakeholders to deploy knowledge to commercial ends is contingent on their geographic and domain proximity (Rosiello et al., 2022). Spillover theory posits that the geographic concentration of assets, knowledge and networks in specific locations yields benefits through relational alignments that generate synergies among participants (Jaffe et al., 1993).

We focus on the most important cities in each country analysed in the previous section (Bogotá, Buenos Aires, Mexico City, Lima and São Paulo) to develop a more contextualised understanding of the emergence of unicorns in Latin America. The density of resources, availability of talent and education, access to varied funding sources and culture of innovation position these cities as hubs of technology entrepreneurship. They offer environments where start-ups can launch and scale rapidly to regional or global prominence. As such, and as illustrated by the indicators included in Table 8.3, these major LATAM urban centres play a vital role as resilient and competitive start-up ecosystems.

8.3.2.1 São Paulo, Brazil

According to the Global Start-up Ecosystem Index (Startupblink, 2023), Brazil has twenty-eight cities that rank among the most important city hubs in the world. However, São Paulo stands out as the most significant ecosystem in the country and Latin America by a considerable margin. With a population exceeding twenty-four million residents, São Paulo offers start-ups unparalleled opportunities for reaching minimum efficient scale given the potential for rapidly scaling their businesses without the immediate need for internationalisation. Moreover, São Paulo hosts the largest number of start-ups in Latin America (2,770 technology firms), which provide mentoring opportunities and tangible examples of successful start-up operations. The most important sectors in São Paulo are fintech, e-commerce and retail and transportation, representing 35 per cent of the total industries operating in the city hub.

The city's entrepreneurial ecosystem has contributed to the creation of fifteen unicorns. São Paulo has solidified its position as Brazil's data centre capital, with tech giants such as Microsoft establishing a significant presence in the city. Additionally, the city has access to talented individuals. According to the Times Higher Education ranking, the University of São Paulo and the University of Campinas ranked first and second, respectively, in Latin America for helping start-ups to address their need for skilled labour. São Paulo further enhances its global reach by offering a digital nomad visa, attracting international talent. Government initiatives, such as the ACE Accelerator Program, foster a supportive entrepreneurial environment. São Paulo also faces

Table 8.3 *Key indicators of the most important city hubs analysed in Latin America*

	Brazil	Mexico	Argentina	Colombia	Peru
Cities among 1,000 ranking**	28	13	4	11	1
Most important ecosystem	**São Paulo**	**Mexico City**	**Buenos Aires**	**Bogotá**	**Lima**
Regional ranking main ecosystem*	1	2	3	5	10
Global ranking main ecosystem**	17	48	75	65	201
Number of unicorns main ecosystem (2020–2022)	15	8	3	2	0
Main ecosystem value (2020–2022) in billions	US$113	US$30	US$12	US$13	N/D
Main ecosystem value growth (2018–2022)	47%	107%	164%	52%	N/D
Total VC funding (2018–2022) in billions	US$17	US$6.4	US$1.9	US$4.5	US$0.287
Number of startups surveyed**	798	282	314	755	87
Percentage from the total sample surveyed in each country	46%	50%	55%	59%	90%
Top startup industries in the main city	**Fintech, e-commerce and retail, transportation**	**Fintech, e-commerce and retail, transportation**	**Fintech, edtech, social and leisure**	**Transportation, foodtech and fintech**	**Edtech, foodtech, fintech**
Percentage of top industries over total industries in the main city	35%	53%	30%	15%	41%
Organizations supporting entrepreneurial activities	**InovAtiva, StartOut Brazil, Capital emprendedor, InvestSP**	**Startup Mexico**	**Startup Buenos Aires, Buenos Aires City Government (IncuBAte)**	**Bogotá Chamber of Commerce, Invest in Bogotá, Cemprende**	**Startup Peru, Proinnovate, Pecap**
Digital nomad visa	Yes	No	Yes	Yes	No

Source: Compiled by authors based on PECAP (2023),
* Startup Genome (2023) and
** Startupblink (2023)

challenges. English proficiency levels among the local population, including those in business settings, are relatively low. The time required to execute business-related activities is notably lengthy. Finally, established companies face high interest rates that constrain potential growth.

8.3.2.2 Mexico City, Mexico

Mexico has thirteen cities that rank among the most relevant city hubs in the world. However, Mexico City stands out as the unequivocal tech capital of Mexico, notably giving rise to the country's first unicorn, Kavak(refer to Vignette 8.4), currently valued at US$8.7 billion. The city hub specialises in fintech, e-commerce, retail and transportation, representing 53 per cent of the total industries operating in the hub (Startupblink, 2023). Many prominent domestic and international investors choose Mexico City as the base for their LATAM operations, with firms like ALLVP and Mountain Nazca establishing a significant presence. The strategic location of Mexico City offers a convenient entry point to the US market for LATAM companies and facilitates access to Latin America for US and Canadian entrepreneurs.

Regarding the quality of the city hub, Mexico City has been organically generating unicorns in recent years. The growing presence of these firms provides new generations of start-ups with valuable experiences, strategies and resources to leverage. Furthermore, these unicorns send strong signals to the academic and business communities that promote the appearance of a new generation of start-up firms. In parallel, Mexico City hosts several regional headquarters for multinational corporations in diverse sectors such as IT, manufacturing and services. These companies provide up-to-date practices and resources upon which entrepreneurs may capitalise. A wealth of start-up-focused organisations and government support further contributes critical resources to the local environment. In contrast, Mexico City faces several challenges that negatively impact the start-up business environment. Security concerns pose a notable challenge to the city's attractiveness, and issues such as traffic congestion and air quality may impede start-up operations. At the country level, Mexico ranks poorly in the Corruption Perception Index, adding another layer of complexity to the entrepreneurial environment.

8.3.2.3 Buenos Aires, Argentina

Argentina ranks four cities among the most important hubs globally. However, Buenos Aires has cultivated its own flourishing start-up ecosystem, positioning Argentina as a regional leader. The city is home to several unicorns, including Ualà, Tiendanube and the pioneering e-commerce platform Mercado Libre. Fintech, edtech and social and leisure are the most critical industries in the EE, representing 53 per cent of the total industries operating in the hub (Startupblink, 2023). The government has implemented various initiatives to promote and nurture start-ups. For instance, the Buenos Aires City Government actively participates in an incubator programme known as IncuBAte. Moreover, the city successfully secured a US$200 million World Bank innovation fund, specifically supporting women-led start-ups, reinforcing public-sector backing. Accelerators such as Start-up Argentina and expanded infrastructure like the 12-hectare Buenos Aires Innovation Park contribute to providing targeted support for start-ups.

Buenos Aires not only offers a digital global visa to attract international entrepreneurial talent but also has access to readily available domestic tech talent. Notably, ten universities in Buenos Aires are featured in the QS World University Ranking (Startupblink, 2023). Regarding challenges, Buenos Aires cannot escape the broader economic conditions of Argentina. Economic factors such as poor growth rates, high inflation and significant currency devaluation harm the start-up business environment. Additionally, political instability and the associated regulatory changes further contribute to challenges faced by start-ups operating in Argentina and may drive their rapid i nternationalisation.

8.3.2.4 Bogotá, Colombia

Colombia ranks eleven cities among the most important hubs globally. Colombia's capital, Bogotá, has consolidated its status as a nexus for its start-up environment, with at least 800 venture-funded companies based locally. New initiatives are expanding opportunities for founders, including entrepreneurship centres launched by groups such as the International Chamber of Commerce and the Bogotá Chamber of Commerce. Additionally, planned public-private projects such as the US$300 million Bogotá Science and Technology Innovation District signal a strong future for the ecosystem.

The development of unicorns such as Rappi or Habi not only serve as role models but also help to legitimise the entrepreneurial hub and enhance credibility. Similar to previously described hubs, Bogotá benefits from access to readily available skilled personnel. Further, Colombia offers digital nomad visas to attract foreign entrepreneurs and employees. However, several challenges remain to be addressed, such as security concerns and polarisation regarding the current government's public policy.

8.3.2.5 Lima, Peru

Peru has Lima as the leading local entrepreneurial ecosystem, yet it is a nascent hub. On a positive note, start-ups can innovate and scale up their operations with relatively low competition in the domestic market. However, start-ups do not have entrepreneurs with sufficient experience to scale operations (Startupblink, 2023). This lack of reference prevents the growth of the Peruvian ecosystem. Peru is still lagging behind leading LATAM countries in innovation and growth.

Bridging these gaps will require critical involvement from the public sector to foster a conducive environment for start-ups to thrive and to ensure the development of experienced entrepreneurs capable of scaling operations. Alternatively, weak economic growth, political instability and corruption are country-level characteristics that affect the potential performance of the entrepreneurial hub. In this scenario, it is relevant to analyse the main trends associated with VC funds and their relationship with a unicorn's appearance. VC activities can leverage available resources and promote the rapid growth of start-ups in particular ecosystems.

Vignette 8.2 Rappi

Rappi was founded in Colombia in 2015 by three Colombian entrepreneurs (Simón Borrero, Felipe Villamarin and Sebastian Mejía) as a digital beverage and food delivery service platform. In its initial investment, Rappi joined a prestigious start-up accelerator program called Y Combinator in early 2016, and it was the first LATAM start-up to receive investment from a Silicon Valley accelerator, according to LAVCA (2020). SoftBank became a major stakeholder in Rappi in April 2019, with a US$1 billion investment. This operation valued Rappi at US$3.5 billion. The company became Colombia's first unicorn.

Vignette 8.2 *(cont.)*

The company has since expanded its platform's digital ecosystem into groceries, tech goods, medicine and specialty stores (any item from any store). After 2020, it moved beyond delivery services to travel, entertainment and banking services.

As illustrated in Figure 8.2a, after establishing a core ecosystem for food delivery and its initial user base, the growth strategy involved adding new services that could leverage the existing network of drivers without incurring extra costs to the business. These services included the delivery of medicine, food, alcohol and groceries. Within the same strategy, the offerings have grown to expand the app's service portfolio with RappiMall (e-commerce) and RappiFavor (messaging and on-demand delivery services) in 2020. The expansion beyond delivery came with RappiTravel (online travel agency) and RappiEntertainment (music,

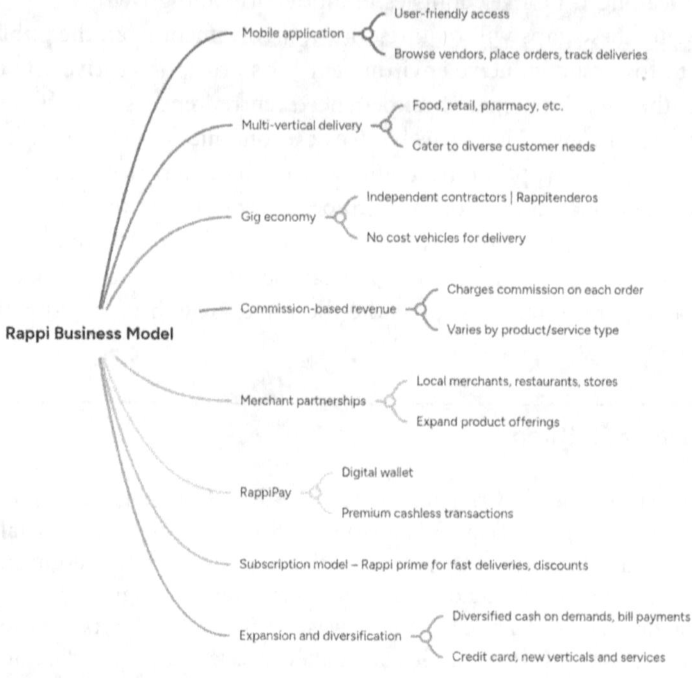

Figure 8.2a Rappi's business model.

Source: Authors' elaboration based on Fieser (2019), Medina and Caparroso (2020), Azevedo (2021) and Rappi (2024).

Vignette 8.2 *(cont.)*

games, events and betting). In 2020, during the peak of the COVID-19 pandemic in LATAM countries, Rappi was also established as the most comprehensive super app in Latin America.

In 2021, Rappi achieved a US$5.2 billion valuation after closing a Series G investment round and raising US$500 million from international investors such as SoftBank, DST Global, Y Combinator, Andreessen Horowitz, Sequoia Capital and others.

The most recent portfolio expansion was in banking services, which has been announced as a primary strategic focus.

Internationalisation is central to the growth strategy of Rappi's ecosystems, as illustrated in Table 8.2b. The company's approach to entering new markets begins with replicating its business model, initially focusing on high-frequency services like restaurant and supermarket deliveries. Later, the company layered new services that could leverage the existing network of drivers and introduce additional features to enrich its portfolio of offerings.

Rappi's primary strategy is to dominate the major cities of Latin America and then strengthen its presence in the region. In 2023 Rappi operated in 250 cities spanning nine countries: Colombia, Argentina, Brazil, Chile, Costa Rica, Ecuador, Mexico, Peru and Uruguay. The company maintains administrative offices in Bogotá, São Paulo and Mexico City. It boasts over 4,000 employees, twenty million active users, 180,000 active partners and 350,000 delivery personnel across

Table 8.2b *Rappi's acquisitions*

Box delivery	Acquired	10 Apr 2023	Food delivery	Brazil/ São Paulo
Avocado	Acquired	1 Jun 2020	Grocery delivery	Brazil/ São Paulo
Payit	Acquired	7 Feb 2019	Mobile payment	Mexico/ Mexico City

Source: Authors' elaboration based on Fieser (2019), Medina and Caparroso (2020), Azevedo (2021) and Rappi (2024).

Vignette 8.2 *(cont.)*

Latin America. To enhance its delivery services, Rappi has strategically acquired three companies in key markets, demonstrating its commitment to expanding and strengthening its ecosystem. begin

Rappi's expansion into financial services has been more cautious due to the complexities of banking regulations and the need for each country's central bank approval to operate as a banking entity. The company introduced its financial services in March 2019, partnering with Visa to launch prepaid cards in Mexico, Colombia and Brazil, along with a QR-code-based digital wallet named RappiPay.

In 2022, Colombia's central bank authorised RappiPay to function as a financial institution within the country in a collaboration between Rappi and the Colombian bank Banco Davivienda. Rappi also provides working capital loans to its restaurant and merchant partners, further integrating financial solutions into its service offerings. In Colombia, RappiPay boasts approximately 750,000 users, has issued over 120,000 credit cards in partnership with Banco Davivienda and aims to offer financial inclusion to the underbanked population, thereby enhancing the digital aspect of its ecosystem. Additionally, Rappi contracted with Mexico's Grupo Financiero Banorte in 2021 to develop a platform dedicated to digital financial services in Mexico, marking another step towards broadening its financial services footprint in Latin America.

Source: Based on Fieser (2019), Medina and Caparroso (2020), Azevedo (2021) and Rappi (2024); authors' analysis.

8.3.3 Evolution of VC Investment in the Region and Unicorn Firm Emergence

National and city-level EEs highlight the importance of resource availability and combination in the local context for start-up firms. However, for a new venture to emerge and become a unicorn, it needs to attract investments generally unavailable locally. Lazarow (2020) highlights the importance of VC firms to unicorns' emergence in emerging economies such as Latin America. Beyond actual investments, VC firms provide strategic guidance, become involved in the governance of firms through representation on the board of directors

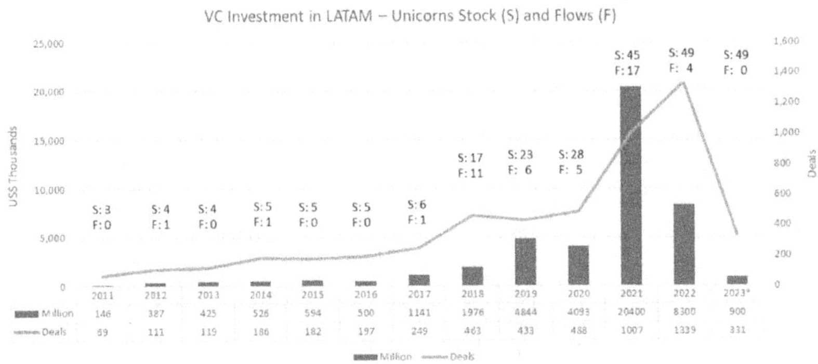

Figure 8.2 VC investment in LATAM: Unicorns stock and flows.
Source: Author generated from LAVCA (2020), CB Insights (2023), Crunchbase (2023) and Kantis et al. (2023).

and share best practices for managing technology and human capital (Mallaby, 2022).

The region has demonstrated considerable dynamism in attracting VC funding to support start-up firms' growth. For instance, investments in start-ups surged by more than twenty-five-fold from 2011 to 2021. Correspondingly, the number of deals during the same period multiplied more than sevenfold. Nevertheless, more recently and in line with global trends in the VC industry, the region has witnessed a diminishing capacity for securing funds for start-ups (refer to Figure 8.2). As of 2023, Latin America is operating at pre-pandemic levels (before the boom), showcasing a substantial contraction in operations both in terms of volume and deals closed. Furthermore, Glasner (2023) mentions that the earlier dynamism observed in the market is anticipated to be notably absent in the short term.

The volume and dynamism of VC investments in the region positively correlate with the emergence and proliferation of unicorns. Since Mercado Libre was the first company to reach unicorn status in Latin America, the evolution of unicorns can be loosely associated[1] with the growth rate of funding activities and the amount of available funds within the region. Notably, an organic growth pattern was discernible

[1] Valuation is not a straightforward measure for start-ups with little or no revenue or profits and uncertain growth potential. It depends on various factors, such as assessment of growth potential, capabilities, product scalability and even the subjective perception of the investor (Silicon Valley Bank, 2025).

between 2011 and 2016. In fact, over this period, unicorns manifested at an approximately biennial frequency.

The relative magnitude of VC investment remained comparatively modest throughout this period, stabilising around the US$500 million mark (per firm). However, the average annual growth rate of VC investments was approximately 40 per cent, while the number of deals undertaken remained consistent from 2014 to 2016. This observation implies a selection effect, where a small number of chosen start-ups are able to secure relatively large amounts per funding round.

In 2017, Latin America attracted more than US$1 billion to support the evolution of start-ups for the first time. From 2017 until 2020, the region consistently set annual records both in terms of volume invested and the number of deals. Simultaneously, the unicorn landscape displayed notable dynamism. Eleven companies attained the US$1 billion valuation in 2018, almost doubling the cumulative total of unicorns created up to that point. This dynamism continued in 2019, with six additional unicorns coming into existence.

For the first time, the growth rate of VC investment in the region witnessed a significant decline in 2020. Despite this challenging environment, five additional firms achieved unicorn status. Relative to 2019, the region experienced a decline in available funds. However, the region still could attract funds to finance start-up activity. An initial signal may suggest the impact of earlier unicorn firms and city-level dynamics on channelling funds to relatively new start-up projects. The region experienced an atypical year in 2021. Venture capital reached a record level of activity, both in terms of volume and secured deals. In parallel, this year marked a record for the number of companies attaining unicorn status in the region. Notably, almost 35 per cent of Latin American unicorns were established in this particular year.

The region has witnessed a negative trend in the growth rate of available funds since 2022. Despite this trend, the funding allocated for supporting start-ups in 2022 exceeded that of most prior years, except for the notably robust funding observed in 2021. Consequently, a total of four new unicorns were announced during 2022. However, the momentum in unicorn creation seems to have subsided, as no new unicorns emerged in 2023. Analysts such as Yanin Alfaro (2023) had indicated that the region may not see the emergence of new unicorns in the near future, suggesting a potential shift or adjustment in the start-up landscape in the short term. Furthermore, there seems to be a connection between the generation of new unicorns and the entrepreneurial dynamics provided by the presence of previous unicorns in specific locations, even in conditions of weak growth. However, it seems that there is a ceiling effect; the capacity to generate new unicorns is contingent on the potential of the ecosystem to attract sufficient funds to generate traction.

Regarding VC investment sectors, fintech emerges as the most dynamic, representing a substantial share of the overall investment landscape. A comprehensive overview indicates that approximately 65 per cent of the total investment is directed toward four pivotal sectors: fintech, e-commerce, health tech and proptech (see Figure 8.3). On the other side, analysing the distribution of unicorns in Latin America reveals a notable concentration in three key sectors – fintech, internet and software and e-commerce – which collectively account for over 70 per cent of the region's unicorn companies (Kantis et al., 2023). This may suggest that Latin American ecosystems may be inclined to favour sectors in which they have experienced success and resource accumulation but potentially divert attention

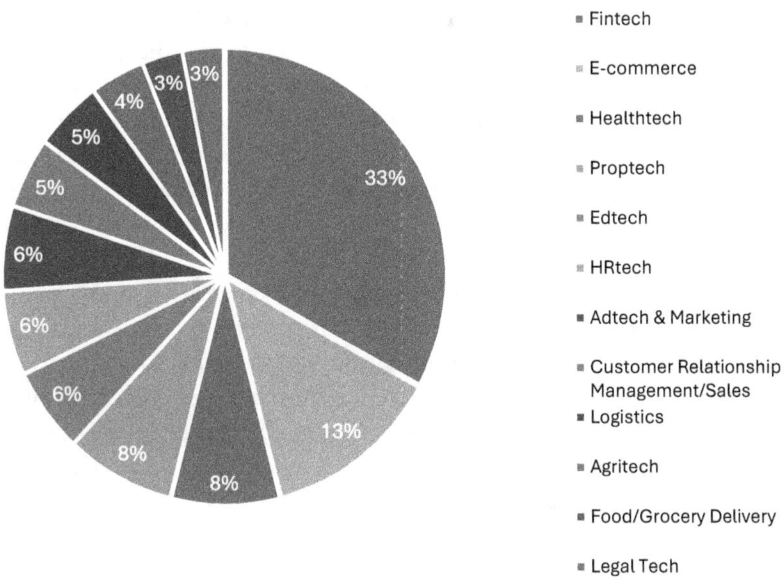

Figure 8.3 VC investment per sector.
Source: Compiled by authors based on LAVCA (2020) and CB Insights (2023).

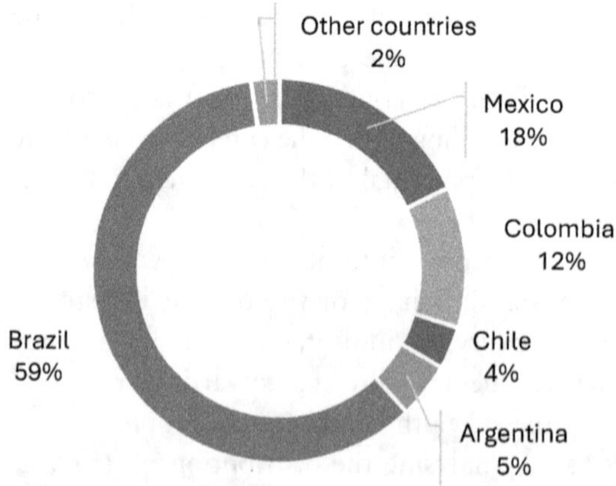

Figure 8.4 VC investment per country 2018–2022.
Source: Compiled by authors based on Dealroom.co (2022).

from emerging sectors with global momentum, such as investments in developing artificial intelligence (AI) capabilities.

Regarding the distribution of VC financing in the region, significant variations cannot be explained by only considering traditional measures such as gross domestic product (GDP), GDP per capita or total population, to name a few. As Figure 8.4 illustrates, there is disproportionate VC activity across selected countries within the region. Brazil dominates the scene, followed by Mexico and Colombia. Among the countries with existing unicorns, Uruguay receives less than 1 per cent of the amount of money received in the region. Similarly, as the 6th largest LATAM economy, Peru attracts less than 1 per cent of the total VC investment in the region.

Our findings indicate that the emergence of unicorns is more closely related to output conditions than to input conditions. However, these favourable conditions are not uniformly distributed across countries, leading to a concentration of resources and capabilities in certain cities. Therefore, we further our analysis by examining the characteristics at the city level. We focus on São Paulo, Buenos Aires, Mexico City and Bogotá, as these cities showcase the most developed EEs among the countries studied. Despite their development, firms within these ecosystems face significant challenges. Thus, in the following sections, we also explore how entrepreneurs respond to these challenges and navigate the limitations they encounter.

Vignette 3 Crehana

Crehana was created in 2015, initially as an edtech dedicated to delivering non-formal education to students from diverse academic, social and economic backgrounds in Latin America. Using a software-as-a-service (Saas) model (as illustrated in Figure 8.3a), the company offered high-quality virtual courses and programmes in Spanish at low cost. The Peruvian start-up has become one of the biggest online learning platforms in the region. Crehana has raised the largest B-Series funding for an edtech in Latin America. By 2023 the company had raised US$95 million in funding.

The company was founded by Diego Olcese and Rodolfo Dañino who continue playing pivotal roles in the top managerial team, with Olcese serving as the chief executive officer and Dañino as the chief operating officer. Following a visit to Silicon Valley in 2013, Olcese made the strategic decision to transition from a Chilean retail company to initiate a new venture, which he named Flikn. He successfully persuaded Dañino to create this edtech company, which centred on photography, music, cuisine and business. Flikn served as the precursor to Crehana.

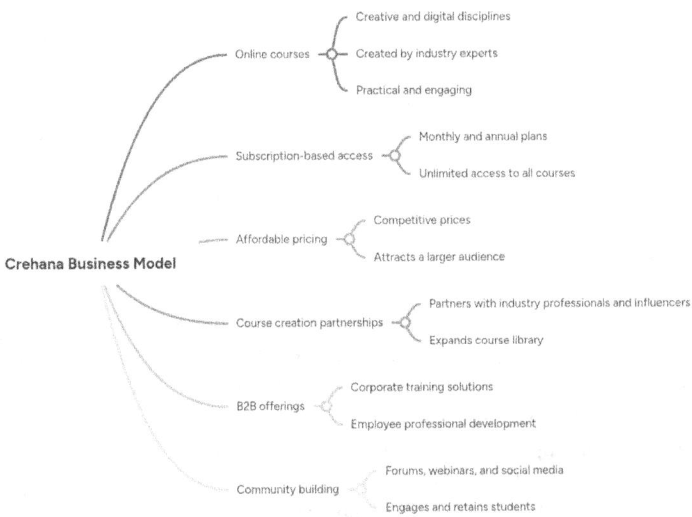

Figure 8.3a Crehana's business model.

Source: Authors' own work based on Atkins (2019), Forbes (2019), Businesswire (2021a), LAVCA (2021), Crehana (2024) and Crunchbase (2024a).

Vignette 3 *(cont.)*

Having garnered valuable insights from their previous venture, the founders established Crehana to cultivate and enhance creative, design and digital competencies among students in the region. In a period when the entire Peruvian ecosystem's funding scarcely exceeded US$5.5 million and with nearly 70 per cent comprised of domestic funds, Olcese and Dañino secured grants from Wayra Peru (Telefonica Group, Spain) in 2014 and from Start-up Peru (Peruvian government) in 2015. Their previous experience with Flikn and their initial traction provided a strong signal for obtaining those grants and support from renowned entities.

To ensure the quality of its operations, Crehana controls nearly the entire process of course creation, commercialisation and consumption. The company has a portfolio comprising over 400 experts responsible for the creation of 700 courses available on the platform. The content created can be organised into three business lines. The first is the online platform that represents a B2C (business to consumer) business model, and the second is Crehana for business, which customises courses to address the specific needs of particular companies. The final line involves the collaborative creation of digital certificates with partner universities (microdegrees).

Most of the funding received by 2020 was allocated towards product development, market penetration and international expansion (Table 8.3b). Indeed, Crehana expanded its presence into the Mexican and Colombian markets in 2019. Nevertheless, both its business model and value proposition have had a significant evolution over time. Initially concentrating on the end user, the start-up is now shifting its focus toward the B2B (business to business) sector. Simultaneously, Crehana's business model has transitioned from being purely edtech to becoming an HRtech company. This transformation marks a substantial shift in its revenue streams.

The company no longer only provides customised courses to companies but now positions itself as its strategic partner, assisting firms in managing and developing their talent. To do so, the company has acquired Acsendo (a Colombian firm specialising in talent management) and Wormhole (an Argentinean start-up specialising in learning management).

As of 2023, the B2B segment constitutes approximately 85 per cent of its revenue, reflecting an impressive growth rate of 400 per cent compared to 2022. The company is firmly committed to this new strategic direction, anticipating a strong growth rate and aiming to achieve financial profitability in the first quarter of 2024.

Vignette 3 *(cont.)*

Table 8.3b *Rounds of funding and recent acquisitions*

Leading investor	Amount	Investment type	Date
Crehana	Undisclosed	Acquisition of Wormhole	20 Jul 2022
Crehana	Undisclosed	Acquisition of Acsendo	3 Apr 2022
Alive Ventures	US$70 M	Series B	5 Aug 2021
Bossanova Investimentos	US$17.5 M	Series A	17 Dec 2020
International Finance Corporation	Undisclosed	Series A	30 Jun 2020
Acumen LatAm Impact Ventures	Undisclosed	Series A	1 May 2020
Acumen LatAm Impact Ventures	US$4.5 M	Series A	31 Jan 2019
Clearly Social Angel	US$900 M	Seed	23 Aug 2017
Clearly Social Angel	US$750 M	Seed	31Oct 2016
Emerge Education	US$96 M	Seed	10 Jan 2016
Start-up Peru	US$40 M	Grant	1 Mar 2015
Wayra	US$50 M	Grant	4 Sep 2014

Source: Compiled by authors based on Atkins (2019), Forbes (2019), Businesswire (2021a), LAVCA (2021), Crehana (2024) and Crunchbase (2024a).

8.4 Firm Strategies in Digital Ecosystems

Whereas the institutional characteristics and resource endowments of local entrepreneurial ecosystems enable and constrain the birth and initial growth of technology-based start-ups, founders' and managers' agency towards further development of start-ups plays an essential role in unicorn emergence. The digital technologies underlying these start-ups' business models allow them to rapidly transcend the local ecosystem, serving clients, engaging in partnerships, developing value chains or receiving funding from investors elsewhere. Drawing on examples from each of the five countries analysed, presented in separate vignettes, we identify some particularities that shape LATAM unicorns' emergence from their local entrepreneurial ecosystem and highlight the active role of founders and managers in developing their firms' own digital ecosystem.

8.4.1 Founders' and Managers' Human and Social Capital

Founders and CEOs play central roles in start-ups' early and scaling phases. Firm leaders' human and social capital is important to unicorn emergence in Latin America, given that alternative sources of such inputs are less readily available. Notwithstanding the persistence of stereotypes that portray founders of unicorn firms as young individuals who come up with a revolutionary idea, research on founders of successful start-ups suggests they are mid-aged and have significant work experience (Azoulay et al., 2020; Lazarow, 2020). This is especially true in the context of Latin America. Many founders were in their 30s or early 40s when they started their company. Additionally, many completed at least a part of their education in more developed markets, particularly in the United States, and frequently had prior work experience in finance, management consulting or established technology firms.

The company-specific vignettes illustrate this founder profile. Ualá's founder Pierpaolo Barbieri studied in the United States and in the United Kingdom and worked for Goldman Sachs, Soros Fund Management and Bridgewater Associates. Kavak founder Carlos García Ottati completed an MBA in the United Kingdom and worked at Amazon and McKinsey. Patrick Sigrist, co-founder and former CEO at iFood, obtained a master's degree and completed specialisation programmes in the United States and worked at several companies before launching iFood. Rappi co-founder and CEO Simón Borrero pursued an MBA in Europe and completed executive education in the United States before starting multiple companies. Crehana co-founder and CEO Diego Olcese may represent an exception, although he was an exchange student in Europe and worked briefly at a corporation before creating his own company.

International education and meaningful work experience prior to starting a company allow for a broader base of human and social capital. Overcoming the challenges of starting a company, especially in the volatile context of Latin America, requires re-imagining strategies and postponing and accelerating plans according to the market's conditions. Research on career development suggests that international experience increases human capital (Dragoni et al., 2014; Le & Kroll, 2017), such as resilience, flexibility and resourcefulness. Additionally, scaling a start-up requires convincing investors, employees, alliance partners and other stakeholders to commit to the company. Early work on the 'strength of weak ties' (Granovetter, 1973; Uzzi, 1999) suggests that wider social networks allow for increased access to information and resources that firms may need to adapt to changing circumstances.

8.4.2 'Tropicalisation' of Business Models

The role of technology as an enabler of new business models, along with increased information exchange via consultancies, investment banks and business schools, explains the emergence of similar unicorns in different regions. Research on the growth of platform companies suggests that firms that engage in active business model imitation and simultaneous strategic development are more likely to outperform their competitors (Zhao et al., 2020). This also applies to the emergence of unicorns in Latin America and emphasises the importance of strategic agency on behalf of founders and managers.

The firms featured in the vignettes represent the dynamics of imitation and adaptation of business models. Kavak's business model had previously been developed in the United States by companies such as CarMax and Carvana. The particularities of LATAM countries' used vehicle markets required Kavak to adapt multiple features of the business model, especially regarding financing and the reconditioning of cars. Similarly, Pizza Hut's launch of Pizzanet in 1994 sparked the development of platform companies that take orders and handle food delivery, such as World Wide Waiter, DoorDash and GrubHub. Rappi and iFood emulated this business model and adapted it to the challenges of LATAM cities, such as informality in the restaurant sector and street criminality affecting riders.

Most unicorns in Latin America started with business models that resemble those of firms in other regions. However, the particularities of local markets represent a strong driver for the 'tropicalisation' of these business models and require strategic agency from founders and managers. The capability for combining business model imitation and innovation speeds up the process of unicorn emergence as firms learn from the experiences of similar firms in other geographies. At the same time, firms' unique responses to challenges specific to the markets in which they operate allow for competitive advantages based on differentiation.

8.4.3 Emphasis on Platform Development

Some LATAM unicorns have emerged due to their development of highly specific capabilities. Examples include cybersecurity and identity authentication service offerings from companies such as Incode, Unico or Auth0[2], or NotCo's use of AI to develop plant-based foods. However, investments in such specific assets involve risk and are costly, especially in contexts characterised by underdeveloped capital markets and macroeconomic volatility, such as Latin America. Boermans and Roelfsema (2013) suggest that firms in emerging economies are more likely to leverage external resources, an approach epitomised by platform companies. This type of firm manages multi-sided markets in which producers of complementary goods on one side compete to sell to users on the other side (Boudreau & Jeppesen, 2015). Not surprisingly, many LATAM unicorn companies are platform companies.

Leveraging external resources comes with two main limitations. Firstly, there is the risk that these resources may not be available when needed, prompting companies to build their own solutions. For instance, Kavak's initiative to establish used car inspection and repair centres across major LATAM cities illustrates this point well. Despite the widespread availability of auto repair shops, it was not possible for Kavak to seamlessly integrate these existing facilities into its platform.

A second challenge refers to the lost opportunities to appropriate the value created within transactions on the platform. External actors whose resources are leveraged through the platform may look for opportunities to divert. For example, food distribution platforms like iFood or Rappi charge restaurants a fee. Restaurant owners may look for ways to encourage customers to order from them directly to avoid such fees. Similarly, financial transactions that take place on platforms may benefit established players such as banks or credit card companies.

[2] Acquired by US-based OKTA in 2021.

Since Ualá's launch, the growth of its platform has allowed the company to handle more transactions internally, decreasing its reliance on payments to third parties.

In analysing unicorns from emerging markets, Lazarow (2020) argues that the speed at which these firms scale is typically slower than those from Silicon Valley. Among the main challenges, he identified the need to develop resources to sustain the implementation of a business strategy. For example, Mercado Libre's development of logistics capabilities was necessary for increasing control of its operations and improving the customer experience. More recently founded LATAM platform companies, such as the firms in our vignettes, replicate this platform development strategy. However, they benefit from a wider offer of complementor firms that provide external resources. This allows newer platform firms to stay focused on developing their digital ecosystem and internal resources they can deploy in multiple markets. Investments in physical resources tend to be limited to those that are critical to success or have a high return on investment.

8.4.4 International Scaling

LATAM unicorn emergence is conditioned by the size of each national economy. This characteristic drives founders and managers to consider internationalisation strategies at an earlier stage compared to Silicon Valley counterparts. Instead of consolidating business models and operating strategies in a single context, internationalisation is typically intertwined with LATAM unicorns' scaling trajectories. This duality is especially challenging for platform companies that need to develop 'a new network of users in [each] foreign country,' because a platform 'only provides value for users if the number of users in a particular market … reaches a critical mass' (Brouthers et al., 2016: 515).

The firms we highlight in the vignettes experience the challenge of scaling through internationalisation. In the case of Crehana, the inter nationalisation of marketing efforts and service delivery mirrored the international profile of its target customers. Companies that invest in virtual training and development frequently do so to prepare geographically distributed teams. In contrast, iFood experienced difficulties in its internationalisation efforts. Having reached an 80 per cent market share in Brazil, it pursued growth opportunities in LATAM's larger markets. However, replicating the network effects it enjoyed in its home market turned out to be challenging. While successful in Mexico, the company was unable to scale in Argentina and Colombia. It merged its Argentine operations with PedidosYa in August 2018 and its Colombian operations with Domicilios.com in March 2021. Ualá's growth strategy combined internationalisation with expanding its service offering, merger and acquisition (M&A) activity and a fast-paced sequence of funding rounds. While conditioned by countries' central bank regulation of fintech activity, it has expanded from Argentina into Mexico and Colombia.

The emphasis on digital operations favours the internationalisation of Latin American unicorns as it allows for replicating business models in foreign markets at a low cost. Additionally, funding provided by international venture capital firms frequently involves expectations or active guidance towards internationalisation. While traditional liabilities of foreignness apply, such as dealing with local regulation or understanding customer preferences, it is arguably competitors that represent the main obstacle to the development of international operations. The firms we illustrate could replicate their digitalised business model in multiple countries and had funding that allowed them to pursue international growth opportunities. However, their direct competitors were in a similar situation. iFood's direct competition with Rappi or Uber Eats or Ualá's competition with fintech companies such as Brazilian Nubank or Argentina's MercadoPago illustrate how market-seeking internationalisa tion may be hampered by similar companies pursuing the same goal.

8.4.5 Reconfiguration Strategies

A final characteristic of LATAM unicorn emergence refers to the active role of founders and managers in the strategic reconfiguration of their companies' digital ecosystems. Scholars refer to this process as resource orchestration, which is defined as the process of structuring, bundling and leveraging firm resources to create sustained value (Sirmon et al., 2010). Departing from ideas for a core business model and a minimum viable product, unicorns develop and acquire the necessary technology, create brands and incorporate human capital. As mentioned in section 8.4.4, the emergence of the LATAM unicorn generally involves early internationalisation. Iterations from prototype to platform typically involve trials in different markets, creating a portfolio of lines of business in constant flux.

The companies featured in our vignettes provide eloquent examples of managerial agency in reconfiguring activities. Having entered the Colombian and Peruvian markets by mid-2022, Kavak announced its withdrawal from these countries in January 2024. The company's management stated that global and local macroeconomic prospects were unfavourable to the company's growth strategy. Similarly, following a trajectory of M&A-driven growth, Ualà announced it needed to lay off employees in redundant positions. Rappi's attempt to diversify into financial services in Peru based on an alliance with Interbank was cancelled after only two years of operations. In contrast, it increasingly leverages information on its user base to offer specific services, including travel and targeted publicity.

Active resource orchestration is an essential characteristic of LATAM's unicorns. Developing a core platform that sustains the business model allows for adding services and products that can be replicated in multiple markets at a low cost, a strategy exemplified by the Mexican used-car platform Kavak (Figure 8.4a and Table 8.4b). To the extent that these offerings take off (or do not), founders and managers will quickly decide whether to continue a particular line of business in a market.

Vignette 8.4 Kavak

Founded in 2016, Kavak quickly became a pivotal force in the used car market. It achieved unicorn status within four years, marking it as Mexico's first, with a valuation exceeding US$1 billion in October 2020. This impressive trajectory continued, with its valuation reaching US$4 billion by January 2021, then US$8.7 billion by September 2021. These valuations established Kavak as the second most valuable unicorn in Latin America.

At its core, Kavak operates a user-centric online marketplace for used cars, streamlining sales and purchase processes. The company enhances user confidence by providing personalised financing options and warranty systems, thus ensuring secure and comfortable transactions for both sellers and buyers. By leveraging proprietary algorithms and comprehensive industry data, Kavak ensures transparent pricing and mitigates fraud risk.

Vignette 8.4 *(cont.)*

Kavak's strategic growth plan hinges on both regional and international expansion. In 2020, the company entered various markets through acquisitions. Kavak's global footprint further extends to Peru, Chile, the UAE and Oman.

Technology is the cornerstone of Kavak's business model (see Figure 8.4a). The company employs machine learning across several operations, including credit scoring, price determination and process automation, significantly enhancing its efficiency. For instance, Kavak's algorithms can rapidly analyse various aspects of cars, such as usage and mileage, to reduce vehicle inspection times by over 70 per cent. Integrating AWS (Amazon Web Services) serverless services, such as AWS Glue and AWS Lambda, has been vital for swiftly implementing these machine learning models into production.

Beyond its primary platform, Kavak has broadened its offerings to include financial services through Kavak Capital. This division leverages AI and data algorithms to provide tailored financing. This, in turn, has contributed to the formalisation of the Mexican used car market. This initiative helps customers finance one of their most significant assets: their vehicles.

Kavak's ascent from a nascent start-up to a market leader in the used car industry proves the transformative power of digital innovation and the strategic expansion of ecosystems (see Table 8.4b).

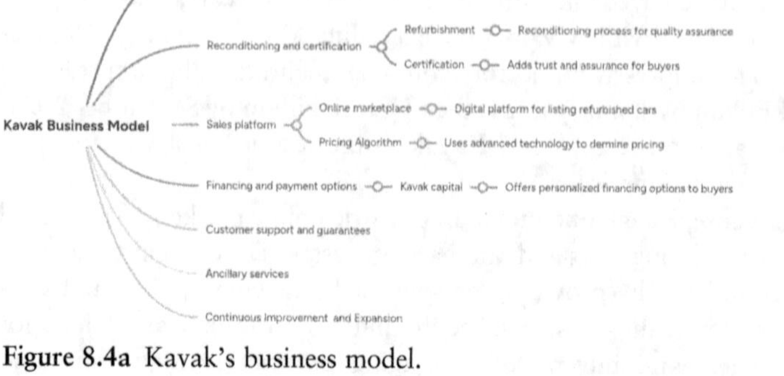

Figure 8.4a Kavak's business model.

Source: Authors' elaboration based on Businesswire (2021b), Enríquez (2021), Leyva (2022), Craft.co (2023), Kavak (2023) and PitchBook (2023).

Vignette 8.4 *(cont.)*

Table 8.4b *Kavak's ecosystem expansion through acquisitions*

Invested companies	Investment type	Deal date	Industry invested company	Country of the invested company
Garaj Sepeti	Acquired	2 Dec 2021	B2B and B2C marketplaces	Turkey
Checkars	Acquired	26 Aug 2020	Used car e-commerce	Argentina
Carzaty	Acquired	10 Dec 2022	Car e-commerce/ finance	Oman
Credijusto	Acquired	15 Nov 2021	Fintech	Mexico
OPI Analytics	Acquired	4 Dec 2023	Data analytics	Mexico

Source: Compiled by authors based on Businesswire (2021b), Enríquez (2021), Leyva (2022), Craft.co (2023), Kavak (2023) and PitchBook (2023).

8.5 Discussion

This chapter analyses the evolution of EEs and common features of unicorns in Latin America. Notwithstanding the emergence of unicorns such as Mercado Libre and Despegar during the first decade of the 2000s, the decade between 2014 and 2024 has witnessed an increased number of firms reaching unicorn status in the region with exponential growth.

Unicorn emergence in Latin America is concentrated in only a few large cities. Several interrelated factors enabled the emergence of thriving entrepreneurial hubs in cities like São Paulo, Buenos Aires, Mexico City and Bogotá. In this context, we have argued that an interplay between national and especially local entrepreneurial and digital ecosystems provides room for entrepreneurial agency to respond to environmental constraints. While EEs are suitable to respond to the needs of start-ups at early stages, start-ups need to overcome existing institutional limitations to reach minimum efficient scale in their operations and eventually gain unicorn status.

At the country level, input conditions commonly associated with innovation and start-up activity are less related to the emergence of unicorns in the region than to output dimensions. For instance, Peru is the only country that has not developed a unicorn in the sample despite outperforming other countries in most input conditions included in the GII. It seems that, while important, input dimensions are more associated with long-term outcomes that are not necessarily easily absorbed by actors in domestic markets. On the contrary, entrepreneurs and other agents can leverage outcome conditions (like patent and trademark generation) in the marketplace. Peru consistently lags in most output dimensions in the GII. Firstly, economic and political reforms established better foundations for start-ups and VC investment. Secondly, proliferating accelerators and government start-up programmes boosted deal flows. Thirdly, enhanced fundraising capabilities allowed VC firms to ramp up spending. VC involvement is relevant because they provide financial support to start-ups at different stages but also because of their role in providing mentoring and transferring best practices associated with the entrepreneurial scene (incubators, accelerators, angel investors, among others). Hence, the presence of international VC helps to dynamise entrepreneurial hubs and generate a new breed of scalable start-ups with the potential to become unicorns.

However, as of the mid-2020s, the environment has shifted, with declining global VC appetite presenting headwinds. Much capital now flows into specialised sectors, such as AI and machine learning, which have limited presence in LATAM hubs. This could constrain the emergence of the high-potential start-ups required to drive ongoing momentum.

The LATAM context presents start-up firms with many challenges. Navigating these challenges requires emerging unicorns to simultaneously manage multiple growth aspects, including adapting business models, securing funding, leveraging technology, internationalisation, lack of regulation and acquiring human capital. In this sense, the role of founders and managers of unicorns is fundamental for cultivating the EE. Generally, this involves local activities such as mentoring other entrepreneurs. However, 'giving back' behaviour has become more regional, as founders and managers collaborate with organisations such as Endeavor or initiate their own VC fund.

Strategic moves by pioneers like iFood and Kavak also accelerated ecosystems' growth. Leveraging cloud infrastructure and digital assets, these unicorns expanded across the region and diversified into adjacent spaces. For example, Argentina's early appearance of unicorns in the region could provide not only a role model or signal but also dynamise the local environment with the active involvement of successful entrepreneurs. Figure 8.5a illustrates an example from Argentina. In contrast, Peru (and Lima) is a nascent hub with few reference models to provide guidance and help in scaling new businesses created in the ecosystem.

Is there more to come? Whereas many cities have developed a vibrant start-up scene and aspirant founders can take advantage of the experiences of established unicorns, several trends warrant a less optimistic view. Firstly, the higher cost of capital in global markets constrains available funding. 'Learning on the go' approaches are no longer feasible, requiring founders to pitch well-developed ideas and functioning minimum viable products (MVPs). Secondly, existing unicorns' ongoing expansion into new markets limits opportunities for new unicorn emergence. The 'winner-takes-all' logic of many markets, along with the development of super-apps intending to monopolise interactions with end users, makes it more challenging for new firms to develop a competitive position. Thirdly, the importance of firm-level strategic characteristics to unicorn emergence in Latin America implies a risk of 'de-location'. Founders and managers may leverage information and communication technology to coordinate local operations virtually while residing physically in other places. LATAM start-up firms increasingly relocate to the United States or Spain, seeking proximity to clients, stability in regulation and taxation and access to specialised human capital pools.

Navigating these contradictory forces requires coordinated efforts from entrepreneurs and policymakers. Governments should promote targeted incubation in promising tech areas while incentivising global VC engagement. Entrepreneurs must creatively address updated pain points with digital solutions and strategically expand their networks globally.

If ecosystems can adapt on both fronts, the foundation exists for LATAM's hubs to move to the next level. Failure to adjust, however, risks losing hard-won gains. It is therefore imperative to build local resilience and secure the future of technology entrepreneurship across the region.

Vignette 8.5 Ualà

Ualà is an Argentine fintech company in financial services in Latin America. The core of Ualà's operational model is the combination of an app and an international Mastercard debit card that can be used free of issuance, renewal, maintenance and closing costs. Through the app, Ualà's customers have convenient and cheap access to a range of financial services that would typically involve several steps, different service providers and high transaction fees. Examples include making purchases on any website served by Mastercard, transferring money, paying bills and topping up mobile phones or transportation cards. Additionally, the app allows customers to track expenses, apply for loans and make investments. In 2023, the company had over five million users in Argentina, Colombia and Mexico.

Officially founded in October 2017 by Pierpaolo Barbieri, the company's story began in 2015.

> …with a couple of team members, we began to think about how to revolutionise the Argentine financial system. We were ashamed that more than 50 percent of the country had never had access to the formal financial system and wanted to change that …. We worked for more than a year and a half, almost 2 years, without being able to launch the product because we had to build the entire structure that would allow us to do what we wanted to do. (Ualà, 2025: 22)

Ualà launched its app in 2017. The underlying logic of the business model was to use digitalisation to develop a credit history, even for individuals not included in the traditional financial system (see Figure 8.5a). A more accurate credit rating would allow the company to offer products, services and financial instruments according to a customer's risk profile. In less than four months following its launch, the app had been downloaded more than 200,000 times and 65,000 cards were issued. In September 2020, the company expanded into Mexico and began operations in Colombia in January 2022.

As a platform company, Ualà developed its merchant-focused vertical, Ualà Bis. It offers a range of products and services based on QR, mobile point of sale solutions, payment links or integration with online stores. Likewise, following the acquisitions of online banks Wilobank in Argentina and ABC Capital in Mexico in 2021, and Argentinian credit company Ceibo Creditos in 2022, it branched out into offering consumer loans and instalment plans. The 2022 acquisition of Empretienda, an e-commerce platform that allows business owners to

Vignette 8.5 *(cont.)*

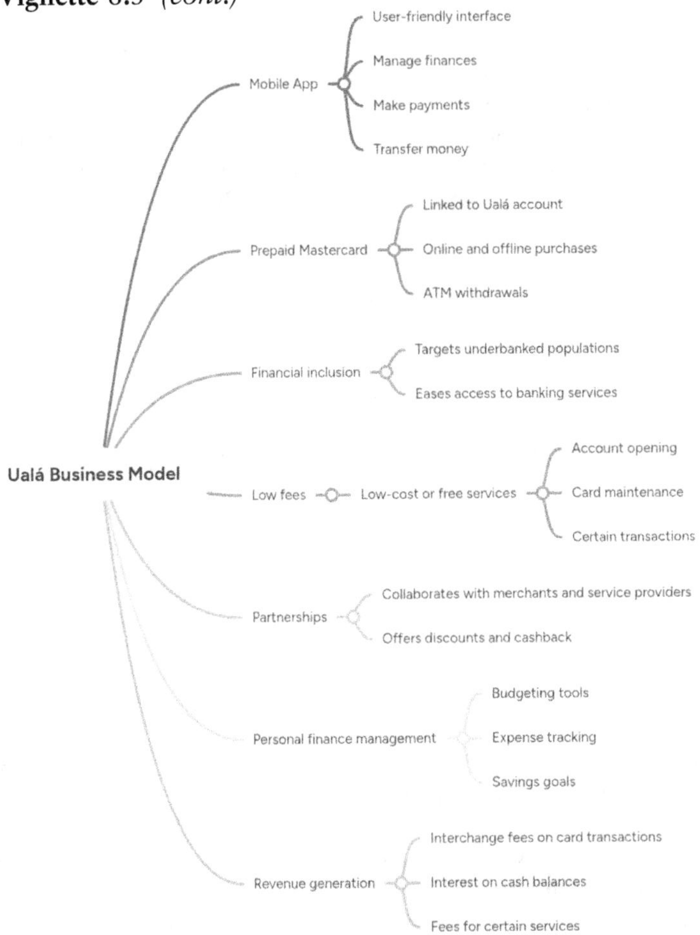

Figure 8.5a Ualà's business model.
Source: Authors' elaboration based on Misculín (2022), Noguez (2023), Crunchbase (2024b) and Ualá (2024).

create and manage their own virtual store, enhanced the B2B service offering. Finally, through Ualintec and Uanex, its trades and exchange companies, the company offers its customers the possibility to invest in mutual funds and buy stocks, foreign currencies and cryptocurrency.

Ualà went through several funding rounds before it became a unicorn company, with a valuation of US$2.45 billion in 2021. In January

Vignette 8.5 *(cont.)*

2018 Ualà had its series A round, intended to hire employees and consolidate the business model, backed by Soros Fund Management LLC, Jefferies LLC, Point72 Ventures, Greyhound Capital and investor Kevin Ryan for the amount of US$10 million. Only months later, the series B round yielded US$34 million granted by Goldman Sachs Asset Management, Ribbit Capital and Monashees. In April of 2019 the company received an investment from Tencent for an undisclosed amount and a US$150 million series C investment from the SoftBank Latin America Fund, Endeavor Catalyst and other investors. The Series D investment round, organised in August 2021, was led by SoftBank Latin America Fund and Tencent. The company received US$350 million to enhance its operations and push its growth efforts in Argentina and Mexico.

Source: Authors' work based on Misculín (2022), Noguez (2023), Crunchbase (2024b) and Ualà (2024).

References

Acs, Z. J., Stam, E., Audretsch, D. B., and O'Connor, A. (2017). The lineages of the entrepreneurial ecosystem approach. *Small Business Economics 49*(1), 1–10.

Alfaro, Y. (2023). *Goodbye unicorns: See you until mid-2024*. Contxto. contxto.com/en/venture-capital/goodbye-unicorns-see-you-until-mid-2024/

Amorós, J. E., Leiva, J. C., Bonomo, A., and Sosa Varela, J. C. (2021). Guest editorial: The entrepreneurship challenges in Latin America. *European Business Review 33*(6), 837–848.

Andonova, V., Nikolova, M. S., and Dimitrov, D. (2019). *Entrepreneurial Ecosystems in UnexpectedPplaces*. Springer. doi.org/10.1007/978-3-319-98219-9

Atkins, J. (2019). *Crehana raises US$4.5 million to accelerate growth in Latin America*. Contxto.

AWS. (2018). *Estudo de caso da AWS: iFood*. aws.amazon.com/pt/solutions/case-studies/IFood61/

Azevedo, M. A. (2021). *Colombian on-demand delivery startup Rappi raises 'over' $500M at a $5.25B valuation*. Tech Crunch. tinyurl.com/2bpm46yw

Azoulay, P., Jones, B. F., Kim, J. D., and Miranda, J. (2020). Age and high-growth entrepreneurship. *AER: Insights* 2(1), 65–82. doi.org/10.1257/aeri.20180582

Banalieva, E. R., and Dhanaraj, C. (2019). Internalization theory for the digital economy. *Journal of International Business Studies* *50*(8), 1372–1387.

Boermans, M. A., and Roelfsema, H. (2013). The effects of managerial capabilities on export, FDI and innovation: Evidence from Indian firms. *Asian Business and Management* *12*(4), 387–408.

Bohnsack, R., Rennings, M., Block, C., and Bröring, S. (2024). Profiting from innovation when digital business ecosystems emerge: A control point perspective. *Research Policy* *53*(3), 104961. doi.org/10.1016/J.RESPOL.2024.104961

Boudreau, K. J., and Jeppesen, L. B. (2015). Unpaid crowd complementors: The platform network effect mirage. *Strategic Management Journal* *36*(12), 1761–1777. doi.org/10.1002/smj.2324

Brouthers, K. D., Geisser, K. D., and Rothlauf, F. (2016). Explaining the internationalization of ibusiness firms. *Journal of International Business Studies* *47*(5), 513–534.

Brown, R., and Mason, C. (2017). Looking inside the spiky bits: a critical review and conceptualisation of entrepreneurial ecosystems. *Small Business Economics* *49*(1), 11–30.

Buitrago R., R. E., and Barbosa Camargo, M. I. (2021). Institutions, institutional quality, and international competitiveness: Review and examination of future research directions. *Journal of Business Research* *128*(May 2021), 423–435.

Buitrago R., R. E., Torralba Barreto, D. R., and Reyes, G. E. (2023). Are competitiveness rankings and institutional measures helping emerging economies to improve? *Competitiveness Review: An International Business Journal* *33*(5), 861–888. doi.org/10.1108/CR-04-2021-0064

Businesswire. (2021a). *Crehana raises largest series B for Edtech in Latin America*. Businesswire.

Businesswire. (2021b). *Kavak boosts its global expansion by investing US$500 million in Brazil*. Businesswire. tinyurl.com/4bsdvmyt

Cahen, F., and Borini, F. M. (2020). International digital competence. *Journal of International Management* *26*(1), 100691. doi.org/10.1016/J.INTMAN.2019.100691

Cahen, F., Borini, F. M., and Dhanaraj, C. (2022). Measuring digital globalization competence. *Academy of Management Proceedings* *1*, 14667.

Cavallo, A., Ghezzi, A., and Balocco, R. (2019). Entrepreneurial ecosystem research: present debates and future directions. *International Entrepreneurship and Management Journal* *15*(4), 1291–1321.

CB Insights. (2023). *State of venture global – Q3 2022.*

(2025). *The complete list of unicorn companies.* www.cbinsights.com/research-unicorn-companies

Craft.co. (2023). *KAVAK company profile – Office locations, competitors, revenue, financials, employees, key people, subsidiaries.* craft.co/kavak

Crehana. (2024). *Así nació Crehana.*

Crunchbase. (2023). *Latin American startup funding fell again in 2023.* news.crunchbase.com/venture/latin-america-startup-funding-eoy-2023/

(2024a). *Crehana.*

(2024b). *Uala.*

Cuervo-Cazurra, A., and Dau, L. A. (2009). Structural reform and firm exports. *Management International Review 49*(4), 479–507.

Daniel, L., Medlin, C. J., O'Connor, A., Statsenko, L., Vnuk, R., and Hancock, G. (2018). Deconstructing the entrepreneurial ecosystem concept. *International Studies in Entrepreneurship 38*, 23–44. doi.org/10.1007/978-3-319-63531-6_2

Dealroom.co. (2022). *Latin America – Overview & top startups.* dealroom.co/guides/latin-america

Dragoni, L., Oh, I. S., Tesluk, P. E., Moore, O. A., VanKatwyk, P., and Hazucha, J. (2014). Developing leaders' strategic thinking through global work experience: The moderating role of cultural distance. *Journal of Applied Psychology 99*(5), 867–882. doi.org/10.1037/A0036628

Edquist, C. (Ed.). (1997). *Systems of Innovation: Technologies,Iinstitutions and Organizations* (1st ed.). Routledge.

Enríquez, A. (2021). *Kavak: Story of a US$4 billion company.* Mexico Business News. mexicobusiness.news/automotive/news/kavak-story-us4-billion-company#

Fieser, E. (2019). *Rappi is the super app that's transforming Latin America.* Bloomberg. www.bloomberg.com/news/articles/2019-12-04/rappi-is-the-super-app-that-s-transforming-latin-america

Forbes. (2019). *Crehana, la plataforma que revoluciona a la educación digital.* Forbes Centroamerica.

Glasner, J. (2023). *Latin America's startup funding continued to fall sharply in first half of 2023.* Crunchbase News.

Granovetter, M. S. (1973). The strength of weak ties. *American Journal of Sociology, 78*(6), 1360–1380.

iFood. (2023). *Foodtech at iFood.* carreiras.ifood.com.br/en/

Jaffe, A. B., Trajtenberg, M., and Henderson, R. (1993). Geographic localization of knowledge spillovers as evidenced by patent citations. *The Quarterly Journal of Economics 108*(3), 577–598. doi.org/10.2307/2118401

Kantis, H., Caicedo, V., and Ibarra García, S. (2023). *Unicornios y Ecosistemas en América Latina: ¿Del Boom al Final de Fiesta?* Prodem, Working Paper. tinyurl.com/45s7wf7j

Kavak. (2023). *KAVAK – Changing the car industry around the world.* www.kavak.com/

Latitude. (2023). *LatAm tech report 2023.* www.latitud.com/latam-tech-report-2023

LAVCA. (2020). *LAVCA's Annual review of tech investment in Latin America. General Atlantic leads USD70m series B for Edtech Crehana.* www.lavca.org/general-atlantic-leads-usd70m-series-b-for-edtech-crehana/

Lazarow, A. (2020). Out-innovate: How global entrepreneurs – from Delhi to Detroit – are rewriting the rules of Silicon Valley. *Harvard Business Review Press.*

Le, S., and Kroll, M. (2017). CEO international experience: Effects on strategic change and firm performance. *Journal of International Business Studies 48*(5), 573–595.

Leyva, P. (2022). *Kavak: Leveraging data to become the most valuable startup in Latin America – Digital innovation and transformation.* Harvard MBA Students Perspectives. tinyurl.com/3j57k7wm

Malecki, E. J. (2018). Entrepreneurship and entrepreneurial ecosystems. *Geography Compass 12*(3), 1–21. doi.org/10.1111/GEC3.12359

Mallaby, S. (2022). *The Power Law: Venture Capital and the Making of the New Future.* Penguin Press.

Martins, I., Romaní, G., and Atienza, M. (2021). An institutional approach to the development of business angel networks in Latin American emerging countries. *European Business Review 33*(6), 918–941.

Medina, A., and Caparroso, J. (2020). *Rappi vive un buen 2020: Sus planes de crecimiento se aceleraron con la pandemia.* Forbes. tinyurl.com/3xtcacuz

Misculín, N. (2022). *Argentine fintech Uala to invest $150 mln on Mexico, Colombia expansion, CEO says.* Reuters.

Monaghan, S., Tippmann, E., and Coviello, N. (2020). Born digitals: Thoughts on their internationalization and a research agenda. *Journal of International Business Studies 51*(1), 11–22.

Mova. (2023). *Como o iFood aumentou 100x sua receita com produtos de crédito.* blog.mova.vc/caso-de-sucesso-ifood/

Nambisan, S., Zahra, S. A., and Luo, Y. (2019). Global platforms and ecosystems: Implications for international business theories. *Journal of International Business Studies 50*(9), 1464–1486.

Noguez, R. (2023). *De fintech a banco: Este es el plan de Uala tras la compra de ABC Capital.* Forbes Mexico. www.forbes.com.mx/de-fintech-a-banco-este-es-el-plan-de-uala-tras-la-compra-de-abc-capital/

Parker, G., Van, A., and Jiang, X. (2017). Platform ecosystems. *MIS Quarterly 41*(1), 255–266.

PECAP. (2023). *Reporte Anual 2022: Inversiones de capital emprendedor en Perú 2022.* www.pecap.pe/reportes2023

PitchBook. (2023). *Kavak company profile: Valuation, funding & investors.* pitchbook.com/profiles/company/180502-93#overview

Pooler, M. (2022, March 14). *Brazilian delivery group iFood corners meals market.* Financial Times. www.ft.com/content/39f004b7-cda8-4f63-bc95-d6958dbbbf45

Rappi. (2024). *Rappi Corporativo.* blog.rappi.com/rappi-corporativo/

Rosiello, A., Vidmar, M., and Marsan, G. A. (2022). *Mapping innovation-driven entrepreneurial ecosystems: An Overview.* Economic Research Institute for ASEAN and East Asia. tinyurl.com/3k4sa2jw

Silicon Valley Bank. (2025). *Valuing your seed-stage startup: Key methods & metrics.* www.svb.com/startup-insights/raising-capital/determining-seed-startup-valuation/

Sirmon, D. G., Hitt, M. A., Ireland, R. D., and Gilbert, B. A. (2010). Resource orchestration to create competitive advantage. *Journal of Management 37*(5), 1390–1412. doi.org/10.1177/0149206310385695

Stam, E. (2018). Measuring entrepreneurial ecosystems. In A. O'Connor, E. Stam, F. Sussan, and D. Audretsch, eds. *International Studies in Entrepreneurship* (Vol. 38). Springer, pp. 173–197.

Stam, E., and van de Ven, A. (2021). Entrepreneurial ecosystem elements. *Small Business Economics 56*(2), 809–832.

Startup Genome. (2023). *The global startup ecosystem report 2023 (GSER 2023).* startupgenome.com/library

Startupblink. (2023). *Global startup ecosystem index.*

Sussan, F., and Acs, Z. J. (2017). The digital entrepreneurial ecosystem. *Small Business Economics 49*(1), 55–73.

Teece, D. J. (2017). Dynamic capabilities and (digital) platform lifecycles. *Advances in Strategic Management 37*, 211–225.

Ualà. (2024). *Somos Ualà.* www.uala.com.ar/nosotros

Institutional video (0:22). YouTube. www.youtube.com/watch?v=_noKYrhsb3I

Uzzi, B. (1999). Embeddedness in the making of financial capital: How social relations and networks benefit firms seeking financing. *American Sociological Review 64*(4), 481–505. doi.org/10.1177/000312249906400402

WIPO. (2023). *Global innovation index.* www.wipo.int/global_innovation_index/en/

Zhao, Y., von Delft, S., Morgan-Thomas, A., and Buck, T. (2020). The evolution of platform business models: Exploring competitive battles in the world of platforms. *Long Range Planning 53*(4), Article 101892. doi.org/10.1016/j.lrp.2019.101892

9 Can the MENA Region Build Its Indigenous Start-Up Unicorns? Analysis of Unicorns and Soonicorns and the Supporting Entrepreneurship Ecosystem

AYMAN ISMAIL AND SHERIF KAMEL

9.1 Introduction

Since the beginning of the 2010s, the Middle East and North Africa (MENA) region has witnessed an acceleration of growth in technology-based entrepreneurship, particularly in the e-commerce, fintech, logistics and transportation sectors. This evolution has been particularly visible in countries like Egypt, the United Arab Emirates (UAE) and the Kingdom of Saudi Arabia (KSA), where several start-ups successfully attained unicorn status. Other countries such as Jordan, Morocco, Tunisia and Lebanon also had similar evolutions, although the smaller size of their domestic markets has arguably been a challenge to their accelerated growth. However, in a region with a combined population of more than 450 million and a gross domestic product (GDP) of US$3.5 trillion, along with unlimited prospects across a more diverse portfolio of economic sectors, unicorns remain rare.

In this chapter, we examine the entrepreneurship ecosystems in the MENA region and how they have supported the rise of unicorns, which are considered to be of substantial value for the national and regional economies. We offer business profiles of the region's current and soon-to-be unicorns (soonicorns) and analyse the existing supporting ecosystem in terms of talent, investments, markets, regulations and enablers. We also look at what needs to change to scale and maximise their impact (Kamel, 2023).

The key findings indicate that while the current unicorns are based in only three MENA markets, namely Egypt, the UAE and the KSA, their scope of operations and reach is regional. Unicorns support and build on regional integration and complementarities between markets, talent and investments. Regionalisation is the key enabler for the expansion of the number of tech unicorns across the MENA region.

9.2 The Evolution of the Tech Entrepreneurship Ecosystem in the MENA Region

State-owned enterprises, family businesses, small and medium enterprises (SMEs) and multinational corporations have traditionally dominated economies in the MENA region, focusing on extractive and low-tech manufacturing industries (Ismail et al., 2017). Since the 2010s, many countries have started building entrepreneurship ecosystems for technology-enabled start-ups with scalable business models backed by venture capital (VC) investments. These tech start-ups became popular with the evolution of mobile connectivity, the internet, smartphones and, more generally, the connecting ecosystem of information and communication technologies (ICTs). These technologies, along with the start-ups that popularised their offerings, have been transforming people's lives, creating economic value and accelerating the digital transformation of the economy. Still, in a constantly rapid and transformative global environment, emerging economies, including countries in the MENA region, need a conducive nationwide entrepreneurial ecosystem that is government-enabled, private sector-led, innovation-driven and future-oriented (Kamel, 2022).

The MENA region includes countries with very diverse economic, social and political backgrounds. To analyse the findings, we have grouped them into three broad types of economies: economies heavily endowed with natural resources, diversified emerging economies and conflict/post-conflict economies.

Economies endowed with natural resources include the Gulf Cooperation Council (GCC) countries and Algeria, whose economies are powered by the abundance of oil and gas. The cumulative GDP of these countries is US$2.4 trillion, with a population of 104 million and a GDP per capita of US$22,949 (World Bank, 2022). While oil and gas remain the main industry powering those economies, they continue to diversify their economic activities with a growing focus on the services, retail and entertainment sectors. In a strategy aimed at evolving into international business hubs, they have started to open their markets by updating their regulations and offering incentives to attract companies, start-ups and talent to operate in and/or relocate to their economies.

Currently, the UAE, followed by the KSA, is leading in efforts to attract talent, entrepreneurs and start-ups. Algeria is still in its nascent stage, while the remaining resource-endowed economies are naturally characterised by their small populations and markets.

On the other hand, despite a population of 113 million, economies riddled with internal and regional conflict, including Iraq, Libya, Syria and Yemen, have a combined GDP of only US$342 billion, translating into a GDP per capita of US$3,037. This GDP represents 14 per cent and 13 per cent, respectively, of those of the resource-endowed economies (World Bank, 2022). The growth of these economies is dependent on their ability to restore political stability and security.

In contrast, diversified emerging economies including Egypt, Morocco, Tunisia and Jordan have an abundance of human capital. They have a combined population of 172 million, yet their GDP totals US$703 billion, less than a third of resource-endowed economies. Their average GDP per capita of US$4,083 equals 18 per cent of the economies with abundant natural resources (World Bank, 2022). These emerging economies, especially Egypt and Morocco, are working hard on developing their entrepreneurial ecosystems by capitalising on the size of their population, talent pool and large internal markets. While internally developing their ecosystems, emerging economies also provide endowed economies with high-quality talent and more cost-efficient back-office opportunities, leading to what some might consider a brain drain phenomenon. Tables 9.1 and 9.2 provide key macroeconomic and innovation indicators for MENA economies.

9.3 Building the Business Case for MENA Entrepreneurial Success: Maktoob and Linkdotnet as Mavericks

The two signature stories of tech start-ups with substantial exits occurred in Jordan and Egypt. In 2009, Maktoob, a Jordanian start-up providing Arabic language email service to the region, was acquired by Yahoo! at a valuation of $175 million (Toukan, 2015). In 2010, Linkdotnet, an Egyptian internet service provider, was acquired by Orascom Telecom at a valuation of $140 million (Ismail, 2024). These were substantial valuations for technology start-ups with no physical assets in traditional markets like Egypt and Jordan and at the infancy of the internet and tech start-ups in the MENA region.

Table 9.1 *Key macroeconomic indicators for MENA economies*

	GDP, 2022	GDP per capita, 2022	Population, 2022	Human capital index, 2020	Gini index		Adult (15+) literacy rate		% Population using the internet		Mobile cellular subscriptions (per 100 people)	
Economy	Current US$ ($M)	Current US$		0–1	Latest year	Value	Latest year	Value (%)	Latest year	Value (%)	Latest year	Value
Algeria	194,998	4,343	44,903,225	0.53	2011	27.6	2018	81	2021	71	2022	109
Bahrain	44,383	30,147	1,472,233	0.65	N/A	N/A	2011	92	2021	100	2022	145
Egypt	476,748	4,295	110,990,103	0.49	2019	31.9	2022	75	2022	72	2022	93
Iraq	264,182	5,937	44,496,122	0.41	2012	29.5	2017	86	2022	79	2022	98
Jordan	48,653	4,311	11,285,869	0.55	2010	33.7	2021	98	2021	86	2022	68
Kuwait	175,363	41,080	4,268,873	0.56	N/A	N/A	2020	96	2021	100	2022	181
Lebanon	23,132	4,136	5,489,739	0.52	2011	31.8	2019	95	2021	87	2021	77
Libya	45,752	6,716	6,812,341	N/A	N/A	N/A	1994	77	2014	18	2022	205
Morocco	130,913	3,442	37,457,971	0.50	2013	39.5	2022	77	2021	88	2021	137
Oman	114,667	25,057	4,576,298	0.61	N/A	N/A	2022	97	2021	96	2021	135
Qatar	236,258	87,661	2,695,122	0.64	N/A	N/A	2014	98	2021	100	2022	174
Saudi Arabia	1,108,572	30,448	36,408,820	0.58	N/A	N/A	2020	98	2022	100	2022	132
Syria	8,970	421	22,125,249	0.52	2003	37.5	2014	86	2021	36	2021	80
Tunisia	46,304	3,747	12,356,117	0.67	2015	32.8	2022	84	2021	79	2022	129
United Arab Emirates	507,064	53,708	9,441,129	0.58	2018	26	2022	98	2022	100	2022	212
Yemen	N/A	650	33,696,614	0.38	2013	36.7	2004	54	2017	27	2021	46

Source: Compiled by authors based on data from the World Bank (2022).

Table 9.2 *Key innovation indicators for MENA economies*

Economy	GII ranking	Institutions	Human capital and research	Infrastructure	Market sophistication	Business sophistication	Knowledge and technology outputs	Creative outputs
Algeria	119	97	113	102	125	120	128	107
Bahrain	67	28	77	37	78	92	74	98
Egypt	86	103	95	90	88	100	77	73
Iraq	N/A	N/A	N/A	N/A	N/A	N/A	N/A	N/A
Jordan	71	51	82	87	53	70	76	75
Kuwait	64	86	55	46	62	103	73	64
Lebanon	92	125	72	96	46	76	86	96
Libya	N/A	N/A	N/A	N/A	N/A	N/A	N/A	N/A
Morocco	70	83	86	94	80	107	65	55
Oman	69	62	52	61	74	95	75	79
Qatar	50	23	54	39	44	73	82	65
Saudi Arabia	48	45	35	48	28	45	68	66
Syria	N/A	N/A	N/A	N/A	N/A	N/A	N/A	N/A
Tunisia	79	107	46	89	98	119	50	72
United Arab Emirates	32	10	16	15	25	23	59	50
Yemen	N/A	N/A	N/A	N/A	N/A	N/A	N/A	N/A

Source: Compiled by authors based on data from the Global Innovation Index (GII) (2023) and WIPO (2023).

Maktoob was founded in 1999 by two Jordanians, Hussam Khoury and Samih Toukan, with the goal of expanding email services to Arabic language users who were not well served by global email providers like Yahoo! and Google. They provided expanded Arabic language capabilities through a free platform, supported by advertising, to a growing user base that had reached sixteen million users by 2009. Enjoying a rapid growth rate and a scalable business model, Maktoob became profitable in 2004 and was ranked among the top 10 websites in the Arab region (Wamda, 2013).

By 2015, Maktoob products were fully integrated into the Yahoo! offerings, and their regional offices closed. As an early success case of building a tech start-up from idea to exit and attracting such an acquisition valuation, Maktoob inspired other entrepreneurs to launch their tech start-ups and attracted regional and international investors to expand their VC investments in the region (Toukan, 2015). It also drew the attention of government leaders to the potential value such start-ups could unlock, especially in Jordan, a country with limited natural resources. Over the following decade, a home-grown start-up and VC ecosystem grew in Jordan, inspired by Maktoob and its founders as role models.

Linkdotnet, an Egyptian internet service provider (ISP), had a similar effect in Egypt. Link Egypt was started by the Egyptian entrepreneur Khaled Bishara and other co-founders in 1996 to provide internet services to the emerging local market. The company grew into a leading regional internet provider, serving customers in Saudi Arabia, Jordan, Algeria, Pakistan and Bangladesh, offering a wide range of products including hosting and web development. In addition to its organic growth, Link Egypt grew through mergers and acquisitions, including other ISPs as well as internet content and commerce start-ups, rebranding into Linkdotnet. By 2009, the company grew into one of the most prominent technology players in Egypt and the region, with more than 2,500 employees and US$120 million in revenue. Linkdotnet was acquired by Mobinil (now Orange), Egypt's largest mobile operator, for $140 million (Ismail, 2024) in 2010.

Maktoob and Linkdotnet became the mandatory references for regional venture-backed technology start-ups and were instrumental in shaping the tech start-up ecosystem. They inspired future entrepreneurs and provided validation for investors regarding the actual potential of technology start-ups across MENA. The start-up, investor and mentor community that rapidly grew around the co-founders turned into a support network for other technology-driven start-ups through investments, talent and advice. It also helped shape the next entrepreneurial wave that had the potential to raise some of the start-ups to unicorn status.

9.4 Building Entrepreneurial Ecosystems across MENA: Egypt, UAE and Saudi Arabia

The tech-enabled entrepreneurship ecosystem in Egypt was among the earliest in the region. A technology development fund was established with the support of the Ministry of Communications and Information Technology (MCIT) in 2004. The fund was managed by Ideavelopers, a subsidiary of EFG-Hermes private equity aimed at investing US$50 million in early-stage start-ups in Egypt and the region (Turki, 2015). The fund seeded several start-ups that grew to become large players in the ecosystem and the economy, such as Vezeeta and Fawry (Ismail, 2009). Other home-grown VC funds started to appear, including Algebra Ventures, Sawari Ventures, A15, Egypt Ventures, Camel Ventures, NClude Fund, Endure Capital and Foundation Ventures, among others (Ismail, 2022). By 2024, these funds had collectively raised over US$500 million to invest in the regional entrepreneurial ecosystem.

In addition to these VC funds, several angel investor networks supported entrepreneurs in their early stages, such as Cairo Angels, Alex Angels and AUC Angels (Ismail, 2022). Start-up incubators and accelerators, such as The Venture Lab at The American University in Cairo (AUC Venture Lab), Flat6Labs, EdVentures and Nahdet El-Mahrousa provided support services and, sometimes, pre-seed funding to entrepreneurs.

In parallel, an ecosystem of enablers supporting entrepreneurs grew, including government agencies such as the Technology, Innovation and Entrepreneurship Center (TIEC) and the Micro, Small and Medium Enterprise Development Agency (MSMEDA). It also included international development agencies such as the World Bank, USAID and GIZ and international foundations such as the Drosos and Hivos foundations, that grew more active with time. Local and regional summits such as RiseUp and Techne Summits attracted a broader regional and global community of entrepreneurs, investors and enablers to explore opportunities in Egyptian start-ups (Ismail, 2022).

This growing ecosystem led to an expansion in the pipeline of start-ups and VC investments. According to MAGNiTT, VC investments in Egypt reached US$491 million invested in 165 start-ups in 2021 and US$517 million invested in 160 start-ups in 2022. These figures represent steep growth from the US$22 million invested in 2017 (MAGNiTT, 2022, 2023).

In the UAE, a similar entrepreneurial movement was unfolding, mostly propelled by a profile of entrepreneurs coming from more seasoned corporate or consulting backgrounds. The entrepreneurship ecosystem in UAE was driven by two signature start-up stories: Souq.com and Careem.

In 2005, Ronaldo Mouchawar, a Syrian entrepreneur, founded Souq.com. Over the next decade, Souq.com became the region's most prominent e-commerce platform. Amazon acquired Souq.com for US$580 million in 2017, giving them a strong footprint in the region (Russell, 2017). In 2012, Magnus Olsson and Mudassir Sheikha, two McKinsey consultants based in Dubai, saw an opportunity in ride-hailing and launched Careem. Careem grew to become the region's biggest ride-hailing service provider, following Uber's model. In 2019, Uber acquired Careem for US$3.1 billion in one of the region's largest exits to date (Motte, 2022).

These two technology-driven venture success stories gave UAE entrepreneurs the role models necessary for building their own unicorns. They also provided the UAE's growing VC investment industry with strong momentum to validate their investment theses. Several UAE regional funds emerged with a strong investment portfolio, such as Arzan, Global Ventures, Wamda Capital, BECO Capital, Shorooq Partners, Venture Souq and Middle East Venture Partners (MEVP). UAE VC funds invested over US$1.2 billion in 2021 (MAGNiTT, 2022). To cover smaller tickets, several angel investing groups emerged in the UAE, including Womena, Dubai Angel Investors and Emirates Angels Investors Association (Tracxn, 2024). In addition, the UAE government launched its own investment funds, including the Khalifa Fund for Enterprise Development and the Mohammed Bin Rashid Innovation Fund, to support start-ups and SMEs by providing them with the financial assistance and training needed to accelerate growth and attain unicorn status (Knecht, 2024).

In addition to financial support, other enablers in the ecosystem included innovation hubs such as Dubai's Internet City, Abu Dhabi's

Hub71, Sharjah's Research Technology and Innovation Park (Elcheik, 2023) and the Mohammed bin Rashid Innovation Centre (Elements Next Generation, 2023). Incubators/accelerators such as Flat6Labs, Innova MENA, Start AD and Plug and Play (Abu Dhabi SME Hub, 2021) play a pivotal role by providing educational and mentorship programmes and, sometimes, funding. Similarly, some governmental organisations-led initiatives to support start-ups, such as the Abu Dhabi Investment Office (ADIO)'s Innovation Programme and Abu Dhabi Global Market's (ADGM) Tech Startup Commercial License for Incorporation. The UAE also hosted monthly events, such as Startup Grind, and annual large-scale events including GITEX, Hub71 Impact Event and Step Conference to attract local and regional start-ups and entrepreneurs.

A significant force in the development of the entrepreneurship ecosystem in the UAE was the governmental initiatives aiming to make the UAE an entrepreneurial nation by 2031. Launched in 2021/2022, the Entrepreneurial Nation 2.0 initiative aimed at developing 8,000 SMEs and start-ups by 2030 (Cabral, 2022). In 2021, 2022 and 2023, the UAE ranked 1st worldwide in the Global Entrepreneurship Monitor (GEM) National Entrepreneurship Context Index (GEM, 2024). Furthermore, the government sought to bring talent into the UAE by offering international entrepreneurs and founders long-term residence visas, known as the Golden Visa, enabling them to live, work or study in the UAE (IFZA, 2022). In addition, to encourage start-ups to locate themselves in the UAE, they created several free zones, such as Dubai's International Free Zone Authority (IFZA). The UAE also allowed foreigners to own 100 per cent of a company, imposed no corporate tax or import/export duties, up to 50 per cent reductions in 1,500+ government fees and allowed them to repatriate all their profits (Seed Group, 2022).

The start-up movement in the KSA started later than in other countries in the region. However, it has made rapid progress, and KSA was among the top 3 countries in 2024, both by the number of start-ups and the size of investments. VC investments in start-ups increased from US$59 million in 2018 to US$987 million in 2022. The KSA also emerged as a lucrative market for regional start-ups to base their headquarters, attract investments and potentially plan their exits. Their first unicorn entered the news in 2022 when Jahez, an online food delivery platform, completed its initial public offering (IPO) at a valuation of US$2.4 billion (Al Taasis, 2023).

By modernising the regulatory landscape to streamline operations for both VCs and start-ups, the KSA government fostered and regulated entrepreneurship through the Small and Medium Enterprises General Authority (known as Monsha'at), offering training services through the Monsha'at Academy, incentives, grants and community building events for members of the ecosystem (Al Taasis, 2023). KSA has several tier 1 VC funds, including privately-backed STV, Khwarizmi Ventures, Vision Ventures, RAED Ventures, Riyad Taqnia Fund, Hala Ventures and Impact 46, as well as government-backed funds, including Jada, the King Abdullah University of Science and Technology (KAUST) Innovation Fund, and SVC (Aad, 2023). Angel investment networks include OQAL Angel Investors, Riyadh Angel Investors, Falak Angels and Saudi Angel Investors (Attar, 2023).

Enablers in the KSA included the local start-up accelerators TAQADAM, Falak and Misk accelerators, as well as regional accelerators such as Sanabil 500 MENA and Techstars accelerators. Government-backed initiatives, such as the Saudi Unicorn programme, launched by the Misk Foundation, the Ministry of Communications and Information Technology (MCIT) and the National Technology Development Programme, aimed at increasing the number of unicorns in the KSA by supporting early-stage start-ups. The Garage, a hub for local and regional start-ups based at KAUST, offered accelerator and incubator programmes, coworking spaces and events hosting (Al Taasis, 2023). The KSA's most significant entrepreneurial events included the LEAP Conference, the Global Entrepreneurship Congress and Step Saudi (Misk Foundation, 2022). Additionally, the KSA's Monsha'at holds the Biban conference to connect entrepreneurs, investors and policymakers to help address obstacles faced by stakeholders, including various governmental procedures and regulatory requirements (Entrepreneur, 2023). The local chapter of Startup Grind also hosts periodical events and meetings for entrepreneurs to encourage networking and community building.

Since the launch of 'Vision 2030' in 2016, the KSA has been diversifying its economy away from oil by investing in various sectors, including the local entrepreneurial ecosystem start-up and entrepreneurship sector. To achieve their ambitious vision, the government has been encouraging investors and entrepreneurs to direct their efforts towards the KSA, aiming to become a key hub for global entrepreneurs by 2030 (El-Shaeri, 2023). The KSA was ranked second in the GEM National Entrepreneurship Context Index in 2022 (GEM, 2022).

9.5 Profiling the MENA Region Unicorns and Soonicorns

Like in most emerging markets, most of the region's unicorns build their business models around the digital transformation of traditional sectors, such as financial services (payments and lending), logistics and transportation and e-commerce. These three sectors have the highest share of VC investments in the region and the highest share of unicorns in emerging markets globally. Table 9.3 provides a list and the profiles of the region's unicorns and soonicorns. We include the two start-ups that did not technically reach the US$1 billion valuation mark but had very influential exits at substantial valuations, paving the way for the unicorn phenomenon in the MENA region: Souq.com and Anghami.

Within the fintech space, digital payments ventures like Fawry, STC Pay, PayMob and Geidia are transforming this space, mostly in collaboration with banks and other financial institutions. Lending is another area for business success for fintechs, with start-ups like MNT-Halan for microfinance and Tamara and Tabby for 'buy now pay later' and consumer finance. Several other local companies are also pursuing similar business models in the region but are at earlier stages. Start-ups from other sectors, such as Bosta in logistics or Souq (now Amazon) in e-commerce, are also focused on embedded financing models, providing their customers or vendors with financing to accelerate their own sales.

Logistics and transportation are emerging as another strong domain for unicorn success. Start-ups such as Careem, Swvl and Yassir provide consumers and businesses with a tech-enabled, safe, cost-effective transportation service with a seamless user experience. Others, like Trukker and Maxab, provide logistics services to businesses such as trucking, warehousing and distribution. Food delivery has emerged as another high-growth category, with ventures such as Jahez, Careem and a myriad of early-stage players. Despite their digitally enabled business models, most of these businesses are capital-intensive. However, they promise to transform the sector, pushing traditional players to accelerate their digital transformation processes.

E-commerce is another attractive focal area for unicorns, with start-ups such as Souq.com, Breadfast and Flowered adopting different models to serve consumers. Many other e-commerce players are attempting to enter this space in the region. However, most of them are still in earlier stages or struggling to scale their customer base.

Table 9.3 *Profiles of MENA unicorns and soonicorns*

Category	Start-up	Sector	Origin	Founded	Entrepreneurs	Profile
Unicorn	Fawry	Financial services, payments	Egypt	2008	Ashraf Sabry, Mohamed Okasha	Electronic payments and financial services
Unicorn	Careem	Logistics, transportation	UAE	2012	Magnus Olsson, Abdullah Elyas and Mudassir Sheikha	Ride sharing, along with food delivery, bike rentals, and financial services
Unicorn	EMPG^2	Marketplace, classifieds	UAE	2015	Imran Ali Khan, Zeeshan Ali Khan	(Now Dubizzle) Classifieds portals in emerging markets, including OLX, Bayut, Zameen, and others
Unicorn	Jahez	F&B, logistics	KSA	2016	Ghassab Al-Mandil	Food delivery platform for meal orders from restaurants
Unicorn	MNT-Halan	Financial services, micro lending	Egypt	2017	Ahmed Mohsen, Mohamed Aboulnaga, Mounir Nakhla	Super-app providing microfinance, BNPL, lending and digital payments
Unicorn	Swvl	Logistics, transportation	Egypt	2017	Mostafa Kandil, Mahmoud Nouh, and Ahmed Sabbah	Bus and van ride sharing
Unicorn	Kitopi	F&B, cloud infrastructure	UAE	2018	Mohamad Ballout, Saman Darkan, Bader Ataya, and Andres Arenas	Cloud kitchen providing delivery only services for restaurants
Unicorn	STC Pay	Financial services, payments	KSA	2018	Abdulkarim Giraud, Abdulqader Alharbi, Ahmed Alenazi, Iyas Alhabib, Khalid Algarni	Digital wallet fintech
Unicorn	Vista Global	Aerospace	UAE	2018	Thomas Flohr	AI-driven subscription-based private jet booking
Unicorn	Tamara	Financial services, BNPL	KSA	2020	Abdulmajeed Alsukhan (CEO), Turki Bin Zarah (COO), Abdulmohsen Albabtain (CPO)	BNPL shopping and payments platform
Almost unicorn	Souq	E-commerce, retail	UAE	2005	Ronaldo Mouchawar	Online e-commerce website

Almost unicorn	Anghami	Media, music streaming	Lebanon	2011	Eddy Maroun, Elie Habib	Streaming platform for Arabic and international music
Soonicorn	Unifonic	Information technology, messaging	KSA	2006	Ahmed Hamdan (CEO), Hasson Hamdan (CTO)	Customer engagement platform providing unified communication channels
Soonicorn	Property Finder	Real estate, property management	UAE	2007	Michael Lahyani, Renan Bourdeau	Online real estate listing
Soonicorn	Geidea	Financial services, payments	KSA	2008	Abdullah Al-Othman	Distributor payment solution
Soonicorn	Vezeeta	Information technology, healthcare	Egypt	2012	Amir Barsoum	Digital health booking and management platform
Soonicorn	Instabug	Information technology, testing	Egypt	2013	Moataz Soliman, Omar Gabr	Software enabling developers to test their mobile apps
Soonicorn	Foodics	F&B, MIS	KSA	2014	Ahmad AlZaini (CEO), Mosab Alothmani	Restaurant management system managing sales, transactions, inventory, employee schedules, and customer relationships.
Soonicorn	Starzplay	Media, video streaming	UAE	2014	Maaz Sheikh (CEO), Danny Bates (COO), Karin Baggstrom, Khaled Benchouche,	Streaming platform for films, Hollywood series, documentaries, and kids' entertainment
Soonicorn	Paymob	Financial services, payments	Egypt	2015	Islam Shawky (CEO), Alain El Hajj (COO), Mostafa Menessy (CTO)	Omni-channel digital payments enabler for SMEs providing online and in-store payments acceptance
Soonicorn	TruKKer	Logistics, transportation	KSA	2016	Gaurav Biswas (CEO), Pradeep Mallavarapu	Tech-enabled truck aggregator for multiple truck types
Soonicorn	Nana	E-commerce, grocery	KSA	2016	Sami Alhelwah (CEO), Abdulmajeed Alsukhan, Bakr Elsherif, Ahmed Alsamani	Grocery shopping and delivery platform

Table 9.3 (*cont.*)

Category	Start-up	Sector	Origin	Founded	Entrepreneurs	Profile
Soonicorn	One Moto	Logistics, transportation	UAE	2016	Adam Ridgway, Stephen Wood	Electric vehicle developer
Soonicorn	Pure Harvest	Agriculture, agritech	UAE	2017	Sky Kurtz (CEO), Robert Kupstas, Mahmoud Adi	Tech-enabled agribusiness for year-round production of premium fruits & vegetables
Soonicorn	Yassir	Logistics, transportation	Algeria	2017	Noureddine Tayebi (CEO)	Super app offering on-demand services, ride-hailing, delivery and payments
Soonicorn	Bosta	Logistics, transportation	Egypt	2017	Ahmed Gaber, Mohamed El-Houssainy, Mohamed Ezzat	E-commerce last mile shipping and logistics provider
Soonicorn	Breadfast	E-commerce, F&B logistics	Egypt	2017	Abdallah Nofal, Mostafa Amin, Muhammad S. Habib	Same-day delivery for household essentials, grocery and F&B
Soonicorn	Rain	Financial services, cryptocurrency	Bahrain	2017	Abdullah Almoaiqel, AJ Nelson, Joe Dallago, Yehia Badawy	Digital currency exchange
Soonicorn	Floward	E-commerce, retail	Kuwait	2017	Abdulaziz Al Loughani	Online flowers and gifts store
Soonicorn	Maxab	Logistics, transportation	Egypt	2018	Belal EL-Megharbel, Mohamed Ben Halim	B2B e-commerce platform connecting F&B retailers with suppliers
Soonicorn	Sary	E-commerce, marketplace	KSA	2018	Khaled Alsiari, Mohammed Aldossary	B2B supplies marketplace
Soonicorn	Tabby	Financial services, BNPL	UAE	2019	Hosam Arab (CEO), Daniil Barkalov (COO)	BNPL payments and shopping app

Source: Compiled by authors based on data from crunchbase.com, tracxn.com and a compilation of data from company websites and press releases.

Other sectors that have facilitated the emergence of unicorns include classified advertising (EMPG^2), cloud kitchens (Kitopi), private jet booking (Vista Global) and media and music streaming (Anghami) in addition to food and agriculture (Pure Harvest) and digital currencies (Rain).

The healthcare sector is visibly missing from this list, with only one start-up, Vezeeta, operating in healthtech. Despite growing spending on healthcare services in the region, the start-up pipeline remains limited, and the sector remains dominated by governments and large private sector service providers.

In essence, most of these start-ups operate in traditional sectors where they digitally transform traditional products and services through innovative business models. However, what is missing are start-ups that build on deeptech, such as those offering products that leverage science and technology with strong research-based intellectual property (IP). This might be seen as an indication of the weak research and development (R&D) infrastructure in the region, with limited government and private sector funding. Growing research-based commercialisation requires a more knowledge-intensive ecosystem that is deeply embedded in R&D universities with long-term strategic funding.

Looking at the aggregate country portfolios, Table 9.4 groups MENA unicorns and soonicorns by country and highlights their distribution. The ten unicorns in the region in 2023 were concentrated in the UAE (four), Egypt (three) and KSA (three). Most of the start-ups

Table 9.4 *MENA unicorns and soonicorns by country*

Economy	Unicorn	Almost unicorn	Soonicorn	Total
UAE	4	1	5	10
Egypt	3		6	9
KSA	3		6	9
Lebanon		1		1
Kuwait			1	1
Bahrain			1	1
Algeria			1	1
Total	10	2	20	32

Source: Compiled by authors based on crunchbase.com, tracxn.com and data from company websites and press releases.

on the list (unicorns, almost unicorns and soonicorns) were also concentrated in these three countries, with twenty-eight out of the thirty-two start-ups. The top 3 countries were also those with pipelines of soonicorns, indicating the ecosystems' future potential. Lebanon, Kuwait, Bahrain and Algeria had one start-up each (soonicorn or almost unicorn). This concentration of unicorns points to the importance of multiple drivers, such as talent, large domestic markets and availability of VC investments, among others. These are generally recognised as the three most important propellers for attaining unicorn status within the MENA entrepreneurial ecosystem.

9.6 Key Elements of the Supporting Ecosystem

Entrepreneurial ecosystems have emerged as a framework for studying the enabling environment for start-ups. In this section we focus on the most impactful elements of an entrepreneurial ecosystem for supporting the creation of regional unicorns in MENA: talent, investments, market opportunity, sophistication and government support.

9.6.1 Talent and Human Capital Development

The pool of talent in the region, both with business and technical experience, is promising. However, culturally, the idea of starting a tech start-up had not appealed to most of the seasoned talent until relatively recently. Most of the early start-ups were founded by entrepreneurs with limited business experience who managed to make it in an environment that was not used to building scalable, venture-based start-ups (e.g., Linkdotnet, Maktoob, Swvl, PayMob). Over time, the business opportunities became more attractive to a more seasoned breed of entrepreneurs, including consultants (for example, Careem and Vezeeta), seasoned executives (Anghami) and serial entrepreneurs (MNT-Halan). This evolution of founder profile was driven by the growth of the regional VC industry, providing significant investments to promising teams with lucrative high-growth opportunities and demonstrating the exit potential evidenced by Careem, Souq and others.

This emerging talent and human capital development builds on several patterns. The MENA population is young and rapidly growing, with a population growth rate of 1.6 per cent (World Bank, 2022), almost double that of the global population growth rate of 0.83 per cent (Macrotrends, 2024). The youth population under the age of thirty constitutes around 55 per cent of the MENA population (United Nations, 2022).

MENA economies spend around 14 per cent of their government budgets on education, with a particular focus on higher education. MENA economies host 634 universities (Times Higher Education, 2024), with a growing share of the youth population having access to higher education opportunities, especially in business and engineering disciplines. However, of these 634 universities only fifteen were internationally ranked in 2024: These were universities in KSA (four), UAE (three), Egypt (two), Lebanon (two), Qatar (two), Jordan (one) and Oman (one) (QS Universities Rankings, 2024). These ranked universities provide access to international knowledge and quality higher education, producing strong talent for high-growth tech start-ups.

Among this young and increasingly educated population, interest in entrepreneurship is growing, as the GEM MENA report (2016) highlighted. Among the surveyed MENA economies, entrepreneurial intentions (individuals indicating an intention to start a business) were at approximately 38 per cent, scoring higher than Latin America (36 per cent) and more than double North America and Europe (13 and 12 per cent, respectively). Entrepreneurial intentions in the region were led by Egypt, which ranked second worldwide with a score of 64 per cent, followed by the UAE, scoring 48 per cent and Morocco, scoring 36 per cent (Ismail et al., 2017). Other countries in the region enjoyed high entrepreneurial intention scores and/or rapid increases in their scores. While these figures measure interest in starting a business in general, they are also a good indicator of the interest in tech start-ups. Table 9.5 provides an overview of the indicators of entrepreneurial behaviour and attitudes among MENA economies.

Throughout the MENA region, entrepreneurs are regarded highly, with 80–95 per cent of the population having a positive perception of entrepreneurs and business owners. In addition, 70–95 per cent of the MENA population indicates that becoming an entrepreneur is a good career option. These figures are significantly higher among the youth (Ismail et al., 2017).

Egypt has emerged as the region's talent pool, both in the business and technology domains, as it is also home to some of the best universities in MENA. Many start-ups with a regional focus have core teams located in Egypt, regardless of their geographic footprint. This is

Table 9.5 *Entrepreneurial behaviour and attitudes for select MENA economies*

Economy	Year	Perceived opportunities	Perceived capabilities	Fear of failure rate	Entrepreneurial intentions	Total early-stage entrepreneurial activity (TEA)	Established business ownership	Female/male TEA	High job creation expectation	Business services sector	High status to successful entrepreneurs	Entrepreneurship as a good career choice
Egypt	2022	63.71	62.76	50.64	47.26	6.62	2.6	0.39	25.53	7.43	78.31	71.24
Jordan	2023	47.65	73.22	52.13	46.97	15.7	7.2	0.54	14.28	7.21	86.33	78.09
Morocco	2023	70.73	68.17	32.62	23.44	6.29	6.84	0.56	16.98	4.39	82.21	83.02
Saudi Arabia	2023	93.21	90.82	60.81	38.47	25.34	13.59	0.85	29.46	4.41	95.36	95.72
Tunisia	2022	61.8	78.62	42.59	50.67	17.14	10.04	0.75	21.71	6.85	83.72	80.65
United Arab Emirates	2022	72.16	71.66	39.18	44.46	25.52	4.53	0.71	76.74	19.5	87.02	82.8

Source: Created by authors using Global Entrepreneurship Monitor (GEM, 2022, 2023) data.

particularly true for technical and engineering talent. UAE has emerged as an attractive location for international talent with an interest in building start-ups, who are focused on the region and who increasingly embrace a global perspective. Many of the co-founders of UAE start-ups are foreign-born, coming from international backgrounds with diverse professional stories. Meanwhile, KSA has begun to develop their entrepreneurial ecosystem relatively recently and is growing its talent pool. Most Saudi start-ups were created with a mix of local talent who has an understanding of the local market and culture, together with international talent, providing exposure to business and technology skills. Both UAE and KSA are intentionally active in attracting regional and international talent with the promise of investments, an open business environment, a large market and strong government support.

9.6.2 *Entrepreneurial Finance and Investments*

Start-ups in the MENA region raised over US$4 billion in VC through 795 transactions in 2022 – a record figure, compared to US$700 million in 2019. UAE start-ups raised the highest amount of US$1.85 billion in 252 transactions. Saudi start-ups came second in the number of investments, with US$907 million in 154 transactions, while Egypt came second in the number of transactions, with US$736 million invested in 180 transactions (Wamda, 2023). While this significant increase can be partially attributed to the global liquidity bubble that affected VC investments everywhere, it was also largely due to real growth in the sector. This growth was backed by regional funds that saw opportunities for investments and were further encouraged by the forward-thinking initiatives, policies and regulations adopted by the respective countries. Table 9.6 provides a list of investors in MENA unicorns and soonicorns. The list includes regional funds which usually invest in the early seed and Series A rounds, such as Algebra Ventures and Sawari Ventures from Egypt, Shorooq Capital, BECO Capital, MEVP Ventures and Wamda Capital from the UAE and Raed Ventures and STC Ventures from KSA (Forbes Middle East, 2023).

However, as the MENA start-ups successfully progressed to larger investment rounds, other top global investors started joining, including global VCs, development finance institutions (DFIs), corporations and corporate VCs. Global VCs such as Vostok Ventures, SoftBank Vision

Table 9.6 *Investments in MENA unicorns and soonicorns*

Category	Start-up	# Rounds	Total raised	Latest round	Date	Investors
Unicorn	Fawry	4	$122M	IPO	2019	Egyptian American Enterprise Fund (EAEF), Helios Investment Partners, Ideavelopers, IFC Venture Capital Group, ResponsAbility Investments (the MENA Long Term Value Fund)
Unicorn	Careem	7	$772M	Series F	2018	Al Tayyar Travel Group, BECO Capital, Coatue, DCM Ventures, Didi, Endure Capital, Impulse, Kingdom Holding Company, Lumia Capital, Mercedes-Benz, Rakuten Capital, Saudi Telecom, STC Ventures, STV, The Abraaj Group, Wamda Capital
Unicorn	EMPG^2	6	$479M	Private equity	2022	Acacia Partners, Affinity Partners, Exor Ventures, KCK, OLX Group, Prosus & Naspers
Unicorn	Jahez	1	$36.5M	IPO	2021	Impact46
Unicorn	MNT-Halan	3	$470M	Venture	2023	Abu Dhabi Commercial Bank, Agricultural Bank of Egypt, Al Ahli Bank of Kuwait - Egypt, Al Baraka Banking Group, Algebra Ventures, Apis Growth Fund II, Arab African International Bank, Bank ABC, Battery Road Digital Holdings, Chimera Investment, Commercial International Bank, Development Partners International (DPI), Disruptech Ventures, Egypt Ventures, Endeavor Catalyst, GB Capital, Housing and Development Bank, International Finance Corporation, Lorax Capital Partners, Middle East Venture Partners (MEVP), National Bank of Egypt, NI Capital, Nowais Capital, Shaka Ventures, Unidelta, Wamda Capital
Unicorn	Swvl	8	$264M	PIPE	2022	Agility Ventures, Arzan Venture Capital, Autotech Ventures, BECO Capital, Blu Stone Management, Careem, Chimera, DASH Ventures, DiGAME, Emilian Popa, Endeavor Catalyst, Esther Dyson, European Bank for Reconstruction and Development (EBRD), Luxor Capital, Michael Lahyani, MSA Capital, Oman Technology Fund, Property Finder, Queen's Gambit Growth Capital, Raed Ventures, Sawari Ventures, Silicon Badia, VNV Global, Vostok Ventures, Zain

Unicorn	Kitopi	5	$804M	Series C	2022	B. Riley Financial, BECO Capital, Bossanova Investimentos, Chimera Investment, Crescent Enterprises Venture Capital, DisruptAD, Doğuş Grubu, Endeavor Catalyst, HB Investments, Knollwood Investment Advisory, Lumia Capital, Next Play Capital, Nordstar, Omakase Investment Club, Reshape, Rise Capital, SoftBank Vision Fund, VentureSouq
Unicorn	STC pay	1	$200M	Corporate	2020	Western Union
Unicorn	Vista Global	1	$200M	Private equity	2018	Rhone Group
Unicorn	Tamara	8	$955.6M	Series C	2023	Checkout.com, Coatue, Endeavor Catalyst, Goldman Sachs, HALA Ventures, Impact46, Khwarizmi Ventures, Musaab Hakami, Nama Ventures, Pinnacle Capital, Sanabil, Saudi National Bank, SEEDRA Ventures, Shorooq Partners, Vision Ventures, Wealth Well
Almost Unicorn	Souq	5	$460M	Venture	2016	Baillie Gifford, IFC Venture Capital Group, Jabbar Internet Group, MVI (MENA Venture Investments), Naspers, Standard Chartered Bank, Tiger Global Management
Almost Unicorn	Anghami	10	$63.5M	Post-IPO	2023	Abu Dhabi Investment Office (ADIO), Endeavor Catalyst, Franklin Templeton, MBC Ventures, Middle East Venture Partners (MEVP), Mobily Ventures, Samena Capital, Shuaa Capital psc, SRMG Ventures, Vistas Media Capital
Soonicorn	Unifonic	2	$146M	Series B	2021	Elm, Endeavor Catalyst, Highgoal Capital, Riyad Bank, Riyad TAQNIA Fund (RTF), Sanabil, SoftBank Vision Fund, STV
Soonicorn	Property Finder	3	$140M	Series B	2018	Bossanova Investimentos, Endeavor Catalyst, General Atlantic, Pegasus Capital, VNV Global, Vostok Ventures, Xplorer Capital
Soonicorn	Geidea	1	$266M	Private equity	2018	Gulf Capital
Soonicorn	Vezeeta	11	$71.5M	Venture	2022	BECO Capital, Bossanova Investimentos, Crescent Enterprises Venture Capital, Endeavor Catalyst, Gulf Capital, International Finance Corporation, Sahra Growth Capital, Silicon Badia, STV, TDF Capital, Technology Development Fund, VNV Global, Vulcan Capital

Table 9.6 (*cont.*)

Category	Start-up	# Rounds	Total raised	Latest round	Date	Investors
Soonicorn	Instabug	6	$53.1M	Series B	2022	Accel, Amr Awadallah, Cairo Angels, Endeavor Catalyst, Flat6Labs, Forgepoint Capital, Georges Harik, Global Forward Capital, Ihab Hinnawi, Insight Partners, Jim Payne, Middle East Venture Partners (MEVP), Sharif El-Badawi, Y Combinator
Soonicorn	Foodics	5	$198M	Series C	2022	500 Global, BADIR, Bossanova Investimentos, Derayah Venture Capital, Elm, Endeavor Catalyst, Faith Capital, Naseel, Peak XV Partners, Prosus & Naspers, Raed Ventures, Riyad TAQNIA Fund (RTF), Sanabil, Saudi Venture Capital, Savour Ventures, STV, Tech Invest Com, Vision Ventures
Soonicorn	Starzplay	2	$150M	Debt financing	2021	Delta Partners, Ruya Partners, SEQ Capital Partners, Starz Entertainment, State Street Global Advisors
Soonicorn	Paymob	4	$68.5M	Series B	2022	A15, AMK Investment Office, British International Investment, Capria Ventures, CDC Group, Clay Point Investors, FMO, Global Ventures, Helios Climate Ventures, Helios Investment Partners, Kora, Nclude, PayPal Ventures
Soonicorn	TruKKer	16	$320.4M	Series C	2022	500 Global, ADQ, Arzan Venture Capital, Bossanova Investimentos, Endeavor Catalyst, International Finance Corporation, Investcorp, LIQUiDITY Group, March Holding, Mars Growth Capital, Middle East Venture Partners (MEVP), Mubadala, Oman Technology Fund, Partners for Growth, Raed Ventures, Reliance Egypt, Riyad TAQNIA Fund (RTF), Riyadh Valley Company, Select Venture Equity, Shorooq Partners, STV
Soonicorn	Nana	7	$212.2M	Series C	2023	AlJammaz Group, Al-Jasser Holding, Dallah Albaraka Holding, Faith Capital, FIM Partners, Impact46, Jahez International Company, Kingdom Holding Company, Middle East Venture Partners (MEVP), Quencia Capital, Red Diamond Foodservice, Saudi Venture Capital, STV, Sultan Holdings, Sunbulah Group, Uni-Ventures, Wamda Capital, Watar Partners, Zamil Group

Soonicorn	One Moto	8	$191.5M	Debt financing	2023	Adam Ridgway, Pyse, (majority of rounds, including $150M round are undisclosed)
Soonicorn	Pure Harvest Smart Farms	11	$334.4M	Venture	2022	Abu Dhabi Investment Office (ADIO), IMM Investment, Metric Capital Partners, Sancta Capital Group, Shorooq Partners, Shuaa Capital psc, The Olayan Group, Wafra international investment
Soonicorn	Yassir	10	$217.6M	Series B	2022	Alumni Ventures, Andrew Vigneault, Bond, Bossanova Investimentos, Claire Diaz-Ortiz, Cleo Sham, Daniel Curran, DN Capital, Dorsal Capital, Dorsal Capital, Edward Lando, Erik Peterson, Erik Peterson, FJ Labs, French Partners, George Godula, Hannes Graah, Incisive Ventures, Inference Partners, K3 Diversity Ventures, K50 Ventures, Karman Ventures (fka Moving Capital), Kismet Capital Group, Lars Fjeldsoe-Nielsen, Mandeep Singh, Nadav Ben-Chanoch, Nellore Capital, Palm Drive Capital, Pareto Holdings, PowerPlay Capital, Quiet Capital, Rebel Fund, Rohan Monga, Spike Ventures, Tahseen Consulting, Thomas Layton, Two Culture Capital, Unpopular Ventures, VentureSouq, Walid Aradi, Wes Schwalje, WndrCo, Y Combinator
Soonicorn	Bosta	9	$7.7M	Venture	2024	4DX Ventures, AUC Venture Lab, Avanz Capital, AXIAN, Beltone Venture Capital, Cairo Angels, DPD group, Fawry, Hassan Allam Holding, Khwarizmi Ventures, Numu Capital, Plug and Play, Silicon Badia, Wealth Well
Soonicorn	Breadfast	5	$29M	Series A	2021	4DX Ventures, 500 Global, Ahmed Abdel-Wahab, Amr ElGabry, Endure Capital, Flexport, JAM Fund, Mohammed Elsewedy, NHN Investment, Outliers Venture Capital, Paul Buchheit, Paul Graham, Pioneer Fund, Pontem Ventures, Sherif Nagui, VNV Global, Vostok Ventures, Y Combinator
Soonicorn	Rain	9	$228.7M	Series B	2022	500 Global, A'Z Angels, Cadenza Ventures, CMT Digital Ventures, Coinbase Ventures, Dennis Porto, Dubai International Financial Centre (DIFC), Global Founders Capital, Jimco, Kleiner Perkins, Middle East Venture Partners (MEVP), Musaab Hakami, Paradigm, Storm Global, VentureSouq, Vision Ventures, Taibah Valley

Table 9.6 (*cont.*)

Category	Start-up	# Rounds	Total raised	Latest round	Date	Investors
Soonicorn	Floward	4	$186.3M	Series C	2023	500 Global, Aljazira Capital, BNK Ventures, Faith Capital, Impact46, Rainwater Partners, STV
Soonicorn	Maxab	5	$101.2M	Series A	2022	4DX Ventures, 500 Global, Africa Platform Capital, BECO Capital, Bossanova Investimentos, British International Investment, Crystal Stream Capital, DisruptAD, Endeavor Catalyst, Endure Capital, Flourish Ventures, International Finance Corporation, Outlierz Ventures, Rise Capital, RMBV
Soonicorn	Sary	5	$112.1M	Series C	2021	Bossanova Investimentos, Derayah Financial, Derayah Venture Capital, Endeavor Catalyst, MSA Capital, Musaab Hakami, Nour Nouf, Raed Ventures, Rocketship.vc, Sanabil, STV, VentureSouq, Wafra international investment
Soonicorn	Tabby	13	$1.7B	Pre-IPO Debt Financing	2023	AB Accelerator, Arab Bank, Arbor Ventures, Atalaya Capital Management, Blue Pool Capital, Coventure, Delivery Hero, Endeavor Catalyst, Global Founders Capital, Global Ventures, Hassana, HOF Capital, J P Morgan, Jimco, MSA Capital, Mubadala, Outliers Venture Capital, Partners For Growth, PayPal Ventures, Peak XV Partners, Raed Ventures, Sequoia Capital, Soros Capital Management, STV, VentureSouq, Wamda Capital, Wellington

Source: Authors' adaptation of data from crunchbase.com, tracxn.com and from company websites and press releases.

Fund, Tiger Global Management, Naspers and General Atlantic joined some of the advanced investment rounds. Pan-African funds such as Helios Investment Partners and Development Partners International (DPI) also contributed to several transactions in Egypt. DFIs such as the International Finance Corporation (IFC) Venture Capital Group, the European Bank for Reconstruction and Development (EBRD) and the Dutch Entrepreneurial Development Bank (FMO) contributed to investments in start-ups with a developmental impact in areas such as financial inclusion. Corporations and corporate VCs also joined some transactions relevant to their core business, such as Mercedes-Benz, Agility Ventures and Checkout.com. This increase in the appeal of the region's late-stage start-ups to global investors has been interpreted as a positive sign of their investment potential.

Despite the success of MENA start-ups in attracting a wide group of international investors, the number of large investment rounds remains limited compared to other emerging markets such as India, Latin America and Asia, both in size and number of investments. Moreover, there are important structural problems in the investment landscape: There are funding gaps in the early-stage seed investments which are needed to create an early-stage start-up pipeline.

9.6.3 Market Infrastructure and Sophistication

The top 3 markets for MENA unicorns vary significantly in size and demographics. Egypt has a large young population of more than 110 million; however, nearly one third live in poverty, with a narrow segment that enjoys strong purchasing power. This is indicative of the sharp income inequality that characterises most emerging economies. Extreme income inequalities provide an opportunity for start-ups that are focused on efficiency, cost savings and expanding market access through inclusion in sectors such as finance and health-care. This is why unicorns from Egypt include ventures such as Fawry, MNT-Halan and PayMob, with a focus on digital payments and microfinance, Swvl focused on affordable transportation and Vezeeta, which focuses on healthcare access. Egypt's market offers entrepreneurs a good environment for piloting their products and services with low starting costs compared to other countries in the region. However, the business environment remains challenging and slow to navigate. Historically, most Egyptian start-ups used to focus on Egypt until they reached a certain size and scale, when they would start looking for regional growth. Some unicorns such as Fawry started looking beyond Egypt after more than fifteen years of operations and an IPO!

UAE, on the other hand, provides a relatively smaller market of ten million inhabitants, 90 per cent of whom are expatriates. However, customers in the UAE market enjoy strong purchasing power across the different segments: Emirati citizens (around 1.2 million), professional expatriates and high-net-worth tourists and visitors. The openness and cultural diversity in the UAE market, especially in Dubai, makes it a highly competitive market with demanding consumers. It opens up opportunities for start-ups that are more focused on lifestyle and cater to a more affluent market. Unicorns in the UAE include companies with sectoral diversity such as Careem (ride-hailing), Kitopi (cloud kitchen), EMPG^2 (classified advertising), Anghami (music streaming) and Pure Harvest (organic agriculture). With an open and friendly business environment, the UAE is becoming a favoured location for launching start-ups with rapid regional and global growth aspirations. Most Emirate start-ups internationalise to other neighbouring GCC countries and then branch out to Egypt and Pakistan. An increasing number are born global and start operating with plans for global growth.

KSA has a different demographic and market mix; the Saudi population is young and sizable with strong purchasing power; they have a young population of around thirty-seven million, 40 per cent of whom are expatriates. Family-owned businesses and multinational corporations have traditionally dominated the market. However, the start-up movement is growing rapidly, along with the many other social and economic reforms the Kingdom has been experiencing. Driven by ambitious government plans, the Saudi market is opening up to regional start-ups with the promise of strong purchasing power, access to investments and ease of doing business. Most of the Saudi unicorns were created more recently than their counterparts in Egypt and UAE. However, they have enjoyed faster growth rates propelled by better access to the market and investments as, for example, in the case of Jahez (2016), STC Pay (2018) and Tamara (2020). As of 2024, KSA had attracted some fast-growing start-ups from other parts of the region to relocate there. The country had also supported many of these to grow into unicorns and exit through the Saudi financial markets.

In addition to these three markets, other countries in the MENA region are competing for start-ups. Jordan has a solid pool of talent but a small market. Despite this, Jordanian entrepreneurs are known to 'pilot in Jordan, launch in the GCC'; many are building companies targeting the sizable KSA and UAE markets while keeping their back offices in Jordan. Bahrain is small compared its GCC neighbours. Nevertheless, historically it has offered an open and progressive business and regulatory environment, especially for financial institutions and fintech start-ups. This competitive space, however, has been shrinking since their Saudi neighbour started opening up. Thinking big from the outset definitely helps spread an innovative entrepreneurial culture. For emerging economies such as Egypt and other countries in the MENA region, it could be the ideal game changer and transformational platform for socioeconomic development and growth (Kamel, 2016).

9.6.4 Government Support and Regulatory Reforms

Entrepreneurship is a private sector activity by definition, powered by individual entrepreneurs, investors and dynamic, open markets. However, MENA· demonstrates that a national or regional entrepreneurship ecosystem capable of producing unicorns is highly dependent on government policies and regulatory frameworks.

The starting point is often the overall business environment and ease of doing business. However, as most start-ups enter traditional sectors with innovative business models, they need more than this overall ease of operation. They often require the opening up and deregulation of specific sectors to be able to operate under their new business models. Fintech is a good example. For a start-up to be able to operate in digital payments, lending or investments, it needs to operate within the financial sector, which is typically highly regulated by central banks and other financial agencies. In most countries, a boom in fintech is preceded by an opening up of the regulatory framework to allow start-ups to operate and integrate with banks, stock markets and other traditional financial institutions. Egypt, UAE and KSA all made major changes in their financial regulatory frameworks over the past decade, allowing start-ups such as Fawry, STC Pay, PayMob, Tamara and Tabby to emerge. Sectors where these regulatory reforms were not implemented, most visibly healthcare, did not witness a similar unicorn surge. Similarly, some of the most promising regional markets, such as

Morocco and Algeria, did not experience similar entrepreneurial ecosystem development, primarily due to traditional or conservative regulatory frameworks.

From a government policy and regulatory reforms perspective, the UAE has led the region in creating progressive regulatory designs to attract entrepreneurs and investors. Egypt provides a mixed example, with sectors such as fintech leading while others, like healthcare, lag behind. The KSA is rapidly moving to upgrade its markets and regulatory frameworks, promising massive potential for entrepreneurs to access its large market. Other large countries in the region need a regulatory update if they aspire to support their tech-driven start-ups to attain unicorn status.

9.7 Conclusions and Key Insights

Examining the unicorns from entrepreneurial ecosystems in the MENA region, particularly in the three leading countries, Egypt, UAE and KSA, highlights two key insights regarding exits and regionalisation as significant common aspects among unicorns from emerging economies.

9.7.1 Exits Remain Limited and Acquisitions Are Common

Venture-backed start-ups are built with an exit opportunity in mind as a mechanism for investors to cash out on their capital gains. However, exits have been sparse in the region and have mostly occurred through acquisitions rather than IPOs.

The two largest acquisitions in the region over the past decade were Careem (US$3.1 billion by Uber) and Souq.com (US$580 million by Amazon). These two acquisitions were notable because they were made by large multinationals as a way to accelerate their entry into MENA markets. There were several other acquisitions beyond these two deals for smaller start-ups at smaller valuations, with a wide variation in returns on investments.

Exit through IPOs in public stock markets was also sparse and with mixed success. In Egypt, Fawry was the most successful exit story. The company completed an IPO at a valuation of close to US$400 million, which later grew to around US$2 billion then recessed again below the US$1 billion mark. Despite these fluctuations, Fawry offers an example of a successful tech company focused on a single market. In KSA, online food delivery platform Jahez completed an IPO in 2022 at a valuation of US$2.4 billion (Al Taasis, 2023), marking the first KSA unicorn exit.

The two other IPOs in the region, Swvl and Anghami, took a different approach by listing through special purpose acquisition vehicles (SPACs) in the US Nasdaq stock market. SPACs are controversial exit vehicles that offer a shortcut to an IPO, although with extreme risks. Swvl and Anghami used SPACs to IPO at Nasdaq, and both saw their valuations plummet post-IPO. However, both companies remain alive and have managed to recover from their bad IPOs experiences.

With the limited number of exits up to 2024, most of the VC funds that made investments in MENA start-ups are yet to recoup their investments. Moreover, with the current challenges in financial markets and the decline in valuations from 2021/2022 levels, entrepreneurs and funds are both under pressure to be more selective and explore opportunities for exits. As they explore their options, KSA is emerging as a market with high potential for exits through acquisitions and IPOs. Large Saudi corporations are likely to hunt for technology start-ups that could propel their growth beyond traditional markets. At the right valuation, they are likely to explore acquisition opportunities. Saudi stock markets enjoy strong liquidity, and investors are interested in regional technology start-ups.

9.7.2 Regionalisation is a Major Driver for Value Creation

With few exceptions, start-ups from MENA that reached unicorn status had to build a regional footprint. For Egyptian start-ups, growing in the GCC market, particularly UAE and KSA, is a natural opportunity for expansion. Some continue to grow into the rest of the GCC market, others grow to Pakistan and some look towards the African continent. KSA is a natural expansion for UAE start-ups, followed by Egypt, GCC and Pakistan. For Saudi start-ups, many remain focused on capturing their sizable local Saudi market, while others grow into the UAE, Egypt and Pakistan. Growing into Egypt and the GCC countries is an immediate natural move for start-ups from smaller markets like Jordan, Lebanon or Bahrain.

Table 9.7 profiles the geographic footprint of the MENA unicorns and soonicorns. Some patterns emerge when we examine the growth

Table 9.7 *Geographic footprint of MENA unicorns and soonicorns*

Category	Start-up	Origin	Geographic presence
Unicorn	Fawry	Egypt	Egypt
Unicorn	Careem	UAE	Bahrain, Egypt, Iraq, Jordan, KSA, Kuwait, Morocco, Pakistan, UAE
Unicorn	EMPG^2	UAE	Egypt, KSA, Pakistan, Romania, UAE
Unicorn	Jahez	KSA	KSA
Unicorn	MNT-Halan	Egypt	Egypt
Unicorn	Swvl	Egypt	Egypt, Europe, Jordan, Kenya, KSA, Latin America, Mexico, Pakistan, UAE (exited all but Egypt and KSA in 2023)
Unicorn	Kitopi	UAE	Bahrain, KSA, Kuwait, UAE (entered USA in 2019, but exited in 2020)
Unicorn	STC pay	KSA	KSA
Unicorn	Vista Global	UAE	Austria, France, Germany, Hong Kong, Malta, Portugal, UAE, UK, USA
Unicorn	Tamara	KSA	Egypt, Germany, KSA, UAE, Vietnam
Almost unicorn	Souq	UAE	Global
Almost unicorn	Anghami	Lebanon	Algeria, Bahrain, Egypt, Jordan, KSA, Kuwait, Lebanon, Morocco, Oman, Palestine, Qatar, Tunisia, UAE
Soonicorn	Unifonic	KSA	Egypt, Jordan, Pakistan, KSA, Serbia, UAE
Soonicorn	Property Finder	UAE	Bahrain, Egypt, KSA, Qatar, Turkey, UAE
Soonicorn	Geidea	KSA	KSA
Soonicorn	Vezeeta	Egypt	Egypt, Jordan, Kenya, KSA, Lebanon, Nigeria
Soonicorn	Instabug	Egypt	Global
Soonicorn	Foodics	KSA	35+ countries including KSA, UAE, Egypt, Jordan, Kuwait, Netherlands
Soonicorn	Starzplay	UAE	Global
Soonicorn	Paymob	Egypt	Egypt, KSA, Oman, Pakistan, UAE
Soonicorn	TruKKer	KSA	Bahrain, Egypt, Jordan, Kazakhstan, KSA, Kuwait, Oman, Pakistan, Poland, Turkey, UAE
Soonicorn	Nana	KSA	KSA

Table 9.7 (*cont.*)

Category	Start-up	Origin	Geographic presence
Soonicorn	One Moto	UAE	Kenya, KSA, UAE, UK
Soonicorn	Pure Harvest	UAE	KSA, UAE
Soonicorn	Yassir	Algeria	Algeria, Canada, Egypt, France, Morocco, Senegal, South Africa, Tunisia
Soonicorn	Bosta	Egypt	Egypt, KSA
Soonicorn	Breadfast	Egypt	Egypt, KSA
Soonicorn	Rain	Bahrain	Global
Soonicorn	Floward	Kuwait	Bahrain, Egypt, Jordan, KSA, Kuwait, Oman, Qatar, UAE, UK
Soonicorn	Maxab	Egypt	Egypt, Morocco
Soonicorn	Sary	KSA	KSA
Soonicorn	Tabby	UAE	Egypt

Source: Compiled by authors based on crunchbase.com, tracxn.com and from company websites and press releases.

path of these start-ups. Egypt, GCC and, to a great extent, Pakistan represent a highly integrated potential market for regional start-up growth. They offer a favourable mix of market size (Egypt and Pakistan) and purchasing power, investment and exit opportunities (KSA and UAE). Other North African MENA countries (Algeria, Morocco and Tunisia) are less integrated within this geographic region. Algeria is lagging in entrepreneurship and ecosystem development; Moroccan start-ups are looking towards the West African francophone countries for expansion; and Tunisia is small and more connected with France. Levant countries are also lagging in their entrepreneurial ecosystem development.

Despite the limited formal regional integration, entrepreneurs and investors quickly learned that building start-ups with sizable valuations required large, addressable markets beyond what a single country in the region could offer. Hence, the drive for regional growth has become more urgent and an indispensable part of the unicorn playbook. It should be noted that MENA unicorns pay limited attention to other African markets. Few Egyptian start-ups operated in Kenya and Morocco, and none seem interested in or able to enter the large Nigerian market or other smaller African markets. These specific inter nationalisation patterns are consistent with the familiarity offered by neighbouring markets due to large expatriates' movements and cultural and language commonalities. However, regulatory differences among these countries make it harder for entrepreneurs to grow their regional operations quickly (as opposed to the US and EU common markets). Regulatory harmonisation and regional soft-landing programmes can accelerate start-up growth for the common benefit of all participating countries and the emergence of more MENA unicorns.

9.7.3 The Future of MENA Entrepreneurial Ecosystems and Unicorns

The future of MENA unicorns will be shaped by three major drivers: firstly, establishing and institutionalising a vibrant entrepreneurship and venture investment ecosystem; secondly, moving beyond local markets towards broader regionalisation and internationalisation as a growth enabler; and thirdly, moving up the value chain and building start-ups around more advanced technologies, particularly in deep tech.

One of the major accomplishments of the entrepreneurship ecosystem over the past decade is the transition from its position as an 'anomaly', driven by the efforts of a few individuals, to being more 'institutionalised' through investment vehicles, enablers, universities, policymakers, regulatory frameworks, media attention and other dimensions. This institutionalisation is a potent trigger in shaping the future growth trend in the creation, funding and growth of tech start-ups. It therefore provides a higher potential for the creation of unicorns. The idea of an integrated ecosystem is becoming popular among policymakers, enablers and investors, backed by data assessing the quality of these ecosystems and the institutional and policy changes needed to improve them. For example, the GEM National Entrepreneurship Context Index (NECI) quantifies the entrepreneurial framework by evaluating economies based on a multitude of factors such as entrepreneurial financing, governmental support, market dynamics, commercial and physical infrastructure and entrepreneurial training. Table 9.8 contains the entrepreneurial framework conditions in the MENA region and their respective rankings. The latest GEM

Table 9.8 *GEM entrepreneurial framework conditions for select MENA economies*

Economy	Year	Financing for entrepreneurs	Governmental Support and Policies	Taxes and bureaucracy	Governmental programs	Basic school entrepreneurial education and training	Post school entrepreneurial education and training	R&D transfer	Commercial and professional infrastructure	Internal market dynamics	Internal market openness	Physical and services infrastructure	Cultural and social norms	National entrepreneurship context index (NECI)
Egypt	2022	4.22	4.25	3.68	3.68	2.33	3.64	2.77	4.95	6.33	4.48	6.63	5.16	4.3
Jordan	2023	4.25	4.95	4.74	5.07	2.87	3.71	3.69	5.58	5.12	4.43	6.92	5.05	4.7
Morocco	2023	3.72	5.72	4.55	4.4	2.11	4.13	3.16	5.26	4.91	3.45	6.18	4.47	4.3
Saudi Arabia	2023	6.47	6.57	6.38	6.39	4.44	5.54	5.14	6.34	7.17	6.01	7.96	7.4	6.3
Tunisia	2022	3.5	3.57	3.76	3.78	2.04	3.96	3.4	4.71	4.29	3.5	4.85	3.71	3.8
United Arab		**Emirates**	2023	7.28	7.92	7.46	7.46	7.65	7.81	7.75	7.76	8.01	7.34	7.6
8.12	7.7													

Source: Compiled by authors based on data from Global Entrepreneurship Monitor (GEM, 2022, 2023).
Note: Scores are on a scale of 1–9.

global report (GEM, 2024) highlights the UAE and KSA as top ecosystems, with other economies in the region lagging behind but gradually moving forward.

As the regionalisation and internationalisation trend manifests, ecosystem enablers and policymakers need to think of the region in a more integrated way, seeking talent, capital and market access where they are best available and building companies that are regional or global from the start. Moreover, policymakers in the leading MENA economies need to move beyond the narrow local angle of advocating local start-ups to a wider perspective, looking at regional opportunities using a more integrated approach. This includes providing investment vehicles that are regional in perspective, building soft-landing programmes that allow for rapid regionalisation and developing connections with international investors and research communities.

Most of the current unicorns and the pipeline of VC investments are targeted towards tech-enabled start-ups that are using ICTs to improve efficiencies in the economy in areas such as fintech, logistics and transportation, e-commerce, supply chain and healthcare. However, as the ecosystem grows in depth it is likely to start seeing start-ups in areas that are driven by deeptech and IP on innovation produced by universities and research institutions. Today, the pipeline in these areas remains nascent or at the early stages of investment (Series A). However, some examples of start-ups in this space indicate that local talent can create innovation that quickly commercialises if backed by the right investors. For example, InCurA (nanotech medical material), Proteinia (engineering proteins to tackle diseases) and Nawah Scientific (cloud lab for R&D services) are the ventures to follow.

This trend may be supported by the evolution of artificial intelligence (AI) technologies backed by open infrastructure that allows innovators to quickly test and develop ideas with limited capital. These include Velents (an AI interview and hiring platform), Brightskies (high-performance computing for self-driving cars) and Rology (an AI teleradiology platform). The future of unicorns from MENA looks much more dynamic that what the world has seen so far.

References

Aad, E. (2023). *The rise of entrepreneurship in Saudi Arabia: A transformative landscape.* Roland Berger. tinyurl.com/378f6ezu

Abu Dhabi SME Hub. (2021). *Abu Dhabi entrepreneurship ecosystem map out report.* Setup in Abu Dhabi. www.setupinabudhabi.ae/assets/uploads/ADSMEHubReport2021.pdf

Al Taasis. (2023). *Saudi entrepreneurial landscape: A global hub for startups and investors.* altaasis.sa/blog/entrepreneur-license-in-saudi-arabia/

Attar, H. (2023). *Angel investor groups.* Hussein Attar. www.husseinattar.com/en/angel-investor-groups-saudi-arabia/

Cabral, A. (2022). *UAE launches updated programme to develop 8,000 SMEs and start-ups by 2030.* The National. tinyurl.com/ysb8vbev

Elcheik, L. (2023). *How the UAE's start-up ecosystem is leading the charge in tackling youth unemployment.* Abu Dhabi SME Hub. tinyurl.com/cybx8smx

Elements Next Generation. (2023). *The UAE's start-up ecosystem: A thriving hub.* Elements Next Generation. tinyurl.com/yvs6jss4

El-Shaeri, N. (2023). *Saudi Arabia's entrepreneurial ecosystem demonstrating significant change.* Arab News. www.arabnews.com/node/2228301/business-economy

Entrepreneur. (2023). *Save the date: Here are the key entrepreneurship conferences in Saudi Arabia that you need to keep an eye out for.* tinyurl.com/mr44xrsd

Forbes Middle East. (2023). *The 50 most active investors in the Arab world.* www.forbesmiddleeast.com/list/the-50-most-active-investors-in-the-arab-world

GEM. (2022). *Ten notable numbers from the GEM Kingdom of Saudi Arabia national report.* Global Entrepreneurship Monitor. tinyurl.com/bcueztyr

(2023). *Dataset.* Global Entrepreneurship Monitor. www.gemconsortium.org/data

(2024). *GEM 2023/2024 global report: 25 years and growing.* Global Entrepreneurship Monitor. www.gemconsortium.org/report/51377

IFZA. (2022). *Dubai: A thriving ecosystem for entrepreneurial success.* International Free Zone Authority. ifza.com/en/dubai-a-thriving-ecosystem-for-entrepreneurial-success/

Ismail, A. (2009). *Private equity and venture capital in emerging markets: A case study of Egypt and the MENA region.* Unpublished dissertation, MIT. dspace.mit.edu/handle/1721.1/55105

(2022). *Entrepreneurship in Egypt: 2022 ecosystem overview.* African Development Bank. www.afdb.org/en/documents/entrepreneurship-egypt-2022-ecosystem-overview

(2024). *From idea to exit: The story of Egypt's Linkdotnet.*

Ismail, A., Schøtt, T., Bazargon, A., Dudokh, D., Al Kubaisi, H., Hassen, M., and et al. (2017). *GEM Middle East and North Africa regional report.*

Global Entrepreneurship Research Association. Global Entrepreneurship Monitor. www.gemconsortium.org/report/gem-2017-middle-east-and-north-africa-report

Ismail, A., Tolba, A., Schott, T., Meshreki, H., Barakat, S., and Ghalwash, S. (2022). *Global Entrepreneurship Monitor Egypt national report 2021–s22*. The American University in Cairo. Global Entrepreneurship Monitor. www.gemconsortium.org/economy-profiles/egypt

Kamel, S. (2016). Start-up. Global focus: The European Foundation for Management Development (EFMD) *Business Magazine 10*(3), 52–55.

(2022). The influence of entrepreneurship on the Arab cultures and economies: Reflections from Egypt's entrepreneurial journey. In N. Azoury and T. Hafsi, eds. *Entrepreneurship and Social Entrepreneurship in the MENA Region*. Palgrave MacMillan, pp. 255–279.

(2023). The role of business schools in creating national entrepreneurial ecosystems: The case of Egypt and the AUC School of Business. In E. Cornuel, H. Thomas, and M. Wood, eds. *Business School Research: Excellence, Academic Quality and Positive Impact, Annual Research Global Focus*, Vol. 2. The European Foundation for Management Development, pp. 68–77.

Knecht, J. (2024). *SMEs strengthening the entrepreneurial ecosystem*. Khaleej Times. tinyurl.com/t9andu54

Macrotrends. (2024). *World population growth rate 1950–2024*. www.macrotrends.net/global-metrics/countries/WLD/world/population-growth-rate

MAGNiTT. (2022). *2021 Egypt venture investment report*. magnitt.com/research/2021-egypt-venture-investment-report-50810

(2023). *2022 Egypt venture investment report*. magnitt.com/research/2022-egypt-venture-investment-report-50861

Misk Foundation. (2022). *6 entrepreneurship events in Saudi that are a must-visit in 2022*. tinyurl.com/mr3ah6k2

Motte, T. (2022). *The story of Careem, MENA's most important start-up to date*. Realistic Optimist. www.realisticoptimist.io/p/the-story-of-careem-the-worlds-first

QS Universities Rankings. (2024). *QS world university rankings 2024*. Top Universities. www.topuniversities.com/world-university-rankings

Russell J. (2017). *Amazon completes its acquisition of Middle Eastern e-commerce firm Souq*. TechCrunch. techcrunch.com/2017/07/03/amazon-souq-com-completed

Seed Group. (2022). *The UAE's entrepreneurial ecosystem and how to be a part of it*. seedgroup.com/2022/01/the-uaes-entrepreneurial-ecosystem-and-how-to-be-a-part-of-it/

Times Higher Education. (2024). *Where to study: Which university is right for you?* www.timeshighereducation.com/student/where-to-study

Toukan, S. (2015). *Yahoo! Closes, but Maktoob's legacy continues.* Wamda. www.wamda.com/2015/12/yahoo-closes-but-maktoobs-legacy-continues

Tracxn. (2024). *Angel network in GCC.* tinyurl.com/3mdfxuz2

Turki, A. (2015). *Public venture capital in Egypt: An assessment.* Master's thesis, American University in Cairo. AUC Knowledge Fountain. fount.aucegypt.edu/etds/137

United Nations. (2022). *World population prospects.* population.un.org/wpp/

Wamda. (2013). *The story of Yahoo's acquisition of Maktoob (case study).* www.wamda.com/2013/10/case-study-yahoo-acquisition-maktoob

(2023). *Startups in MENA raised almost $4 billion in 2022.* www.wamda.com/2023/01/startups-mena-raised-4-billion-2022

World Bank. (2022). *World Bank open data.* data.worldbank.org/

10 Nurturing Unicorns and Entrepreneurial Ecosystems in Africa: Harnessing Policy Innovation for Digital Transformation

FRED OLAYELE AND MZUKISI QOBO

10.1 Introduction

The venture capital and entrepreneurial ecosystem in Africa is thriving and one indicator of this is the number of start-ups that have achieved unicorn status. With multiple large fundraises and exits, the continent transitioned from having not a single unicorn to seven start-ups worth over US$1 billion in less than a decade. Prior to the recent downturn in global venture capital, Africa attracted international private capital at historic levels, reflecting growing investor confidence in the continent's potential. Starting with Airbnb's Brian Chesky and Microsoft's Satya Nadella in 2015 (followed by Facebook's Mark Zuckerberg, Google's Sundar Pichai, Alphabet's Sergey Brin, Alibaba's Jack Ma and Twitter's Jack Dorsey in subsequent years) high-profile tech hub visits and tours by these executives of global tech giants to the continent have amplified the emergence of Africa's tech entrepreneurship.

The upward trends in talent attraction, capital raising, market development and exits have generated interest, while new digital technology platforms are disrupting traditional industries by reshaping the way they operate. Even though many technology-driven start-ups gain traction organically, this is no substitute for finding a regional model that offers a sustainable flow of successful start-up ventures that go on to obtain unicorn status. To the extent that demographic, political and market nuances are key determinants of jurisdictional investment competitiveness, the leapfrog effect triggered by successful start-ups is generating incremental innovations in the governance infrastructure of several African countries. It is thereby tilting the risk–reward balance and incentivising some hitherto fearful investors to commit.

Among other factors, Africa's challenges to development can mainly be attributed to inadequate human capital development, weak governance and a poor institutional framework. Structural transformation and governance challenges are at the core of the political economy of African development. Poverty and high levels of inequality remain among the key challenges for the continent. From fragmentation and low productivity to poor infrastructure and the presence of large informal sectors, economic diversification remains a mirage, despite its prominence on the front burner of the economic policy debate dating back at least to the immediate post-independence period.

The majority of countries in sub-Saharan Africa perform poorly on key indicators of human development like years of schooling, life expectancy and poverty rates. This continues to limit the ability of the continent to deploy its vast human resources for longer-term growth. For instance, with the exception of Mauritius and Seychelles (which were ranked 63rd and 72nd, respectively), the rest of sub-Saharan African countries were ranked after 100th place of the 191 countries included in the Human Development Reports (UNDP) Human Development Index (HDI) in 2022. South Africa, with the third-highest HDI in sub-Saharan Africa, was ranked 109th (UNDP, 2022).

For a long time, conventional wisdom in the development orthodoxy rested largely on the notion that economic modernisation only occurred when workers transitioned from lower productivity employment in agrarian and extraction sectors to higher productivity employment in manufacturing and ultimately service industries (Rostow, 1960). Arguably, due to institutional and structural constraints, this model failed to deliver industrial diversification, particularly in the poorest countries in sub-Saharan Africa (Qobo, 2022). Despite the continent's inability to harness the benefits of both the agricultural and industrial revolutions, the rise of the digital knowledge economy is generating a lot of hope for the socioeconomic transformation of the continent, albeit with cautious optimism. The digital knowledge economy beckons, particularly in the context of leapfrogging, according to which a low-income country can skip stages in its development journey by leveraging the digital revolution to move directly from a traditional to a modern industrialised economy. As digital entrepreneurship matures in Africa, fostering venture capital and entrepreneurial ecosystems that can support and nurture unicorns as they adapt and innovate becomes increasingly important. Policy innovation can play a key role in this regard.

This chapter argues in favour of policy innovation in the context of Africa's burgeoning venture capital growth. As such, we subscribe to the Schumpeterian innovation model that explains industry growth through three channels: creative accumulation, creative destruction and rejection of competitive market equilibria. These channels underscore evolutionary growth and endogenous innovation. In this context, innovation is the vital force behind capitalism, as is the presence of an entrepreneur who is willing to make things happen through market dynamics, profit expectations and long-run growth expectations (Schumpeter, 1942).

10.1.1 *Institutional Prerequisites*

Africa's success in developing cutting-edge start-ups with the ability to attract the requisite investment hinges on building institutional capabilities and investing in human capital, including creating an ecosystem of digital economy underpinned by digital skills. The African continent does not need to be a twin of Silicon Valley in the sense of exactly replicating the entire ecosystem found in the US start-up capital. There is a vast difference in institutional structure, resources and capabilities between countries on the continent. Furthermore, what is found in the United States or in other advanced industrial economies is rarely available in Africa.

Beyond capabilities such as well-developed knowledge resources that are in abundance in the leading academic institutions of the Global North, as well as the agglomeration of venture capital, government resources and deep networks, there are specific challenges with which Africa contends that require a different approach to venture creation. As Christensen (2019) proposes, context matters for innovation.

Public investment in innovation broadens the possibilities for dynamic growth and entrepreneurial success. It is unlikely that a single successful model could be implemented across Africa in this respect. There are diverse paths to the emergence of unicorns around the globe, including transforming and deploying state capacities and support to promote tech innovation and the emergence of technological ventures. Still, it is important that institutional reforms for enabling the venture capital and tech start-up ecosystems reflect the inherent contextual pros and cons to ensure resources are allocated where they can have the biggest impact. In this chapter we argue that reforms enabling the strengthening of existing policy frameworks, skills development initiatives and a financing architecture that supports entrepreneurship along the entire value chain will be critical to the success of African unicorns.

We have organised the rest of the chapter in the following way. Section 10.2 examines Africa's political economy regarding digital entrepreneurship. Section 10.3 focuses on the prospects and challenges of tech entrepreneurship for the creation of African unicorns. The importance of agglomeration economies and regional innovation are seen as instrumental for harnessing the potential of the digital economy. Finally, Section 10.4 concludes and offers a discussion of possible implications.

10.2 Digital Entrepreneurship and Africa's Political Economy

Technology remains the backbone of the modern global economy due to, among other things, its impact on productivity growth in a knowledge-based economy. Africa is home to dynamic and growing digital ventures that drive growth in tech innovation, an influx of international capital and multiple large investment rounds and exits. According to a report by BusinessTech (2023), 2022 was a record year for tech start-ups across the continent, with 600 start-ups receiving US$3.3 billion, representing 55.1 per cent growth from the previous year. While the rise of the digital economy provides a unique opportunity for reforms that can help unlock further private investments, important caveats beckon. We discuss these below.

10.2.1 The Digital Economy as a Catalyst for Africa's Development

To attain a place of significance in the world, Africans should focus on improving the structural conditions of their economic systems, a process that requires the right kind of leadership and institutions in place. This is truer in the age of digital transformation and growing interest in tech start-ups. There is a window of opportunity for the African continent to overcome its institutional voids and create an enabling environment for the growth of investment in start-ups that could potentially become unicorns. The Boston Consulting Group report on tech start-ups in 2021 bemoaned the fact that Africa only had three unicorns compared to approximately fifty in the European Union,

100 in China and 200 in the United States (Boston Consulting Group, 2021). Developing digital skills, investing in technological assets including research and development (R&D) and having enabling institutions in place are some of the key interventions African countries need to prioritise to support their start-up ecosystems.

Africa's demographics have often been singled out as a source of strong future growth. This demographic potential can only be realised if African countries invest in skills development and the creation of job opportunities, especially in the industrial sector. Moreover, innovative high-tech companies receiving financial backing grew at 46 per cent between 2020 and 2021 (Boston Consulting Group, 2021). However, these positive developments are unlikely to trigger a leapfrogging process if the markets of fifty-four countries on the continent remain fragmented, with weak purchasing power, complex and inconsistent regulations and a dearth of capital and talent.

The digital economy grows on the back of stable internet connectivity, which provides the basis for innovation and the expansion of economic activity, including through the development of new applications and growth in e-commerce. For this reason, African countries must invest in digital assets, including infrastructure and human capital. Internet connectivity, the backbone for the digital economy, is relatively weak and unstable in many African countries. It is no wonder that the adoption of new, artificial intelligence (AI)-driven technologies is low in Africa compared to the rest of the world (Marwala, 2020: 148).

Given the strong linkages between internet connectivity and electricity (which powers the towers that provide internet), Africa's energy constraints have an adverse impact on the reliability of internet connectivity. This, in turn, has a negative bearing on productivity, further dampening investor sentiment in African start-ups.

Many African countries have only partial broadband coverage. Without access to quality broadband, building a digital economy that enables the scale of start-ups to unicorn status becomes a challenge. The digital economy can undoubtedly be a critical source of start-up growth on the continent if the right kind of investments are made and if government regulation acts as an enabler rather than an obstacle. A 10 per cent increase in broadband penetration in developing countries generates 1.4 per cent increase in gross domestic product (GDP) (Broadband Commission, 2011), a fact that should motivate a change in government priorities. The various channels through which such connectivity enhances a country's development path include bridging information divides and improving communication, especially for citizens in remote areas. Another channel includes reducing information asymmetries in the economy, for example, between consumers, producers and other nodes of the value chain. Finally, increasing productivity, lowering transaction costs and optimising supply chains is another.

UN Trade and Development (UNCTAD) (2019) highlights three dimensions of the digital economy: the core aspects that comprise fundamental innovations such as semiconductors and processors, core technologies such as computers and telecommunication devices and enabling infrastructures such as internet and telecoms networks; digital and information technology sectors, which produce key products or services that rely on core digital technologies, for example, mobile applications and payment services; and a wider set of sectors, such as e-commerce, and changes in business models to respond to digitalisation, including a reformatting of activities such as media, finance and transportation.

African countries engage in only a few of these dimensions due to their weak economies, shallow digital infrastructure and lack of requisite skills. Although there have been some innovations in the domains of applications and e-commerce, albeit on a lower scale, African countries lag on the core aspects of technology infrastructure. These are the constraints to which African governments need to pay more attention.

Human capital development and public investment in innovation will have to be at the centre of development strategies in African countries. It is not enough to push for structural transformation; it is crucial to search for more dynamism through public investment in innovation, digital infrastructure and upgrading human capital. These policy drivers should aim at advantageously positioning the African continent in a changing global economy and help in shifting negative perceptions that view Africa as a permanent problem with which others should deal through development aid. With the development of the right set of institutions and the presence of a policy environment conducive to innovation, Africa can hope to leapfrog certain stages of development.

10.2.2 A New Era of Africa's Tech Entrepreneurs

An army of innovators and entrepreneurs has emerged at the forefront of shaping Africa's nascent digital economy in recent times. They are creating products and services that respond to social and economic challenges that are specific to the continent. They lack scale but are impressive nonetheless, given that the continent has lagged behind on the use of digital products and services. For example, the Boston Consulting Group highlighted several African tech start-ups that have achieved zebra valuations (those with a valuation of at least US$200 million) and identified some of the structural barriers that suffocate the emergence of national champions that are key to driving the development of new technologies. The key observation of the report is that collaboration (including through strategic alliances) between large incumbents that have significant capabilities and resources may perhaps be the best avenue for growing tech start-ups at the zebra valuation level, which could then scale to unicorn level. Examples of such high-potential ventures include Ghana's Jumo that describes its services as offering mobile wallet technology with data-driven credit prediction models to provide digital financial services infrastructure to partners. It also shares credit scoring with its financial partners, thus providing a valuable service in expanding credit. Fawry, also part of the financial services sector, offers e-payments and digital finance solutions in Egypt, as does Interswitch in Nigeria. The growth of digital or e-payment services meets the critical need for financial inclusion and holds huge potential for low-cost growth in financial intermediation. Partnerships with incumbents make sense given the dearth of financial markets and low activity of venture capital on the African continent. The newly emergent high-net-worth foundations on the continent and their associated family offices could also ignite a spark of entrepreneurial growth. We should avoid a narrow view of the sources of financial succour as only originating in Africa. They can also come from outside of the continent, including impact funds and other sources of patient capital.

Beyond digital finance and banking, Africa's rising entrepreneur and serial investor in tech start-ups, Sangu Delle, has surveyed digital trends that are pioneered by various entrepreneurs across different countries on the continent (Delle, 2020). He observes that the investments various African countries have made in information and communication technology (ICT) have begun to bear fruit, enabling African entrepreneurs to spawn innovations and build businesses that had not existed before

For some time, the signs of digital adoption have been evident on the African continent through the platform of mobile phones, which serve as conduits for financial transactions in an environment where the majority of poor people are excluded from financial services, or where there is 'nonconsumption' (Christensen, 2019). Such transactions go beyond just receiving remittances from relatives in the diaspora and making payments for products and services. Much has been written about Kenya's pioneering foray into this area through M-Pesa, and how this has transformed the way individuals and entrepreneurs transact.

Remittance flows to sub-Saharan Africa grew by 10 per cent to US$46 billion in 2018. Much of this was due to the convenience offered by mobile payments platforms. Digital banking, and to a broad extent fintech, hold great potential for expanding on the African continent and becoming a preferred route for mediating transactions, since bank charges in Africa tend to be prohibitively high. Various mobile companies can find profitable ways to make strategic shifts towards building digital banking platforms or fintech in ways that could disrupt retail banking on the continent, just like when mobile network operators rendered fixed-line telephony obsolete in the 1990s. Some retail banks are expected to join the party by acquiring fintech start-ups or incubating in-house innovations. Apart from mobile payments, there have been various other exciting developments and experiments that point to the continent's appetite for making advances in the digital economy.

There are tech entrepreneurs in Kenya, who have overcome logistical or marketing constraints in agriculture value chains, mainly serving smallholder rural farmers. Some local entrepreneurs have created technology-based solutions to aggregate farmers' produce and facilitate their routes to markets, thereby cutting intermediaries that push up transaction costs.

Entrepreneurs in Nigeria such as Chinny Ogunro have tapped into digital tools to solve healthcare challenges, adapting solutions applied in India to deliver quality healthcare at affordable prices through a network of new generation hospitals in Africa. Various other digital solutions have been applied in the education sector to deliver high-quality education that trains work-ready graduates or skilful entrepreneurs willing to start their businesses, thereby creating opportunities to absorb young Africans who would otherwise face a jobless future.

There is also an increase in technology-driven solutions to address challenges in payments systems using fintech and platforms such as the unicorn Flutterwave, created by Nigerian entrepreneur Olugbenga

Agboola. In Ghana, Wefarm taps into AI to work alongside humans to enlarge the scope of knowledge of smallholder farmers. This tech start-up and its technology solution avoid the step-by-step modernisation paradigm and integrate technology into primary production processes. Wefarm aims to connect every smallholder farmer on earth and offers solutions that help them better understand data related to crop production and overcome constraints posed by market information asymmetry.

There are also major firms that support the development of a digital ecosystem that fosters entrepreneurial growth in a broader sense. Naspers had pioneered a venture capital initiative called Naspers Foundry, which had set aside R1.4 billion (roughly US$100 million when the initiative was announced) of investment over three years from 2018 to support technology start-ups in South Africa, especially Series A and B funding. This mainly targeted black-owned technology start-ups with the aim of addressing the lack of inclusion in the country's digital business ecosystem. The initiative was closed down in 2022 due to the global downturn and tight regulatory conditions in South Africa.

Another pan-African mobile company, MTN, founded in 1994, has lent a hand in broadening the commercial space for tech start-ups. Its investments have included the meteoric e-commerce platform Jumia. The company also works through universities on tech challenge contests to support a new generation of tech entrepreneurs among young South Africans. It has been active in working towards universal connectivity and supporting social enterprise initiatives to ensure the availability of smartphone devices to enable access.

10.2.3 The Data Governance Imperative

There are, however, marked skills shortages on the African continent for more complex AI processes. These capabilities can be built over time, however, as Lee (2013) has shown, a country does not need a great abundance of elite engineering skills to take advantage of the technological breakthrough. Africa's focus should be on supporting entrepreneurs and making investment alongside public funding agencies attractive for venture capital. Africa needs heavy and smart investment in human capital and ambitious public investment in innovation. Investment in R&D is crucial for spurring invention and innovation. Enabling policies that can improve the tech start-up ecosystem are essential. In the absence of strong intellectual property (IP) rights protection, inventions become a mere public good. Under the right regulatory framework and enforcement, IP rights could become a major tool for unlocking additional dynamism in the African entrepreneurial scene.

The African continent is a potentially data-rich market from a demographic point of view and in various dimensions such as language, culture, consumer patterns, decision-making structures, talents, arts and craft, natural systems and biodiversity, to name but a few. Africa should build innovation systems that fuse technology and indigenous knowledge structures to create solutions to problems that are specific to the continent and rely on local data generation. Webb (2019: 5) notes that human data is possibly the most important natural resource in the era of AI. According to Ramge and Mayer-Schonberger (2018: 63), 'data is the new grease for the wheels of the market ... the most obvious difference between conventional markets and data-rich ones is the volume and variety of data that flows among market participants'. The importance of data markets is not just about matching buyers and sellers, but also about identifying the problems that need solving and how best to solve them.

It is worth highlighting that foreign companies control the data produced in Africa, making it all the more necessary for Africans to have sound data governance and data sharing frameworks to safeguard data ownership and control. Such data could be directed towards solving a defined set of problems or achieving a critical mission; for example, making advances in health, rural enterprises, food production systems or any number of socioeconomic challenges.

Africa's potentially data rich markets partly explain why major tech firms such as Amazon Web Services, Microsoft and Google have established a footprint in this burgeoning data market. For the same reasons, Huawei has worked closely with the security forces in Zimbabwe to build voice and facial-recognition systems and exports its 'smart cities' technology, which integrates surveillance and data collection practices, to other countries with weak privacy or personal data collection norms (International Institute for Strategic Studies, 2021).

Challenges related to market information asymmetry in agriculture value chains, healthcare (including modelling for future diseases), education constraints, delivery of public services through e-government and responding to the effect of climate change on biodiversity, among others, are some of the candidates for Africa's technology solutions and domains within which future African unicorns could be created.

10.3 Unicorns and Tech Entrepreneurship in Africa: Promises and Challenges

Africa is ranked as the youngest, fastest-urbanising region in the world, as well as one of the most entrepreneurial (Duffy, 2021). Fuelled by a burgeoning population and urbanisation, the growth of megacities and smaller towns across the continent presents an opportunity to defragment markets, reduce inefficiency and boost productivity. These are all key preconditions for an entrenched and sustainable entrepreneurial ecosystem.

Compared to established global tech innovation hubs like Silicon Valley, New York, London and Hong Kong, venture capital investment in Africa is still negligible. In addition, only four countries (Nigeria, Egypt, South Africa and Kenya) account for about one third of the continent's start-up incubators and accelerators and 80 per cent of foreign capital inflows. For this reason the distribution of venture capital in Africa has major implications for inclusive economic development across the continent (African Development Bank, 2021).

Before 2016, when Africa's e-commerce company Jumia raised US$493 million to reach the billion-dollar valuation mark, no single unicorn had existed on the continent. Since then, African start-ups have received record levels of funding in relation to previous years, leading to a robust start-up ecosystem that now boasts seven unicorns: Interswitch, Flutterwave, OPay, Wave, Andela, Chipper Cash and MNT-Halan (Afridigest, 2023). While Interswitch became a unicorn in 2019, Flutterwave, OPay, Wave, Andela and Chipper Cash hit the US$1 billion valuation threshold in 2021. The latest entrant, MNT-Halan, joined the list in 2023. Four of the seven companies are Nigerian, two are Ghanaian and one is Egyptian.

Innovators and entrepreneurs still need to overcome various hurdles in the African institutional setting. These include a shallow base of venture capital, the lack of a rich innovation ecosystem to bring universities, government, industry, entrepreneurs and venture capitalists together, reasonably high education levels and data skills and governance frameworks to set the rules of the game involving the uses of personal data and IP. Policies aimed at supporting the development of ICT as well as regulatory instruments for the digital economy remain poorly developed.

Technological breakthroughs are not only an individual effort but also benefit from corporate-level initiatives and broader institutional cooperation; all these elements interact together for successful innovation (Sun, 2018). Mazzucato (2015: 30) underlines the importance of innovation as part of an ecosystem that is based on the symbiotic relationships between the public and private sectors. Further, she argues that policymaking regarding innovation should focus on outcomes. Such outcomes can be achieved through collaboration between the public and private sectors 'on investing in solutions, having a long-run view, and governing the process [of collaboration] to make sure it is done in the public interest' (Mazzucato, 2021). African governments will need to learn to work closely with both small and large businesses in the private sector and take feedback from holders of capital such as venture capitalists. Such strategic interactions can help improve the investment climate, especially for high-risk tech-based investments.

10.3.1 The Venture Capital Landscape

Based on data from Disrupt Africa and data analytics firm MAGNiTT, the African start-up ecosystem witnessed record levels of venture capital investment in 2021, with more start-ups raising more money from more investors than in any other year on record. While other traditional tech hubs on the continent witnessed a significant increase across funded ventures and total secured capital, Africa's 'big four' start-up ecosystems (Nigeria, Egypt, South Africa and Kenya) received over 92 per cent of the total funding (Figure 10.1).

Venture capital funding for Africa more than tripled between 2020 and 2021, standing just shy of US$3 billion in 2021 (MAGNiTT, 2022). Also, the number of deals closed reached an all-time-high with unprecedented growth in the influx of international private capital.

Funding for start-ups in Nigeria increased by 431 per cent compared to 2020, a record-high, with 43 per cent of all financing coming from the African fintech sector. Kenya, another leading fintech hub in Africa, witnessed a 5 per cent increase in venture capital investment between 2020 and 2021. While lower than its 2019 record in terms of the number of deals, this was a record-high for 2021.

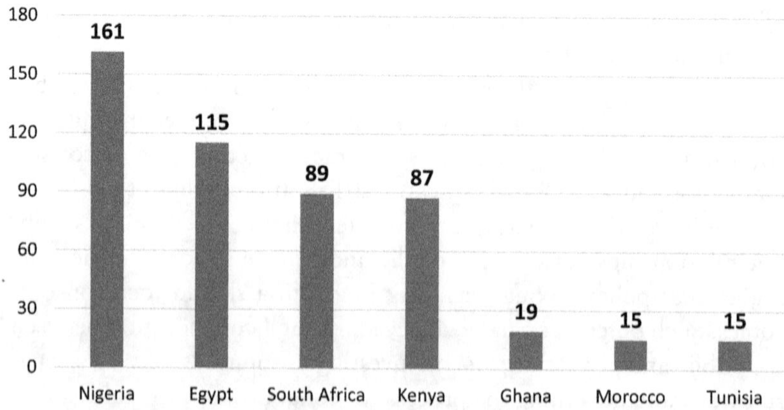

Figure 10.1 Number of funded African start-ups (by country).
Source: Statista (2024).

The South African start-up ecosystem witnessed record levels of venture capital investment in 2021, with an increase of 445 per cent from 2020. The number of deals increased by 8 per cent year-over-year in 2021, while the country recorded a yearly all-time-high venture capital investment.

Funding for start-ups in Egypt increased for the fifth year in a row in 2022 when it rose by 3 per cent to US$517 million. The country saw a total of 160 venture capital deals in the same year, emerging first in the entire Middle East and North Africa (MENA) region in terms of total deals.

10.4 Agglomeration Economies and the Case for Regional Innovation

Agglomeration economies remain the basic logic behind building innovation ecosystems in cities and industrial clusters, as Porter's (1990; 1998) diamond model of regional/national competitive advantage largely highlights. It entails using efficiency gains and productivity increases from the interactions between firms and people located near one another. This logic has major implications for Africa.

Fragmentation, subsistence, informality and low productivity, which drive contemporary economic outcomes across Africa, limit the ability to leverage much of the innovation that occurs in large metropolitan areas due to agglomeration economies. As already discussed, the economic ascent of many of today's highly industrialised nations occurred through agricultural transformation and transition to the modern service economy. However, in the African context, due to the leapfrog effect and the drastic changes in the post-industrial economy in the face of digitalisation, there is a limit to the application of this reasoning. This includes important caveats related to access to non-local critical resources such as international venture capital.

Still, as the global economy continues to rapidly digitalise, sustainable value creation within the innovation economy is important for regional output maximisation. To achieve this objective, it is important to conduct a critical assessment of the other key ingredients needed for success, aside from digital technologies. Among others, the availability of top talent, creativity, start-up and growth capital, intellectual capital and a robust ecosystem that can connect start-ups to programmes and funds for expansion are vital (Gutiérrez & Olayele, 2021). Clusters are becoming an important vehicle in the development of the entrepreneurial ecosystem because of their potential for driving innovation on a large scale. Innovation clusters are increasingly being deployed across Africa to help boost private sector financing, attract top talent and prioritise the role of intellectual capital in the innovation value chain.

10.4.1 Digital Transformation and the AfCFTA

Efforts towards deepening economic integration on the African continent, especially in the context of the African Continental Free Trade Area (AfCFTA) need to be made for greater investment in innovation.

Africa's public institutions and development agencies should work collaboratively to enable large-scale digital markets and harmonise regulatory frameworks for the digital economy. The urge should not be a defensive one; that is, to regulate in a way that throttles the continental digital ecosystem, nor should it be laissez-faire and ignore the risks that come with data-rich markets. The focus, rather, should be on co-creating the right regulatory framework through collaboration with market agents, learning from norm champions in a framework of experimentation and development of sandbox approaches.

The AfCFTA comprised fifty-five member states of the African Union and created a market of over 1.2 billion people at the time the mechanism was officially announced in January 2021. The single market had an estimated combined GDP of more than US$3.4 trillion at the time of its launch. Apart from promoting intra-regional trade and improving the structural profile of goods traded, this mechanism also aims to support infrastructure expansion and the development of cross-border value chains. There is increasing emphasis on using the AfCFTA as an enabler for digital transformation on the African continent. Beyond instruments of restraints such as data localisation or risk assessment for cyber threats, public institutions and development agencies should create an enabling environment for tech entrepreneurs and large companies that want to invest in the digital ecosystem in Africa. Building a thriving digital economy alongside the quest to industrialise should be central to AfCFTA's long-term efforts.

The various innovations that have trickled in over the last decade suggest that the African continent has better prospects if governments put critical success factors of institutional support and the right regulatory framework in place. Sims (2012) makes an important point that major innovative breakthroughs happen on the back of initiatives that are based on 'little bets', through a process of discovery aimed at solving a defined set of problems. This should not be confused with a step-by-step structural change following Rostow's (1960) pattern or the idea of moving to the next product space that Hausmann and Klinger (2006) propounded. These constitute little bets along technology curves rather than shifting from producing cotton to manufacturing a complete garment. Sims (2012: 8) notes that this idea of pushing knowledge through discovery 'is based on the proposition that we can use a lot of little bets and certain creative methods to identify possibilities and build up to great outcomes'; such little bets 'are concrete actions taken to discover, test, and develop ideas that are achievable and affordable'. Such ideas could be scalable. This would become more true if African governments placed a strong focus on making significant investments in innovation and public infrastructure, particularly on supporting the market-creating innovations that Christensen (2019) alluded to.

10.4.2 Regional Innovation Models in Africa

From the private and public sectors to international development and philanthropy, successful regional innovation models abound across the continent. The Water and Energy for Food (WE4F) initiative is a global development effort based on regional innovation hubs. With a hub located in Pretoria, South Africa, the WE4F programme focuses on sustainability and climate resilience in southern and central Africa. From providing access to financing and technical assistance to grants and investment facilitation, it supports smallholder farmers in the region to overcome fragmentation challenges and scale their business by unlocking missing inputs, finance, technology and markets (WE4F, 2024).

Another regional innovation model is the African-European Digital Innovation Bridge Network (AEDIB|NET), which aims to support local digital innovation and start-up ecosystems on the continent. This support takes the form of facilitating, developing and strengthening activities focused on building technical capacity and technology transfer between African and European innovators and start-ups, small- and medium-sized enterprises, private sector actors, academia, local governments and investors (European Commission, 2021–2024).

We will now discuss some of the constraints and opportunities for leading regional countries in harvesting nascent digital infrastructure-enabled opportunities. We focus on Kenya, Nigeria, Rwanda and South Africa for their regional economic weight, reform trajectory and leadership in attracting investments in the digital economy.

10.4.3 Kenya

Kenya has received accolades as a result of the impressive developments in its digital economy and the contribution this has made to overall economic growth. Mobile telephones, rising internet usage and the uptake of e-commerce has propelled the country's digital economy (World Bank, 2019a: 26). As the World Bank report points out, the country had forty-seven million active mobile subscribers in 2019, with mobile penetration at 90 per cent. About 46 per cent of citizens were connected to broadband by the end of 2018. Early adoption of digital payments and the unflagging entrepreneurial spirit lifted Kenya's digital economy.

The role of digital technologies in Africa as drivers of socioeconomic development tends to be constrained by regulation and policy, especially those that relate to radio communications and the frequency spectrum. Even a country like Kenya, which has acted as an example for digital tools such as mobile banking and money transactions, suffers significant regulatory challenges that limit the telecoms sector's potential to be fully used for e-commerce (World Bank, 2019a). This throttles the development of rich digital markets. Furthermore, data protection remains a weakness in Kenya as it does in many other African countries.

Kenya suffers market concentration in the interlinked telecoms and mobile money markets. As a report of the World Bank (2019a) points out, Kenya's tech start-ups are on the rise, but these require more government support to improve their success rate in reaching high growth stages. Regulatory barriers to doing business affect these start-ups and interfere with their scaling up trajectories. Mentorship, training and the development of managerial skills are essential. The inequitable provision of broadband infrastructure between the urban and the rural parts constitutes a structural inequality for digital product access. This must be overcome if universal connectivity is to be achieved and if digital products are to act as a source of development and inclusion.

Digital payment platforms have been a boon for users and improved the way consumers transact in the marketplace. This is one example of the kinds of market-creating innovations that Christensen (2019) encouraged and has helped to reduce poverty in Kenya, acting as a testament to the role of digital markets in generating socioeconomic benefits. The value of mobile transfers constituted 44.7 per cent of the GDP in 2018 (World Bank, 2019a: 28).

The Kenyan government has committed to positioning the country as a hub for information and communication, e-commerce and digital services. The dynamic business and innovation environment has attracted the IBM African Research Lab, Google and General Electric to set up headquarters there. According to the World Bank (2019a), digital transformation in sub-Saharan African countries can increase growth by nearly two percentage points per year, with poverty coming down one percentage point per year.

Human capital development will be vital to reaping the gains of the digital shifts. There are five key foundational pillars for success in the digital economy: digital infrastructure, digital skills, digital platforms and services, digital financial services and digital entrepreneurship (World Bank, 2019a: 26). Developing these five elements could position African countries and specifically Kenya at the forefront of digital transformation in the Global South. These foundational pillars are still missing in many African countries and should be a priority for governments at both the national and continental institutional levels.

10.4.4 Nigeria

The Nigeria Communications Commission developed an eight-point agenda in 2015. This was aimed at supporting Nigeria's transition to the digital economy through investment in digital infrastructure, facilitating broadband penetration, improving quality of service, maximising usage and benefits of the spectrum and promoting ICT innovation and investment opportunities in the country (World Bank, 2019a: 11). Nigeria launched a presidential initiative for innovative entrepreneurship in 2018, focusing on supporting start-up and tech ecosystems.

Nigeria ranked 152 out of 157 countries in the World Bank's 2018 human capital index. The country has low overall internet usage with a 27.7 per cent penetration rate (International Telecommunications Union, 2018). Africa's average is even lower, at 22.1 per cent. This means that connectivity is lacking in much of the continent, possibly exacerbated by deficiencies in energy infrastructure. Nigeria had a 0.004 per cent household penetration rate for broadband at the end of 2018, while Africa's average stood at 0.6 per cent and the world average at 13.6 (International Telecommunications Union, 2018). Furthermore, digital divides along rural–urban and gender lines are a frequent common feature across the continent. The country faces difficulties such as the opaqueness of its regulatory system and overlapping and conflicting regulatory bodies. Specifically, there are significant infrastructural challenges and market failures in the provision of broadband connectivity in rural areas. Additionally, the urban–rural divide undermines economic inclusion in most African countries.

10.4.5 Rwanda

Like many other African countries, Rwanda must overcome challenges related to digital skills and the affordability of digital devices and services. Computer literacy in Rwanda was estimated at under 10 per cent in 2019, making it harder for many to participate in the digital economy in any meaningful way. Building skills, widening internet access and improving connectivity could go a long way towards increasing participation; these objectives are already built into the government's programmes.

Rwanda has bet on the digital economy. The country's government perceives the adoption of digital platforms as key to improving productivity across various sectors of the economy. The government also partners with non-profit and for-profit organisations to increase the country's digital skills base. The uptake of digital tools, especially by the government, has improved public service delivery.

At 93.5 per cent, Rwanda's 3G network coverage is higher than the regional average of 76 per cent. However, the internet penetration rate is low and with weak access to smartphones and 4G-compatible devices. There is under-utilisation of the 4G network, mainly because mobile phone devices with 4G capability are not affordable to most consumers. The country has tapped into international networks to build public–private partnerships with Korean Telecom to provide 4G network coverage.

The government has also ramped up the focus on basic digital skills in partnership with the World Economic Forum and Digital Opportunities Trust. It will be hard for Rwanda and other African countries to attract venture capital at scale with deficient digital skills and lacking government support for the tech ecosystem. This is a key challenge for African governments if they are to leapfrog several development stages and meaningfully participate in the increasingly digitised global value chains.

10.4.6 South Africa

According to the World Bank, in 2019 the tech start-up sector was 'overwhelmingly white, male and middle class' (World Bank, 2019c: xv). Initiatives such as Naspers Foundry aim to change this profile. Some of the factors that hinder tech entrepreneurship highlighted by the World Bank report include policies related to IP legislation, R&D, tax incentive schemes, exchange controls and labour legislation. Finance gaps are still persistent throughout most of a digital start-up's lifecycle, with 'later stage funds lacking sufficient capacity, inclusiveness, and critical size to fund and facilitate rapid internationalisa tion of South African digital businesses' (World Bank, 2019c: xv). Data costs in South Africa are exceptionally high.

In 2019 South Africa's Competition Commission found that South Africa's mobile network operators charged consumers excessive data prices. The enquiry undertaken by competition authorities into data costs revealed evidence of monopolistic behaviour. The report found that South Africans paid higher prices compared to other countries, including African countries. Lower-income consumers were found to be 'exploited to a far greater degree relative to wealthier consumers for mobile data prices' (Competition Commission, 2020: 11). This was not surprising given that two operators dominate South Africa's mobile telecommunications market; Vodacom and MTN command 78 per cent of the market share (National Planning Commission, 2020). The other two operators, Cell C and Telkom Mobile, have a subscriber market share estimated at 17 per cent and 5 per cent, respectively.

According to a report by the National Planning Commission (2020: 4), 'the failure of the broadcast digital migration process and the debacle over the release of the high-demand spectrum are two of the more striking examples of what appears to be the institutional failure.' In December 2020 and at the beginning of 2021, mobile network operators took the government to court to challenge aspects of the high-demand radio frequency spectrum auction process. There is also a lack of technical capacity at the institutional policy and regulatory levels. The government's slow progress in releasing the high-demand spectrum is due to delays in digital migration from analogue to digital, a process that has been caught up in litigation. This has left mobile operators with both insufficient spectrum and a lack of access to favourable low-frequency bands. This has a potentially cost-raising effect on data plans.

When the spectrum is not readily available, operators are forced to increase the volume of base stations, which pushes up their capital and operational costs. The operators then recuperate these costs by raising consumer prices. When digital migration finally happens and the low-frequency spectrum is abundantly available, operators could use it for coverage in less populated areas in ways that could close the urban–rural digital divide and yield new digitally empowered businesses. South Africa's ongoing energy crisis could be an albatross to digital innovations because the data tower signals rely on old electricity infrastructure. This is an example of how infrastructural deficiencies could undermine progress. Absence of economies of scale in rural areas is a reality that more systemic interventions could overcome. This is where market-creating innovations through public policy support, public private partnership initiatives, skills development and a range of incentives to attract private sector investment are required; they hold the key to unleashing prosperity.

In sum, South Africa still faces challenges in its transition to a digital economy that promotes inclusiveness. There are major policy and human capital bottlenecks that hinder the meaningful participation of many citizens in the digital economy. Measured by the commonly used Gini index, South Africa (at 0.63) had the highest level of inequality in the world in 2022 (World Bank, 2022). Given the poverty-reducing effects of digitalisation that come from access to a reliable and affordable internet connection, we cannot overemphasise the importance of the digital economy in addressing South Africa's pervasive challenge of inequality.

Another constraint is the country's lack of skills. South Africa lacks sufficient skills for the digital economy. The country had internet usage of more than 54 per cent in 2017, with smartphone penetration rates of over 80 per cent. The usage rate is below the profile of an aspirational middle-income country like South Africa that is, in relative terms, an economic giant in sub-Saharan Africa. Of greater importance is the value that the digital economy could generate for the country's socioeconomic development. Christensen (2019) argues that the creation of new markets through innovation, especially in areas blighted by socioeconomic challenges, yields new jobs and other economic activities. Africa is a fertile terrain for market-creating innovations, but governments will need to play a more visible role in making interventions that could uncover new opportunities.

The government will need to direct its efforts towards narrowing the socioeconomic divide that is also starkly reflected in the digital divide. This is especially visible between well-off suburbia and underserved townships, and between the urban centres and rural areas. Co-investing in building digital infrastructure in underserved areas and releasing the much-awaited spectrum are as important for socioeconomic development as they are for economic value generation.

In the context of policy diffusion, ample innovation lessons abound from both established global venture capital hotspots and success stories from across the continent. Africa has the potential to become a superpower in the tech innovation sector, but this will require filling the existing void to ensure the continent's tech start-ups continue to attract private equity, offering attractive returns for investors. Not only is this paradigm key for talent attraction and high-quality ideas that drive funding and unlock wealth, but it is also necessary for other activities along the value chain. These include, but are not limited to, secondary sales to growth-focused and private equity investors and deepening of commercial and technology linkages with established local and global unicorns as well as burdenless exit options.

10.5 Concluding Reflections and Lessons for Policy Innovation

The digital economy can contribute significantly to value generation under an economic policy paradigm that prioritises strategic investments in broadband infrastructure and access to new digital technologies for a skilled and globally competitive workforce. Many African countries share common challenges for the implementation of such a paradigm.

The beneficial impacts of Africa's unicorns and their start-up ecosystems can be understood in the context of the innovation economy, which derives its primary value from digital technologies, the continent's young demographic, an abundance of innovative talent and an unprecedented availability of risk capital. We can see the multiplier effect of these critical ingredients which has at least two broad implications.

Firstly, given the importance of venture capital funding for enabling start-ups to scale, develop new products and enter new markets, aspiring unicorns generate significant economic impacts through new jobs, tax revenue and foreign exchange inflows. The increased level of private investment in digital infrastructure is attracting many young graduates to embrace digital entrepreneurship, thereby becoming job creators and helping to address endemic poverty and high levels of unemployment across the continent.

Secondly, consistent with the concept of Schumpeterian entrepreneurship, innovation is a key driver of economic change. This is because new ideas, experimentations and technological disruptions are needed to create the so-called perennial gale of creative destruction[1] which is largely spurred by entrepreneurs and innovators (Olayele, 2022). Given their dominance in new and emerging sectors of the regional economy, African start-ups play a major role in

[1] Coined by Joseph Schumpeter in his 1942 work *Capitalism, Socialism and Democracy*.

diversifying value creation activities across the continent, thereby making them more resilient to economic shocks.

In addition to cost factors, many rural communities lack the internet speeds available in urban areas due to under-investment in broadband infrastructure. This is unacceptable, as it sustains apartheid geographies and throttles the potential of a country. As the vice president of Microsoft Brad Smith points out, 'broadband has become the electricity of the twenty-first century. It is fundamental to the way people work, live, and learn. The future of medicine [especially in rural areas] is telemedicine. The future of education is online education [or a blended mode]. And the future of agriculture is precision farming' (Smith & Browne, 2019: 156).

Digital infrastructure and affordable internet connectivity could enable rural and poor communities in Africa to accelerate their economic progress. Today, rural areas that lack broadband are living in the twentieth century. This is also the relative position of Africa in the global economy today. Making significant improvements in economic development and building momentum for digital transformation will be a crucial step in changing global perceptions about Africa. Importantly, it will infuse the younger generation of Africans with self-confidence and a sense of pride in their continent.

Growing digitisation requires that African governments nurture the digital ecosystem while also developing appropriate regulatory frameworks for data governance and technology partnerships with external partners. Based on the analysis and discussion so far, the rise of Africa's digital economy provides a unique opportunity for reforms that can help unlock further private investments. By its very nature, venture capital is not long-term funding. Its basic tenet is to invest in a start-up until it reaches a sufficient size and credibility that can enable it to sustainably commercialise its innovation. This underscores the role of a robust support system across the African start-up value chain.

It is not lost on us that while a handful of players are bountifully reaping the benefits of the acceleration of technological uptake across key sectors and digital innovation ecosystems on the continent, in reality many Africans still do not have access to digital resources at a scale large enough to spark a continent-wide digital revolution that could move a significant number of Africans above the poverty line. This shall be the primary aspiration of African unicorns and local ecosystem actors.

References

African Development Bank. (2021). *Entrepreneurship and free trade: Africa's catalysts for a new era of economic prosperity*. tinyurl.com/4kmatxzu

Afridigest. (2023). *The complete list of African unicorns today*. afridigest.com/complete-list-african-unicorns-today/

Boston Consulting Group. (2021, 12 April). *Overcoming tech startup obstacles*. tinyurl.com/5w9d5zpk

Broadband Commission. (2011, June). *Broadband: A platform for progress. A report by the Broadband Commission for digital development, ITU and UNESCO*.

BusinessTech. (2023, 23 April). *Rough start to 2023 for tech startups in South Africa*. tinyurl.com/35hjuyc5

Christensen, C. M. (2019). *Targeting nonconsumption: Who are the best customers for our products?* Harvard Business School Module Note 420-015, July 2019.

Competition Commission. (2020). *Competition in the digital economy*. (A Paper for Public Comments). September 2020.

Delle, S. (2020). *Making futures: Young entrepreneurs in a dynamic Africa*. Cassava Republic.

Duffy, A. (2021). *African tech ecosystems of the future – The dawn of a new era: South Africa has come out on top of the inaugural African tech ecosystems of the future ranking*. FDI Intelligence. www.fdiintelligence.com/article/79638?saveConsentPreferences=success

European Commission. (2021–2024). *African-European digital innovation bridge network*. cordis.europa.eu/project/id/101017105

Gutiérrez, A., and Olayele, F. (2021). Urban innovation and reinvention: The case of New York. *ICE. Revista De Economía* (920), 29–48. revistasice.com/index.php/ICE/article/view/7211

Hausmann, R., and Klinger, B. (2006). *Structural transformation and patterns of comparative advantage in the product space*. Centre for International Development, Kennedy School of Government, Harvard University.

International Institute for Strategic Studies (ed.). (2021). *The Strategic Survey 2021* (1st ed.). Routledge.

International Telecommunications Union. (2018). *Measuring the information society report*. International Telecommunications Union.

Lee, A. (2013). *Welcome to the unicorn club: Learning from billion-dollar startups*. TechCrunch. techcrunch.com/2013/11/02/welcome-to-the-unicorn-club/

MAGNiTT. (2022). Home page. magnitt.com/research/

Marwala, T. (2020). *Closing the Gap*. Pan Macmillan.

Mazzucato, M. (2015). *The Entrepreneurial State*. Public Affairs.

(2021). *Mission Economy: A Moonshot Guide to Changing Capitalism.* Allen Lane.

National Planning Commission. (2020). *Digital futures: South Africa's digital readiness for the 'fourth industrial revolution'.*

Olayele, F. (2022). *African policy innovation and the political economy of public-private policy partnerships.* IGI Global

Porter, M. (1990). The competitive advantage of nations. *Harvard Business Review.* hbr.org/1990/03/the-competitive-advantage-of-nations

(1998). *Competitive Strategy Techniques for Analyzing Industries and Competitors* (1st ed.). New York Free Press.

Qobo, M. (2022). *The Political Economy of China-US Relations: Digital Futures and African Agency.* Palgrave Macmillan.

Ramge, T., and Mayer-Schonberger, V. (2018). *Reinventing Capitalism in the Age of Big Data.* John Murray.

Rostow, W. W. (1960). *Stages of Economic Growth.* Cambridge University Press.

Schumpeter, J. (1942). *Capitalism, Socialism, and Democracy* (3rd ed.). Harper and Brothers.

Sims, P. (2012). Little Bets: How Breakthrough Ideas Emerge from Small Discoveries. Free Press.

Smith, B., and Browne, C. A. (2019). Tools and Weapons: The Promise and the Peril of the Digital Age. Penguin Press.

Statista. (2024). *Start-up funding raised in Africa in 2023 (in million USD).*

Sun, Z. (2018, July). *Innovation and Entrepreneurship in the 4th Industrial Revolution.* In Joint Workshop on Entrepreneurship (pp. 1–34).

UNCTAD. (2019). *Digital economy report 2019.* UN Trade and Development.

UNDP. (2022). *Human development index.* Human Development Reports. hdr.undp.org/data-center/human-development-index#/indicies/HDI

Water and Energy for Food (We4F). (2024). If webpage (we4f.org) unavailable, see capacity4dev.europa.eu/projects/desira/info/we4f_en

Webb, R., O'Donnell, T., Auty, K., Bai, X., Barnett, G., Costanza, R., . . . and Stafford Smith, M. (2023). Enabling urban systems transformations: Co-developing national and local strategies. *Urban Transformations 5*(1), 5.

World Bank. (2019a). *Kenya economic update: Securing future growth – Policies to support Kenya's digital transformation.* Edition 20. *The World Bank Group. tinyurl.com/bdm53m53*

(2019b). *Nigeria digital economy diagnostic report.* tinyurl.com/4jdk3ek8

(2019c). South Africa: Digital economy diagnostic. The World Bank Group. tinyurl.com/382rzyc3

(2022). *Inequality in Southern Africa: An assessment of the Southern African customs union.* The World Bank Group. tinyurl .com/y24w2x4y

11 China Private Sector Innovators: Established Disruptors and New Challengers

LOURDES CASANOVA, ANNE MIROUX AND XINGQI YE*

11.1 Introduction

One of the key reasons for China's rise as an innovation and technology powerhouse since the early 2000s (see Chapter 5) has been the remarkable growth of Chinese start-ups. They have contributed not only through technological advancements and innovation, but also by fostering the entrepreneurial spirit of the younger generation and nurturing talent, exchange and collaboration. Several of these start-ups achieved unicorn status and evolved into industry leaders, such as Alibaba, Tencent and, later, ByteDance. The transformation was fast: The number of Chinese unicorns rose from an estimated 120 in 2017 to 316, a quarter of the world total, in 2023 according to data from the Global Unicorn Index 2023 (Hurun Research Institute, 2023). By comparison, the United States accounts for about half of the world's unicorns. The number of unicorns in the Guangzhou province alone was equal to that of Israel or France in 2023, while the number of unicorns in the Greater Bay Area (Guangdong, Hong Kong, Macau and Shenzhen) was equivalent to that of India.

In the following sections, we will use case studies to review the innovation strategies of Chinese companies and show the roles of what we call the incumbents or 'established disruptors' and the new start-ups and innovators in China's innovation ecosystem.

11.2 The 'Established' Disruptors

We first examine the most famous (past) unicorns, Tencent (founded 1998) and Alibaba (founded 1999). Although since going public they

* The contribution of Noel Liu, Cornell Class of 2025 and research assistant at the Emerging Markets Institute, Cornell University, is gratefully acknowledged.

are no longer unicorns, with Tencent launching its initial public offering in 2004 on the Hong Kong stock exchange and Alibaba in 2014 in New York, their journey in the last twenty-five years sheds light on their role as disruptive innovators and corporate venture capitalists. These tech leaders helped China move towards a cashless society and inspired a new generation of entrepreneurs.

11.2.1 Alibaba and Tencent: Behind the Mobile Payments Triumph in China

Alibaba and Tencent have been and still are drivers of entrepreneurial ecosystems in China. Offering mobile payments services to meet the needs of a largely unbanked Chinese population, they rapidly evolved from their original business activity (messaging, social media and gaming for Tencent and e-commerce for Alibaba). Both progressively built a holistic ecosystem around mobile payments, where users could manage their finances, make investments, transfer money, shop online or in physical stores, order food deliveries, pay for bills, use public transportation and nearly everything else, using a single platform. Tencent and Alibaba captured this opportunity to make mobile payment a key pillar of their corporate ecosystems.

Over 904 million Chinese people, roughly 64 per cent of the total population, used mobile payments in 2021 (Statista, 2023), and about 54 per cent of all e-commerce payments were made through digital wallets, while only 10 per cent were made through cash (J. P. Morgan, 2019). In addition to the digital wallet, QR payments expanded quickly in China. Facilitating the shift of mobile payment from online-only to offline transactions, they contributed to the surge in digital payments. By the end of 2022, about US$3.5 trillion had been transacted through digital payment in China, nearly twice the figure in the United States (Daxue Consulting, 2022).

In our book *The Era of Chinese Multinationals: Competing for Global Dominance* (Casanova & Miroux, 2019), we discussed the three phases of the history of the online payment industry in China, which started with the growth of PC-based online payment, followed by the rise of digital wallet and mobile payment and is now transitioning into digital financial services. Alipay and WeChat Pay, the two-payment systems set up by Alibaba and Tencent, respectively, have driven this revolution.

While Alibaba launched Alipay about ten years before Tencent introduced its WeChat Pay, the latter was the more disruptive innovator in the early stages of mobile payment competition. As early as 2005, Tencent started playing with digital currency by launching the 'Q coin', which could be purchased with real money on its website and then used to purchase digital products and services such as game coins or virtual pets on its QQ platform (an instant messaging and social media software and web portal). In 2013, WeChat Pay debuted as a new digital wallet service incorporated into WeChat, Tencent's app and the largest Chinese messaging and social media app (Casanova & Miroux, 2019). Two key functions of the service were introduced in the next year that drove the take-off of mobile payment adoption: WeChat Red Packet and QR code payment.

Based on the Chinese tradition of distributing *hongbao*, a traditional Chinese gift of money presented in a red envelope on Chinese New Year and other important holidays and events, WeChat's Red Packet (or red envelope) was essentially a digital *hongbao*. The service did not gain massive popularity until the 2015 Chinese New Year, when the Spring Festival Gala show distributed digital red envelopes (worth US$80 million in total) through WeChat. To receive the red envelopes, the audience needed to shake their WeChat app by entering WeChat, tapping 'Discover', selecting 'Shake' and shaking the phone. Eleven billion shakes were made during that single night (Forbes, 2015). At the same time, users also discovered the fun of sending virtual red envelopes to families and friends. Moreover, the red envelope-based transaction was further gamified through the 'catching red envelopes competition', where people in a WeChat group can send a red envelope, which will be randomly divided among group members into different size packets. Only when the packet is open is the amount known to the recipient and to the whole group through a billboard posting. The integration of social elements, competition and cultural traditions helped make the virtual red envelope a big success, driving the use of WeChat Pay. During the 2015 Chinese New Year's Eve, a total of one billion red envelopes were sent via WeChat, five times the total number for 2014. Alipay followed suit with its own red envelope campaigns with innovative gamification designs, including augmented reality games.

Developed in 1994 by a subsidiary of Toyota Motor Co. for tracking car assembly parts (Kneese, 2014), QR codes had been widely adopted across diverse sectors including e-commerce before WeChat Pay began to use them. The QR code offered Tencent the optimal enabling technique for its offline payment strategy, and the Chinese context was particularly conducive to its adoption for several reasons. Firstly, mobile payment was generally perceived as a major technological advancement in China, much more than in developed economies, because people were less aware of the convenience of using credit cards. Secondly, the barriers for merchants, especially small merchants, to adopt the method are lower in China because there is less of a need to replace existing technology. For instance, small restaurants typically did not have point of sales (POS) machines. QR codes, on the other hand, offer a low-cost and high-convenience alternative to cash payment. A street food vendor, for example, can simply print out his or her own QR code. The cost is zero and the benefit is visible, so its presence in the market quickly skyrocketed. One can see QR codes for WeChat Pay and Alipay in nearly every physical commercial outlet in China today (convenience stores, supermarkets, restaurants, hotels, hospitals, schools, carparks, etc.) as well as on nearly every website that receives payment.

Just as Tencent did, Alibaba significantly disrupted the financial services industry in China. It created Alipay in 2004 to provide a reliable and secure online payment system for purchases on its site. More than 190 million Chinese consumers generated 42.3 billion transactions via Alipay ten years later, in 2014 (Investor's Business Daily, 2020), and there were over 330 million active users on Alibaba's e-commerce sites (Alibaba, 2014). The enormous user base and the voluminous amount of user data generated provided Alipay with a significant competitive advantage over other fintech players. Within financial services such data can be used in various ways, from credit score ratings to personalised financial marketing and fraud risk management. As a natural step, Alibaba spun Alipay off into a more independent financial service arm in 2014, the Ant Financial Group. It offered a large portfolio of services in addition to payment such as digital banking, personal wealth management, micro-loans, credit reference and insurance. All those services were incorporated into the Alipay app, in line with its mobile-first strategy.

One of Alibaba group's most important innovations in recent years is its "Smile to Pay" system. Initially introduced in 2017, the system uses facial recognition to replace traditional passwords and is incorporated into self-service check-out devices in stores, instead of relying on a mobile phone camera.[1] This represents a renovation of the 'mobile' component of mobile payment: While the term originally refers to "payment through a mobile device", it may now extend to payment without carrying a device. Tencent followed suit, launching its own facial payment system called 'Frog Pro' in 2019. The uptake of facial-recognition payment technology accelerated during the COVID-19 pandemic, with nearly 500 million Chinese customers using this method to pay in 2021 (Tang, 2022).

As Ant Financial Group gradually transformed into a real bank and leveraged its access to user information to achieve scale and scope, it started to threaten traditional banks, most of which are state-owned, triggering regulatory scrutiny from Beijing. Following a meeting with regulatory authorities in 2020, its planned initial public offering (IPO) was cancelled. To align itself better with the government's vision for the financial sector in China, Ant Financial shifted its focus away from customer finance to technology services (Zhang & Ruwitch, 2018). It also restructured the business to enable stricter user data protection and reduce Alibaba's control over the data. Following pressure from the government, Alibaba created a new subsidiary allowing customers' financial data to be accessible to the government and other financial institutions. In 2023 Alibaba then announced it would split the company into six different groups, each independently managed and free to go public with its own IPO, which has been delayed several times. It remains to be seen, in this new phase and under increasing government scrutiny, how the company will maintain its e-commerce leadership in China and globally.

11.2.2 How Will the Digital Yuan Affect the Duopoly of Tencent and Alibaba in Mobile Payments?

A recent challenge and potential opportunity for Tencent and Alibaba's mobile payment businesses is the launch of the Digital Yuan, the e-CNY, a digital currency issued by China's central bank, the People's Bank of China. China started piloting the e-CNY in 2019,

[1] Point of sales machines are equipped with a device connected to a small camera that has access to the facial information database of Alipay. To be able to use this technology, the customer first needs to link his/her facial image to Alipay.

introducing this digital currency for four main reasons (BIS, 2022). Firstly, China wants to improve the efficiency of its payment systems. Just as Alipay and WeChat Pay brought convenience to individual customers, the digital yuan could remove friction from business transactions. Secondly, the risks associated with the dominance of big tech companies like Alibaba and Tencent, where key payment infrastructure is built and maintained by private and profit-driven players, are a matter of concern for the government. Thirdly, the digital yuan aligns with digitalisation trends while maintaining the public's access to cash. Finally, it may contribute to the internationalisation of the e-yuan. Additionally, the digital yuan could help the Chinese government to directly compete with less regulated digital currencies such as Bitcoin. Moreover, the introduction of a new, accessible digital payment method could drive up competition in what has become an oligopolistic market dominated by Alipay and WeChat Pay.

Some observers have suggested that the digital yuan could not succeed through a stand-alone app without the help of established platforms (Shen, 2023). Their array of interconnected services makes payment settlement a seamless process. For instance, to buy a new phone, it is easier to do it all (from product selection to payment) on the Tmall app (one of Alibaba's e-commerce platforms) than to open the separate digital yuan app and then jumping back to the e-commerce platform. Given how Chinese customers are used to paying with Alipay and WeChat pay, it would be hard to make them switch to the e-CNY wallet. As a result, China's central bank granted WeChat Pay and Alipay the right to provide digital yuan, in addition to state-owned banks. Both Alipay and WeChat Pay have now set up digital yuan wallet services, integrating them directly through their apps, and accept digital yuan for their other services.

11.2.3 *Alibaba and Tencent as Providers of Venture Capital*

Alibaba and Tencent also have played a key role in Chinese entrepreneurial ecosystems as providers of corporate venture capital, investing heavily in domestic and overseas technology start-ups and actively bringing those firms into their own innovation ecosystems. In 2022, Tencent's corporate venture arm was ranked as the fourth largest venture capital in the world by the number of investments, following Sequoia Capital, SoftBank and Tiger Global. It was also ranked as the one of the top among Chinese venture capital based on value, followed by CICC Capital (Hurun Research Institute, 2022). Since the establishment of its corporate venture arm, Tencent has funded over 1,300 companies including Discord (an instant messaging platform headquartered in San Francisco), Lynda (an online learning platform located in Carpinteria, USA), Nubank (a Brazilian online bank) and Xiaohongshu (a Chinese social media and e-commerce platform). Spending over US$12 billion on 163 firms across several industries in 2020 (Nikkei Asia, 2021), Tencent has been following a long-term growth strategy, leading sometimes to full mergers and acquisitions or long-term collaborations. This strategy is like what Su et al. described as a 'long-tail strategy for IT outsourcing', where the innovation model consists of a few key partnerships and many dynamically changing connections with other firms (Su et al., 2015). The investment in and integration of start-ups help Tencent maintain a continuous in-flow of new capabilities while remaining competitive in a turbulent market environment. Alibaba followed a similar path, with Alibaba Capital Partners investing in several digital start-ups such as the Chinese leading AI company SenseTime; however, it has moved less aggressively than Tencent.

11.3 The Next Generation: Innovative Start-Ups and Unicorns

Although Alibaba and Tencent (as well as Huawei) are the most well-known and most innovative Chinese technology companies abroad, the start-up scene in the country is vibrant, and China has now become home to a significant number of highly valued privately held enterprises. Based on valuations, several of these firms are among the top-ranked unicorns. In April 2023, five of the ten most valuable unicorns in the world were Chinese, with ByteDance, the owner of TikTok in the top position with a valuation of about US$200 billion, and Ant Group and SHEIN (e-commerce) in the third and fourth position, respectively (Table 11.1). Some other major names in the world of Chinese unicorns include WeBank (fintech), DJI (high-end hardware) and Cainiao (logistics) among others.

While e-commerce, fintech and other consumer related services tend to dominate the unicorn landscape in China, new unicorns belong industries favoured by the government like semiconductors, artificial intelligence (AI), robotics, healthtech, green technology and green

Table 11.1 *List of the ten most valuable unicorns in the world, April 2023*

Unicorn	Valuation (US$ bn)	Country	Industry
ByteDance	200	China	Social media
SpaceX	137	USA	Aerospace
Ant Group	120	China	Fintech
SHEIN	65	China	E-commerce
Stripe	50	USA	Fintech
WeBank	33	China	Fintech
Databricks	31	USA	Big data
Telegram	30	UAE	Social media
Revolut	28	UK	Fintech
Cainiao	27	China	Logistics

Source: Based on data from the Global Unicorn Index, Hurun Research Institute (2023).

energy. This is in line with China's strategic technology development goal and its efforts to become self-sufficient, hence less dependence on foreign technology. These unicorns benefit from strong government support, including state-backed funding (see discussion in the next paragraph). AI and semiconductors accounted for 11 and 9 per cent of the total number of Chinese unicorns, respectively in 2023, more than e-commerce (8 per cent), green energy and healthtech (7 per cent each), according to data from the Hurun Research Institute (2023). The semiconductor industry saw a remarkable rise: While there was no unicorn in the industry in 2017, there were thirty Chinese semiconductor unicorns in 2023 (see Table 11.2). Similarly, AI saw its number of unicorns rise from three in 2017 to thirty-five in 2023.

Driven by its strategy to turn China into a leading industrial nation with innovation and technology at its core, the government has been instrumental in the development of a start-up ecosystem in China through its Made in China 2025 and its Mass Entrepreneurship and Mass Innovation initiative launched in 2015. Hence, high tech and new technology companies, venture capitalists and angel investors benefit from preferential tax policies, and graduate students have preferential policies to promote entrepreneurship. The state has also become a key player in Chinese start-up financing, an area that used to be dominated by privately owned tech giants. Alibaba, Tencent, Xiaomi, Baidu and JD.com, for instance, collectively invested in about

Table 11.2 ***Chinese unicorns: Top 5 industries (by numbers of firms) 2017 and 2023***

	Number of unicorns	%		Number of unicorns	%
Internet services	22	18	Artificial intelligence	35	11
E-commerce	22	18	Semiconductor	28	9
Fintech	17	14	E-commerce	25	8
Culture & entertainment	10	8	Green energy	22	7
Automobile & transport	9	8	Healthtech	22	7
2017 Total: **120**			2023 Total: **316**		

Source: Author-generated based on data from the Hurun China Greater Unicorn Index (2017), KrAsia (2017) and Global Unicorn Index (Hurun Research Institute, 2023).

half of China's unicorns in 2017, with Alibaba and Tencent playing a primary role in the venture capital industry as seen in the previous section. However, the end of easy money in the United States and Europe, combined with inflation and higher interest rates in those regions, has tempered private investors' appetites. In addition, the crackdown on tech giants such as Tencent and Alibaba has led them to reduce their start-up investments. At the same time, the Chinese government established several funds to invest in start-ups, such as the National Venture Capital Fund for Emerging Industries. Regional funds also provide financial support to start-ups across different provinces and cities (most notably Beijing, Shanghai, Shenzen, Guangdong, Hangzhou and Chengdu), often working in collaboration with venture capital firms. State entities and state-owned enterprises are also direct investors in Chinese start-ups. For instance, Guangzhou Automobile, a state-owned car maker, has invested in several automobile and transport start-ups, such as Greater Bay Technology (a developer of fast-charging power batteries and energy storage systems of which Tencent is also a significant investor), Aion (an electric vehicle manufacturer), Ruqi Mobility (a ride hailing platform) and CanSemi Technology (a chip manufacturer). The State Power Investment Corporation has a stake in Qiyuan Green Power Technology, a Shanghai-based start-up that provides electric heavy truck battery charging and swapping services. Five of the fourteen major investors in early-stage business in China in 2023 were fully or partially state-owned (see Table 11.3).

In the next section, we present case studies that draw on a variety of examples of Chinese unicorns, focusing on AI, drones, robotics and entertainment. The case studies allow a deeper understanding of Chinese unicorns and their role in advancing China's innovation and technology.

11.3.1 DJI: The World's Leading Commercial Drone Manufacturer, A Global Born Company

Founded in 2006 in Shenzhen (part of the Greater Bay Area formed by Shenzhen, Guangzhou and Hong Kong), SZ Da Jiang Innovation Sciences and Technologies Ltd (DJI), is the largest drone manufacturer in the world. As a privately owned company, it has reportedly received investment from Chinese state-owned entities such as the China's State Development and Investment Corporation and the Shanghai Venture Capital Fund, owned by the Shanghai Municipality (*Washington Post*, 2023). Drones were originally used for military purposes but have increasingly been used in civilian applications. These can include search, rescue and security, shopping and delivery for e-commerce, healthcare, mapping, agriculture and filmmaking, among many other applications. DJI has said that its drones were for civilian (not military) use. However, drones can be controlled using modified firmware obtainable on the black market, and many drone companies have found their products used, for instance, in the war in Ukraine.

DJI was born global, pushing its products abroad while still facing significant market uncertainties at home. It entered Western markets in 2009, just as it was starting to sell its drone control system in China. Offering sophisticated products such as the Phantom, its hit product, at competitive prices, it quickly became the global leader in the industry. DJI North America was founded in Los Angeles in 2011, and it had 77 per cent of the market share of the consumer drone market in the United States by 2020 (Bloomberg, 2022). In 2021, DJI accounted for 76 per cent of the global market, followed by Intel with a market share of about 4 per cent (Statista, 2022). Demand, especially for commercial use, has grown quickly as companies increasingly recognise the business potential of the technology. The global drone market is expected

Table 11.3 *Major investors in early-stage business in China (2023): Type of investments, ownership and estimated assets under management (AUM)*

Name	Investment Type	Estimated AUM (billion)	Ownership	Headquarters
Hillhouse Capital Management	Growth, balanced	US$100	Private	Singapore
Shenzhen Capital Group	Venture, early stage, growth, buyout	US$63.8	State-owned	China
China International Capital Corporation (Private Equity Arm)	Venture, growth, fund of funds (FoFs)	US$61.6	Partially state-owned	China
HongShan (Sequoia Capital China)	Seed, venture, growth, expansion	US$56	Private	China
PAG	Growth, buyout	US$50	Private	Hong Kong
CCT Fund Management (China Structural Reform Fund)	Growth, FoFs	US$49.1	State-owned	China
China Merchants Capital	Venture, growth, balanced	US$42.1	State-owned	China
Boyu Capital	Venture, growth	US$40	Private	Hong Kong
IDG Capital	Growth	US$23	Private	China
BPEA EQT (Private Equity Arm)	Growth, buyout	US$22	Private	Hong Kong
Asia Alternatives	FoFs	US$15.4	Private	Hong Kong
National Green Development Fund	FoFs	US$14	State-owned	China
FountainVest Partners	Growth	US$11	Private	Hong Kong
Qiming Venture Partners	Venture	US$9.5	Private	China

Source: Authors and Noel Liu, based on data from Pitchbook (2023) and Preqin (2023).

Note: Assets Under Managements (AUM) refers to the global assets of the firms. They were used as a basis for this table as most of these assets are invested in China. However, the precise amount of AUM held in China by those funds was not publicly available.

to almost double from US$30 billion in 2022 to about US$55 billion by 2030, with the commercial drone segment alone growing at a 7.7 per cent compound annual growth rate (CAGR) per year (Drone Industry Insight, 2023). DJI entered the intelligent driving systems business through the launch of DJI Automotive in 2022.[2]

Shenzen's manufacturing ecosystem, including its physical infrastructure, logistics services and highly skilled workforce, has helped DJI. The company started competing as an innovator, with innovative technology, while others typically experience the transition from imitator to innovator. DJI's first product prototype was developed in the dorm room of its founder, Tao Wang, who then built the company around the technology while he was still a graduate student in Hong Kong. Over time, DJI has focused on both basic and applied research to push the technological frontier. For instance, DJI's consumer segment has focused on camera drone technology and has spent tremendous research and development (R&D) resources to improve the image quality during the flying process, making its Phantom series one of the top choices for film studios all over the world as well as for professional and amateur photographers (Xu & Muneyoshi, 2017). A quarter of DJI's 14,000 employees are in R&D, and in 2022 the firm held the largest number of drone related patents in the world (about 8,000) (Global Data, 2023).

The nature of the product and its potential use for surveillance, data collection and military application is such, however, that DJI has been facing increased scrutiny in the United States, one of its largest markets. In 2021, DJI was blacklisted in the United States for its alleged participation in the surveillance of the Muslim Uyghur minority in Xinjiang province. Despite the blacklisting, DJI's private valuation was estimated at about US$15 billion in 2022 (Bloomberg, 2022).

11.3.2 Royole: Pioneering Flexible Display Technology

Shenzhen-based Royole Technology manufactures flexible displays, sensors and smart devices used in human–machine interface products (Royole Technology, 2023). Founded in 2012, the company holds over

[2] DJI Automotive has been launched as a Division of DJI. As of November 2023, DJI was not a separate company.

3,000 international patent rights and has offices in China (including Hong Kong), Japan and California and sells its products to over twenty countries (Japan External Trade Organization, 2020). Its main investors include IDG Capital, Shenzhen Capital Group Co. (a venture capital fund founded by the Shenzen Municipal Government), Kunpeng Capital (a state-owned fund, set up by the Shenzen Municipality), Poly Capital and CITIC (state-owned). Being a leader in flexible technology, the company is known for developing ultra-thin LED displays and foldable screens. Its innovations include the world's thinnest fully flexible colour display, the world's first foldable mobile phone FlexPai and the first micro-LED elastic flexible screen technology.

Royole leverages a global partnership model, collaborating with diverse partners across different industries to explore new applications of its core technology. For instance, the company has assisted in the digital transformation of an aeronautics company, helping the client replace traditional paper magazines and outdated digital LED displays with thin digital displays. This reduces the weight of an aircraft by about one ton, which would save each plane over 1,000 tons of carbon emissions annually (Royole Technology, 2023). Similarly, Royole has also worked with the world's largest supplier of rail transit equipment to develop light entertainment screens integrated into the seats of a new magnetic levitation (maglev) train, minimising weight and reducing carbon emissions. Collaboration with different industries has allowed the firm to move up the innovation chain.

Royole has also been trying to extend the applications of its products outside traditional settings like rear seat displays. For example, it partnered with one of the largest Chinese alcohol companies to develop the world's first alcohol bottle with an interactive display for its high-end Baijiu brand, Guojiao 1573 (Royole Technology, 2023). In China, Baijiu is largely considered a 'social drink'. By incorporating a customisable digital display, Royole helps the alcohol company further boost the social value of its products. Moreover, Royole's collaboration with a leading French fashion and luxury goods company, which integrated its touchscreen interface into clients' iconic leather bags to allow customers to personalise the products, manifests their expertise in integrating new digital technology into unexpected settings.

Royole went through thirteen rounds of financing between 2012 and 2020, and its valuation exceeded US$7.5 billion (50 billion yuan) at its peak. However, despite its technological capabilities and innovative products, the company has faced financial difficulties since 2020, failing to go public three times. As has been the case for many other start-ups all over the world affected by a funding chill since 2022, Royole's financial difficulties have been growing. The firm saw US$5.5 million in assets frozen by a court in September 2022 (Caixin Global, 2022). For some observers, the missing link in Royole's strategy was in the commercialisation stage of the global value chain and the poor attention paid to the market. Its FlexPai foldable phone, for instance, faced tough competition when Samsung and Huawei launched their own foldable devices. As of late 2023, it remains to be seen whether the company will manage to adjust and overcome such troubled times.

11.3.3 Cloudwalk Technology—AI Unicorn Driving Facial Recognition

Cloudwalk Technology, one of the leading Chinese AI technology firms, was a unicorn until May 2022 when it launched an IPO on the Shanghai stock exchange. Incubated from the Chinese Academy of Sciences and based in Shanghai, it focuses on developing facial recognition technology driven by AI (Cloudwalk, 2023). It was founded in 2015 and made several major technological breakthroughs. For instance, in March 2018 its Re-ID technology moved the technology from face scanning to 'human recognition'. In October 2019, its natural language processing, developed in alliance with Shanghai Jiaotong University, surpassed humans in a deep reading comprehension task. In November 2019, the company's 3D human body reconstruction technology achieved a computational algorithmic speed of 5 milliseconds. As of 2021, Cloudwalk had over 300 patents and more than 100 technological products used in diverse industries including finance, transportation, governance and retail (EqualOcean, 2022). During the year prior to its IPO in 2021, the company spent over US$80 million (nearly 77% of its total investments) on R&D. Although the company is no longer a unicorn, it is another example of a fast-rising Chinese high-tech firm, one of the so-called four AI dragons.

The company is the largest supplier of AI in China's financial industry. Risk management and payment are key areas for the application of its technology. It offers facial recognition in ATMs and self-service systems for fraud prevention to over 100,000 bank branches and some of the biggest Chinese banks: the Industrial and Commerce

Bank of China (ICBC), the Bank of China and the Agricultural Bank of China (Cloudwalk, 2023). In 2020, Cloudwalk partnered with ICBC to create an 'AI + finance' initiative which deepened the involvement of the company in fintech, especially in security aspects. Around the same time, it also announced a deal with UnionPay, the largest Chinese credit card company. The deal involved pushing the adoption of face-scanning payment in Zhejiang with the aim of improving payment efficiency and card user experience through contactless payment (Cloudwalk, 2023). Outside traditional banking, the company also engages with e-commerce and offline retail industries. For instance, it partnered with shopping malls to not only increase the adoption of intelligent payment solutions but also to develop new AI-driven systems for customer services such as AI assistants.

Going beyond the financial and e-commerce payments on which it initially focused, Cloudwalk has added facial-recognition access control, voice recognition systems, interactive screens and various sensors. The technologies have been widely adopted by airports and railways (for identity verification and passenger self-service) and police (for crime risk analysis and criminal identification) as well as in office buildings, hospitals, parks, schools and tourism sites (Cloudwalk, 2023). As of March 2019, Cloudwalk's technology had reportedly helped Chinese police make 10,000 arrests (Deng, 2019). During the COVID-19 pandemic, Cloudwalk also introduced a series of 'Smart Epidemic Solutions' used for identifying people wearing protective masks in crowds, measuring body temperature from long distances and sending alerts when detecting high temperature and screening international passengers at airports, et cetera (Cloudwalk, 2023).

However, concerns and controversies have arisen regarding this firm, as for a number of other Chinese firms working on facial recognition. The US government has added CloudWalk to the United States Entity List, which found the firm complicit in aiding the Chinese government in mass surveillance of the Uyghur population. Cloudwalk, together with other Chinese firms such as Hikvision, has also been providing face recognition technology to Zimbabwe's government, raising concerns among human and civil rights advocates that such technology would be used against political opponents.

Before going public, Cloudwalk benefited from a propitious funding environment, receiving multiple rounds of financing from its creation. However, just like other Chinese AI companies such as SenseTime, it did not fully meet investors' expectations. The company remained unprofitable with revenues declining by 51 per cent in 2022 and by a further 25 per cent during the first nine months of 2023, and a net income of minus US$130 million in 2022 and minus US$100 million in September 2023 (Pitchbook, 2023). In November 2023, its market value showed a 70 per cent decline from its peak value.

11.3.4 Horizon Robotics Technology, Machine Learning and Artificial Intelligence

Horizon Robotics Technology was founded in 2015 by Dr Kai Yu, a recognised researcher in machine learning and deep learning who previously headed Baidu Institute of Deep Learning, the first AI lab in China. Horizon Robotics designs and develops AI chips and computing solutions with a focus on advanced driver assistance systems and automated driving vehicles. Its major product lines include automotive-inference processors, smart processor optimisation, scalable reception commuters for autonomous robotics mobility, toolkits for neural network performance, optimisation, ecosystems for smart driving and internet of things (IoT) solutions.

Horizon positions itself as a tier 2 supplier to major original equipment manufacturers and automakers and has secured contracts with the Chinese automotive firms BYD and SAIC, as well as with Continental Auto Parts, for instance. However, the market for automated driving processors has been increasingly competitive in recent years. Chipmaking giants like Nvidia (Orin SoC), Qualcomm (Snapdragon Ride Flex SoC) and Intel/Mobileye are making significant investments. In China, Huawei has launched Huawei Ascend auto chips through its semiconductor arm HiSilicon. Newer entrants like Cambricon Technologies and Semidrive may pose greater threats to Horizon.

High-profile venture capitalists (5Y capital, Hillhouse, Sequoia and linear ventures) and leading Chinese car makers (state-owned firms, SAIC Motor, China FAW, Chery Auto, BYD) are major investors in Horizon. In October 2022, Volkswagen announced that its software unit Cariad would invest US$1 billion in Horizon and a further US$1.26 billion to take a 60 per cent stake in the new joint venture formed with the company. The transaction was completed in 2023.

11.3.5 ByteDance and Tiktok, the Global Chinese Social Media Platform

Zhang Yiming founded ByteDance Ltd in 2012 together with Liang Rubo. It is a privately owned Chinese internet technology company focusing on social networking and content creation and distribution. Its main products include TikTok, the short-video platform, Douyin (TikTok China), Toutiao (or 'Today's Headlines', a news and information content platform) and Xigua Video, a long-form video-sharing platform. Bytedance was the most highly valued unicorn in the world in 2022 (Table 11.2). Its investors are mostly global, including the American venture capitalists Sequoia, General Atlantic, Susquehanna International Group and GGV Capital, as well as the United Arab Emirates' G42 and the Japanese Softbank (Crunchbase, 2023; Forbes, 2023). The government keeps a 1 per cent stake together with a board seat and a golden share (The China Project, 2023; Reuters, 2023).

One of the company's most successful applications is TikTok. Its merger with Musical.ly, a Shanghai-based social media service focused on the US market, accelerated ByteDance's international expansion from 2018 onwards. TikTok became the fifth application in the world to exceed one billion daily active users (DAUs) in October 2022, after Facebook, WhatsApp, Instagram and YouTube. The Chinese super-app, WeChat, had 900 million DAUs. The group's other products are heavily based in China, and ByteDance still generates most of its revenues from China.

ByteDance uses sophisticated algorithms powered by AI to personalise users' feeds across its applications. These algorithms analyse data such as users' past behaviours and interactions to maximise user engagement. The group has made heavy R&D investments in the area by setting up an AI lab in 2016 and employing thousands of software engineers worldwide since then (Market Power Analytics, 2024). Its AI research capability is highly regarded by the industry.

The group monetises its user base through advertising, which represented about two thirds of its revenue in 2021. The average cost per mile on TikTok (the price an advertiser pays for 1,000 views) is US$10 higher than its peers such as Instagram (US$7.91) and YouTube (US$3.41) (Varos, 2023). This premium reflects the highly effective advertising campaigns on TikTok backed by advanced data analytics and a strong sales team serving the needs of business owners/e-commerce operators. Hence, the group's profits (before interest, tax, depreciation and amortisation) rose to US$25 billion in 2022, more than Tencent and Alibaba, with revenues reaching US$85 billion (*Financial Times*, 2023).

The group has had mixed outcomes in diversifying its income sources. Its online K–12 education fell apart in 2020 as the Chinese government imposed strict restrictions on extracurricular activities. It faced fierce competition in the gaming industry (especially from the two leaders Tencent and NetEase) and it had to wind down Nuverse by the end of 2023. The group is re-focusing on its core business: short videos and e-commerce. While the gross merchandise value of TikTok Shop reached US$4.4 billion in Southeast Asia in 2022, its domestic arm, Douyin, recorded a gross value of US$208 billion during the same period, representing a 76 per cent increase in one year (Tech in Asia, 2023).

Lawmakers and regulators are increasingly concerned that TikTok and its parent company could be asked by the Chinese government to hand over sensitive user data. They have imposed restrictions and bans in foreign markets, which has caused problems for the group. TikTok has strongly denied such allegations. Yet, sixteen countries had banned the usage of TikTok by civil servants and universities by 2023. India imposed a nationwide ban. Such developments, combined with a much less favourable financing environment, contributed to a decline in the group's valuation. ByteDance was valued at US$220 billion by the UAE-based AI company G42 in March 2023, half of its estimated valuation in 2021.

As shown by the case studies and Table 11.4:

- Meta leads in revenues at US$117,929 million, with ByteDance second (US$61,700 million) and Kuai Shou third (US$11,777 million), followed by Bilibili (US$2815 million) and Snap Inc. (US$4,117 million).
- In terms of employees, ByteDance has the greatest number at 130,000 people, followed by Meta at 86,482 and Kuai Shou at 28,098, then Bilibili at 12,281 and Snap Inc. at 5,288.
- Restrictions imposed on ByteDance's TikTok have clearly hindered its ability to profit from a global market. As such, compared to Meta, which has a gross profit of US$95,280 million, ByteDance only has a gross profit of US$34,300 million.

Table 11.4 *Basic data of major social media Chinese and US unicorns, 2021 (USD million)*

Company Name	ByteDance (China)	Kuai Shou (China)	Bilibili (China)	Snap Inc (US)	Meta (US)
Revenues	61,700	11,777	2,815	4,117	117,929
Est. MAU (mm)	> 1,900	626	332.6	750	3,700
Gross profit	34,300	4,943	587	2,367	95,280
Opt. income / loss	(7,150)	(4,024)	(579)	(583)	54,720
Net income	N.A.	(11,341)	(986)	(488)	39,370
Total employees	130,000	28,098	12,281	5,288	86,482

Source: EMI research team with data compiled from WSJ articles, company annual reports, Capital IQ database and Statista.

11.3.6 Chipone, Leading in CHIPS

Chipone Technology is a China-based semiconductor company founded in 2008 by Jinfang Zhang. It specialises in designing and researching display driver integrated circuits (ICs) and touch controllers for electronic devices. Known for its high-performance, low-power and cost-effective solutions, the company has become a leading supplier of these ICs to the consumer electronics industry. Chipone's direct clients include major panel manufacturers like BOE group, CSOT, Absen and LG Corporation. Its end-product has been widely adopted by many high-profile brands such as TCL, LG, Xiaomi and OPPO.

The display market is a highly competitive space, traditionally dominated by Taiwanese and South Korean companies. In that market, Chipone is a relatively small company compared to firms such as Huawei's Hisilicon and TSMC, not to mention Intel, that have a much wider range of semiconductor products and services. As a mainland China IC solution provider, however, Chipone is a leader in the global LED driver market. It is also quickly expanding in other segments like liquid crystal display (LCD) drives and large-format display drivers. The firm places a heavy focus on R&D, with expenses in this area registering a 246 per cent increase in 2021. R&D also accounts for about 14 per cent of the company's operating income. More than 60 per cent of Chipone's employees are R&D personnel (Chipone,

Table 11.5 *Chipone's main investors as of 2023 – Ownership stake (percentage)*

Selected Shareholders	Percentage (%)
Jinfang Zhang	17.79
State Strategic Emerging Industry Fund	9.55
Xiaomi Venture Fund	3.73
State Development and Investment Corporation	2.50
Hubble Investment (Huawei's VC arm)	2.45
Vivo Global	1.59

Source: Authors and Noel Liu based on data from Pitchbook (2023) and Preqin (2023).

2023). Available information indicates that Chipone revenues amounted to about US$800 million in 2021 and its net profits to US$135 million (DealstreetAsia, 2023).

The company is backed by a line of Chinese venture capital funds, state-owned investment funds and consumer electronics firms (Vivo Global, Xiaomi Venture, TCL venture) (Table 11.5). The company filed for initial public offering on the Shanghai stock exchange in July 2022, but the offering was withdrawn in March 2023, partly due to the downturn of the global semiconductor market.

The case studies show the companies behind China's successful technology and innovation drive. Table 11.6 summarises the main features: sources of funding, type of government support, their competitive advantage and main strategies as well as possible risks.

Almost all the companies listed in Table 11.6 use some kind of cutting-edge technology and innovation that has differentiated them from their competitors. While each of these companies bring their own set of risks and concerns, they do have strong customer bases and/or government support backing their mission.

11.4 What Next for Chinese Unicorns?

Alibaba and Tencent, two former unicorns, and Huawei, are all emblematic of those firms that transformed China into a global innovation leader from the early 2000s. Since the late 2010s, a new start-up and unicorn landscape has emerged in China, whose number of unicorns alone increased massively to exceed 300 in 2022, second

Table 11.6 *Main features of selected Chinese unicorns*

	Founding team	Industry	Funding strategy	China govt support	Competitive strategy	Competitive advantage	Risks
DJI	Engineer	Drones	Local VC, govt funding, intl investor	high	Cost leadership, internationalisation	Low-cost manufacturing, R&D capability, product innovation	Military & surveillance-related products, human rights violation
Royole	Engineer	Flexible displays, sensors, and smart devices	Local VC, govt funding	medium	New products, differentiation, internationalisation	Global partnerships, product innovation	Poor commercialisation, financial difficulties
Cloudwalk Technology	Academia	Facial recognition	CVC, local VC, govt funding	high	New products and applications, differentiation	R&D capability, large SOE clients, government support	Data privacy concerns, human rights violation, geopolitical risks
Horizon Robotics	Industry expert	AI chips and computing solutions (advanced and autonomous driving)	CVC, local VC, intl investor	low	New products, differentiation, focused	R&D Capability, economies of scale, reputation & strong customer base	Geopolitical risks
ByteDance/ Tiktok	Serial entrepreneur	Social network	Local VC, intl investor	low	New products and services, differentiation, internationalisation	Unique culture, massive user base, AI research capability	Data privacy concerns, geopolitical risk
Chipone	Engineer	Semiconductors	CVC, local VC, govt funding	medium	Cost leadership, focused	Strong customer base, R&D capability	High entry barriers, cyclical industry, poor internal control

Source: Authors.

only to the United States. This new breed of entrepreneurs includes firms that are among the most valued in the world. They concentrate on leading sectors such as AI, semiconductors, robotics, health and green energy, reflecting the instrumental guiding role played by the state in the Chinese start-up ecosystem. While privately held tech giants such as Tencent and Alibaba used to dominate the start-up landscape, many of the new start-ups and unicorns have state backing. With technology and innovation at their core, many of the new start-ups and unicorns in China are moving away from the imitation-then-innovation model, engaging in 'real innovation' from the outset, and many start to expand internationally at an early stage.

Chinese start-ups can build upon China's four key attributes: excellent manufacturing ecosystems in Beijing, Shanghai or the Greater Bay area, a high skilled labour force, a huge domestic market and strong government support. They also face several challenges, some of which are global. For instance, as their peers elsewhere, Chinese tech firms have been impacted by the uncertain global environment that developed following the pandemic and regional conflicts. Accessing venture capital is becoming increasingly difficult, even if in China the fall in venture capital (VC) funding has been less marked than in other markets.[3] Others arise from China, such as the regulatory changes introduced by the government in sectors like fintech and education that have substantially modified the business models of firms operating in those sectors. Some prominent Chinese tech companies have also faced increased scrutiny on monopolistic behaviour and unfair competition (such as Alibaba, Tencent, Did Chuxing, Meituan and JD.com) or on data security and privacy (TikTok, Did Chuxing, Ant Group, Xiaomi and Tencent's WeChat). This has led to fines for alleged antitrust violations, for instance. In addition, many of the new Chinese start-ups and unicorns that operate in industries spanning from semiconductors to entertainment related business are the subject of intense scrutiny and restrictions from advanced economies. It remains to be seen how the Chinese start-ups and unicorns will adapt to this evolving environment both at home and abroad.

[3] Venture capital funding in China declined by 25 percent in the first three quarters of 2023 – considerably less than in the United States (down 45 percent) and the United Kingdom (down 43 percent). In India, the decline was even sharper, reaching 70 percent (The Hindu Business Line, 2023). United Kingdom (minus 43 per cent). The decline was as high as 70 per cent in India.

References

Alibaba. (2014). *United States securities and exchange commission form 20-F.* tinyurl.com/yc54bp26

BIS. (2022). *E-CNY: Main objectives, guiding principles and inclusion considerations People's Bank of China.* In CBDCs in Emerging Market Economies, BIS Papers No 123, 14 April 2022.

Bloomberg. (2022). *DJI won the drone wars, and now it's paying the price.* tinyurl.com/ms5nepzw

Caixin Global. (2022). *Flexible-screen maker Royole has $5.3 million in assets frozen amid 'contract disputes'.* tinyurl.com/3un8284u

Casanova, L., and Miroux, A. (2019.) *The Era of Chinese Multinationals: Competing for Global Dominance.* Academic Press. Elsevier. doi.org/10.1016/C2018-0-01595-9

China Project. (2023). *TikTok is mostly owned by the Americans.* thechinaproject.com/2023/04/26/who-really-owns-bytedance-its-complicated/

Chipone. (2023). Company website. www.chiponeic.com/en/

Cloudwalk. (2023). Company website. www.cloudwalk.com/en/

Crunchbase. (2023). *Beijing software companies.* www.crunchbase.com/hub/beijing-software-companies

Daxue Consulting. (2022). *Payment methods in China: How China became a mobile-first nation.* daxueconsulting.com/payment-methods-in-china/

DealstreetAsia. (2023). *Chinese chip designer Chipone valued at $4.7b after Oceanpine-led $1b Series E round.* www.dealstreetasia.com/stories/chipone-oceanpine-274307

Deng, I. (2019). *This state-backed AI unicorn has helped Chinese police arrest 10,000 criminals.* South China Morning Post. tinyurl.com/mpewkxfs

Drone Industry Insight. (2023). *Global drone market report 2023–2020.* droneii.com/product/drone-market-report

EqualOcean. (2022). *CloudWalk Technology, a rocket taken off in the China AI market.* equalocean.com/analysis/2022060718219

Financial Times. (2023). *ByteDance posts record profit despite TikTok losses.*

Forbes. (2015). *Tencent's WeChat sends 1 billion virtual red envelopes on New Year's Eve.* tinyurl.com/375uuzr8

Global Data. (2023). *Global: Top drones patents holders (2002–2022).* tinyurl.com/t5herjry

The Hindu Business Line. (2023). *VC funding plunges 25% in China; US, UK, India fare worse.* tinyurl.com/2jz6ja5a

Hurun Research Institute. (2022). *Hurun global venture capitalists 2022 half-year report.* www.hurun.net/en-US/Info/Detail?num=FSTQO6FY1G4E

(2023). *Global unicorn index 2023*. www.hurun.co.uk/global-unicorn-index-2023

Investor's Business Daily. (2020). *Alipay boasts more than 42 billion total transactions.* www.investors.com/news/technology/alipay-sends-payment-reports-to-chinese-users/

J. P. Morgan. (2019). *E-commerce payments trends: China*. www.jpmorgan.com/merchant-services/insights/reports/china

Japan External Trade Organization. (2020). *Royole, a pioneer in the flexible technology industry has established its Japanese subsidiary in Tokyo.*

Kneese, T. (2014). *QR codes for the dead.* The Atlantic. www.theatlantic.com/technology/archive/2014/05/qr-codes-for-the-dead/370901/

KrAsia. (2017, December). *This report counts 120 greater China unicorns in 2021 with 21 backed by Tencent and 11 by AliBaba.*

Market Report Analytic. (2024). *ByteDance: AI powerhouse behind TikTok* tinyurl.com/mreh5h7t

Nikkei Asia. (2021). *Tencent spent more than Alibaba on start-ups in 2020.* tinyurl.com/2e8sfucd

Pitchbook. (2023). *Profiles*. pitchbook.com/profiles/company/222518-53#stock

Prequin. (2023). *Preqin's benchmark report 2023: China's private capital landscape*. tinyurl.com/bd7mm786

Reuters. (2023). *Beijing took stake and board seat in key ByteDance domestic entity this year.* tinyurl.com/52jmhufz

Royole Technology. (2023). *About us*. global.royole.com/us

Shen, T. (2023). *China's digital yuan needs WeChat, Alipay to boost adoption, experts say*. Yahoo! www.yahoo.com/now/china-digital-yuan-needs-wechat-090212132.html?guccounter=1

Snap Inc. (2023). *2023 Investor Day – Recap*. newsroom.snap.com/investor-day-2023

Statista. (2022). *Global market share of consumer and commercial drone manufacturers in March 2021, based on sales volume.* www.statista.com/statistics/1254982/global-market-share-of-drone-manufacturers/

(2023). *Number of mobile payment users in China from 2013 to 2022.* www.statista.com/statistics/278487/number-of-mobile-payment-users-in-china/

Su, N., Levina, N., and Ross, J. W. (2015). *The long-tail strategy for IT outsourcing*. MIT Sloan Management Review. sloanreview.mit.edu/article/the-long-tail-strategy-for-it-outsourcing/

Tang, L. (2022). *Revisiting facial-recognition payment: Old problems still lingering*. Nielsen Norman Group. www.nngroup.com/articles/facial-recognition-payment/

Tech in Asia. (2023). *TikTok Shop's GMV in SEA topped $4.4b in 2022*. www.techinasia.com/bytedance-sees-208b-spending-douyins-ecommerce-service

Varos. (2023). *How much do TikTok ads CPM cost in 2024?* www.varos.com/blog/tiktok-ads-cpm-cost

The Washington Post. (2023). *Drone company DJI obscured ties to Chinese state funding, documents show.* 1 February 2022. tinyurl.com/mrydyx65

Xu, F., and Muneyoshi, H. (2017). A case study of DJI, the top drone maker in the world. *Kindai Management Review 5*, 97–104.

Zhang, S., and Ruwitch, J. (2018). *Exclusive: Ant Financial shifts focus from finance to tech services: Sources.* Reuters. www.reuters.com/article/us-china-ant-financial-regulation-exclus-idUKKCN1J10WV

12 *Brazilian Unicorns and Their Triggers of Scalability*

MOACIR DE MIRANDA OLIVEIRA JR AND LEANDRO LIMA DOS SANTOS

12.1 Start-Ups and the Challenge of Scalability

Start-ups are emerging companies, generally technology-based, that seek to develop and commercialise innovative products or services. As start-ups use emerging technologies to develop products and generate new business models, they are considered a source of innovation. They are characterised by their agility, flexibility and ability to grow quickly, and they generally take on high-risk and uncertain projects, seeking to create disruptions in established markets with new ideas, business models or technologies (Aulet, 2013; Dorf et al., 2014; Giardino et al., 2014).

The term 'start-up' is most commonly associated with companies in the technology sector, but it can be applied to companies across various sectors that share similar characteristics of innovation, rapid growth and a pursuit of scale. Additionally, start-ups often begin with limited resources and a lean team but with an ambitious vision of making an impact on the market. They typically seek initial funding from investors, such as angel investors or venture capital funds, to finance growth and development.

One of the biggest challenges for start-ups concerns their scalability. Scalability is the process of quickly expanding the number of customers and profitability of a start-up. Prior studies (Blank, 2010; List, 2022; Neves & Zilber, 2023; Rayport et al., 2023) have identified several factors that contribute to the scalability of start-ups, such as a scalable business model, business management talent, resource orchestration skills, data-based decision making, a favourable business environment and abundant investment.

A scalable business model is innovative in its value proposition and establishes achievable long-term goals, in addition to being difficult to imitate. Finding a service idea with scaling potential is a challenge for most start-ups. In this sense, it is essential to understand the practical problem the product or service must solve before its full development, and it is mandatory to validate the concept through a minimum viable product (MVP). Furthermore, during product or service development it is essential to implement iterative improvements based on customer feedback.

For example, Brazilian Gympass, founded in 2012 by César Carvalho, Vinicius Ferriani and João Thayro, was a start-up whose innovative value proposition consisted in building a platform that provided a flexible and convenient way for people to access a wide range of gyms and fitness classes with a single membership. The MVP service of Gympass was built around the B2C (business to consumer) model, with fitness services sold to individuals. Soon the founders realised that by focusing on the end consumer, the service ended up competing with offers from their partner gyms. In 2014, the company decided to change its business strategy to B2B (business to business): A single client company immediately doubled the size of the start-up. Switching to B2B enabled them to keep scaling up.

Scalability becomes necessary when a start-up identifies new business opportunities requiring flexibility and agility, therefore business management also becomes a critical factor. When a start-up decides to make rapid transformations to stimulate its growth, it typically chooses between enhancing performance through new technologies, expanding its portfolio of offerings or creating new features for the service or product, all of which require adjustments to its business plan. This adaptation in business management demonstrates that the focus and challenges of the business can change as the company progresses through the stages of the life cycle. This is because in the early stages, concerns generally relate more to product development and finances, whereas subsequent challenges are more likely to involve customer acquisition and business scaling. In both cases, start-ups need to adjust their business plans, primarily in terms of sales, as some initially operate with negative cash flows, since their strategies may result in high initial costs due to the disruptive potential of the offering.

An example of the agile decision-making and adaptability of a Brazilian unicorn is Wildlife Studios, a mobile game developer. Founded in 2011, Wildlife Studios has demonstrated impressive agility and adaptability in the highly competitive and fast-paced gaming industry. The company has developed a reputation for quickly bringing high-quality games to market as their agile development process allows them to rapidly prototype, test and implement new game ideas. In order to achieve this, the company uses extensive data analytics to understand player behaviour and preferences. By analysing in-game data, they can make real-time adjustments to game mechanics, features and monetisation strategies. This adaptability ensures that their games continuously meet the evolving needs and desires of their players.

Resource orchestration encompasses the search for the best way to adjust human capital, processes and financial resources to the company's scalability. As start-ups grow, especially those which do so at a fast pace, hiring or developing competent and experienced employees with specialised knowledge becomes an important factor for scalability. In this sense, the need to hire employees with appropriate skills may vary according to the start-up's life cycle. In addition, if the company does not have qualified people or access to them through networking, the need for financial resources to hire these people increases. In this regard, the start-up may fail due to the lack of financial resources from its investors or the lack of investors themselves. Furthermore, resource orchestration is related to making decisions at the opportune moment regarding technology acquisition for the business and the ability to obtain investments and strategically allocate resources.

A notable example of a start-up that invested in human capital to scale up is Gympass, whose platform offers access to a wide network of gyms and physical activities to the employees of partner companies. Gympass decided to focus heavily on developing its team, understanding that motivated and well-trained employees would be the key to growing the company in a sustainable and efficient way. In this case, Gympass created intensive training programmes for its sales teams, ensuring all representatives had in-depth product knowledge and refined sales skills. With a highly qualified and motivated team capable of meeting the demands of a rapidly expanding market, Gympass was able to scale its operations globally, expanding its presence to several countries and establishing partnerships with large corporations around the world.

Loft is another example. Founded in 2018, the start-up quickly grew in the Brazilian real estate market, offering a technological platform that facilitates the purchase and sale of properties. Loft invested heavily in hiring experienced and highly qualified professionals in technology, data engineering and product development. To ensure its employees continued to grow and develop, Loft implemented robust training and development programmes. Additionally, they promoted a culture of constant feedback, where employees received regular guidance on their performance and areas for improvement. As a result, the focus on attracting, developing and retaining the best professionals helped the company maintain its competitive position and continue to grow at a rapid pace, ensuring it had the necessary human base to support its long-term ambitions.

Data-based decision-making highlights that obtaining customer feedback, analysing data and making constant adaptations are crucial aspects to the start-up's scalability success. In other words, through the data obtained from interactions with customers, a start-up is able to develop their service in an agile way, identifying which adaptations must be made for the scalability of the business model. Meanwhile, lack of customer feedback limits the support for decision-making aimed at this growth strategy. Furthermore, data-based decision-making indicates the relevance of using technologies such as artificial intelligence (AI) for data analysis, as this supports decision-making regarding new businesses, enables experimentation and allows for the exploration of opportunities and improvement of processes. It thus modifies a company's outcomes and consequently drives its growth.

A Brazilian unicorn that is particularly sensitive to consumer feedback is QuintoAndar, a real estate tech company that revolutionises the rental market by simplifying the process for both landlords and tenants. The company continuously refines its platform based on user feedback to ensure it is easy to navigate and use. This includes simplifying the process of finding, renting and managing properties online, making it as seamless as possible for users. QuintoAndar also offers robust customer support to address any issues or concerns promptly. Therefore, feedback from these interactions is used to improve the overall user experience and service quality. In addition, the company leverages technology and data analytics to interpret consumer feedback efficiently. Innovations such as a digital contract signing process, secure online payments and virtual property tours were all influenced by consumer feedback.

In turn, another notable example of a Brazilian unicorn that applied an advanced data analytics model to scaling is StoneCo, a leading fintech company that provides financial technology solutions, primarily focusing on payment processing and financial services for merchants. The data analytics model provides deep insights into customer behaviour and preferences. This allows the company to segment its customer base accurately and offer targeted marketing and personalised financial solutions. In addition, advanced data analytics streamline StoneCo's operations by optimising processes, reducing costs and enhancing productivity, as well as identifying inefficiencies and implementing improvements. The company also employs machine learning and AI to predict customer behaviour, detect fraud and personalise services. These technologies helped the company optimise operations and improve customer experiences.

The business environment is fundamental, which means that external factors impacting business performance such as customers' needs, behaviours and lifestyle in the target market require monitoring as they affect the size of business opportunities. In other words, for start-ups to sustain the growth of their businesses in a particular market, it is important to understand the unique behaviour of local consumers and the social aspects that could leverage the business and then develop an appropriate business model. Another important aspect of the business environment is the role of governments, as they create rules and regulations that affect the size of business opportunities. Additionally, in terms of location, the integration of the start-up into a business ecosystem increases access to skilled workers, customers and investments, generating advantages over competitors and new entrants.

For example, iFood is a Brazilian food delivery unicorn that successfully capitalised on a market opportunity and developed an effective strategy to become a leader in its segment. This position was further solidified during the pandemic, when the service was heavily utilised as people were unable to leave their homes. The combination of various factors, such as strong demand for delivery services, an efficient business model, robust technology and an experienced team resulted in exponential growth and established the company as the symbol of the Brazilian delivery market.

The level of investment is undoubtedly another relevant factor because a start-up needs investments to scale up. The role of investors is critical during periods of high spending and low revenue. Venture capital investors allocate financial resources to start-ups with disruptive potential, even if they may operate at a loss for long periods. This is because when start-ups receive investments, they are expected not only to become extremely valuable in the long term but also because they are expected to change the economic logic in economic sectors or high-valued market niches.

Among the main venture capital funds in Brazil is Bossanova Investments, which invests from R$100,000 to R$500,000 (approx. US$18,500 to US$92,500) in technology companies in the pre-seed and seed stages, focusing on B2B or B2B2C business models. As of 2024, Bossanova Investments has supported around 900 start-ups in all regions of Brazil with capital, mentoring and connections. Monashees was created in 2005 as one of the first venture capital managers in Brazil. Among the companies in its portfolio are the Colombian Rappi and the Brazilian companies 99, Loft, Loggi and Neon, all companies that have reached unicorn status. Monashees finished raising US$700 million for two new venture capital funds in December 2021. Half of that amount was for a new fund that focuses on newly born start-ups, and half went to another fund aimed at companies in advanced stages of development and growth. Still, many of the venture capital funds that joined investment rounds for Brazilian start-ups are based outside the country, such as SoftBank, Tiger Global Management, Tencent, Riverwood Capital, Accel, Ribbit Capital and QED Investors.

In short, start-ups represent a dynamic facet of the business world, driving innovation, challenging established paradigms and shaping the future of markets. The ability to quickly adapt to market changes, make decisions based on data and attract strategic investments are critical elements for the success of start-ups. Furthermore, understanding the business environment and the ability to orchestrate resources, especially human capital, plays a crucial role in the journey towards scalability.

12.2 Scalability Triggers: Combining Distinctive Competencies with Market Opportunities

According to Dorf et al. (2014), start-ups are new organisations in search of a scalable business model in uncertain environments. In this sense, we can assume that the long-term goal of the start-up is not to remain as it is, but rather to become a unicorn through leveraging scalability triggers. A central question, then, is to identify what these scalability triggers would be for a given start-up to become a unicorn. We suggest that such triggers result from a combination of the start-up's distinctive competencies and the market opportunities.

12.2.1 Market Opportunities

Start-ups are usually aware of constant technological changes and take advantage of opportunities to reduce costs and increase availability through the adoption of technologies such as cloud computing. Uber, for example, took advantage of the constant evolution of mobile technology to create a disruptive business model and continually improve its service. The objective was to offer value to customers, continually increasing market share and the number of customers based on the technological advances associated with its service. In this regard, Uber's scalability was driven both by the market opportunity provided by the sharing economy and by the technological advances that facilitated its service.

One way to illustrate and analyse the potential of a new business based on a market opportunity can be through the business model canvas template (Osterwalder, 2004). Business model canvas is a simple tool for depicting and analysing new business models in a systematic way. The first step consists of defining which customer segments the business aims to prioritise. Identifying the target audience allows for a more realistic projection of the value proposition that will be offered to these potential customers. Next, a start-up should decide on the communication channels they will use to communicate with customers, in order to make their product or service visible. Options to be considered include physical channels, such as stores, or digital channels such as marketplaces and websites. Then, the customer relationship strategy needs to be defined, that is, whether the relationship with the consumer will be automatic or personalised. Considerations include customer service strategies, loyalty programmes or personalised marketing, for example. A key element is the revenue flow design. In this case, the aspects to be considered involve the primary and secondary sources of revenue, pricing strategies, costs and profit margins, among other things. Finally, it is important to identify the resources and activities essential to creating proposed value for customers, as well as key partners. Developing in-depth specialised resources and competences in one or more of these domains, such as customer relationship marketing, product or service innovation, market research and development, et cetera, puts start-ups on the path to building valuable distinctive competencies – that is, starting with a tangible and verified market opportunity.

The business model canvas consists of nine main components: key partnerships, key activities, key resources, value propositions, customer relationships, communication channels, customer segment, cost structure and revenue streams.

12.2.2 Distinctive Competencies

The combination of distinctive competencies across different links of the value chain that match market opportunities ultimately creates the triggers necessary for achieving scalability for start-ups. This process requires a deep understanding of the market, a careful analysis of internal competencies and a clear strategy for taking advantage of identified opportunities.

Again, the fundamental condition for a start-up to create a unique value proposition is to find a market with paying customers. The main premise is that based on its distinctive competencies and market opportunities, a start-up can develop a unique value proposition that differentiates it from the competition. This value proposition should highlight the benefits that the company offers to customers and how its distinctive competencies make it capable of delivering significant benefits, creating the perception of enhanced value for potential customers.

Furthermore, it is essential that start-ups understand the complete value chain of the market in which they operate. This involves identifying all links in the chain, from production to the final delivery of the product or service to the customer. In this sense, a start-up also needs to strategically identify its distinctive competencies at each link in the value chain. These capabilities may include its own technology, innovative processes, specialised knowledge or access to specific valuable resources.

Finally, once a unique value proposition is established and aligned with market opportunities, the start-up can focus its efforts on scaling up. This may involve expanding into new national and international markets, increasing production, expanding the team, redesigning the value proposition or seeking strategic partnerships.

The combination of distinctive competencies with market opportunities give rise to the appropriate scalability triggers. Start-ups that have become unicorns generally capitalise on promising market opportunities, gaps in the market and unmet demands or emerging trends that could be successfully exploited. When such opportunities are matched with distinctive competencies such as the unique skills, resources and technologies that start-ups possess, the chances to scale up to unicorn status increase. However, it is important to note that there are many other factors at play, including funding, market strategy and incumbents' reactions, effective growth management and appropriate timing. The right combination of these elements propels start-ups to exceptional success.

12.3 Cases of Brazilian Unicorns and Their Scalability Triggers

Becoming a unicorn is seen as a milestone of success for a start-up, offering benefits that include validation and recognition, as well as access to capital through venture capitalists, growth capital funds or debt financing. Additional benefits include access to talent, growth based on expansion of operations or penetration into new markets and a likely profitable alternative through its acquisition by a larger company or an initial public offering (IPO). Both cases generate significant returns on the initial investment. However, it is important to remember that unicorn status does not guarantee a company's continued success and that many start-ups face challenges even after reaching this milestone.

According to the consulting company CB Insights (2024) there are more than 1,200 unicorns around the world to date, and among them forty-five are located in Latin America. Despite being the largest open innovation hub in Latin America, Brazil only began to reveal its first unicorns in 2018. The consensus is that there are twenty-four start-ups that have achieved unicorn status in Brazil. They are: 99, C6 Bank, CloudWalk, Creditas, Dock Tech, Ebanx, Facily, Frete.com, Gympass, HotMart, iFood, Loft, Loggi, Madeira Madeira, Merama, Mercado Bitcoin, Neon, Nubank, Olist, Pismo, QuintoAndar, Unico, Vtex and Wildlife Studios.

12.3.1 Nubank: Fulfilling Dreams

Nubank was born as a simple idea: to bring an end to the complexity of the financial system for average consumers, offering users independence in managing their own bank accounts. The company is what we call a fintech, a start-up or a company that digitally develops financial products, in which the use of technology is the main differentiator in relation to traditional companies in the sector. In doing so, Nubank has opened the doors of financial services to unbanked market segments, allowing them to fulfil their purchasing aspirations for the first time.

The company was founded in 2013 by David Vélez, Vagner S. Teves Jr, Edward Wible and Cristina Junqueira, gaining notoriety with its first product, a credit card free of annual fees. In addition to not having an annual fee, the bank became popular due to its simple application with which users could control and monitor all expenses directly from the screen of a smartphone. In a concentrated market dominated by large traditional banks such as Itaú, Bradesco, Santander and Banco do Brasil the ease of service through digital media was also a standout feature for the company.

Nubank reached the unicorn mark in 2018 after participating in an investment round in which the fintech company reached a value of US$1 billion and became the third Brazilian unicorn. Other products were offered as the service became popular, such as NuConta, a digital account that initially yielded 100 per cent of the CDI (Interbank Deposit Certificate), which is an interest rate used in loans between banks. The company also expanded in 2021 with the acquisition of NuInvest (formerly Esynvest), and started offering insurance, loans and even the option of purchasing cryptocurrency.

With all these moves, Nubank even managed to reach the title of 'decacorn', an expression used for companies valued at more than US$10 billion, being the first Brazilian company to reach this status before going public. In December 2021, Nubank held its IPO on the New York stock exchange. At the time, it was valued at US$41.7 billion.

12.3.2 Nubank's Business Model Canvas

Nubank's business model canvas is the following:

Value proposition – A digital credit card with no annual fee.

Customer segment – Young people up to thirty-five years old open to innovation and new technologies.

Channel – A mobile app.

Customer relationships – Personalised customer attendance service on a mobile app.

Revenue stream – Percentage on transactions (interchange) and interest on invoice financing.
Cost structure – Operational team; physical and technological structure.
Key resources – Strong brand and culture; advanced technology; security.
Key activities – Customer service; credit analysis, evaluation, and approval.
Key partnerships – Mastercard, investment funds.

From these elements, it is easy to comprehend that Nubank's financial intermediation business model was structured around offering a credit card that works as a platform for transferring financial resources between consumers and companies during purchases. With the main revenue rate being the interchange, every time a purchase is made on a credit card, the merchant pays a fee of around 5 per cent. Part of this money goes to the card machine, another part to the brand (in the case of Nubank, it is Mastercard) and a third part goes to Nubank.

To guarantee profitability in a model like this, Nubank invests heavily in efficiency. Therefore, the focus is on technology and experience via a mobile application, which reduces the need for agencies and call centres.

12.3.3 Market Opportunity Analysis, Strategy and Scalability

Nubank had around eighty-five million Brazilian customers as of 2023, and satisfaction rates such as the net promoter score were the highest in the sector. Nubank's market share was still relatively low: 14 per cent in credit cards, 6 per cent in personal credit and 3 per cent in deposits. On the other hand, in 2024 the average revenue per active customer for customers who used Nubank's card, digital account and personal credit was US$37, while for the average customer base it was US$10. At the same time, the cost of serving each of these customers is estimated at around US$1 per month, given the efficiency of the fintech platform.

With the initial success of the credit card, Nubank quickly expanded its presence in the Brazilian financial market. Thus, the company diversified its services, introducing digital accounts, investments, contactless payments and personal loans. In this way, Nubank's strategy evolved into offering a complete range of financial products with the same simplicity and transparency that had been the pillars of the credit card.

Unlike the bureaucratic procedures and excessive fees associated with traditional banks, Nubank has offered a simplified application process with no annual fee and the possibility of managing the card through an intuitive mobile application. It is expected that Nubank's offering of digital financial services could capture a larger share of the traditional banking market in the future, especially among younger and more technologically inclined consumers. Furthermore, international expansion in emerging countries with limited banking infrastructure offers a vast scope for growth.

12.3.4 Lessons from Nubank

There are three main lessons from the scaling up of Nubank. Firstly, the disruptive way in which Nubank entered the traditional banking market with no annual credit card fee and a fully digital alternative, combined with an intuitive and less bureaucratic experience, allowed it to expand its range of customers quickly and with high levels of satisfaction.

The second lesson is that the company's structured financial intermediation business model, with an emphasis on credit cards and the use of technology to reduce operational costs, was a crucial scalability element in the growth of this unicorn. With its expansion it managed to open other market niches and grow further. Thirdly, the search for a greater market share becomes achievable with low-cost strategies, digitalisation, growth potential driven by younger audiences and a successful IPO in 2021.

In short, Nubank stands out as an example of a successful unicorn in the financial industry, consolidating itself as a disruptive force. Its fundamental scaling drivers range from innovative digital solutions to the effective execution of a financial intermediation model, which is also scalable and technology based. While the challenge of expanding market share persists in 2024, the company has benefited from well-formulated strategies and has been recognised as a company that has not only revolutionised the banking experience but also serves as an example for companies seeking to innovate, scale and thrive in a very dynamic business context.

12.4 QuintoAndar: A Revolution in the Real Estate Market

QuintoAndar is a Brazilian start-up for buying, selling and renting properties. Valued at more than US$5.1 billion, it is the largest real estate agency in Brazil, and the second most valuable unicorn in the country, having reached unicorn status in September 2019. The idea for the company was born in 2012, and the company was formally founded in February 2013 by André Penha and Gabriel Braga.

Initially, it only served the geographic area of Campinas, a city of the state of São Paulo, but the company quickly reached the capital of the same state. Currently, QuintoAndar operates in more than seventy-five cities spread across all regions of the country, except the north region. It has a presence in nine of the twenty-seven Brazilian federative units.

The business idea arose from the common challenges faced by the founders themselves. Braga had difficulty finding a rental property due to insufficient information about available properties and the lack of a guarantor. Penha, on the other hand, owned a property in Campinas but was unable to rent it out because he lived in the United States. From their shared frustration, they decided to conduct a qualitative market research study with 400 people, discovering that their challenges were shared by many potential customers. This contributed to their decision to turn their idea into a start-up.

The success of QuintoAndar was due to its effort in the de-bureaucratisation and simplification of the rental, purchase and sale of real estate in Brazil. Its founders initially intended to make life easier for those seeking a new home, using technology to provide a safe and totally digital platform for the task. For property owners, the entire process was extremely convenient and agile, as QuintoAndar provided a professional photographer to take photos and even recorded videos of each property. The owner could even make their property available for rent or sale while they were abroad, which was a significant benefit. For tenants, the website had a user-friendly layout and useful filters for finding the ideal home, as well as the ability to schedule visits and sign contracts digitally, eliminating the need to show up in person at a notary's office.

Furthermore, QuintoAndar added value to its services by making it financially simpler and more secure for both parties involved. Tenants did not need to pay a security deposit or have a guarantor – standard practices in the real estate industry – rather they only needed to prove they had a certain income level. QuintoAndar guarantees the monthly rent payment for property owners even if the tenant defaults. In certain cases, it also offers the possibility for the owner to receive up to six rent payments in advance.

12.4.1 QuintoAndar's Business Model Canvas

Value proposition – It offers tenants a hassle-free renting process with no need for a co-signer or rental insurance, a wide selection of verified properties, an online tour booking and digital contracts. For landlords, it offers guaranteed rent payments, comprehensive tenant vetting, property management services and reduced vacancy periods.

Customer segment – This is for tenants looking for an easy and secure way to find and lease properties and landlords looking to rent out their properties quickly and with minimal hassle, in addition to property owners who might consider selling their properties through QuintoAndar.

Channel – QuintoAndar's website and mobile app for property searches, virtual tours and transactions.

Customer relationships – Automated services through the platform for searching, booking visits and signing contracts; community and feedback opportunities through user reviews, ratings and additional feedback mechanisms.

Revenue stream – Fees charged to tenants when they successfully rent a property and to property owners for rental management services. Eventually, additional services are added such as property photography, insurance and maintenance.

Cost structure – Platform development and maintenance, marketing and sales, customer support, operational costs, commissions and fees.

Key resources – The digital platform (website and app) that facilitates the entire rental process and strong data analytics for personalised service offerings and market insights.

Key activities – Development and maintenance of the digital platform. Marketing and sales for attracting and retaining both tenants and landlords through advertising and partnerships, as well as providing support and ensuring satisfaction for both tenants and landlords.

Key partnerships – Real estate agencies and brokers, insurance companies, financial institutions and tech partners.

12.4.2 Market Opportunity Analysis, Strategy and Scalability

QuintoAndar operates within what is perceived as an old-fashioned, traditional market, that of property rental and sales. However, its focus on a 100 per cent digital environment revolutionised this market in 2013, after its founders noticed that the penetration of the rental market in Brazil was very low compared to other countries and was highly focused on the brick-and-mortar experience.

As highlighted by StartSe, only 18 per cent of residences were rented in Brazil when the company was created, compared to 36 per cent in the United States and 48 per cent in Germany. Upon analysing the issue, the start-up founders noticed that one of the reasons was the market's heavy reliance on the brick-and-mortar experience, in addition to extremely high levels of bureaucracy. Thus, an opportunity to enter into a giant underexplored market became evident to its founders.

It was then that the company was born with a product–market fit proposal, encompassing a greater focus on the digital user experience, intensive use of data, feedback and partnerships into its business model. Furthermore, the model connected all of these elements through an overarching process of digitalisation and technology adoption. In this way, the company allowed customers to carry out virtual visits, electronic signatures and credit card payments over a user-friendly online platform to reduce the market's biggest issue: bureaucracy. Over time, these advantages were further developed to strengthen the company's positioning.

As of 2024, QuintoAndar also offered a payment guarantee to property owners and options without a guarantor for the landlord, as well as maintenance and repair services. Additionally, with the centralisation of property portfolio management into a digital format, its business model allowed the company to achieve an efficient distribution of fixed costs. This formed another strong pillar in the model that enabled scalability. Thus, the start-up not only achieved better margins but also passed a share of these savings on to its end customers by offering better rates.

The start-up developed valuable competence in uniting a huge and traditionally bureaucratic market through the process of digitalisation and customer experience offerings. These elements represented powerful scalability triggers that turned the company into a Brazilian unicorn. With entirely digital processes, the cost structure and management of client/property portfolios further enhanced this trigger, enabling QuintoAndar to scale up growth around the entire country.

Furthermore, the company launched operations in Mexico due to the similarity between the two real estate markets, both in size and problems faced by tenants and landlords, with an eye to expanding the rental vertical. The Mexican expansion via Benvi represented the digital replication of QuintoAndar's core business activities at home.

12.4.3 Lessons from QuintoAndar

The lessons provided by QuintoAndar go beyond the combination of technology and innovation. Through the need that the founders themselves faced with bureaucracy and difficulties when renting properties, they saw an opportunity to penetrate a consolidated and rigid market, bringing greater agility, autonomy and transparency for both tenants and property owners via a digital platform.

Digital functions such as virtual tours, the speed and convenience of electronic contract signatures and resolving property issues through the platform as well as laser focus on user experience, intensive use of data analytics, valuing feedback from customers and partners, continuous investing in technology, strategic partnerships, rent payment guarantee to property owners and bureaucracy reduction all ensured a unique selling point for QuintoAndar compared to the traditional competitors in the market.

Thus, QuintoAndar is an example of incremental innovation which allowed it to become profitable early on. Steadily gaining initial market share and improving customer experience, the company would eventually experience exponential growth, with its valuation multiplying with each new investment round.

This favourable scenario was also due to the company's operational choices, as part of its business strategy was to focus on operating in a virtual environment, ensuring greater scalability. Additionally, the less centralised and more robust platform model allowed for the dilution of fixed costs, making QuintoAndar's operation leaner and yielding higher margins. Part of this gain was passed on to customers, who paid lower fees than those charged by traditional real estate agencies. This led to improved customer satisfaction.

The company also aimed to diversify its revenue. Its value proposition was focused exclusively on property rentals until January 2020. Subsequently, it launched the option for buying and selling properties on its platform. The company expanded vertically in mid-2022 and entered the Mexican market with a new international brand named Benvi. Market similarities with Brazil, particularly regarding the bureaucratic burden, meant they could offer Mexicans the same rental experience.

12.5 iFood: The Brazilian Delivery Giant

iFood was founded in May 2011. Its operations began with Disk Cook, a delivery service featuring a printed menu guide, where orders were placed through a call centre. The company transitioned to the internet the following year, launching the iFood website and app, with the aim of improving the consumer experience. In 2013, it received investments from Movile, a company that invests in technology businesses. Movile gained a controlling share in iFood in 2022.

The idea of connecting restaurants to the end consumer using a digital platform in a simple and practical manner quickly expanded to other establishments, including pharmacies and pet shops, among others. The technological platform solution revolutionised the delivery market by enabling access to various options and updated information from each user, allowing the entire purchasing journey to be completed in one place. This innovation made the company the second most popular unicorn in Latin America, serving more than 1,700 cities in Brazil. In addition to delivering meals and other products, the company invests in fintech solutions with the iFood Benefícios card.

iFood recorded approximately seventy million orders per month in 2023, a 55.6 per cent increase compared to the forty-five million transactions in August 2020. A study conducted in 2020 by the Economic Research Institute Foundation indicates that the company alone contributed 0.43 per cent to the national gross domestic product (GDP), creating around 730,000 jobs.

In essence, the company identified a potential market that had not yet been explored. It successfully entered the delivery market, which was already well-known and widely used in Brazil, by transitioning to a digital platform, thus initiating its activities in a blue ocean, that is, in the absence of competition.

12.5.1 iFood's Business Model Canvas

iFood is acknowledged for consolidating the country's delivery business model and transforming it through its app. The model is based on three fundamental relationships: with customers, establishments and delivery personnel. The company's innovative proposition effectively delivered value to all key stakeholders. We can summarise iFood's business model canvas as follows:

Value proposition – Convenient delivery.

Customer segment – Customers willing to trade convenience for a small fee.

Channel – An online platform and increasing offerings following a continuous territorial expansion. It reached a broader audience by expanding into new municipalities.

Customer relationships – Automated services through the platform and building a strong brand with structured and constant communication to reach customers. Customer satisfaction is a priority at every stage of the journey, from selecting the restaurant to the delivery of the order, with a focus on food quality, delivery time, customer service and app usability.

Revenue stream – The main revenue stream is based on fees per transaction.

Cost structure – Platform development and maintenance, marketing and sales, customer support, operational costs, commissions and fees.

Key resources – State of the art technology and a privileged first-mover advantage.

Key activities – Continuous optimisation of operations, enhancing the customer experience and increasing delivery efficiency through investment in AI and other tools. Service diversification includes delivery of beverages, grocery products and financial services such as the iFood Card.

Key partnerships – Complete ecosystem of partnerships with restaurants, supermarkets, banks and other market players to expand possibilities and generate value for all stakeholders. To strengthen these partnerships, iFood has introduced innovations such as drone deliveries and the iFood Box, a temporary storage locker for orders in residential and commercial buildings.

In the past, consumers had to keep track of several establishment phone numbers and menu pamphlets. Options were limited, requiring phone call confirmation. However, iFood integrated all this information into one place, providing updated and extensive options, allowing users to choose, order and pay on the same platform. Establishments also experienced significant advantages. Despite commission rates, the app provides access to a larger audience, offering a guaranteed and updated showcase, allowing the use of registered delivery personnel and eliminating the need to invest in an in-house delivery team.

iFood's scalability was perhaps one of the most notable aspects of its success. iFood revolutionised the food delivery sector in Brazil by offering a digital platform that connected restaurants and consumers, allowing food delivery on demand. This market opportunity came from the growing trend of convenience for eating out that offered a wide variety of restaurant options and a fast and reliable delivery experience. iFood has also invested heavily in technology to improve user experience and optimise delivery operations, which is one of its distinct competencies. Furthermore, the company expanded its international presence, entering the markets of Mexico and Colombia. Significant investments from large venture capital funds and the acquisition of local competitors have also contributed to its billion-dollar valuation and unicorn status.

iFood's strategy benefited from several scalability triggers that propelled the company's rapid growth. In a nutshell, the strong demand for food delivery in Brazil, iFood's efficient digital business model, the robust technology employed by the company and the experienced team behind it are the key factors explaining its success. The success of iFood is not the result of a single factor, but rather the combination of various factors that complement and reinforce each other. The company is expected to continue evolving and adapting to market changes, maintain its leadership position and offer the best possible experience for its customers.

12.5.2 Lessons from iFood

Considering that iFood has become one of the main players in the Brazilian market, the organisation capitalised on an opportunity to deliver a service/product to consumers in an efficient and entirely innovative manner. In this regard, as the organisation sought to modernise a simple food delivery process into something more practical and accessible from anywhere, solely requiring a smartphone connected to the internet, iFood pursued a strategy based on the growth of the internet and mobile usability.

iFood solidified its position as the leading delivery platform in Brazil in 2024, which brought certain obligations and demands for the app to perform to its maximum capacity. As a result, the company provides a vast array of services and products to their customers in most Brazilian cities and have become extremely renowned for their agility, speed and process optimisation. All these competencies have been built out of a commitment to maximum efficiency. In other words, the platform's priority is to simplify the daily lives of its users and be recognised not just as a delivery platform but as a tool that assists and facilitates their users' daily routines.

The success of iFood is based on the use of technology (internet, mobile, etc.) to transform a task that was previously carried out in a much more restricted manner. To ensure coherence, the platform employs AI and customer data in a highly refined and articulated manner so that ordering, confirmation and delivery processes are conducted according to user expectations. iFood has also solidified itself as a strategic partner to restaurants, enabling them to expand their businesses beyond their physical capacity through the orders and deliveries enabled by the app.

Finally, the primary concern for iFood is the entry of new players into the market. Despite being pioneers and leaders, the market is open to innovations that could potentially further upgrade simple activities like ordering food. Therefore, continuous improvement is a fundamental barrier to imitation in the case of iFood.

12.6 The Importance of Unicorns in Wealth Creation, Employment and Income Generation

According to Matos and Radaelli (2020), start-ups play a crucial role in wealth creation, employment and income generation in emerging economies. The emergence of unicorns in Brazil garners international attention and foreign investments to the country. Investors and venture capital funds are increasingly inclined to support promising start-ups in the Global South, which foster the growth of the local entrepreneurial ecosystem and the development of a more dynamic and innovative economy. Indeed, according to the report published by the Association for Private Capital Investment in Latin America (LAVCA, 2020), the Brazilian entrepreneurial ecosystem has stood out in Latin America, and Brazil has accounted for half of the investments made in start-ups in the region in 2020, with approximately US$2.49 billion across over 220 investments.

Wealth generation is also tied to access to capital. The emergence of unicorns often attracts investors from around the world interested in investing in a country. This not only provides capital for existing companies but also increases access to funding for start-ups, further promoting innovation and economic growth. For instance, Latin America ranked 7th in the list of regions with the highest venture capital activity. According to a report by Distrito (2023) in collaboration with SoftBank, US$36.9 billion was invested between 2019 and 2023. Brazil is the largest country in terms of land area and population in Latin America, and this significantly translates into the start-up scene: Brazil represents 62.9 per cent of total start-ups across the region, followed by Mexico (11.7 per cent), Argentina (7.1 per cent), Colombia (6.2 per cent) and Chile (5.1 per cent). Brazil is also at the forefront in terms of participation in the volume of venture capital, with 63.9 per cent of total resources invested in 2023.

Regarding job creation, unicorns typically grow rapidly and require both skilled and unskilled labour to support their operations. This process increases employment opportunities across various sectors, from technology development to marketing and sales, thus positively impacting the country's employment rate. Furthermore, these start-ups often attract both local and international talent, offering attractive career opportunities and competitive remuneration. This positive loop helps retain talent within the country and contributes to the development of a skilled and diverse domestic workforce. Moreover, unicorns can positively affect knowledge generation and technology development. This is because a successful unicorn can stimulate innovation in other sectors of the economy, promote the development of the local innovation ecosystem and increase the global competitiveness of local companies. Finally, the more successful start-ups reach the unicorn status, the more that country becomes a reference for the development of promising new businesses, generating optimism and increased investments.

On the other hand, the higher the number of unemployed individuals in a country or region, the lower the wealth generation and consequently, the lower the consumption. This negative cycle directly impacts the size of a country's GDP. Income generation is directly linked to entrepreneurship and employment. New companies create jobs in various areas as they grow, including software development, marketing, sales and customer support. This is particularly significant in a country like Brazil, where unemployment is a major concern and where start-up success can make a big difference to alleviating this structural economic problem.

In a country as geographically vast as Brazil, the emergence of start-ups and unicorns can contribute to regional development. This is because start-ups are not created only in major regions but can also arise in less developed regions of Brazil. For instance, Recife's Porto Digital is a technology park that hosts numerous start-ups. It has revitalised the local economy, promoting technological innovation and providing jobs for skilled workers. Cases such as this can help reduce regional disparities by creating economic opportunities and promoting development in areas that have historically faced economic challenges, such as the northeast of Brazil. Overall, start-ups and unicorns play a crucial role in the economic development of emerging countries by driving innovation, creating jobs, enhancing competitiveness and contributing to the overall prosperity of the economy.

The home country of a start-up that becomes a unicorn also benefits from economic diversification. The emergence of a successful unicorn can contribute to diversifying the country's economy, reducing the dependence on traditional sectors. This can make the economy more resilient to external shocks and promote more sustainable long-term economic growth. Additionally, the success of a unicorn can elevate the country's international reputation as a hub of innovation and entrepreneurship with all the associated benefits.

Santos et al. (2023) also highlighted the importance of start-ups in the socioeconomic landscape of Brazil for meeting sustainable development goals (SDGs). The authors conducted a mapping exercise to identify the main impacts of start-ups on Brazil's socioeconomic landscape concerning the UN's SDGs for the 2030 agenda. According to their findings, Brazilian start-ups have a greater association those SDGs that prioritise decent work and economic growth, reduction of inequalities and emphasis on the country's industry, innovation and infrastructure. Furthermore, it was observed that the sector with the highest start-up contribution to socioeconomic development in Brazil was the energy field, aiding investment in clean and renewable energies. The second most impactful vertical was the agribusiness sector, which contributes to the goals of sustainable agriculture, sustainable communities and responsible production and consumption.

It is clear that start-ups and unicorns in Brazil contribute to job creation and income generation, democratising services that were previously often restricted to certain groups. Unicorns are also a source of innovation in various traditional markets and established sectors of the industry through new products and business models, favouring the country's economic development. However, despite its leading role in Latin America, Brazil still has a small number of unicorns in relation to its GDP when compared to other emerging countries. This is because there are still structural challenges to be addressed, such as regulatory barriers and difficulties in training qualified professionals to be prepared for technological innovation and digital transformation.

Finally, unicorns do not only affect tangible aspects of economic prosperity. They also increase the expectations and confidence of investors and citizens in the country. This can lead to capital inflow and stimulate job creation, which result in economic growth.

12.7 Conclusions

In this chapter we have briefly explored the emergence of start-ups and the challenges they face to trigger scalability that will eventually lead them to unicorn status. We described three cases of Brazilian start-ups that reached unicorn status using the business model canvas. Finally, we discussed the systemic importance of unicorns in emerging economies, highlighting their impact on wealth creation, employment, regional development, income generation and sustainability.

Scalability, understood as the ability to rapidly expand the customer base and profitability, is a fundamental challenge for start-ups. Understanding the triggers of scalability is crucial for start-ups to overcome growth challenges and achieve success in highly competitive and constantly changing markets. By adapting quickly, exploiting opportunities and attracting strategic resources, start-ups gain the potential to drive innovation, challenge established paradigms and shape the future of the markets in which they operate.

Scalability is driven by a combination of distinctive competencies and market opportunities. In this context, for start-ups to identify the path towards scalability, they need to develop a deep understanding of the market and a unique value proposition, and to align internal competencies with external demands. The three cases of Brazilian unicorns illustrate how start-ups can achieve this status by identifying market opportunities and developing distinctive competencies. Nubank, QuintoAndar and iFood capitalised on market opportunities, invested in technology and innovation and rapidly expanded their operations. These cases highlight the importance of a well-planned strategy, a differentiated business model and a commitment to operational excellence in the pursuit of scalability and market success.

When start-ups achieve unicorn status, they bring several tangible and intangible benefits to their home country, including international prestige, increased investments, the development of the entrepreneurial ecosystem, job and income generation, knowledge transfer and economic diversification. These benefits can have a significant long-term impact on a country's economic and social development.

Acknowledgement

This chapter is part of Project 2021/10599-3 FAPESP – Fundação de Amparo à Pesquisa no Estado de São Paulo. We are grateful to FAPESP for their support.

References

Aulet, B. (2013). *Disciplined Entrepreneurship: 24 Steps to a Successful Startup*. John Wiley and Sons, Inc.

Blank, S. (2010, 4 January). *Make no little plans – defining the scalable startup*. tinyurl.com/374mupr4

CB Insights. (2024). *The complete list of unicorn companies*. www.cbinsights.com/research-unicorn-companies

Distrito. (2023). *Panorama Tech América Latina 2023*. materiais.distrito.me/report/panorama-tech-america-latina-2023

Dorf, B., Blank, S., Högsdal, N., and Bartel, D. (2014). *Das Handbuch für Startups: Schritt für Shritt zum Erfolgreichen Unternehmen*. O'Reilly Germany.

Giardino, C., Unterkalmsteiner, M., Paternoster, N., Gorschek, T., and Abrahamsson, P. (2014). What do we know about software development in startups? *IEEE Software 31*(5), 28–32.

LAVCA. (2020). *Annual review of tech investment in Latin America*. www.lavca.org/research/lavcas-annual-review-of-tech-investment-in-latam/

List, J. A. (2022, 5 May). Scaling entrepreneurial ventures: Why it's so hard to scale a great idea. *Harvard Business Review*. hbr.org/2022/05/why-its-so-hard-to-scale-a-great-idea

Matos, F., and Radaelli, V. (2020). *Ecossistema de startups no Brasil: Estudo de caracterização do ecossistema de empreendedorismo de alto impacto Brasileiro*. Working Paper, BID. tinyurl.com/bdbcr6we

Neves, A. P. Z., and Zilber, S. N. (2023). Digital startups survivor and scalability: Identifying variables for accelerated growth. *Open Journal of Business and Management, 11*, 1927-1947.

Osterwalder, A. (2004). *The business model ontology – A proposition in a design science approach*. PhD thesis, Faculté des Hautes Etudes Commerciales de l'Université de Lausanne.

Rayport, J.F., Sola, D., and Kupp, M. (2023). The overlooked key to a successful scale-up. *Harvard Business Review*.

13 A Unicorn under Sanctions: The Case of Yandex

ANDREI PANIBRATOV AND KALMAN KALOTAY

13.1 Introduction

There is plenty of anecdotal evidence of unicorns with strong domestic and international standing whose fate is influenced by strong invisible (and visible) struggles during their international expansion due to the geopolitical factors. BRICS (Brazilian, Russian, Indian, Chinese, South African, Egyptian, Ethiopian, Indonesian, Iranian and Emirati) unicorns are prominent examples. These are well known for their excellence in high-end technologies and widely recognised around the world, while failing to access markets in the United States and Western Europe. It is mandatory to address the critical role of the (geo)political factors for unicorns from emerging economies.

In this chapter we analyse the strategic response of and consequences for the former Russian unicorn Yandex, nicknamed 'Russia's Google', in the face of sanctions levied against the Russian Federation due to its conflict with Ukraine starting in February 2022. We focus on explaining the impact of political pressures on Yandex, Russia's largest internet company, examining its international expansion before and during the sanctions, when its global ambitions were strongly challenged by its status as a Russian firm operating in a strategic industry.

Events after February 2022 negatively impacted the macroeconomic climate in Russia and resulted in increased Ruble volatility, currency controls, significant increases in interest rates and inflation, an expected reduction in consumer spending and a withdrawal of foreign enterprises and suppliers from the Russian market. In addition, as of 2024 there were rumours about new laws and regulations that could adversely affect foreign shareholders and the value of their Yandex shares.

The first line of defence of this systematically important company in the face of the crisis was to conserve cash and effectively allocate capital and budget, while continuing to invest in the development of key businesses and products. Yandex was closely monitoring the evolution of sanctions and the export control situation, as well as the macroeconomic climate and consumer sentiment in Russia. It was also evaluating various contingency plans in case of unforeseen changes. The board of directors and management of the company prioritised the well-being of employees in the face of the recent partial mobilisation while doing everything possible to protect the interests of shareholders and other stakeholders.

In July 2024 a consortium of only Russian entities bought Yandex for US$5.4 billion (RBC, 2024). This was one of the largest corporate exits from Russia since February 2022: The sold businesses accounted for most of the company's assets and employed the bulk of its 26,000 employees (*New York Times*, 2024). It was more and more difficult for Yandex to navigate between the Kremlin's policies and a Western sanction imposed on the Russian economy, which led to the dramatic transformation of what once was Russia's most prominent unicorn.

13.2 Regional Context

Russia and the region of the transition economies of Central and Eastern Europe (CEE) have not emerged as a major locus for unicorns. By 2023, the twenty-eight United Nations member countries of the region[1] had become the birthplace of fifty-three unicorns. Twenty-eight of these kept their headquarters in their countries of origin, while twenty-five relocated to either Western Europe or North America, while maintaining a significant presence in their countries and region of origin, mainly in relation to technical and back-office activities.

Russia has the largest economy within the CEE region and has produced the third highest number of unicorns (seven), behind Poland (eleven) and Estonia (eight) (Table 13.1). Russia has not been recognised as a major hub for tech firms, either globally or regionally, especially compared with the scientific and technological tradition and potential of the country. However, certain Russia-based national champions possess specific dynamic capabilities which could distinguish them and even mark them as superior to other (Western-)

[1] We do not count those regional entities that have declared independence or quasi-independence but have not been unanimously recognised as such by the United Nations.

European firms within their respective industries (Panibratov & Klishevich, 2020). There is little understanding of the factors that have led to this outcome and the occasional technological supremacy that nourished the growth of these unicorns. Any generalisations are extremely difficult because Russian unicorns are very diverse in terms of their home-grown characteristics and internationalisation patterns, an aspect that has precluded the emergence of an evident pattern in relation to unicorn emergence and growth.

According to Table 13.1, the region of CEE countries hosts a mere 1 per cent of the world's unicorns, plus close to another 1 per cent is accounted for by unicorns that were established in the region but relocated their headquarters elsewhere. Most countries within the region host no unicorns. There are also marked differences related to the population size, gross domestic product (GDP) per capita and

Table 13.1 *The universe of Central and Eastern European unicorns, 2023 (Number of firms)*

Country/ region	Headquartered	Founded but "exited"	Total
Poland	11	0	11
Estonia	2	6	8
Russia	5	2	7
Ukraine	0	6	6
Czechia	4	1	5
Lithuania	3	0	3
Croatia	2	1	3
Belarus	0	3	3
Kazakhstan	1	0	1
Latvia	0	1	1
Slovenia	0	1	1
Armenia	0	1	1
Bulgaria	0	1	1
Hungary	0	1	1
Romania	0	1	1
Remaining 13 countries of the region	0	0	0
Total CEE	28	25	53

Source: Compiled by the authors based on data from Dealroom.co (2023).

migration patterns of the countries in CEE. Notably, a relatively high number of unicorns have been created in small countries such as Estonia, Lithuania and Croatia. It is important to stress that the negative demographic and social developments of CEE countries following the fall of the iron curtain in 1991, including a significant and persistent brain drain, affected the competitiveness of these economies and their human potential. For example, in relation to the direction of unicorn founders' migration flows, Russia, Romania, Poland, Bulgaria and Ukraine are found to fall into the 'losing all unicorn founders' category, indicating that the phenomenon of brain drain of unicorn founders is extreme (Kutsenko et al., 2022). This trend, along with the economic sanctions imposed on Russia in 2022, turns the analysis of Yandex into an enlightening inquiry into the birth of unicorns under extreme circumstances, which are probably tougher than in most emerging economies.

Yandex was one of the largest Russian CEE unicorns. It specialised in internet-related products and services, including search and information services, e-commerce, transportation, navigation, mobile applications and online advertising. Its founders began the development of Yandex's search technology back in 1989 and launched the yandex.ru website in 1997. In fact, the company was set up as a combination of two small start-ups, Arcadia and Comptek, that were founded a few years earlier by two Russian information technology (IT) specialists. The principal Russia-based headquarters was founded in 2000. The team consisted of twenty-five people at that time, and all the data was on one server. The company had indexed the Russian internet, which consisted of only a few thousand websites and contained just a few gigabits of data. From these modest beginnings and over its few years Yandex became the leading internet company in Russia.

The unique attribute of Yandex as a search engine was its first-mover advantage in Russia. Launched almost immediately after Russia got internet connectivity, it benefited from a rapidly growing market, especially in terms of contextual advertising. Investing in the Russian market from the start, as well as a superior time and language alignment, allowed Yandex to have a larger market share than Google, the leader of the global search engine industry. Yandex remains strong in the Russian market to this day.

After a decade of fast growth, Yandex moved its holding company to the Netherlands in 2007, though it kept most of the central corporate operations in Russia. It became a unicorn by exceeding the US$1 billion valuation mark in 2011. With the fast spread of internet in the country, from less than 1 per cent of the population when the company was first established to more than 85 per cent in 2020, Yandex's standing, image and competitiveness expanded. It became one of Russia's most desired IT employers, even a 'symbol of freedom' (MacFarquhar, 2022). By successfully competing with Google and offering dozens of digitally based services, the company became the hub of Russia's internet market and the flagship search engine in the country. Such developments helped Yandex transform into a unicorn and being a major player in Russia's internet ecosystem further promoted its domestic growth (Seddon, 2020). The company became profitable in 2002, very soon after its creation. Nine years later, in May 2011, Yandex held a public offering on the Nasdaq. The Yandex ticker is YNDX. According to Dealroom.co (2024), its valuation in 2023 reached US$7.7 billion. The same year it had offices in ten countries worldwide and employed about 21,000 people.

13.3 The Early Years: Growing the Service Ecosystem

Like any major market participant, Yandex's existence and activities affected the whole internet ecosystem. Yandex tried to use this central role to best serve the interests of users. To provide them with good searches, Yandex needed an open, diverse internet infrastructure with multiple high-quality resources. Developing services for users was only possible in partnership with other market players, taking their interests into account. The company managed to create platform solutions and developed transparent rules of interaction for diverse businesses, from shops to taxi depots. Yandex created new tools that people could use to interact with these businesses, no matter where they were and on what they were working.

The top two largest segments were the search portal and taxi hailing, which together accounted for 88 per cent of Yandex's group revenue. They were the most profitable businesses for Yandex, helping to fund its initiatives in FoodTech and Yandex Delivery. The goal was to develop Yandex into a super app, under whose umbrella users could find all kinds of services. By taking such a central role within the internet ecosystem, Yandex did not regulate the internet usage rules. Rather, it ran multiple platforms that aggregated and enabled users to transmit content online. The company aimed to operate these services by referring to the guidance of various frameworks of international standards for human rights, such as the International Covenant on Civil and Political Rights.

Thus, Yandex demonstrated technological orientation towards service ecosystem development and prioritisation of the independent development of new services within the company. It did not strive to create joint ventures and had a minimal level of acquisitions. The company preferred to develop the service ecosystem internally, even with the risk of limiting areas of growth (Panibratov, 2012).

The fast growth of the Russian IT market has facilitated the growth of Yandex. The growth rate was still at 20 per cent in 2021 and the size of the market reached 2.22 trillion Rubles (equivalent to US$38.36 billion). This happened largely due to the large-scale digitisation of companies and an increase in demand for information security solutions and products developed by Russian companies.

13.4 Yandex Goes Global

The internationalisation of Yandex started with the launch of search engines in the geographically and linguistically proximate former Soviet Union countries. This proximity sustained a strong regional advantage for the company due to the opportunity of the 'soft' inter nationalisation to the neighbouring countries of Belarus, Kazakhstan and Ukraine, with short geographic and cultural distances, common history and similar institutions. Building on innovations and growing via international expansion into the former Soviet space, Yandex accumulated the knowledge and adaptability necessary for successful internationalisation without the significant effort and costs traditionally associated with aggressive expansion in remote and alien geographies. In turn, this allowed Yandex to strengthen its position in the neighbouring locations and limit the power of Google in Russia and in the former Soviet sphere.

By the end of 2010 two domains were opened in Ukraine (yandex.ua) and in Kazakhstan (yandex.kz), both working in Russian but geographically oriented towards Ukraine and Kazakhstan in keywording. The internet markets of Belarus and Poland were the next important host markets for Yandex. Most of the Belarusian population spoke Russian and used it in daily life (along with Byelorussian). As for

Poland, the company expected many obstacles. Only part of the population understood Russian or read the Cyrillic alphabet. Besides, an aversion to everything Russia-related lingered in the country. Moreover, Yahoo and Google were very strong in this market. Both companies had their domains in Poland running in Polish.

Yandex, like many internet firms, was born global. Yet, within its internationalisation the only physical international asset that Yandex had abroad was its subsidiary, Yandex Labs. This was founded in Silicon Valley, California in 2009, at the time of the launch of its English twin, Yandex.com. This investment initiative was undertaken to develop its core technological capabilities and attract foreign talent (Dorofeev, 2013). It was used mainly for research rather than to provide services in the USA.

Yandex was a market leader not only in countries where Russian language was commonly used, but also in places where large Russian-speaking diasporas lived. As such, it occupied a leading position in Russia, Belarus and Kazakhstan, and had a major presence in Turkey (Panibratov, 2012). In Russia, where it was founded, it achieved a search engine share of up to 61 per cent in 2022 (Yandex.Radar, 2022).

Yandex received a significant part of its income from the sale of advertising. Yandex technologies allowed customers to place ads on desktop and mobile devices and target them to a specific audience. The company offered a comprehensive service for working with all types of advertising: Yandex.Direct. It also offered analytical tools for evaluating the effectiveness of advertising campaigns. Yet, the company's software was primarily developed for the Russian market and maintained the internet search engine for the same market, where it had a strong brand. It introduced innovations to the industry in the form of the pay-per-click system of pricing for advertising and contriving to operate successfully in Cyrillic. However, competition with Google had grown tougher. While Yandex had a strong, established brand in Russia, Google started expanding into Eastern Europe with technology that was fully attuned to the Cyrillic alphabet, something it long lacked. Between 2010 and 2013, Google and Yandex were in direct competition in Russia, Belarus and Ukraine. In Turkey, Yandex was the second most popular search engine after Google (Panibratov, 2012).

The company was engaged in a number of strategic tech partnerships with foreign companies, such as ride-hailing service Uber, food-delivery group Grubhub and search engine DuckDuckGo (*Financial*

Times, 2022). In addition, the Yandex Taxi app expanded to about twenty countries across the globe including Norway, Uzbekistan and Ivory Coast, and the Yandex Delivery service reached destinations such as London, Paris and Tel Aviv (*New York Times,* 2024).

13.5 Sanctions Coming to Russia and Its Unicorns

Since February 2022 the impact of sanctions against Russia have become of paramount importance for all Russian firms, whether they were directly put under such sanctions or not (Meyer et al., 2023). With the outbreak of the military conflict in Ukraine, the IT market in Russia started declining. Analysts suggested that the main factors of market decline were the sanctions and disruption to supply chains, suspension of activities of foreign IT companies and the global economic situation (Borak, 2023). Among the key factors keeping the sector afloat were the increase in import substitution projects, the increased demand for information security and the support from the state.

The role of the government was particularly important for Yandex, due to the expectation that this and other IT firms could still derive a large share of their revenue from abroad on the bases of their intangible assets as they had high levels of international investments in a large number of countries (Sawant et al., 2021). For this reason, the Russian government shielded sanctioned firms with international operations, such as Yandex, by facilitating the development of new business networks that were built in friendly foreign markets.

On one hand, sanctions imposed in 2022 did not create a dramatic change in the Russian business environment as they were the continuation of measures applied against Russian firms and individuals after the annexation of Crimea in 2014. On the other hand, the new sanctions were more severe, making the Russian Federation one of the most sanctioned country in the world with close to 14,000 measures by March 2023 (Castellum AI, 2023).[2]

[2] Analysing the impact of political factors on Russian multinational enterprises' strategic choices to divest their foreign operations due to sanctions, Panibratov and Gaur (2022) found that firms operating in countries that did not join the economic sanctions against Russia were less inclined to divest their subsidiaries than those in countries that supported sanctions. In their findings, the authors emphasised the political dimension of the foreign market exit, a factor largely confirmed by the events after 24 February 2022.

Regarding sanctions, Yandex was in a difficult position. On the one hand, its board insisted that neither Yandex nor any of its group companies was a target of sanctions in the United States, European Union, Switzerland or United Kingdom, and the Yandex group was not owned or controlled by any persons who had been designated as under such sanctions (Yandex, 2023a). On the other hand, Arkady Volozh, one of the founders, was on the sanctions list, although he was no longer formally with the firm. In any case, Yandex operated in cyberspace, which is a highly sensitive domain in modern warfare. Against this backdrop, Nasdaq suspended the company's listing in March 2023 (Yandex, 2023b).

After February 2022, Russian businesses reacted to the new situation using defensive strategies to minimise their losses, mostly through reverse internationalisation (Kalotay & Weiner, 2022). This was in line with experts' predictions and the prescriptions of international business literature on sanctions (cf. Meyer et al., 2023). As non-military coercive measures (coined as 'jus ad vim' by Michael Walzer, 1977), sanctions have the potential to disrupt the international business environment, especially the institutional environment (Meyer et al., 2023), and change the rules of the game. Like many other large Russian companies, Yandex had to adapt accordingly under the geopolitical pressures of 2022. The company's capitalisation had been declining since the second half of 2021, along with the entire Russian market, and had dropped sharply after February 2022. Later, there was a period of gradual recovery and a sharp fall against the backdrop of the announcement of partial mobilisation. In 2022, capitalisation was partially recovered to about 700 billion Rubles (approximately US$10.24 billion) (Vedomosti, 2022).

The 2023 share value was still at 35 per cent of the peak values, since trading of the company's shares abroad had been suspended in February 2022. The share price on the Moscow Exchange served as a reference point: At the peak of 2022, the share price was around 6,000 Rubles per share, while at the lowest levels of this year the price was around 1,350 Rubles. By the end of 2022 Yandex was more than two times cheaper than the year before (Vedomosti, 2022).

Even though the Yandex group itself did not fall under the sanctions of any countries, its top managers were put under the restrictions. In mid-March, Tigran Khudaverdyan, chief executive officer (CEO) of Yandex in Russia, fell under EU sanctions, after which he left his post (YLE, 2023). Mr Volozh was sanctioned in June; his name was included in the EU sanctions list as part of the sixth package of restrictions imposed as a result of the Russian military operation in Ukraine. To avoid the transfer of sanctions to the company, Mr Volozh left all positions in Yandex and its divisions and transferred the right to vote to the board of directors, the Dutch parent company Yandex N.V. The company then announced that he was leaving the posts of executive and general director with the parent company of the Yandex N.V. group in the Netherlands and transferred his voting rights to the board of directors. Mr Volozh considered the decision to impose sanctions against him 'misguided and ultimately counter-productive' (EQS.News, 2022). Eventually, neither Yandex nor the group's subsidiaries were included in the sanctions.

Western companies exiting from Russia have faced hurdles. For example, Russian authorities signed off on buyers, price and terms, and often forced the exiting companies to sell at fire-sale prices (*New York Times*, 2024). Due to the anti-war position of Mr Volozh, the domestic situation was complex and a possible scenario in which Yandex could be sold started to crystalise.

13.6 Yandex Management Structure

In 2019, after discussions in the State Duma about a draft law on limiting foreign ownership in significant internet companies, Yandex changed its management structure. The Public Interest Fund was created, to which the so-called golden share was transferred. The fund could block transactions geared towards the consolidation of 10 per cent or more of the voting or economic shares of an internet company. A bill to limit foreign ownership in such companies was never passed.

Yandex's revenue under the International Financial Reporting Standards, the most widespread set of globally comparable accounting rules for the financial statements of publicly traded companies, grew by 54 per cent in 2021, to 356.2 billion Rubles (about US$4.83 billion). For nine months of 2022 it amounted to 356.9 billion Rubles (about US$5.22 billion), exceeding the total annual revenue for the entire previous year. The earnings before interest, taxes, depreciation and amortisation (EBITDA) for those nine months of 2022 amounted to 46 billion Rubles (about US$673 million), and the net profit was 40.56

billion Rubles (about US$593 million). This growth came as a result of the increase in the company's customer base that was only possible after foreign firms (including providers of IT services and applications) left Russia. Being unable to use services such as Booking.com or SkyScanner anymore, Russians turned to the Yandex-based search for alternative solutions, which significantly increased the respective market share of the company's services.

As of September 30, 2022, Arkady Volozh's family fund controlled 45.1 per cent of voting shares and 8.5 per cent of ordinary shares, according to the Yandex website. Another 46.3 per cent of the voting shares and 87.6 per cent of the company's share capital were free floating. Employees of the company, including top management, held 6.6 per cent of voting shares and 3.2 per cent of ordinary shares.

In total, the Volozh trust and other employees of the company had more than 50 per cent of the votes. At the same time, almost 88 per cent of the economic rights to the company were held by class A traded shareholders, which were accounted for in free float (Vedomosti, 2022).

13.7 Changes in the Company Governance Structure

Restructuring usually occurs in situations of deep crisis, which was the case of almost all sanctioned Russian firms. Facing sanctions, Yandex's board of directors announced intentions to make changes to the ownership and corporate governance structure. These were seen as solutions that would allow Yandex to continue to focus on creating innovative technological products and services, as well as to develop the company in the interest of its users, employees and shareholders.

Yandex was also considering spinning off the main part of the business and including several foreign ventures into a separate holding of companies that would retain the Yandex brand. Dutch Yandex N.V. planned to eventually sell its shares in this holding and change its name. The possibility of changing the corporate structure was also considered, as well as the possibility of management of the new holding to be transferred to Yandex's management.

On the one hand, such a reorganisation of business would protect Yandex from financial losses. The results after the first nine months in 2022 were worrisome: The adjusted EBITDA of other business segments and initiatives was 19.2 billion Rubles (about US$281 million) in the red, which was 124 per cent higher than the previous year's.

At the same time, the associated revenue for the same period grew by 70 per cent, indicating that losses grew much faster than revenue.

On the other hand, the reorganisation was expected to lead to an outflow of personnel, and it was impossible to evaluate this factor in terms of its impact on financial results. According to various estimates, between 2,000 and 6,000 Yandex employees left Russia after the spring of 2022 and were working remotely (MacFarquhar, 2022). Whether they would return or accept the option of working within the new structure was an open question. The company never officially confirmed these numbers because of concerns that such an outflow of qualified personnel could lead to a decrease in productivity, a drop in the quality of services and loss of customers. Detailed plans for reorganisation were not disclosed and remained to be approved by Yandex shareholders.

13.8 New Roof

In November 2022, Russia's chief government auditor and former prime minister of Russia Alexei Kudrin officially confirmed that he was moving to Yandex. Kudrin was known not only as an old associate of Vladimir Putin, with whom he worked for a long time, but also as one of the last 'systemic liberals' in the government. His main objective was to ensure the survival of the largest Russian IT company, which was divided into two parts against the backdrop of armed conflict and sanctions.

According to Kudrin, at Yandex he would 'develop the new holding company's corporate structure, along with the existing management team' which 'will ensure the company's long-term and sustainable development in all markets, including international ones' (Reuters, 2022).

One of his main tasks in the new position entailed helping to preserve 'Yandex's unique management and technology culture so that it could remain independent, and the best IT company in Russia, where the most talented people strive to work.' Almost immediately, the question as to whether the state would have tighter control over the company arose, given that a person who had spent most of his life in the civil service in President Putin's inner circle became the corporate leader. *The Financial Times* called Kudrin a 'roof' for Yandex (*Financial Times*, 2022). Given the company's strategic and systemic importance, no one expected much to change because Yandex used to be closely supported by the Russian state, and this was expected to continue.

As of 2024 Yandex was an example of what was happening in the Russian economy: Thanks in large part to the structure created through the reorganisation, the company remained relatively stable. The crisis triggered by the armed conflict and the subsequent sanctions turned out to be mild; however, there were concerns about the ability of Yandex to keep its innovation pace while isolated from the West and faced with its hostility.

13.9 Sanctioning Yandex Data Centres in Finland

One of Yandex's important initiatives was the development of data centres; the company operated them in Russia and rented space in co-location centres in Amsterdam, the Netherlands and Ashburn, Virginia. The geographic distribution of the servers decreased the cost of internet usage for the users and increased access speed for the services and stability and dependability of the offerings. This structure provided redundant fail-safe capacity such that the failure of a single facility would not cause the company's websites to stop functioning. Considering the projected demand for services, Yandex continuously evaluated the capacity and locations of its data centres to determine the most cost-effective manner in which to deliver reliable service to users.

One of the key projects in this area was the 2015 construction of a data centre in Mäntsälä, Finland, a small city located about 60 kilometres north of Helsinki. Yandex data centre management offered operational flexibility, as the servers' workload depended on business needs and could change on a daily basis.

The choice of the data centre location was based on several criteria. The first was the availability of a cheap and stable energy supply, and the second, the existence of high-quality optical fibre infrastructure. According to these criteria, several possible locations in Russia were excluded from the list: For example, an area near Baikal has a lot of cheap energy, but it is located far from the European part of Russia, where most Yandex search users reside. Additionally, signal transfer from Siberia would cause a substantial delay in search engine responses to users' queries. Eventually, Yandex managers prioritised the Nordic region of Europe for the data centre's location.

Finland was geographically close to Russia, it had favourable regulation towards the data centre industry, power supply was sufficient and optical fibre infrastructure was going to be extended through creation of new cable to Western Europe. A qualified workforce was usually mentioned as a key advantage to locating IT skill-intensive enterprises in Finland. However, in this case it was a minor concern because employees still needed to be retrained in order to qualify for specific data centre operations. One of the main factors in the decision-making process was the personal experience of one of the Yandex managers, who worked in Finland for several years. As a company representative said, 'Finland was an ideal choice for the company, as it provided opportunities for sustainable development and an excellent infrastructure' (YLE, 2023). In the Finnish subsidiary, Yandex senior management's participation was minimal, as data centres were not the company's main business; rather they were treated as infrastructure expenses.

A bleak situation was emerging in Finland and the Baltic countries in 2022. The authorities were backing Yandex into a tight corner. In particular, the taxi service was suspected of transferring passengers' personal data to Russian special services, and governments forbade the operation of this branch of the business in their territories (Valitsus, 2022). No specific facts or evidence were found, but a law had indeed been adopted in the Russian Federation with such requirements for taxi aggregators. In addition, electricity to the Finnish data centre was cut off, as the power engineers are not ready to accept payments from the sanctioned parent company.

Starting with the Finnish transport and communications minister Timo Harakka's statement that 'Yandex is being closely monitored' (YLE, 2023), Finnish authorities confiscated Yandex's assets in Finland in August 2022, which constituted the company's only data centre outside Russia, after the company's founder and former chief executive Arkady Volozh had been put on a European Union list of sanctions (Reuters, 2023). The firm's Finnish subsidiary was renamed Global DC Oy in 2023 (YLE, 2023).

13.10 Geopolitics and Unicorns

In order to gauge how the environment evolved for Yandex and the options it had, we systematise the environmental characteristics and highlight the potential impact on Yandex's decision-making process and specifics of the IT industry. In this analysis, sanctions constitute one of the key geopolitical factors affecting Yandex.

Politically – While operating internationally and with Russia under sanctions, Yandex exposed itself to different types of political environments and a number of political system risks. To achieve success in a strategically important and innovation-driven industry across various countries it was important for Yandex to diversify the systemic risks of the political environment. For this reason, the former unicorn had to address the following issues: attempts to isolate Russia geopolitically, which severely restricted opportunities for internationalisation ; political instability including risk of military invasion and regime change; sanctions against Yandex from geographically close European countries; and government bureaucracy and interference in the internet industry, which could affect costs and brand image.

Economically – It was necessary for Yandex to have a clear understanding of the economic condition in the countries where it operated or intended to operate, paying special attention to inflation, interest rates and foreign exchange dynamism, among other factors. Specifically for Yandex, critical issues were: volatility in share price; labour force dynamics including skill levels, specialists' relocation costs and brain drain; and the rise of the new contender, 'Sber' Corporation (formerly Sberbank), as an ecosystem-wide competitor in Russia, which built a tech-driven ecosystem around its banking business.

Socially – Yandex had to account for: demographics dynamism, which could dramatically affect the number of users; the rise of digitalisation in everyday life, including online services competing with Yandex; education levels and standards in the IT industry; and digital culture, for example, the tendency to spend more time online and socialise on the web.

Technologically – The company was aware of the cutting-edge technologies that sustained a competitive advantage at home and abroad, and the speed at which technology disrupted the IT industry and left firms with little chance to respond timely. Critical factors for Yandex included: recent technological developments by Yandex competitors; a trend in favour and technologies supporting remote work; the development of a super-app for the Russian market; and opportunities in foreign markets related to self-driving cars, cloud computing, education technology and data science.

Legally – Legal frameworks and institutions were an important factor for protecting Yandex's intellectual property (IP) rights. The company carefully monitored the risks for theft of the organisation's competitive advantage thus its overall competitive edge. Important domains that Yandex considered were: IP protection including copyright, patents and cybersecurity; data protection laws; consumer protection and e-commerce; and changes in labour law and new regulations related to the military context.

Special attention was paid to protecting customers' personal data. The food delivery app Yandex Food had a major data leak in March 2022. This led to Roskomnadzor, an executive body supervising communications and media, drawing up an administrative protocol against Yandex.Eda for violating Russian legislation in the personal data sphere.

The system of Western sanctions and the Russian response created difficulties for the proper functioning of the former unicorn. The most salient problems were, firstly, that there was a growing contradiction between the requirements of Russian authorities and Western governments in a number of domains, specifically in terms of access to data used by Yandex. While most of the data had no direct military use, a large amount of information could be used indirectly for strategic military purposes.

Secondly, the general difficulties of doing business in Russia, for example, in terms of access to international finance, affected the operations of Yandex, too. They manifested themselves in the form of higher costs of doing international business.

Thirdly, as the potential of new sanctions loomed and the propaganda war escalated, customer confidence in Yandex' services ran the risk of weakening. For most users, it took extra effort to work with companies of Russian origin.

In addition, foreign operations were becoming more difficult. One example occurred in March 2023, when the takeover of Tecnologia Intelligente in Italy by Nebius, a Netherlands-based company owned by Yandex, was blocked (Reuters, 2023).

It remained to be seen how Yandex would navigate such an unfavourable business environment that looked unlikely to change for a long time. Its rise took place in an atmosphere that used to be more favourable. In addition, its technology and dominant position made it vulnerable to regulatory changes. The environment of heavy sanctions tested the company's resilience to a maximum.

The Yandex case is particularly relevant for understanding the complex geopolitical context, as it highlights how Russian government policy and the company's Russian origins strongly influence its patterns and mechanisms of internationalisation. With growing nationalism and increasing geopolitical concerns, the strategy of unicorns is likely to integrate many of the components of Yandex's survival kit.

Yandex was not the only unicorn established by Russian entrepreneurs whose headquarters were transferred abroad due to the geopolitical challenges which were further aggravated after 2022. For example, the messaging company Telegram and financial services company Revolut were also among the unicorns created fully or partly by Russian nationals whose headquarters were relocated abroad. This was due to the contradictory requirements of Russian and foreign authorities. Put under intense pressure, most unicorns opted for the larger, global market that gave them access to the United States and Western European countries. In addition, many CEE unicorns established in EU member countries such as Croatia, Czechia, Estonia, Lithuania and Poland (see Table 13.1) were forced to scale down or divest their operations in Russia by the geopolitical situation. As a result, the overall presence of unicorns in the country has been diminishing since 2022. Although unicorns are particularly vulnerable due to the highly international character of their activities, the geopolitical divisions affected all types of companies under sanctions. It is yet to be seen how the new international realities will affect the unicorn phenomenon in geographies under extreme circumstances and heavy sanctions. More importantly, the role of some of these companies for shaping geopolitical realities needs to be seriously addressed.

References

Borak, M. (2023, 4 April). How Russia killed its tech industry. *MIT Technology Review*. www.technologyreview.com/2023/04/04/1070352/

Castellum AI. (2023, 31 March). *Russia Sanctions Dashboard*. www.castellum.ai/russia-sanctions-dashboard

Dealroom.co. (2023). *Dashboard*. app.dealroom.co/dashboard

(2024). *Yandex*. app.dealroom.co/companies/yandex

Dorofeev, V. Y. (2013). *Yandex Volozh. History of dreams*. Alpina.

EQS.News. (2022, 3 June). *Arkady Volozh resigns as Executive Director and CEO of Yandex N.V. and transfers his voting power to the Board*. tinyurl.com/5n8f73b9

Financial Times. (2022, 24 November). *Yandex seeks Putin approval for restructuring plan.* www.ft.com/content/5ac72014-d7af-4435-aaaf-2a15033fb2a1

Kalotay, K., and Weiner, C. (2022). The impact of sanctions on Russian business abroad and Hungarian business in Russia: Parallel stories of adjustment. In L. Casanova and A. Miroux, eds. *Emerging Market Multinationals Report 2022: Reinventing Global Value Chains.* Cornell S. C. Johnson College of Business, pp. 92–100.

Kutsenko E., Tyurchev K., and Ostashchenko T. (2022). Relocation as a driver of innovative activity: A global study of unicorn founders' migration. *Foresight and STI Governance* 16(4), 6–23. foresight-journal.hse.ru/article/view/19124

MacFarquhar, N. (2022, 6 July). *How war in Ukraine roiled Russia's 'coolest company'.* New York Times. www.nytimes.com/2022/07/06/world/europe/yandex-russia-ukraine.html

Meyer, K. E., Fang, T., Panibratov, A., Peng, M. W., and Gaur, A. (2023). International business under sanctions. *Journal of World Business* 58, 101426. doi.org/10.1016/j.jwb.2023.101426

New York Times. (2024, 5 February). *Russian tech giant reaches $5 billion deal to quit Russia.* www.nytimes.com/2024/02/05/world/europe/yandex-russia-sale.html

Panibratov, A. (2012). *Russian Multinationals: From Regional Supremacy to Global Lead.* Routledge.

Panibratov, A., and Gaur, A. (2022). Political drivers of international divestments of Russian MNEs. *BRICS Journal of Economics* 3(1), 5–25. doi.org/10.3897/brics-econ.3.e84707

Panibratov, A., and Klishevich, D. (2020). Dynamic capabilities during the internationalization of MNCs from post-socialist emerging markets. *Multinational Business Review* 28(3), 307–331. doi.org/10.1108/MBR-06-2019-0052

Reuters. (2022, 5 December). *Putin ally Kudrin accepts tech giant Yandex's offer of advisory role.* tinyurl.com/34rpbkza

(2023, 23 March). *Italy's Meloni vetoes Russian-linked takeover of tech company.* tinyurl.com/ycyzhccx

RBC. (2024, 24 July). *Yandex is back on the stock exchange* (in Russian). www.rbc.ru/quote/news/article/669a4f6c9a7947a3cd98f8b5%0A

Sawant, R., Nachum, L., and Panibratov, A. (2021). The effect of interpersonal political embeddedness on firm internationalization scope. *British Journal of Management* 32(3), 812–831. doi.org/10.1111/1467-8551.12430

Seddon, M. (2020, 11 May). *In lockdown, Yandex evolves from Russia's Google to its Amazon.* Financial Times.

Valitsus. (2022, 31 March). *The government prohibits Yandex from offering taxi services in Estonia.* valitsus.ee/en/news/government-prohibits-yandex-offering-taxi-services-estonia

Vedomosti. (2022, 28 November). *'Yandex' announced plans to split the company* (in Russian). www.vedomosti.ru/technology/articles/2022/11/28/952360-yandeks-obyavil-o-planah-po-razdelu-kompanii

Walzer, M. (1977). *Just and Unjust Wars.* Basic Books.

Yandex. (2023a, 6 March). *Yandex announces changes to the board of directors.* yandex.com/company/press_center/press_releases/2023/06-03-23

(2023b, 15 March). *Yandex receives notice of delisting from Nasdaq and intends to appeal.* yandex.com/company/press_center/press_releases/2023/15-03-2023

Yandex.Radar. (2022, Q1). *Search engines in Russia.* radar.yandex.com/search

YLE. (2023, 6 May). *Minister Harakka: Yandex data centre 'closely monitored' as power firms pull the plug.* yle.fi/a/3-12434064

14 What Lies Ahead for Unicorns from Emerging Economies

DIEGO FINCHELSTEIN, VENETA ANDONOVA AND JUANA GARCÍA DUQUE

14.1 Unicorns from Emerging Economies Deserve Attention

Throughout the book, we have shown the importance of unicorns as a distinctive phenomenon. Unicorns have been on the rise, and they have almost quintupled their number since 2019. Even more importantly, unicorns are no longer just a phenomenon in advanced economies; they have been transforming emerging economies, too. At first glance, the rapid growth of unicorns in emerging economies seems surprising. *Ceteris paribus*, they have fewer resources or resources of inferior quality (research and development (R&D), for example), weaker institutional arrangements and/or structural disadvantages that could have prevented unicorns from rising. Nevertheless, unicorns from the Global South have flourished, and in many cases, they have even used the systemic disadvantages of their context instrumentally to build uniquely successful business models.

Given the challenges that the contexts of emerging economies impose, the innovation capabilities for value creation and business venture growth are crucial. With this book we have offered evidence of how unicorns surpass the weaknesses of emerging markets and occasionally convert institutional drawbacks into advantages. In this sense, their innovation approach is different from that of ventures from developed countries (Cahen et al., 2021). Insights into the innovation strategies employed by unicorns from the emerging economies and the source of their competitive advantage have practical managerial and public policy implications. Namely, as these firms have been able to overcome many of the challenges posed by emerging markets, public policies that support their emergence and learn from their success can be quite useful for accelerating development trajectories around the globe. Adding to the knowledge and hope that this process brings about has been the main driver behind this book.

With global mega trends as a backdrop, the structural conditions that emerging economies frequently face such as poverty, extremely skewed income distribution, inefficient public services, poor quality of education and lack of healthcare provision, to name but a few, are seen as hard challenges to prosperity and business growth, let alone exponential growth. Yet, unicorns represent unique success stories of overcoming these drawbacks. Moreover, such businesses have occasionally used local challenges to build their business models as they are better suited to deal with the imperfect entrepreneurial ecosystem conditions. Examples can be found in this book from Central and Eastern Europe (Chapter 1), China (Chapter 5), India (Chapter 6), Southeast Asia (Chapter 7), Latin America (Chapter 8), the Middle East and North Africa (MENA) (Chapter 9) and Africa (Chapter 10).

The examples of unicorns from the Global South contained in this book can be used by entrepreneurs and managers as inspiration and as a practical model for promoting business success, growth and development under less-than-ideal circumstances.

Rapid unicorn growth across the Global South is a relevant dimension of private wealth creation and societal development. Emerging economies have found it difficult to bridge the rich–poor divide and catch up with the standards set by economically developed economies. Not only can the leapfrogging potential of unicorns be an inspiration, their multiplier effect across different economic sectors also raises hopes for these countries' gross domestic product (GDP) growth, prosperity levels and other macroeconomic variables that are crucial to achieving a better quality of life. Unicorns from the Global South can act as engines for accelerating economic convergence and de facto facilitate leapfrogging opportunities for different sectors of emerging economies.

It is revealing to analyse the type of activities through which unicorns from emerging economies evolve. Unicorns need an engine for exponential growth, and this usually comes from innovation- and technology-related activities, often digital in nature. The universe of these companies belongs to sectors with higher added value than most other companies from emerging economies. Most successful business ventures from the Global South have traditionally belonged to commodity sectors or other low added value activities. For instance, in Latin America there is only one country – Mexico – whose main export is not in a commodity but an industrial sector (car manufacturing) linked to global value chains. In the past, scholars conjectured that the dependency on commodities may not be the answer to emerging economies' search for progress (North et al., 2013; Tröster & Küblböck, 2020) as it negatively reinforces the inequality of the terms of trade between advanced economies and emerging ones. Hence, the fact that unicorns from the Global South appear in non-traditional sectors with higher added value could be seen with additional optimism as, arguably, the process can directly and indirectly contribute to economic development through better technology and human capital improvements.

Many unicorns from emerging economies have been able to obtain a competitive advantage by alleviating some facets of the profound structural problems characterising the Global South. Throughout the different chapters of this book, we have illustrated how fintechs, edtechs and healthtech have offered solutions that in many cases have transformed structural shortcomings into competitive business advantages. A myriad of studies have anticipated such solutions. For example, unicorns frequently develop unique innovation capabilities (Hermans et al., 2024) and particular ways of providing solutions that make them different from simple copycats (Cahen et al., 2021) because their technology-driven innovations are context-specific and tropicalised (Cuervo Cazurra et al., 2019a). In line with such ideas, the evidence provided in this book suggests that unicorns operationalise innovations contingent on the context of the Global South with unique models that are better suited and more efficient than traditional strategies transplanted from the Global North (Kumar et al., 2013). Such solutions are also connected to the overall business strategy and the development of disruptive models (Cuervo Cazurra et al., 2019b). To be effective, the solutions unicorns from emerging economies find must overcome the challenges of their own context while also competing with local incumbents or multinationals. Thus, the business model components of unicorns from the Global South stand out as well designed and particularly resilient.

Of course, the rise of unicorns from emerging economies is also relevant for analysts and scholars interested in the macro trends and influence of context on business development (Finchelstein, 2017; Gao et al., 2017; Cuervo Cazurra et al., 2019b; Mariotti & Marzano, 2020). An interest in the direct or indirect mechanisms used by firms to adapt their strategies to the different institutional settings is common among such studies. In emerging contexts, a wide range of institutions provide diverging signals and incentives to companies. There can therefore be a mistaken perception that companies regularly underperform because of distorted incentives; institutional transplants can seem to be a quick fix. We advise caution and encourage genuine and in-depth research into the unique institutional details of emerging economies before recommending any kind of transplanted solutions (for the dangers of institutional transplants see Arruñada & Andonova, 2008). For instance, the literature on institutional voids (see, for example, Palepu & Khanna, 1998; Anand et al., 2000) has provided evidence that these voids have created efficient corporate ways of organising business activity in emerging economies that can be very successful under these specific conditions. The present study of unicorns from emerging economies presents similar evidence of uniquely successful local adaptations; we emphasise the existence of very dynamic high-growth ventures in sectors with high added value that often thrive within imperfect entrepreneurial ecosystems because they find unique solutions to long-standing structural shortcomings. Furthermore, once their business model is consolidated, many of the unicorns from emerging economies have actually expanded beyond their national market or region. This book contains examples of this such as the Nigerian unicorn Andela (Chapter 10) and the Chinese Bytedance (Chapter 11).

Encouraging the creation of unicorns and understanding their relevance is particularly important from the perspective of governments and policymakers, as evidenced by the role such ventures play in the geopolitical arena. Of course, unicorns can bring novel solutions to structural societal problems; however, governments can also use them to tackle non-business issues such as access to data and control. On the positive side, fintech unicorns in Latin America, Asia, the Middle East and Africa help reduce the level of informality. These channels, which are easier to track, have partially replaced cash payments that are the base of payments for large segments of unbanked individuals. Still, unicorns can also become tools for unsolicited control and infringement on privacy, which lead them to be treated as threats to national security as argued in Chapter 2.

In essence, this book is a relevant collection of examples, topics and data on understanding unicorns from emerging economies and their transformational potential. By contributing to a clearer picture of their domains and ways in which they operate, all kinds of decision makers, from entrepreneurs to politicians, can comprehend the enormous disruptive force of unicorns. The growth of unicorns from the Global South has been impressive and their impact is exponential. As such, they speed up change at every level, and this book prepares the mind of readers by providing evidence from around the globe of the possibilities that used to seem very distant or imaginary. We chose to bring the optimism that comes with such possibilities to the fore, although there are risks and challenges we cannot ignore.

14.2 A Comparative Analysis of Unicorns from Advanced and Emerging Economies

As Stam and Voogelar (Chapter 3) and Amorós et al. (Chapter 4) have assessed, there are differences related to the characteristics and strategies of unicorns from emerging and developed economies. Without claiming to be exhaustive, Table 14.1 illustrates the dimensions along which such differences stand out, as the research contained in this book demonstrates. For example, take the type and process of innovation. The competitive advantage of many unicorns from advanced economies is based on the development of unique future-centred advanced technologies, frequently protected by patents. Artificial intelligence (AI)-focused companies and those developing products and services around cybersecurity are common within the group of unicorns from these countries as of 2024. Conversely, unicorns in emerging economies frequently emerge out of tropicalised innovations (Cuervo Cazurra et al., 2019a). This means that unicorns find innovative solutions to problems that are common for areas with tropical climates, related to institutional voids or infrastructure deficiencies that are more prominent in such places. Often, these innovations are not based on a proprietary technology advancement but rather on a new (digital) approach that compensates for a long-lasting deficiency. For example, prominent fintech unicorns have emerged in Africa, the Middle East and Latin America. They are not copycats of the models from advanced economies; rather, they focus on inclusion and offer solutions to people who work under informality and/or have not been included in the financial system before. This is the case of the Saudi unicorn Tamara and Egyptian unicorn MNT-Halan which provide micro credits in North Africa and the Middle East, as described by Ismail and Kamel in Chapter 9. Moreover, healthtech projects such as the Indonesian Primaku mentioned by McIntyre and Hoadley in

Table 14.1 *Unicorns from advanced and emerging economies*

	Unicorns from advanced economies	Unicorns from emerging economies
Innovations and innovation process	Future-focused and IP-driven innovation	Tropicalised innovation focused on structural deficiencies
Internationalisation	Global reach	Regional focus that hinges on contextual specificities
Industries	Frontier of knowledge and new industry creation (AI, cybersecurity)	Digitalisation and optimisation of existing industries (e-commerce, fintech, supply chain and direct to consumer activities)
Strategies and environment	Take advantage of available funding, technology and greater purchasing power	Use adaptability and resiliency to turn challenging structural conditions into their favour and develop original business models / First mover advantage in unexplored markets

Source: Authors.

Chapter 7 have also built solutions to compensate for healthcare and infrastructure deficiencies. In the educational domain, Ramamurti argues that Indian unicorns such as Byju's, Physicswallah and UpGrad focus on offering alternative education solutions to students with diverse backgrounds (Chapter 6). In e-commerce, unicorns from emerging economies have found innovative business models instead of transplanting those of advanced economies. As described by Miranda de Oliveira Jr and Lima dos Santos (Chapter 12), the Brazilian unicorn QuintoAndar adapted standard real-estate industry retail models from the Global North that would not have otherwise fit into Brazil's context in their original design due to the regulatory particularities. Again, the new innovative business model of QuintoAndar emerged as a successful creative solution to the local idiosyncrasies.

The international expansion of unicorns from emerging economies has mainly taken place on a regional rather than global scale. This is despite the fact that the acceleration of the digital economy has reduced obstacles to globalisation processes. The reason behind this phenomenon is partially related to the type of innovation at their core, which is context specific and therefore incurs higher transaction costs when taken across borders. Given that their innovation is focused on finding solutions for specific, idiosyncratic environments, and that neighbouring environments tend to have similar challenges, the offerings of unicorns fit better within their specific regions. This is why the Brazilian fintech Nubank (see Chapter 12) has initially expanded to Mexico and Colombia.

As shown by Vogelaar and Stam (Chapter 3), the distribution of unicorns also differs by sector between emerging and advanced economies. E-commerce, fintechs and supply chain related activities are the most salient in emerging economies while software development, cybersecurity and AI are more predominant in advanced economies. This is not to say that there are no future-focused, innovation-driven unicorns from emerging economies. Borda et al. (Chapter 8) highlight the case of Chilean unicorn Notco, which uses AI to create vegan food that emulates traditional non-vegan products. Nevertheless, most unicorns from emerging economies emerge in the domain of 'must have' digitised products or services rather than in the 'nice to have' domain or in the realm of offerings based on fundamental scientific research. As illustrated by Olayele and Qobo in Chapter 10, all but one of the African unicorns in 2024 are either e-commerce or fintech companies. In Chapter 4, Amorós et al. focus on one very significant difference between advanced and emerging economies: *ceteris paribus*, the entrepreneurial education in advanced economies is better. This, along with a continuous brain drain towards advanced economies (Chapter 1 and Chapter 13), can generate a persistent asymmetry in the capabilities of unicorns from emerging economies to participate in the technological race (Andonova & Perez, 2024).

Fundamentally, the differences in the overall contexts of emerging and developed economies are profound and reflect the rich–poor divide at all levels; in emerging economies, inequality is visible. On one hand, unicorns from developed economies can take advantage of the abundance of capital and better technology to build and implement their strategies. In many cases, their solutions rely on finding new ways to take advantage of these resources. Emblematic cases such as Uber (using geo-localisation) or Netflix (adopting streaming) illustrate this method. On the other hand, following research on the role of institutional setup (Hall & Soskice, 2001; Acemoglu et al., 2003; Musacchio et al., 2015; Finchelstein et al., 2022) arguing that companies are shaped by their institutional context, this book highlights that the constraints that exist in emerging markets encourage their unicorns to be adaptable and resilient, as well as to use these features in their strategies. Thus, these companies develop original business models to tackle unique local challenges. Moreover, these conditions can actually become an advantage. For instance, Casanova et al. (Chapter 11) assert that fintech companies have advantages that help them settle in China because there were fewer adoption barriers. There was little resistance to the introduction of a new system because it did not come at the expense of an entrenched incumbent solution; credit cards were not widely used in small shops. These dynamics are also consistent with the greater early-stage entrepreneurial activity as a proxy for constant experimentation found in emerging markets as presented by Amorós et al. (Chapter 4). These authors argue that stricter regulations, long-term job positions and more established incumbent firms may deter entrepreneurial initiatives in advanced economies. Meanwhile, the less stable environment in emerging markets actually encourages entrepreneurial experimentation.

In many cases, the unique structural conditions in the Global South offer their unicorns a first mover advantage given that international competitors are less willing and successful in entering these markets without the creation of unique business models. Such a first mover advantage can also be replicated in neighbouring countries with similar conditions, where multinational players have traditionally been reluctant to enter. Borda et al. present the case of the Mexican unicorn Kavak in Chapter 8 to make this point. The models of such unicorns are inspired by related models that have been successful in developed economies. However, these unicorns include unique features that are crucial to the local context; for example, Kavak helps with the bureaucratic steps involved in buying and selling cars in Latin America. By developing such competences, Kavak has expanded into Oman, Saudi Arabia, Turkey and across South America.

14.2.1 Differences within Emerging Economies

Differences between unicorns from advanced and emerging economies should not obscure the fact that there is also huge heterogeneity among the number and profiles of unicorns coming from the Global South. To be sure, there are shared institutional and developmental challenges that encourage the emergence of a pattern of similarities among these ventures as presented in Table 14.1. However, there are important differences that distinguish unicorns from emerging economies. These differences stem from the relative strengths and weaknesses of the respective entrepreneurial ecosystems.

As shown by Vogelaar and Stam (Chapter 3), China, India and Brazil are among the most dynamic emerging markets in terms of unicorn creation in absolute numbers. Data on Central and Eastern Europe (CEE) and Russia regarding unicorn emergence is possibly the least reliable, representing a significant underestimation. This comes as a result of the long-standing trend of ventures from this part of the world relocating, despite carrying out very large numbers of back-office activities locally, including R&D. This trend is not purely based on business logic but also on geopolitical considerations (as Panibratov and Kalotay describe in Chapter 13) and country brand issues (Andonova et al., 2019). Africa and MENA only have a small number of unicorns; nevertheless, these regions may have a more optimistic perspective for the future given their latent potential, as assessed by Olayele and Qobo (Chapter 10) and by Ismail and Kamel (Chapter 9). Southeast Asia and Latin America are similar in many respects including their historical ability to generate unicorns, as McIntyre and Hoadley (Chapter 7) and Borda et al. (Chapter 8) analyse.

Education is essential to building the knowledge base and innovation capability behind unicorn emergence because these ventures rely on skilled and globally competitive talent. Education and the capacity for innovation linked to it is the agglutinating component that turns start-ups into unicorns and makes societies more prosperous. In terms of education and human capital development across the Global South, India, China and CEE stand out given their traditions in science, technology, engineering and mathematics (STEM) and technical training. Ramamurti (Chapter 6) and Casanova et al. (Chapter 5 and Chapter 11) emphasise the key role of human capital development for the entrepreneurial ecosystem and unicorn creation in India and China, while Panibratov and Kalotay (Chapter 13) call attention to the ongoing brain drain from CEE as a fundamental weakness of the local entrepreneurial ecosystems. There is strong entrepreneurial drive and relatively good access to human capital in

Southeast Asia and Latin America. Ismail and Karmel (Chapter 9) argue that building a tech start-up had not been very appealing for the most talented professionals in the MENA region until recently, despite investing about 14 per cent of the budget in education. Generally, Africa is the region in which access to well-trained talent is most challenging, an aspect that rapidly depletes local entrepreneurial ecosystems of one of the essential components for unicorn creation – well-educated talent.

In parallel to technical learning, experiential knowledge of business development and markets stands out as a driver for attaining unicorn status. Several chapters in this book note that unicorn founders and top executives have had experience and strong relationships to companies or markets from advanced economies. Ramamurti (Chapter 6) highlights that about 60 per cent of Indian unicorn founders used to work for multinational corporations and many unicorn executives studied in the USA. For the Latin American case, Borda et al. (Chapter 8) argue that international business experience has been instrumental in broadening the human talent pool for unicorns.

Domestic market size also plays an important role for unicorn emergence across the Global South, as in the case of India, China and Brazil. Growth potential is realised faster when a scalable business model hits a large potential domestic market. It is not surprising that there is a correlation between the size of the domestic market and the total number of unicorns: Brazil in Latin America, Nigeria in Africa, Egypt in MENA and Thailand and Indonesia in Southeast Asia represent big markets with higher numbers of unicorns. Of course, market scale is not everything. Singapore stands out with an important number of unicorns despite being significantly smaller in size. Easier access to capital, large numbers of expats who represent a diverse talent pool and the development of its financial industry were essential drivers of the initial development of Singapore's entrepreneurial ecosystem, but other countries are catching up along the same dimensions. China and India have had increasingly easier access to capital in addition to the scale of their markets. International venture capital (VC) has had heavy involvement in these countries and has also been instrumental in funding unicorns together with national governments. In Latin America and MENA, VCs have invested less in technological start-ups than in Southeast Asia, but such investments have been growing exponentially. For example, in just a few years VC investment grew 25-fold in Latin America (Chapter 8) whereas in Africa such investments tripled between 2020 and 2021 (Chapter 10), showing significant inter-temporal growth despite smaller tickets. CEE economies, excluding the severely sanctioned Russia, attracted a historic annual investment value in 2020 with US$5 billion . However, macrotrends and geopolitics have severely affected investors' dispositions, lowering this value to US$1.9 billion in 2023 (Invest Europe, 2024).

The role of the government in relation to the development of local entrepreneurial ecosystems and unicorn creation differs. As shown by Casanova et al. (Chapters 5 and 11), the Chinese government has been very supportive of ecosystem development, aiding unicorn creation. In the case of India, Ramamurti (Chapter 6) highlights the role of the government on both the supply and demand sides. Specific policies such as the Digital India initiative and the use of public agencies to promote technology-based companies have been crucial. In MENA, governments have become more active in supporting entrepreneurial ecosystem development as of the early 2020s. In Brazil, Chile and Mexico governments have supported entrepreneurship through different agencies and initiatives (such as Start up Chile), while in Argentina the role of the government has been very small. For the case of Brazil, the role of the National Bank for Economic and Social Development is a distinctive and very important factor in local ecosystem development (Finchelstein, 2017). In Africa, the relative absence of resources has constrained the scope and depth of government initiatives. Besides governments, multilateral organisations such as the Asian Development Bank have played a role in supporting regional entrepreneurial ecosystems, implementing programmes and supporting start-ups. Table 14.2 summarises some of the significant differences among the ecosystems across the Global South in a coarse but revealing way.

14.3 What Lies Ahead for Unicorns from Emerging Economies

Unicorns are a relatively recent phenomenon with a significant transformational potential, raising a very broad range of questions and scenarios for the future. Instead of a conclusion, this section presents a selection of topics that need further study and questions to which satisfactory answers have not yet been found.

Table 14.2 *Comparing entrepreneurial ecosystems from the Global South as per the evidence presented in this book*

	China	India	Latin America	Southeast Asia	MENA	Africa	CEE and Russia
Cumulative number of unicorns	316	108	49	34	10	7	47[1]
Access to human capital	Easy	Easy	Medium	Medium	Difficult	Difficult	Easy
Education quality	High to Medium	High to Medium	Medium to High	Medium to High	Medium to Low	Medium to Low	High to Medium
Availability of capital	High	High	Medium	Medium High	Medium High	Low	Medium
Market size	Large	Large	Large to Medium	Medium	Medium to Small	Small to Large	Small to Large
Role of government	High	High	Medium	Medium	Medium	Small	Medium to High

Source: Authors' analysis based on the evidence and arguments presented in this book.

[1]There has been a strong trend in technology- and innovation-driven start-ups and soonicorns from CEE and Russia that have been showing a trend to relocating to the leading global entrepreneurship hubs and disguising their country and region of origin. The number reported here is very conservative and is based on Henni (2022) and Groszkowska (2023).

14.3.1 Research on Unicorns from Emerging Economies

How resilient can unicorns from emerging economies be over time? Initially, resiliency theory was created to analyse organisations that have to deal with frequent crises (Weick & Sutcliffe, 2011; Sajko et al., 2021). It has been tested on firms from emerging economies given that the institutional, political and economic instability in such countries forces companies to adapt to unexpected challenges quite often. As a matter of fact, resilience is one of the key characteristics that businesses from emerging economies consider to be a competitive advantage. This resilience is acquired over time as a result of exposure to shocks and crises. Yet, most unicorns are quite young and many internationalise very early, while some are born global. This and the fact that many unicorns belong to the fast-paced world of technology and digital innovation introduces an enhanced level of complexity and risk to their survival. Uncovering the mechanisms that unicorns from emerging economies adopt to build resilience and succeed on the global arena is a fascinating avenue for future research.

One possible mechanism for building resilience can potentially emerge from within corporate governance structures. By their own nature, unicorns grow very quickly from small start-ups with very few workers to significantly larger organisations that capitalise on innovation and digitalisation. But are these circumstances sufficient for the emergence of innovative corporate governance arrangements? To be sure, the Anglo-Saxon model of professional management, specialisation of activities and an atomised ownership structure is considered the best way of organising businesses in many advanced economies in the capitalist market system (Demsetz, 1983; Coffee, 1999; La Porta et al., 2000). In many emerging economies, ownership is concentrated in large family-owned businesses, which are largely diversified with a family member in the top managerial position (Granovetter, 2005). This model can be seen in business groups in Latin America and Turkey, the chaebols in Korea, the houses in India, the jituanqiye in Taiwan and the qiyejituan in China. Past research explains how these unique arrangements are better suited to successfully confronting the challenges of emerging markets (Henisz, 2003; Gourevitch & Shinn, 2005; Khanna & Yafeh, 2010; Schneider, 2010; Salvaj & Couyoumdjian, 2016). The success of unicorns from emerging economies hinges on fast-paced technological change, increased international exposure and geopolitical pressures. Hence, it is important to monitor the governance mechanisms they adopt as they face stark inherent trade-offs.

Arguably, start-ups can scale up to unicorn status faster when there are entrepreneurial ecosystems of a certain degree of development and maturity that benefit from a large domestic market. It is no surprise that the two emerging countries with the biggest number of unicorns are also the ones with stronger and larger entrepreneurial ecosystems, as Casanova et al. show for the case of China (Chapter 5) and Ramamurti demonstrates for the case of India (Chapter 6). As argued in Chapter 2, the influences between unicorns and the entrepreneurial ecosystems from which they emerge mutually reinforce each other. Despite this, little is known about the long-term effects of unicorns on local entrepreneurial ecosystems. Which are the most impactful channels and mechanisms of influence? Are they affecting capital availability, role modelling or mentoring the most? When do unicorns turn into engines for new venture building? Do they promote or stifle innovation in specific domains? What positive or negative externalities do they create within the context of emerging economies? While it may be early to give definitive answers, these questions emerge from the research presented in this book and can open future lines of research, particularly in relation to comprehensively measuring the impact of unicorns on their proximate and distal environment.

Focusing on unicorns alone rather than on the growth trajectories of high-growth technology-driven ventures might be a constraint to developing a comprehensive evolutionary perspective on the phenomenon. Soonicorns (companies with the potential to become unicorns) and zebras (fast growing firms that include social and environmental worries within their foundation pillars) are phenomena related to the accelerated process of scaling up. By the same token, the focus on private companies with valuations over a billion dollars leaves aside those that no longer fit the definition but, in some form or another (going public, for example), create enormous impact. On the other hand, there are lower valued ventures which deserve to be better understood despite not having reached the one-billion-dollar milestone given the significant role they play in their local entrepreneurial ecosystems, especially the less mature ones. Reaching a billion-dollar valuation in an emerging economy arguably takes much more effort than in advanced economies as a result of the quality of the entrepreneurial ecosystem. As conjectured in Chapter 9, exploring the growth paths of soonicorns can shed light on the critical hurdles that limit growth and prevent them from reaching unicorn status sooner.

While these effects are clear, there is still a need to measure the impact of unicorns, and new research is needed. Developing specific measures to assess the impact of emerging market unicorns in key growth and development areas would equip policymakers with actionable tools and complement well with the topics of this book.

14.3.2 Geopolitics, Venture Capital Slowdown and Its Effect on Unicorns

Unicorns are very susceptible to global trends and geopolitical factors. While in the process of writing this book, a shift in the global context produced a strong direct effect on the evolution of CEE unicorns. As Panibratov and Kalotay explain in Chapter 13, a new geopolitical scenario preceding and following the Russia–Ukraine armed conflict affected unicorns and soonicorns from the region and beyond. At the same time, there was a sharp global decline in the availability of VC funding. Global funding decreased by 38 per cent in 2023 according to Crunchbase, reaching its lowest level in five years – quite far from the 2021 peak (Teare, 2024). Emerging economies have not been equally affected by this phenomenon: While Brazil managed to keep the decline of venture capital funding in 2023 below the global mean, China reached its lowest level in seven years (KPMG, 2024). Would such circumstances lead to a long-term downward trend in unicorn emergence? What will the new geopolitical map of unicorn creation look like, and will China be able to keep its prominent role? Will China join the category of developed economies where, on the basis of the dynamism and the quality of its entrepreneurial ecosystem, it already belongs?

We can view the relative scarcity of VC capital in many emerging regions from a positive perspective. Start-ups in these economies are thriftier and profit-oriented (less prone to burning cash) and therefore better prepared to work under conditions of scarcity. Scholars have shown that businesses in some emerging markets have developed skills to deal with capital restrictions and have had better saving ratios as a result, mainly caused by the inability to get funding in the capital market (Kornai et al., 2003; Goldstein, 2007; Finchelsein, 2017). Arguably, unicorns from emerging economies exhibit similar adaptation strategies. The inherent characteristics of emerging markets encourage firms to be flexible and adapt under more frequent economic and political crises. If they manage to survive, the resilience they build under these harsh conditions can turn these unicorns into robust economic actors. One of the key characteristics of unicorns from emerging economies is that they tend to develop successful business models by finding solutions to existing structural economic and social problems. The latter are very far from being resolved and may even worsen under more stringent financial constraints and geopolitical tensions. Such a scenario does not bring only negatives, rather can present business opportunities for unicorns from emerging economies.

14.3.3 Potential Challenges and the Future of Emerging Economies Unicorns

The development trajectories of unicorns from emerging economies are hard to predict and many questions about their future role arise. What are the driving forces behind scaling up to unicorn status under conditions of scarcity? In particular, will the demographic dividend of Africa play a determinant role for unicorn creation in the new future? As Olayele and Qobo show in Chapter 10, there is a rapid growth of global VC funding in Africa. Can the smaller size of the domestic market be offset by entrepreneurial ecosystems with stronger innovation and knowledge creation capabilities such as those in Southeast Asia and CEE? Will Southeast Asia continue to grow its number of unicorns? Proximity to China and India and the greater availability and quality of resources place Southeast Asia in an advantageous position. As Ramamurti (Chapter 6) describes, the increasing disputes between China and the United States has reduced international VC funding for Chinese start-ups and therefore indirectly benefited investments in India and the region. The current geopolitical instability in Eastern Europe and the Middle East has affected not only the availability of VC capital there but also talent retention, brain drain and overall investor sentiment.

Stam and Vogelaar (Chapter 3) report that e-commerce and fintech are the verticals with the highest number of unicorns from emerging economies. Software, healthtech and AI are expected to be the industries of growth in the near future. Will unicorns from emerging economies be able to switch to these more knowledge-intensive verticals? Or will they continue to focus on digitalised solutions to long-standing economic and social problems common to emerging economies? Mercado Libre, Jumia, Flikpart and Alibaba appeared in Latin America, Africa, India and China because the unique local conditions delayed the entrance of global players (Casanova et al., 2021). The domains in which unicorns from advanced economies dominate rely on less context-specific knowledge or functionalities such as cybersecurity, where the subsequent emergence of regional entrants is unlikely. If unicorns from emerging economies are to follow a similar path to that of advanced ones, we should expect an attempt at a gradual shift towards verticals with more advanced knowledge bases. This has been the path of China, which has gradually built strong innovation capabilities as Casanova et al. describe in Chapter 5. Bytedance and the Chinese drone manufacturer DJI are examples of creating best-in-class technology. Still, the persistence of structural issues and institutional differences might make this heightened focus on deeptech across the entrepreneurial ecosystems of the Global South more of an aspiration than a reality.

Lastly, the question of ultimate control over the unicorns from emerging economies is an important one. These largely regionally focused high-growth businesses awaken the interest of larger firms from advanced economies and become acquisition targets. Cases such as the Indian unicorn Flipkart (sold to Walmart) or the Argentine Auth0 (sold to Okta) illustrate this phenomenon. Occasionally, global corporations with less sensitivity to local impact can abruptly interrupt the positive role of high-growth ventures on the local entrepreneurial ecosystem. In other instances, geopolitical tensions completely alter the business logic, creating a logic of power and global dominance. While there are cases in which unicorns from emerging markets have resisted and grown to become even larger and more dominant players (see, for instance, Indian unicorn Snapdeal as described by Ramamurti in Chapter 6), others prefer to exit, leaving control over their local or regional operations to long-standing global corporations. This process raises important questions about the relevance of unicorns from emerging economies for the scientific and technological upgrade of the Global South and hints towards a mechanism through which the potential of unicorns from emerging economies to turn into engines for leapfrogging can dissipate.

References

Acemoglu, D., Johnson, S., Robinson, J., and Thaicharoen, Y. (2003). Institutional causes, macroeconomic symptoms. Volatility, crises and growth. The colonial origins of comparative development: An empirical investigation. *Journal of Monetary Economics 50*, 49–123.

Anand, B., Khanna, T., and Rivkin. J. (2000). Market failures. *Harvard Business Review*, April.

Andonova, V., Nikolova, M., and Dimitrov, D. (2019). *Entrepreneurial Ecosystems in Unexpected Places*. Palgrave MacMillan.

Andonova, V., and Perez, J. (2024). Entrepreneurial ecosystems and diaspora: How do remittances and migration affect country of origin early-stage entrepreneurial activity? In J. Cunningham, M. Menter, C. O'Kane, and M. Romano, eds. *The Research Handbook on Entrepreneurial Ecosystems*. Edward Elgar, pp. 238–276.

Arruñada, B., and Andonova, V. (2008). Common law and civil law as pro-market adaptations. *Washington University Journal of Law and Policy* 26, 81–130.

Cahen, F., Casanova, L., and Miroux, A., eds. (2021). *From Copycat to Leaders: Innovation from Emerging Markets*. Cambridge University Press.

Casanova, L., Miroux, A., and Finchelstein, D. (2021). Digital companies driving business model innovation in emerging markets: The cases of Alibaba, Flipkart, Jumia and Mercado Libre. In F. Cahen, L. Casanova, and A. Miroux, eds. *From Copycat to Leaders: Innovation from Emerging Markets*. Cambridge University Press, pp. 122–149.

Coffee, J. (1999). The future as history: The prospects for global convergence in corporate governance and its implications. *Northwestern University Law Review 93*, 641.

Cuervo Cazurra, A., Carneiro, J., Finchelstein, D., Duran, P., Gonzalez-Perez, M. A., Montoya, M. A., Borda, A., Fleury, T., and Newburry, W. (2019a). Uncommoditizing strategies by emerging market firms. *Multinational Business Review* 27(2), 141–177.

Cuervo-Cazurra, A., Mudambi, R., and Pedersen, T. (2019b). Clarifying the relationships between institutions and global strategy. *Global Strategy Journal* 9(2), 151–175.

Demsetz, H. (1983). The structure of ownership and the theory of the fi rm. *The Journal of Law & Economics* 26, 375–390.

Finchelstein, D. (2017). The role of the state in the internationalization of Latin American firms. *Journal of World Business* 52(4), 578–590.

Finchelstein, D., Gonzalez-Perez, M. A., and Salvaj, E. H. (2022). A comparative analysis of the internationalization of sub-national and central state-owned enterprises: Shreds of evidence from Latin America. *Multinational Business Review 30*(2), 259–288.

Gao, C., Zuzul, T., Jones, G., and Khanna, T. (2017). Overcoming institutional voids: A reputation-based view of long-run survival. *Strategic Management Journal 38*(11), 2147–2167.

Goldstein, A. (2007). *Multinational Companies from Emerging Economies. Composition, Conceptualization and Direction in the Global Economy*. Palgrave-MacMillan.

Gourevitch, P., and Shinn, J. (2005). *Political Power and Corporate Control: The New Global Politics of Corporate Governance*. Princeton.

Granovetter, M. (2005). Business groups and social organization. In N. Smelser and R. Swedberg, eds. *Handbook of Economic Sociology*. Princeton, pp. 429–450

Groszkowska, K. (2023). *CEE unicorns: The rise of startup ecosystem in Central & Eastern Europe*. tinyurl.com/48992hn4

Hall, P., and Soskice, D. (eds). (2001). *Varieties of Capitalism: The Institutional Foundations of Comparative Advantage*. Oxford University Press.

Henisz, W. J. (2003). The power of the Buckley and Casson thesis: The ability to manage institutional idiosyncrasies. *Journal of International Business Studies 34*(2), 173–184.

Henni, A. (2022). *Russian tech entrepreneurship on the rise: Forbes identifies 10 'future unicorns'*. tinyurl.com/42kn73hk

Hermans, M., Borda, A., Newburry, W., Cordova Chea, C. O., Finchelstein, D., Gonzalez-Perez, M. A., Montoya, M., Velzco, G., and Velez-Ocampo, J. (2024). Becoming a Multilatina: Strategic capabilities as necessary conditions for the internationalization of Latin American firms. *European Business Review 36*(1), 50–70.

Invest Europe. (2024). *2023 Central & Eastern Europe private equity statistics*. www.investeurope.eu/media/apemo3bx/2023-cee-activity-report_june-2024-final.pdf

Khanna, T., and Yafeh, Y. (2010). Business groups in emerging markets: Paragons or parasites. In A. M. Colpan, T. Hikino, and J. R. Lincoln, eds. *Oxford Handbook of Business Groups*. Oxford University Press, pp. 575–601.

Kornai, J., Maskin, E., and Roland, G. (2003). Understanding the soft budget constraint. *Journal of Economic Literature 41*(4), 1095–1136.

KPMG. (2024). *Venture pulse Q4 2023. Global analysis of venture funding.*

Kumar, V., Mudambi, R., and Gray, S. (2013). Internationalization, innovation and institutions: The 3 I's underpinning the competitiveness of emerging market firms. *Journal of International Management 19*(3), pp. 203–206.

La Porta, R., López-De-Silanes, F., Shleifer, A., and Vishny, R. (2000). Investor protection and corporate governance. *Journal of Financial Economics 58*, 3–27.

Mariotti, S., and Marzano, R. (2020). Relational ownership, institutional context, and internationalization of state-owned enterprises: When and how are multinational co-owners a plus? *Global Strategy Journal 10*(4), 779–812.

Musacchio, A., Lazzarini, S., and Aguilera, R. (2015). New varieties of state capitalism: strategic and governance implications. *Academy of Management Perspectives* 29(1), 1–17.

North, D. C., Wallis, J. J., Webb, S. B., and Weingast, B. R. (eds.). (2013). *In the Shadow of Violence: Politics, Economics, and the Problems of Development*. Cambridge University Press.

Palepu, K. G., and Khanna, T. (1998). Institutional voids and policy challenges in emerging markets. *The Brown Journal of World Affairs 5*(1), 71–78.

Sajko, M., Boone, C., and Buyl, T. (2021). CEO greed, corporate social responsibility, and organizational resilience to systemic shocks. *Journal of Management* 47(4), 957–992.

Salvaj, E., and Couyoumdjian, J. P. (2016). 'Interlocked' business groups and the state in Chile (1970–2010). *Business History 58*(1), 129–148.

Schneider, B. R. (2010). Business groups and the state: The politics of expansion, restructuring, and collapse. In A. Colpan, A. Hikino, and J. Lincoln, eds. *The Oxford Handbook of Business Groups*. Oxford University Press, pp. 650–669.

Teare, G. (2024). *Global startup funding in 2023 clocks in at lowest level in 5 years*. Crunchbase News. news.crunchbase.com/venture/global-funding-data-analysis-ai-eoy-2023/

Tröster, B., and Küblböck, K. (2020). Unprecedented but not unpredictable: Effects of the COVID-19 crisis on commodity-dependent countries. *The European Journal of Development Research 32*(5), 1430–1449.

Weick, K. E., and Sutcliffe, K. M. (2011). *Managing the Unexpected: Resilient Performance in an Age of Uncertainty* (Vol. 8). John Wiley & Sons.

Glossary

A

Accelerator	A programme intended to mentor founders and accelerate the growth and success of a start-up company.
Accredited investor	A person who is permitted to invest in start-ups and other high-risk private company securities based on the net worth, income level and the professional criteria of the potential investor.
Acquisition	A transaction between two companies where one is buying the other.
Adverse change redemption	A type of redemption right whereby a shareholder obtains the right to redeem their shares if something adverse happens to the company.
Advisers	People who advise start-up companies. Normally, these people are paid some sort of compensation for their efforts.
Affirmative covenants	Action a company promises to take during the term of a contract during financing.
Agency costs	The costs associated with an agency/principal relationship that the principal incurs either directly or indirectly.

Alpha The earliest prototype of a product. This is before the beta, which is still a prototype, but a lot more polished.

Amortization terms Terms debt lenders use to better align the debt with the capital strategy of a company.

Analyst A very junior person at a venture capital firm, often a recent college graduate.

B

Blue ocean strategy A business approach that focuses on creating new, uncontested market spaces ('blue oceans') through innovation, making competition irrelevant rather than competing in crowded existing markets ('red oceans').

Burn rate Metric that reflects how fast a start-up consumes or 'burns' money each month to finance its operation. It serves for understanding how the company's cash flow is being affected.

Business to Business (B2B) Business model archetype when the company provides products and services to companies.

Business to Consumer (B2C) Business model archetype when the company provides products and services directly to individuals or end consumers.

C

C-level The top management team of a start-up (founder or not). The most common positions at this level are CEO (Chief Executive Officer), CMO (Marketing), CTO (Technology), CFO (Financial) and COO (Operations).

Conversion price adjustment	The mechanism by which an anti-dilution adjustment takes place. This allows the preferred stock to be converted into more common stock than originally agreed upon and thus allows the preferred to own more stock and voting rights upon converting to common.
Convertible debt	A debt or loan instrument that an investor gives to a company with the intent that it will convert later to equity and not be paid back as a standard bank loan would be.
Corporate venture capital	A venture fund that is sponsored and backed by a corporation.
Co-sale	The right of a shareholder (typically a venture capitalist) to sell shares alongside another shareholder who is selling some or all of its equity to a buyer.
Cost per mile	The price an advertiser pays for 1,000 views.
Cross-fund investment	When a venture capital firm operates more than one fund and more than one fund invests in the same company.
Crowdfunding	When a group of individuals fund a company either through equity purchase, debt purchase, pre-sale ordering of a product or gifting of money.

D

Digital nomad visa	A type of residence permit that allows remote workers to live in a foreign country while working online for an employer or clients based outside that country.
Discount	A standard mechanism in a convertible note agreement that

	allows noteholders the right to convert the amount of the loan, plus interest, at a reduced price (in percentage terms) to the purchase price paid by equity investors who later enter financing.
Dividends	An amount of money or shares of stock that is paid out to investors based on their holdings of stock in a company.
Double-trigger acceleration	A term that describes the situation in which a person would receive accelerated vesting. In a double-trigger situation, two events would trigger accelerated vesting, such as a merger of the company followed by a termination of a person's employment.
Down round	A financing round that is at a lower valuation than the previous round.
Drag-along	A term that sets up a proxy on one's stock ownership to vote the same way as others do on a particular issue.
Draw period	The time during which cash advances may be requested under a loan (also called the availability period).
Due diligence	The process by which investors explore a company that they are thinking of investing in.

E

Early stage	Start-up at an early stage but with a product that is being positively validated by the market and with the potential to be a scalable business.
Early-stage funds	VC funds that invest in Seed and Series A financing.
Earn-out	An amount agreed upon by an acquirer and a target company that

	the former shareholders of the target company will get if certain performance milestones are met post-merger.
Economic terms	Terms that impact the returns of a VC's investment in a company.
Elevator pitch	A short synopsis of what a company does and why it is compelling.
Employee option pool	The shares set aside by a company to provide stock options to employees.
Enterprise value	The post-money valuation plus debt minus cash.
Entrepreneur	Someone who creates a new company, also known as a founder.
Entrepreneur in residence (EIR)	A person at a venture firm that is usually a former entrepreneur who is helping the venture firm by finding deals to invest in or working on their next company that the venture firm will one day fund.
Equity	Ownership or part ownership of a company.
Equity crowdfunding	A financing process made legal by the JOBS Act in 2012 and popularised by AngelList.
Escrow	The amount of consideration that an acquiring company holds back following a merger to make sure that representations and warranties made by the purchased company are valid.
Escrow cap	The amount of money in a merger that is set aside to remedy breaches of the merger agreement.
Executive managing director	A senior partner in a venture capital firm who is superior to a managing director or general partner.

Exercise	The act of purchasing stock pursuant to a stock option or warrant.
Exercise period	The amount of time an employee can exercise their stock after leaving a company.
Exercise price	The price at which a stock option can be exercised (and subsequently the price per share the employee pays for the stock option).
Exited unicorn	A start-up once valued at $1 billion or more that has achieved a successful exit, typically through an initial public offering (IPO) or acquisition, allowing investors to realise returns.
F	
Fair market value	The price that a third party would pay for something in the open market.
Family, Friends and Fans	Those who provide money to start-ups and SMEs in very early stages of business. They do not necessarily expect a return on investment and the probability of losing the money is high. Their main objective is to give moral support to the entrepreneur.
Fiduciary duties	A legal and ethical duty that an individual has to an entity.
Final payments	A fee that is paid at the end of a loan.
First right of refusal	A right that allows an investor to have the first ability to either make another investment in the company or acquire the company.
Flat round	A financing round done at the same post-money valuation as that of the previous round.

Founder	Someone who creates a new company, also known as an entrepreneur.
Founders' stock	Common stock issued to founders at a very low price at the formation of the company.
Founding general partner	A senior partner in a venture capital firm who founded the firm.
Free float	The shares that regular investors can buy and sell freely in the open market.
Full-stack venture capital firms	A venture capital firm that employs many people beyond deal professionals, such as marketing, operations, public relations, engineering and financial executives, to attempt to help companies more than traditional venture capital firms.
Fully diluted	A term explicitly defining that all rights to purchase equity should be in the valuation calculation.
Fundamental rep	A representation made by the seller in an acquisition that survives longer than the escrow period.

G

Game theory	The concept that one's actions depend on what actions other persons may or may not take and the inherent incentives behind these actions.
General partner (GP)	A senior partner in a venture capital firm.
General partnership (GP)	The entity that manages the limited partnership.
General solicitation	Fundraising to potential investors without a substantial pre-existing relationship. Some also consider this to be when a start-up advertises for funding.

GP commitment The amount of money, usually between 1 per cent and 5 per cent of the fund, that the general partners invest in their own fund.

Growth investors VC funds that invest in Series B and later financings.

H

Holdback The amount of consideration that an acquiring company holds back following a merger to make sure that representations and warranties made by the purchased company are true.

I

Indemnification The promise by one party to protect another party should something go wrong.

Information rights The minimum amount of information the company must give its investors on a regular basis.

Initial coin offering A fundraising mechanism where a company sells crypto tokens instead of equity. In the cryptocurrency industry, it is the equivalent of an initial public offering (IPO).

Initial public offering (IPO) The process by which a private company offers its shares to the public for the first time on a stock exchange.

Interest-only (I/O) period A length of time where only interest (and no principal) is paid on a term loan.

Interest rate One of the key pricing mechanisms in a loan.

Investment term The length of time that a venture capital fund can remain active, typically ten years with two 1-year extensions.

IRS Internet Revenue Service (in the United States).

J

JOBS Act Formally known as the Jumpstart Our Business Start-ups Act, enacted in 2012. It created rules around crowdfunding, changed some dynamics around IPOs and gave Congress a way to say they were helping start-ups.

K

Key person clause Contractual provision within the limited partnership agreement that describes what will happen if certain partners leave the venture capital fund.

KISS An acronym for Keep It Simple Security, which can be an alternative for either a debt or equity financing.

Key Performance Indicators (KPIs) They allow evaluating the efficiency, effectiveness and productivity of the different processes, plans, strategies or projects of the start-up.

L

Late stage funds Entities, including VC funds and hedge funds, who invest in the last financing before an IPO.

Lead investor The investor in a start-up company who takes on the leadership position in VC financing.

Lean start-up methodology A business methodology that posits businesses can reduce product development cycles by combining iterative releases and experimentations of their product. Popularised by Eric Ries.

Letter of intent (LOI) A term sheet for a merger or acquisition.

Light preferred	A version of a preferred stock financing that has very simple and watered-down terms.
Limited partners (LPs)	The investors in a VC fund.
Limited partnership (LP)	The entity used by the limited partners to invest in a venture capital fund.
Limited partnership agreement (LPA)	The contract between a venture capital fund and its investors.
Liquidation event/ liquidity event	When a company is sold and ceases to exist as a stand-alone company.
Liquidation preference	A right given to a class of preferred stock allowing that stock to receive proceeds in a liquidation in advance of other classes of stock.
Liquidation preference overhang	The cumulative amount of liquidation preferences that a company has agreed to during their existence. The amount of money owed to investors before common stock will receive proceeds.
Loan fees	A part of a loan agreement that charges a fixed fee for getting the deal done.

M

Major investor	A concept used in venture capital financings that allows a company to distinguish between shareholders who purchase more stock than others.
Management carve-out	An agreement between a company and its preferred shareholders to divert part of the proceeds that would normally flow (pursuant to liquidation preferences) to the preferred shareholders to

	management and employees upon an acquisition.
Management company	The entity that services each fund that a VC raises.
Management fee	The fee that the venture capital funds have a right to receive from their LPs as money to manage their business operations regardless of the performance of the fund.
Managing director (MD)	A senior partner in a venture capital firm.
Mentors	People who advise start-up companies or their executives. Normally, these people are not paid.
Micro VC fund	A super angel who raises a small fund made up of professional investors.
Mid stage funds	Another name for growth investors who are VC funds that invest in Series B and later financings.
Minimum viable product (MVP)	The product with the least number of features necessary to make it useful to ship and learn more about the users. This concept was made popular by Eric Ries as part of the lean start-up methodology.
Most favoured nation (MFN)	The right to get the equivalent terms to anyone who gets better terms than you in the future.
Multiplay game	A term in game theory that deals with a game or situation where there is a continuing relationship after the game is played, like a venture capital financing whereby after the transaction is completed the VC and the entrepreneur will join forces to work together.

N

Negative covenants	Behaviours and actions that the company may not engage in without the lender's consent as a condition of the loan in a debt deal.
North Star Metric	An important start-up metric. The North Star Metric allows understanding how successful the business model is.
Nondisclosure agreement (NDA)	An agreement whereby one party promises not to share information of another party.
Nonparticipating preferred	A simple preferred stock that does not have a participation feature.
No-shop agreement	One of the few binding terms in a term sheet, this provision prohibits a company from seeking other investors (unless approved by the term sheet-issuing VC) once a term sheet has been signed.

O

One pager	One-page document in which the business model is condensed. The elements included are similar to the pitch deck although with less detail. They are useful to present the start-up to potential investors with whom there is no direct contact.
Operating partner	A position at a venture capital firm that is normally under the managing director, but above a principal.
Option budget	The number of options a company plans to allocate to employees over a finite time period.
Option pool	The shares set aside by a company to provide stock options to employees.
Outside director	A member of the company's board of directors who is not an executive or major investor of the company.

P

Pari passu	When all classes of preferred stock have equivalent payment rights in a liquidation.
Partners	An investment professional at a venture firm that may or may not be an actual 'partner' but has some level of deal evaluation and deal-making authority.
Party round	A financing round with many participants, usually at small dollar amounts.
Pay-to-play	A term that forces VCs to continue to invest in future company financings or suffer adverse consequences to their ownership positions.
Perfected lien	A document that has been filed with the appropriate agency allowing for a legal claim to seize assets if a loan borrower defaults on the loan.
Performance warrant	A warrant that is exercisable if certain performance metrics are met by the holder of the warrant.
Pitch	A speech in which the founders usually present

	the business model to investors, allies or potential customers. It has different formats depending on the target audience and purpose.
Pitch Deck	A slide presentation showing in some detail the most important aspects of the business model, problem, solution, market, product, competitive advantage, revenue model, traction, milestones, roadmap and financial projections, et cetera.
Patient capital	An investment that is long-term, flexible and tolerant of lower or delayed financial returns, often used to support businesses or projects that require time to grow, innovate or achieve social impact.
Pivot	A start-up's ability to make radical changes to the business model in the face of product and/or market validation problems.
Post-money	The value of a company after an investor has put money into it.
PowerPoint	Throughout this book, we use PowerPoint to describe presentation

	software that was originally made famous by Microsoft. Many of the presentations we now see are in Google Docs or Apple Keynote, both competitive products to Microsoft PowerPoint.
Preferred stock	A type of stock that has preferential terms, rights and privileges compared to common stock.
Pre-money	The value ascribed to a company by an investor before investing in the company.
Prepayments	The arrangement whereby a borrower can or cannot prepay a loan down before the maturity date. In venture debt, prepayments are generally allowed but may have some additional costs depending on when the prepayment is made.
Pre-seed round	The round before a seed round. This term is now used to refer to the very first financing round in a company.
Price per share	The dollar amount assigned to purchase one share of stock.
Prime rate	A specific reference index that a floating, or variable rate loan, is

	based on. Most venture loans are indexed to the prime rate, either the prime rate of the bank providing the loan or the published benchmark, such as the prime rate published by the Wall Street Journal.
Principal	A junior deal partner at a venture capital firm.
Private placement memorandum (PPM)	A legal document that is prepared by the company, its bankers, and its lawyers that is a long-form business plan created to solicit investors.
Product crowdfunding	An approach to funding product development by using customers to pre-order products that was popularised by Kickstarter.
Proprietary information and inventions agreement (also called **proprietary rights agreement**)	This is a contract that should be signed by anyone who works for a company that specifically states that all intellectual property developed by the person is the property of the company. It also will have the person guarantee that they are not using anyone else's intellectual property while working at the company.

Pro rata	The right of a shareholder to purchase shares in a future financing equal to the percentage the shareholder currently holds at the time of such financing.
Protective provisions	Contractual rights that allow the holders of preferred stock to vote on certain important matters pertaining to a company.

R

Ratchet-based anti-dilution	A style of anti-dilution that re-prices an investor's shares in previous rounds, usually through a conversion price adjustment, to the price paid in the current round.
Redemption rights	The ability of a shareholder to force the company to purchase their shares at a previously agreed-upon price.
Registration rights	The contractual rights allotted to investors pursuant to a financing that detail the ability of shareholders to force the company to register their shares on a public stock market.
Representations and warranties	Provisions in a financing purchase agreement or merger agreement whereby the company makes certain assurances about itself.
Reputation constraints	The impact that reputation has on one's behaviour.
Reserves	The amount of money that a venture capital firm allocates for future investments.

Resource orchestration	The process of structuring, bundling and leveraging firm resources to create sustained value.
Restricted stock units (RSUs)	A substitution for traditional stock options that provides different tax and accounting for the company that issues them.
Restrictions on sales	A right but not an obligation to purchase shares of another shareholder who wishes to sell.
Reverse dilution	The situation in which stock is repurchased by a company, increasing the effective ownership of all shareholders in a company.
Right of first refusal (ROF)	A right but not an obligation for an investor to participate in future rounds of financing.
Right of rescission	The right of shareholders to force the company to buy back their stock, usually given to people who were not supposed to buy the stock in the first place under federal securities law.
Runway	The number of months of cash remaining, based on the projected monthly cash burn.

S

Serviceable Available Market (SAM)	Portion of the market to which the start-up could aspire, taking into account the limitations of the market and the business model. It is a percentage of the total addressable market (TAM). It serves to understand the growth potential of the business.
SAFE	Acronym for 'simple agreement for future equity', which is an

	alternative to the issuance of convertible debt.
Safe harbour	A legally defined way of escaping liability under a law if a party performs certain acts as defined by such law.
Schedule of exceptions	A list of exceptions to representations and warranties in a venture financing or acquisition agreement.
Schmuck insurance	Preferences, including ones that guarantee a return for an investor, especially in a situation where an investor has concerns about overpaying at a particular point in time.
Schumpeterian approach	Describes processes or ideas centred on innovation, entrepreneurship and dynamic market change.
Secondary sale	The sale by a VC of stock in a portfolio company or its entire portfolio to an outside party in a private transaction.
Security	A financial instrument that represents an ownership right in a company.
Seed rounds	What Series Seed financings are sometimes called.
Seed stage	A start-up that is in its infancy.
Seed stage funds	VC funds typically focused on being the first institutional money in a company.
Series A financing	An early round of financing that a company raises.
Series seed financing	A small financing that occurs before the Series A financing and is often the very first financing of a company.

Simple preferred	A very lightweight preferred stock, usually with only a liquidation preference and minimal rights.
Single-play game	A term in game theory that deals with a game or situation in which there is no continuing relationship after the game is played.
Single-trigger acceleration	A term used to describe the situation in which a person would receive accelerated vesting.
Scale up	A venture that has managed to validate its business model, having achieved a Product Market Fit business model and is ready to grow at an accelerated rate without compromising its sustainability as a business in the long term.
Stacked preference	When different classes of preferred stock have senior rights to payment over other classes of preferred stock.
Serviceable Obtainable Market (SOM)	The real target market that the start-up could serve. It serves to understand the current strategy of the business strategy and establish short- and medium-term goals.
Stock option	A right to purchase shares of stock in a company.
Straight line amortisation	The principal balance of a loan is divided up equally among the number of payments.
Strike price	The price at which a stock option may be exercised.

Structure	Multiple liquidation preference or participation in a preferred stock. This is often found in late-stage deals.
Super angel	A very active and experienced angel investor.
Super pro rata rights	The right of shareholders to purchase shares in a future financing equal to some multiple of the percentage they currently hold at the time of such financing.
Syndicate	The group of investors who invest in a start-up.
T	
Term sheet	A summary document of key terms in contemplation of financing.
Total Addressable Market (TAM)	Total size of the available market for the product or service offered by the start-up. It is expressed in total potential revenue. It serves to understand the scalability of the business.
Transaction costs	The direct and indirect costs (time and money) associated with the creation of a business relationship.
U	
Unicorn	A mythical beast that rides on a silver moonbeam and spreads rainbows. Also, a private company that has achieved a valuation of US$1 billion.
Unit economics	These are the key metrics to measure performance, sustainability and profitability of the start-up.
V	
Valuation	The value ascribed to a company by an investor.

Valuation cap	A term in a convertible note deal that sets the maximum conversion price of the debt into equity.
Venture capital fund (VC fund)	An investment fund that pools money from investors to finance early-stage, high-growth start-ups in exchange for equity.
Venture capitalist (VC)	A person who invests in early-stage, high-growth start-up companies.
Venture debt	Debt for an equity-backed company that does not have the cash flows to support traditional debt.
Venture debt fund	A provider of venture debt that is not a bank.
Venture partner	A position at a venture capital firm that is normally under a managing director but above a principal.
Vesting	The notion that a stock award is not earned until some period of time or milestone is reached.
Vesting cliff	The length of time required for an employee to be at a company before any of her stock or options vest. This is typically a year. The specific rights of how preferred stock and common stock vote.

Y

Y Combinator	A start-up accelerator that provides early-stage companies with seed funding, mentorship and resources to rapidly grow, often in exchange for equity.

W

Walking dead portfolio company	A company that has no growth, no exit opportunities and no financing options but just enough revenue, cash or cash flow to stay in business.
Warrant	

	A right to purchase shares of stock in a company.
Weighted average anti-dilution	A style of anti-dilution that re-prices an investor's investment, usually through a conversion price adjustment, to a lower price per share, but considers the relative effect of the number of shares sold in the current round.

Z

Zebra start-ups	Companies that aim for sustainable growth and profitability, while also addressing social or environmental problems.
Zebra valuation	These start-ups prioritise sustainable rather than exponential growth (in contrast to unicorns) and are expected to have a valuation of at least US$200 million.
Zone of insolvency	When a company is nearly insolvent and does not have the assets to pay off its liabilities.

Index

www.ingramcontent.com/pod-product-compliance
Lightning Source LLC
LaVergne TN
LVHW011658200926
848484LV00004B/987
* 9 7 8 1 0 0 9 4 6 9 2 5 8 *